INFORMED CONSENT

THE GUILFORD LAW AND BEHAVIOR SERIES

Alan Meisel, Loren H. Roth, and Elizabeth Loftus, Editors

INFORMED CONSENT
A Study of Decisionmaking in Psychiatry

Charles W. Lidz, Alan Meisel, Eviatar Zerubavel, Mary Carter, Regina M. Sestak, and Loren H. Roth

FORTHCOMING

PSYCHOLOGICAL EVALUATION FOR THE COURTS
A Handbook for the Mental Health Professional and the Lawyer

G. B. Melton, C. Slobogin, and J. Petrila

INFORMED CONSENT
A Study of Decisionmaking in Psychiatry

Charles W. Lidz, Alan Meisel, Eviatar Zerubavel,
Mary Carter, Regina M. Sestak,
and Loren H. Roth

Foreword by Alan A. Stone

The Guilford Press
New York   London

© 1984 The Guilford Press
A Division of Guilford Publications, Inc.
200 Park Avenue South, New York, N.Y. 10003

Printed in the United States of America

LIBRARY OF CONGRESS CATALOGING IN PUBLICATION DATA
Main entry under title:

Informed consent.

   (The Guilford law and behavior series)
   Includes bibliographical references and index.
   1. Mentally ill—Treatment—United States—Decision making.   2. Psychotherapist and patient—United States—Decision making.   3. Informed consent (Medical law)—United States.   I. Lidz, Charles W.   II. Series.
[DNLM: 1. Informed consent.   2. Ethics, Medical.   3. Psychiatry—
Standards.   4. Psychiatry—United States—Legislation.   5. Decision making.   WM 62 I43]
RC443.I53   1984   616.89′06   83-8488
ISBN 0-89862-275-1

TO JAY KATZ

A pioneer in informed consent

ACKNOWLEDGMENTS

Rarely is an academic work with six authors as genuinely collaborative as this one. Each author of this volume played a substantial role in its production. Roth, Meisel, and Lidz did the initial conceptual work and submitted the grant application that provided the funding for data collection. Carter and Zerubavel did the field observations and took the notes that are the empirical basis for this volume. Lidz and Roth supervised these processes and did daily quality control on the notes. Sestak took the notes and turned them into coherent accounts of cases with cross-references for every interaction we observed. Meisel then focused on preparing an elaboration of the legal theory and the empirical literature, while all the others undertook detailed analyses of the notes. These analyses produced drafts of what were to become the empirical chapters of this volume. Everyone then participated in critiques, and the original authors rewrote the drafts (often several times). Finally, Lidz, with substantial help from Meisel, redrafted the whole volume for consistency of content and style. These revisions were again critiqued by the whole group, and a final draft was completed by Lidz, Meisel, and Roth.

We owe substantial debts to a number of people who helped us complete the research. First, and perhaps foremost, Thomas Detre, MD, Chairman of the Department of Psychiatry of the University of Pittsburgh School of Medicine, and David Kupfer, MD, Director of Research, supported this research both personally and with the financial and political resources of the Department of Psychiatry. Without that support, the research would never have been completed. Most of the financial support for this project came from PHS Research Grant No. MH 27553, NIMH Center for Studies of Crime and Delinquency and Mental Health Services Development Branch. We are indebted to Saleem Shah, Thomas Lalley, and Herbert Butler at NIMH for advice and support. We are also indebted to Egon Bittner, PhD, Jay Katz, MD, and Paul Friedman, JD, who met with us periodically during the field work and the analysis of the data to provide us the benefit of their experience and their wisdom. We owe special thanks to Professor Katz, whose pioneering work on informed consent first led us to be interested in the subject and has guided us throughout this research.

John Monahan, PhD, Seymour Halleck, MD, and Elizabeth Loftus, PhD, read an early draft of the complete book and provided helpful comments for rewriting.

We are deeply grateful for the help of the rest of the staff of the Law and Psychiatry Program: Camela Miller, who typed the field notes; Florita Cohen, who worked on the organization of the material and the editing of the manuscript; and Betty Brenneman, who typed numerous drafts and held us all together. Patricia Cavanaugh and Caroline Kaufmann worked on some early phases of the data analysis.

Finally, we wish to thank the staff and patients of "the Hospital," many of whom served as "subjects" of our research. Their patience with our questions and our presence is deeply appreciated.

Some Personal Views: An Introduction

A few months ago, I was sitting on a gurney waiting to be wheeled into an operating room for minor surgery that did not require me to be premedicated. It had been some time since I had been on a surgical floor. It was therefore with great curiosity that I surveyed the comings and goings of the members of the various surgical teams at what is generally considered a great teaching hospital. The hallway in the operating suite served as a last minute waiting room, and on the gurney just ahead of mine I could see an elderly man who seemed sound asleep. I assumed he was well premedicated. Suddenly a frantic young doctor appeared. He shook the old man until his eyes half opened and he tried to focus. The frantic young doctor identified himself as Doctor X, and explained, "I forgot last night to have you sign the informed consent form." Doctor X began to explain the operation, the anesthesia, the risks, et cetera, in an embarrassed and highly abbreviated way to the old man, who was barely conscious. Finally Doctor X took out a pen, placed it in the man's hand and guided the hand to produce the rudiments of a signature.

I had a sense of the young doctor's dilemma. Someone on the operating team had no doubt made a routine check, and with no signed consent form, there would have been no operation. It was also clear that in this busy teaching hospital it would not have been easy to schedule another time in the operating room. What would those charged with utilization review say about the cost of the hospital bed for the day the patient would spend recovering from his preoperative medications so that he could then give truly informed consent? What about the surgeons' busy schedules being thrown off, and those of the anesthesiologists and all the rest of the team? In the world I glimpsed there in the hallway of the great teaching hospital, it was clear that other considerations were far more pressing than informed consent. Yet Dr. X had been unwilling to bring himself simply to forge the signature; he had played out the awkward charade.

At the time, this incident seemed no more than the stuff of which I could make ironic anecdotes to add human interest in my classes on law and medicine at Harvard Law School. Now, however, having read this remarkable book, I realize that my chance observation could in fact be a metaphor for a more general reality. The authors' research reveals how minimal an impact law and the regulation of informed consent have had on the practice of psychiatry. And psychiatry is the specialty in medicine to which the law has paid particular attention. The authors demonstrate that, nonetheless, the patients they studied were given information only after the fact. Further, they demonstrate that patients rarely understood the ritual signing of consent forms. And, finally, they demonstrate that, very much like my chance observation, the psychiatric team functions under systemic constraints that have little if anything to do with providing to patients the information necessary to make informed medical decisions.

This book is a jewel. The authors have brilliantly analyzed the law and the ethics of informed consent; they have critically reviewed the existing empirical literature; they have contributed a carefully crafted empirical study of their own, the best one I have ever seen in law and psychiatry. And they have done all this without polemic, without defensiveness, and without allowing professional self-interest to dominate the work at hand. They claim the work is a truly interdisciplinary effort, and the claim meets the test of a critical reading. The authors have been able to suspend their professional biases and the result is a collaborative effort that should be read and studied by everyone interested in informed consent.

Unlike the authors, I have been unable to overcome my own biases, particularly about the ability of law to achieve fine-tuned regulation of any complex human enterprise. Lawyers seem to be the chief protagonists of "consumer-oriented" informed consent in medicine, yet it is startling how small a part informed consent plays in legal practice. Lawyers bringing class action suits are by no means required to get informed consent from all members of the class. For example, one black legal scholar has argued that the interests of blacks opposed to busing from their neighborhood schools were never taken into account by paternalistic lawyers doing what they thought was correct. Very few trial or appellate lawyers explain their legal strategy and the alternatives to their individual clients. They typically tell the client what his or her chances are, just as the doctor tells the patient. The vast majority of convicted criminals will certainly claim that they did not get the opportunity to offer anything resembling fully informed consent to their lawyers. Indeed, it can be argued that it would be a useful propaedeutic for legal advocates of informed consent to put their own house in order. In the process they might obtain a better understanding of medical resistance.

Whatever its origins, the debate over informed consent in medicine has by now taken on a recognizable pattern. On one side are those who advocate maximal informed consent; they see it as a means of transforming the doctor-patient relationship. The idea is that power will move from the doctor to the patient if the doctor is legally required to give the patient enough information to make an informed decision. Patients will not need to trust the doctor to make the right decisions for them; they will not be helpless; they will become autonomous. This argument stands on four legs. First, doctors make a lot of bad decisions: They favor unnecessary treatments, and there is a growing amount of iatrogenic harm. Patient knowledge and malpractice liability will forestall some of this. Second, treatment is best carried out when patients are cooperative; a patient who understands all of the risks and benefits of treatment, and the alternatives to treatment, will be more cooperative. Third, informed consent demystifies medical treatment and demystification is a good in itself. Fourth, medical decisions are too important to be left to doctors. Modern medicine has in its grasp a powerful armamentarium, most of it developed in the last half century. What is done or not done by doctors is much more crucial than at any time in the past. What is now at stake is life, the quality of life, and the dignity of death; each person should be allowed the right of self-determination in these matters. This last point, of course, is the concern of proponents of the living will. Some of the arguments put forth by advocates are utilitarian: Patients will benefit (e.g., informed consent is a protection against possible iatrogenic harm). But the supporters are also promoting their values about the good of individual autonomy and the evil of authority.

Against the advocates, the medical profession has argued that informed consent simply will not work. Patients, they say, cannot understand or appreciate the necessary medical information that is relevant to even minor treatment decisions. They assert that patients do not want to know, that they will become frightened and upset when confronted with all the risks and the difficult choices.

They also suggest that informed consent soon becomes a meaningless ritual of legal forms which is, if anything, counterproductive. Their objections are mainly practical and utilitarian. Unlike the advocates, however, the opponents offer no important value as a justification for limiting the doctor's responsibility to inform the patient.

Thus, as the authors of this book point out, the pattern of the informed consent debate reveals both deontological and utilitarian considerations motivating informed consent advocates, but only utilitarian concerns being put forward by the opponents. Unless of course the notion of "doctor knows best" can somehow be elevated to a deontological principle.

Since physicians seem to rely on empirical arguments, empirical research should have great significance for them. But in reviewing the literature, the authors have convincingly demonstrated that there is almost no good empirical research in this area. The authors have begun to fill that void. They have begun the laborious process of moving the utilitarian debate from the realm of opinion to the realm of data.

There are, however, enormous difficulties in research of this kind. Even the most carefully conceived social science research may provide only documentation of the history of the moment in the particular context studied, rather than generalizable data about the phenomena we want to understand. The Gluecks' monumental study of delinquency seems to have been such an example. The delinquents they studied were second-generation Irish Catholics from intact families; they could not easily generalize their findings about the etiology of delinquency in pre-World War II Boston to inner city black and Hispanic delinquents from single-parent families in post-World War II New York. But the authors of this study have enormous sophistication: They understand law, medicine, and methodology, not to mention moral philosophy and policy analysis. The study, which is carefully crafted, and the findings, which are cautiously and carefully reported, should permanently alter the contour of the debate on informed consent.

The "consumer-oriented" argument about restructuring the doctor-patient relationship by expanding the legal requirement of informed consent assumes that there is a certain kind of relationship to restructure. But what the authors' research reveals is that the doctor-patient relationship has already been restructured by the team practice of medical care providers, by the constraints of bureaucracy, and by the incentives of third-party payments. These are considerations that have been recognized by many commentators, but this study demonstrates their implications for informed consent. The authors show that just as responsibility for the care of patients now floats among the team, vitiating the stereotypical notion of the doctor-patient relationship, responsibility to inform the patient about treatment also floats among the team.

There may be medical contexts where the team treatment approach is less important than in the psychiatric settings studied by the authors. But I suspect this is only a matter of degree, and that all of medicine is moving in the direction of organized settings where the doctor is part of a team of providers. What this study suggests to me is that those who want patients to be able to make informed medical decisions have a much greater and more complicated relationship to restructure than they imagine. They have assumed that the doctor-patient relationship could be transformed into a contract between equal bargaining parties. But this idea of a two-party contractual context has little to do with the current reality. The reality is that the patient now has a relationship with a complicated bureaucracy that must respond to external considerations that have little to do with particular patients and their autonomous decisions.

The authors explore different settings, but the common features that they found are more impressive than the differences. They demonstrate that typically the decision treatment is a fait accompli before the patient is given much information. The institutional systemic pressures are directed at getting the patient to conform expeditiously to the fait accompli. Based on what the authors report it would require drastic reforms in order for patients to have a realistic opportunity to participate in the process of treatment decisionmaking.

At best, in these settings, one might start by providing an opportunity for the patient to veto the treatment plan that has already been made. The authors doubt that threats of malpractice suits or even regulation will remedy the pattern of systemic pressures they found. But it is clear that they are unwilling to give up, and one can only sympathize with their judicious conclusions. What they have found in their study of informed consent is the dehumanizing bureaucracy of modern medicine. It is a bureaucracy that erodes not only the patient's autonomy but also the doctor's. I doubt that expanding informed consent will solve these problems, but, as this study convincingly demonstrates, the lack of informed consent is symptomatic of a more serious disorder in the healing relationship.

Alan A. Stone, MD
Harvard University

CONTENTS

INFORMED CONSENT

The Background
of the Research

1

Introduction

Substantial ethical and legal changes in any sphere of society are usually controversial. We become accustomed to the rules by which groups to which we belong conduct their affairs, and changes in those rules are, at the least, inconvenient. More important, rules usually have a certain degree of sanctity about them. Group members learn to treat those rules as "right," "just," and "good." Changes in the rules are often seen as a threat to the sanctity of the group. People who practice medicine and its allied professions are no exception to these unspoken rules about rules. Thus when the courts, in a relatively brief period of time, announced a new doctrine for the regulation of research and medical decisionmaking called "informed consent," the reaction of the health professions was not generally favorable. The fact that the proponents of the new doctrine claimed that it did no more than implement existing fundamental legal principles made it little more acceptable. In the past two decades, literally hundreds of articles have appeared in medical, legal, and social science journals and the popular press supporting or condemning the doctrine. While its critics have seen informed consent as a threat to the quality of medical care, its proponents have seen it as promising better patient care, better relationships between doctors and patients, and other benefits.

WHAT IS INFORMED CONSENT?

Although we discuss the matter in more detail in the next chapter, we cannot go any further without some discussion of what the words "informed consent" mean. Unfortunately, they have more than one meaning.

To the clinician who must "get informed consent" from a patient before some procedure can take place, informed consent may mean largely a signed piece of paper containing a description of the procedure written by a lawyer whom the clinician has never met. The lawyer, in turn, may view informed consent as the basis of a liability. Depending on whether he or she serves the plaintiff or the defendant, it may be either an important tool for redressing grievances or something against which the client must be constantly protected.

As a *legal* doctrine, informed consent is in a state of constant flux, as various appellate courts in different jurisdictions extend or contract its coverage in a manner characteristic of the common law in American courts. While there is a general core to the doctrine, the particular boundaries, criteria, and requirements are quite flexible. The core of the legal doctrine is quite simple: Unless a doctor discloses to a patient certain types of information before undertaking a diagnostic, therapeutic, or research procedure, the patient may collect damages from the doctor if he or she is injured by the procedure, even though the procedure itself was properly performed. Although it has been proposed that the law of informed consent might function as "therapy" for the ailing state of the doctor–patient relationship,[1] courts have been hesitant in practice to create the revolution for which some commentators hoped.[2]

Informed consent as an *ethical* doctrine is, however, considerably more expansive. Based on appellate court dicta and the writings of theorists, it urges a reordering of the doctor–patient relationship along more egalitarian–participatory lines. While traditionally patients are supposed to be either completely passive (e.g., the surgical patient) or trusting and cooperative (e.g., the patient who takes medicine as prescribed) in their relations with their doctors, the informed consent doctrine envisions the relationship as one that Szasz and Hollender[3] call "mutual participation."[4]

The ethical doctrine of informed consent can be grounded in either of two ethical positions. It can be grounded either "deontologically," by arguing that informed consent is an inherent good that is a result of the natural obligation of one human being to another, or "consequentially," by arguing that informed consent will provide real substantive benefits to those involved or to others in the society. The former position emphasizes transcendent values, and the latter practical benefits. For our purposes here, the consequentialist position is more relevant, since the deontological position justifies informed consent independent of the empirical consequences that we describe here.

However it is formulated, the basic premise of the ethical doctrine of informed consent is that the patient is an autonomous person who is entitled to make treatment decisions based on relevant, factual information and perhaps advice provided by a doctor or other care-provider. In this regard, it follows a long-standing American legal tradition that protects and encourages the autonomy of the individual.

The doctrine of informed consent, at least in its more expansive ethical form, can be said to have two goals: (1) to promote individual autonomy and (2) to encourage rational decisionmaking.[5] Two specific requirements flow from the goal of promoting individual autonomy. First and most central is the requirement that the ultimate authority to make the decision must belong to the patient and not to the physician, and that the patient must be entitled not only to consent to treatment but to refuse it as well. Second, both the legal and ethical doctrines of informed consent assume that the patient who is to decide is a "free agent." That is, the decision that the patient renders must be voluntary.

Similarly, certain requirements flow from the goal of encouraging rational decisionmaking. Most important is that the patient be provided with information relevant and sufficient to making a rational decision about treatment. A further consideration flowing from the goal of rational decisionmaking is the patient's understanding of the information. Clearly the patient must be competent to understand to make a rational decision; if he or she is not, then the right to decide must be transferred to some other party. But beyond this there is a problem of whether the patient must actually understand the information provided. Although there is no explicit legal requirement that patients understand what their doctors disclose, it seems implicit in the goal of rational decisionmaking that patients actually should understand.

These requirements, derived from the goals of the informed consent doctrine, are the background for the analytical framework of our empirical study of informed consent. The requirements of the doctrine lead to five basic issues amenable to empirical research[6]:

1. *Information*: What was disclosed, how, when, and by whom?
2. *Understanding*: What did the patient understand about the treatment? What were the important ways in which that understanding was developed?
3. *Competency*: If the patient did not understand, did he or she have the cognitive capacity to do so?
4. *Voluntariness*: Was the patient free to choose? Was he or she subject to coercion or undue influence?
5. *Decision*: What was the overall structure of the way in which decisions about treatment were made? What role did the formal disclosure play?

The doctrine of informed consent, and particularly its application to psychiatry, raise a number of interesting policy issues that require empirical data for their evaluation—a task that is undertaken in more detail in the next two chapters. However, first we must place the issues involved in a broader perspective. The conflict over the application of informed consent to medicine generally and to psychiatry specifically can be viewed in a broader context as a struggle between a deeply ingrained pattern of ethical and legal thought on the one hand, and a large and important social institution, the mental health system, on the other. If we are to understand the conflict between the mental health professions and the doctrine of informed consent, we must understand the role of the mental health system in American society.

PSYCHIATRY IN AMERICAN SOCIETY

Formal social control in most societies is primarily the province of the criminal law. The criminal law is a mechanism with which societies protect the values that they hold dear. Each time criminal sanctions are invoked, the boundaries of acceptable behavior are further defined. Indeed, the very existence of the society depends on the clarification of its norms and values that come from the use of the criminal law against deviant behavior.[7] Each instance of invocation of criminal sanctions becomes an opportunity for the community as a whole to unite in support of its norms and values and against the offender. Punishment and the associated condemnation of those whose behavior strays from the norm becomes an educational function and is one of the primary mechanisms by which the members of society learn about their own rules and norms. It is an important mechanism of integration for the society.

However, punishment as a means of clarifying social norms and controlling deviant behavior has faced severe opposition in modern Western societies, as Durkheim pointed out at about the turn of the century. The "liberal" societies of Western Europe and North America developed central values based on secular individualism. Societies whose central moral symbolism derived from Enlightenment concepts of the sanctity of the individual conscience inevitably have trouble with a mechanism of integration that imposes severe constraints on the individual, because it involves the violation of some basic values in an effort to enforce others. The United States and other Western societies have responded by guaranteeing that the individual being punished receives fair and equal treatment and that punishment occurs only if the criminal is convicted in accordance with "due process of law." Nonetheless, the tension between the punitive consequences of criminal law and the liberal values it must defend has remained severe.

This context can help us understand the rise of psychiatry and the mental health movement in Western Europe and the English-speaking countries, particularly the United States. For although psychiatry is a part of medicine and acts to help sick individuals, it also clearly functions to mark off unacceptable behavior. Whether or not that is its intent is beside the point. For, while treating the impaired, psychiatry also acts as a way of marking boundaries between the acceptable and the unacceptable. We can learn and see reinforced our moral code by watching and listening to mental health professionals' interpretations of the psychopathology of a mental patient, just as we can by listening to a judge's summary of the crimes of the criminal during sentencing.

Psychiatry is not without conflict with the individualistic value commitments of American society. These conflicts center in part around the coercion of individuals into treatment—whether legally through involuntary commitment, or informally. Since psychiatry is concerned with individuals who are impaired, there exist extreme cases in which individuals are so impaired that they cannot take care of themselves and need someone to care for them, at least temporarily. Moreover, such impairment may and often does involve an individual's inability to recognize the need for such care.

Psychiatry faces its most serious conflict with American individualistic values in this area.[8] Compulsory treatment or other treatment without meaningful consent requires the particular individual in need of treatment to be temporarily dealt with as though he or she is not entitled to the right of self-direction.[9]

DISCLOSURE REGULATION

One way to temper the intrusion of psychiatry on important social values such as self-determination is by adding a measure of self-determination to the role that psychiatric patients play in their own care. To some extent, this is being done through the application of informed consent to psychiatric treatments and procedures. This is not an unusual pattern in American efforts to regulate the power of the strong against the weak. In area after area over the last two decades, the courts and the legislatures have sought to protect the weak from the strong by requiring that the strong disclose to the weak information that will help the weak party to make a rational decision in his or her best interest. Thus in criminal law, the courts have required that police inform suspects of certain constitutional rights before accepting a confession. In dealing with credit issues, Congress has passed the Truth-in-Lending Act, requiring lenders to inform borrowers of a long list of items designed to permit more rational decisions about borrowing. Recently, the Federal Trade Commission has required disclosures of such diverse groups as makers of goods containing saccharin and people running vocational training programs. The list of disclosure laws and regulations is very long.

What they share in common is a belief in the rationality of the individual. The underlying assumption is that only the individual can truly assess his or her best interests; if the relevant advantages and disadvantages are disclosed, he or she can weigh them and make a rational decision about what to do. They borrow deeply from the utilitarian philosophy of Bentham and Mill and the free-market economics of Adam Smith, which argue that what the individual does is not a proper subject of governmental concern; the government should only concern itself with the maintenance of a free market for goods and services, which is premised on "perfect knowledge."

However, if the formal justification of disclosure laws is to increase contractual freedom, it is also clear that most of their proponents do not see contractual freedom as an end in itself, but rather as a means of producing more equity and justice. For example, the advocates of strict disclosure standards for consent to electroconvulsive treatment (ECT) in psychiatry were, not incidentally, also people who believed that ECT was harmful to patients. They sought to use informed consent as a technique to minimize the use of ECT. In the political context of contemporary American society, they found it hard actually to forbid the use of any medical tool that the medical profession found useful, but it was harder for their opponents to object to requiring disclosure of the "truth." One of our objectives in this book is to describe the ramifications of informed consent law for the way in which psychiatry is currently practiced in one hospital.

THE ORGANIZATION AND PURPOSE OF THIS BOOK

In this volume, we report the results of a 4-year research project involving thousands of hours of systematic observations of mental health professionals and patients. We analyze the information gathered in this study in several ways. First, we describe the problems of implementing the legal model of informed consent. To what degree did the staff follow the requirements of the law? When did they not? Why not? Second, we describe the way the law and the specific behaviors that it produced did or did not produce the type of decisionmaking process mandated by informed consent. Finally, we assess whether or not any disclosure regulation can be expected to produce a more equal and mutual participatory relationship between mental health professionals and their patients.

It would have been easier for both the authors and the readers of this volume if we had simply taken a position and marshaled evidence to support it. However, our aim is to describe what we found with as little prejudice as possible, and our findings do not lead to simple conclusions. We have chosen to lead the reader piece by piece through our findings and to reserve a policy-oriented discussion for the conclusion.

A few things should be noted about our findings. First, the patterns of staff-patient communication and decisionmaking differed markedly from one setting to another. For example, the voluntariness of patients' participation was a serious issue in the Evaluation Center (the admission and referral section) of the Hospital, but not in the Outpatient Clinic. However, nowhere in the Hospital did we see decisionmaking and communication patterns that looked very much the way they were supposed to look under the ethical doctrine of informed consent. We saw only a few examples of either staff members or patients behaving as though they expected patients to be major participants in the decisionmaking or to have good reason to know most of the information necessary to make rational decisions. Likewise, we did not find that the formal informed consent procedures prescribed by state regulations made any substantial difference in this pattern, since decisions were typically made prior to patients' receiving the forms. Incompetency to make decisions was a serious problem with some patients, but no problem at all with others. Nonetheless, patients rarely seemed to understand the treatment issues well enough to make well-informed decisions.

On the other hand, we found that patients often managed to learn a lot about their treatment, and in certain situations they had a substantial influence on what that treatment would be. While informed consent procedures rarely played a major role in promoting these results, it seems possible that more mutual participation in decisionmaking can sometimes be fostered. While few decisions seemed to be completely free of pressures from family and staff, coercion was less of an issue than we had expected it to be.

The book begins with a brief review of the legal and ethical doctrine of informed consent. We have tried to make the complexity of this common-law doctrine simple and clear enough so that the lay reader will understand it without allowing the details of the doctrine to disappear into vague generalities. After that, we review the previous empirical studies of informed consent and try to describe what we believe they have and have not shown.

The analysis of the data itself is divided into three general sections, one on each setting that we observed—an admission and referral section of a hospital, an inpatient research ward for affective (mood) disorders, and an outpatient clinic for patients with thought disorders (schizophrenia). In each section, we have provided a general descriptive overview of the setting and its routine. This is followed by two analytical chapters that describe respectively our findings on the issues of information disclosure and patient understanding, and our findings as to the structure and voluntariness of the decisions. Each section concludes with a general summary of these findings. Finally, we present some conclusions about the current potential effectiveness of the doctrine of informed consent as a regulator of psychiatry.

2

Informed Consent: The Legal Doctrine[1]

INTRODUCTION

What is informed consent? Since its birth about two decades ago, the doctrine of informed consent has spawned untold controversy in the courts, among legal scholars, and within the medical profession. Although often condemned by the medical profession as a myth[2] and a fiction,[3] and sometimes even made the subject of parodies designed to illustrate its absurdity,[4] it has generally been favorably received by legal scholars. The doctrine promotes significant individual rights, and many practicing lawyers think highly of it, though possibly for less altruistic reasons.[5]

Informed consent is an ethical as well as a legal imperative. It has deep and strong roots in the individualistic tradition of the English common law, a tradition reflected in and reinvigorated by the American Constitution. Informed consent is a legal mandate. Nearly half the courts of American jurisdictions have adopted it as law, and only Georgia has rejected it.[6] More recently, 24 state legislatures have enacted statutes dealing with it.[7] In addition, informed consent constitutes a response to the mid-20th-century movements for consumer protection and civil liberties.

Informed consent reflects one of our highest social values, individual autonomy. It reflects a strong emotional need for a sense of control over our own lives and an admission of our dependence upon others, and it deals with a subject of fundamental importance, our health. It is little wonder that it is a source of so much conflict, confusion, and strongly held opinions.

Informed consent is comprised of two legal duties imposed on physicians: to inform patients about treatment, and to obtain their consent to treatment.[8] These duties are imposed in order to assure that a person's right of self-determination may be maintained in one particular sphere of human activity, the acquisition of medical care. In addition to safeguarding the right to determine one's own destiny, the informed consent doctrine encourages, but does not require, patients to make informed or intelligent decisions about medical care.

Viewed broadly, the duties of making disclosures and of obtaining consent are supposed to allow the patient to play the role of primary medical decision-maker. That is, these duties allocate primary decisional authority to the patient in making decisions about whether and how to be treated. The physician's role in decisionmaking is supposed to be to determine the following from a medical perspective: (1) what the patient's problem is (i.e., diagnosis); (2) how, if at all, it may be ameliorated; and (3) what the possible pitfalls of treatment may be. Finally, the doctor is to communicate this information to the patient, who then is to utilize it in the context of his or her own personal values and subjective preferences in order to make a decision.[9]

The physician's role in medical decisionmaking is primarily cognitive, medical, and technical. The patient's role is primarily affective, personal, and subjective. Informed consent views medical decisionmaking as a mix of technical and personal considerations; decisions about medical care are not to be made exclusively by physicians, because only the patient has access to the personal information, which is highly relevant to the making of the decision.

Although decisions about medical care often involve personal considerations, this fact does not necessarily compel the conclusion that primary decisional authority be given to the patient. Two other logical alternatives are available. Rather than requiring the physician to disclose information that the patient does not have but that is relevant to decisionmaking, there could be a requirement that the patient disclose the subjective information that the doctor lacks. The doctor then could decide whether and how to treat. Or both the physician and the patient could be required to disclose the information available to them to a neutral third party, who, on the basis of both kinds of information, would make a decision about treatment.

To a very limited extent, each of these alternative forms of medical decisionmaking does operate—the first, under the aegis of the "waiver"; the second, when the patient is "incompetent." Both situations are discussed later in this chapter. However, the general rule for the vast majority of cases requires that disclosure be made by the physician to the patient, and that the patient then make the final decision.

This is often justified by noting that it is the patient who will, in the most personal way, experience the benefits or the failures of treatment. It is the patient's body, mind, and being that must endure the pain, the uncertainty, the anxiety, and sometimes the cost of medical treatment. Certainly physicians experience benefits and losses from providing care, but the effect upon them is less direct, intense, and personal. It is not critical to every aspect of their lives that a particular treatment on a particular patient succeeds or fails, involves pain and suffering, and entails sacrifice of time, money, and other resources. Thus it is the patient to whom the law ordinarily entrusts primary decisional authority.

The legal rules governing the doctrine of informed consent have undergone and are still undergoing a slow metamorphosis, beginning with what is usually recognized as the first true informed consent case in 1957, the *Salgo*[10] case, and continuing through the rash of legislation in the mid-1970s.[11] Although the development of informed consent began as early as the 18th century,[12] most of the development did not take place until the 1960s and 1970s. This slow metamorphosis was marked by periodic bursts of activity—first in 1960 with the cases of *Natanson v. Kline*[13] and *Mitchell v. Robinson*[14]; next in 1972 with the central case of *Canterbury v. Spence*[15]; followed by important cases in California[16] and Rhode Island.[17] The third period of activity began in 1975 and subsided in 1977, when half of the state legislatures enacted statutes dealing with informed consent.

One informed consent case, *Canterbury v. Spence*, stands far above all others in discussing, if not establishing, the rules governing the obtaining of an informed consent. Although the rules established in *Canterbury* have been adopted in only about half of the jurisdictions that have considered the issue and explicitly rejected in an equal number of others,[18] this case, more comprehensively than any before it, discusses almost all facets of the doctrine: (1) what must be disclosed; (2) how it must be disclosed; (3) when informed consent need not be obtained; and (4) who makes the decision when a patient cannot.

ELEMENTS OF DISCLOSURE

There is little dispute over the kind of information a physician must tell a patient, the so-called "elements of disclosure." The central informational component is that of the possible negative results that may occur from undergoing a particular procedure. While this concept can be expressed in several ways, it is generally referred to as "the risks of the procedure."[19] Although disclosure of the risks neither guarantees that the patient will use the information in making a decision nor assures that the decision reached will be a reasonable one,[20] patients cannot make an informed decision without knowledge of the risks.

Physicians must also explain the nature of the procedure (e.g., whether it is surgical, pharmacological, or radiological; whether it is diagnostic or therapeutic; whether it is experimental or established; and what part of the body is involved, as well as the procedure's purpose). Closely related to the purpose is the benefit that a patient may reasonably expect to accrue from treatment. Although in many cases the benefit of the treatment is self-evident (i.e., the amelioration of the problem for which the patient sought medical care), in many other cases something less than total cure can be expected. There is always a possibility that no benefits may accrue; that is, the treatment may bring neither good nor bad results, but simply may produce no results at all.

Finally, the patient is entitled to be informed of any possible alternative treatments that might be employed, as well as the consequences of these alternatives (i.e., the benefits and the risks likely to be entailed). Since one alternative to any proposed treatment is no treatment at all, the patient should also be apprised of the likely consequences of totally foregoing treatment.

These requirements—risks, benefits, alternatives, and nature of treatment—are the classical elements of disclosure and constitute the basis from which the corpus of disclosure rules and exceptions to informed consent has developed.

THE STANDARD OF DISCLOSURE

Describing the elements of informed consent in general terms is quite simple, and perhaps this is why there is so little debate in the law and so little objection from the medical profession as to what kind of information should be disclosed to patients. But when it comes to determining what particular information should be disclosed, in the context of a particular patient with a particular illness or injury and a particular treatment, the debate increases and the controversy mounts. The issue of how much information a physician must disclose about benefits, about alternatives, and especially about risks causes considerable concern among all interested parties.

Although the informed consent cases often speak in terms of requiring full disclosure, they also acknowledge that the physician is not obliged to tell the patient everything that is medically known about the procedure.[21] There are several reasons for this. First, some of what the physician knows is too complex to be communicated meaningfully to the lay person. The courts have made it quite clear that the physician does not have to disclose such complex information. However, if the physician chooses to do so, simple language must be used that is reasonably calculated for the patient to understand. Second, the process of disclosing all information, if carried to its logical extreme, would involve providing the patient with the equivalent of a medical school education, and time and practicality simply will not permit this.

> The patient's interest in information does not extend to a lengthy polysyllabic discourse on all possible complications. A mini-course in medical science is not required.[22]

Even then there would be no assurance that the patient has been apprised of all of the information that could conceivably fall under the required elements of disclosure. Some of the information that could be disclosed is irrelevant or only marginally relevant to the patient's decisionmaking process and therefore need not be disclosed.

If the problem of defining the standard of disclosure were the only issue, full disclosure would be ideal, since it does most to promote the rationality of patients' decisions. However, since necessity clearly dictates that disclosure be something less than full, there is a need to define the extent of disclosure that is required, so that physicians will have some idea of how to fulfill their duty and patients will know whether their right to information has been denied.

The courts have agreed that the physician must make reasonable disclosure of that information that is "material" to making a decision about treatment. However, the consensus immediately breaks down over the issue of how "materiality" is to be determined, and two separate factions emerge: those courts that believe that materiality should be measured from the physician's perspective, and those that believe that it should be viewed from the patient's perspective.[23]

The early informed consent cases never acknowledged the issue and simply assumed that materiality should be determined from the doctor's perspective. One case indicates that the degree of disclosure made to the patient is "primarily a question of medical judgment,"[24] and, consequently, that

> . . . the duty of the physician to disclose . . . is limited to those disclosures which a reasonable medical practitioner would make under the same or similar circumstances.[25]

This rule closely parallels those in medical negligence cases, in which the standard to which the physician is held is what is customary and usual in the profession.[25,26] The courts of several jurisdictions have explicitly adopted this rule, and few seriously questioned it before 1972.[27] A corollary of this so-called "professional standard of disclosure" was the requirement that expert medical testimony was needed to establish the standard of disclosure to which the physician would be held accountable, despite the problems associated with such a requirement.

Beginning with *Canterbury v. Spence*, a substantial number of courts began to establish a new standard of disclosure based on a different view of materiality. These cases discarded the professional standard of disclosure and replaced it with a lay- or patient-oriented standard, which effectively withdrew from the medical profession the right to determine what information must be disclosed to the patient. A fair statement of the rule that emerged—and there are several different statements in the *Canterbury* case alone—is that the physician is required to disclose all information about a proposed treatment that a reasonable person in the patient's situation would consider material to a decision either to undergo or to forego treatment.[28] The scope of the duty to disclose is to be determined by "the patient's right to self-decision,"[29] rather than by the custom or practice of either the physician making the disclosure or the larger medical profession.

The dust from the storm that this issue has created has not yet settled, and it is unlikely that one rule will emerge to the exclusion of the other. Rather, these two different standards of disclosure probably will remain, with some jurisdictions subscribing to one and the remainder to the other. Despite the problems inherent in the patient-oriented standard, primarily that of how a physician is to know what a reasonable patient would want to know, it is the preferable standard of disclosure because it is most in keeping with the values underlying the informed consent doctrine and the goals that the doctrine seeks to promote, especially that of assuring the patient's primacy in decisionmaking.

However, the failure of the doctor to make reasonable disclosure to the patient (regardless of whether a professional or a lay standard of disclosure is applied) is not sufficient to constitute a violation of the patient's rights under the informed consent doctrine. Two other things must be shown: (1) that some harm occurred to the patient; and (2) that this harm was caused by the doctor's failure to disclose information. The first is referred to as the "materialized risk requirement," and the second is discussed under the aegis of "causation."

If the physician fails to inform the patient adequately, the patient's rights have not been violated unless some bodily injury has been suffered.[30] For example, if the patient agrees to and undergoes surgery without having been informed that the operation may produce paralysis, there is no violation of rights unless the patient is actually paralyzed. The risk that the doctor failed to disclose must materialize for there to be a violation of the informed consent doctrine and a right to recovery of damages.

The materialized risk requirement has received severe criticism for failing to "recognize that a citizen can be wronged without being harmed, that his dignity as a human being has been violated and that an assault has taken place the moment the deceiving authority commences thereby . . . , even if beneficial."[31,32] This criticism goes to the heart of the question of just what rights are actually promoted and protected by the informed consent doctrine.

If the doctrine's avowed individualistic purposes—the promotion of individual self-determination, human dignity, and rational decisionmaking—are to be honored, then the failure to disclose information disserves these purposes. It makes no difference that the patient incurred no bodily harm; the failure to disclose is a harm, and the failure of the cases to recognize this is a betrayal of the lofty ideals of the informed consent doctrine.

Not only must the risk that the physician failed to disclose materialize in order for the patient to recover damages for a lack of informed consent, but the cases all hold that this failure must be the "cause" of the harm that befalls the patient. That is, adequate disclosure must have resulted in a decision to forego the treatment in question. However, controversy exists as to whether causation is found by reference to an objective standard (i.e., would a reasonable person have decided not to undergo treatment had he or she been properly informed?) or to a subjective standard (i.e., would this patient have decided not to undergo treatment had he or she been properly informed?). The early cases seemed unaware of the difference between the two tests,[33] and some commentators assumed that the subjective test should be applied.[34] Surprisingly, since it is otherwise so protective of patients' rights, *Canterbury* and most other cases that have specifically confronted this issue have rejected the subjective test.[35] However, some courts that appear to have adopted a subjective standard of disclosure have not explicitly confronted the issue.[36]

THE EXCEPTIONS TO INFORMED CONSENT

Physicians have duties, and patients have rights, other than those imposed by the informed consent doctrine. Some duties are imposed by law, such as the duty to practice technically proficient medicine. Others derive from the ethics of the profession, such as the duty to "do no harm," and some derive from professional ethics that have been accorded legal recognition, such as the duty of confidentiality.

Some of these duties come into conflict with the doctor's duty to disclose and to obtain consent. In so doing, they impose limits on the informed consent doctrine and help to shape its boundaries. Other limits on the doctrine also exist. Practical considerations often require a more abbreviated or even non-existent disclosure than that contemplated by law. Let us begin with those limitations imposed on the doctrine by the other legal and ethical duties of the physician.

The limitations of the informed consent doctrine take the form of certain exceptions that have developed and acquired judicial or legislative recognition. Although the contours of each of the exceptions and the consequences of invoking them are somewhat unclear, their existence is beyond dispute. The four recognized exceptions are these: (1) an emergency, (2) incompetency, (3) a waiver, and (4) the therapeutic privilege. Each of these exceptions recognizes that the individualistic values that the informed consent doctrine seeks to promote are not the only significant concerns in medical decisionmaking. Health is a value in its own right. The patient, his or her family and friends, and even the society at large have a stake in promoting the patient's health for its own sake. This leads to a parallel concern with assuring that health professionals are not unduly hampered in exercising their skills. The four exceptions are the means by which the law permits health values to be interjected into the process of medical decisionmaking.

THE EMERGENCY EXCEPTION

In an emergency, the doctor may render treatment without the patient's informed consent. The rationale for this exception is, at least where the patient is not also unconscious (in which case the justification for treating without consent ought to be found in the incompetency exception), that there is no time to make disclosure to the patient or to obtain consent without seriously jeopardizing the patient's well-being.

Since there appears to be an intuitive notion of what an "emergency" is, many courts have refrained from attempting to define it even when finding one to exist. Those that have ruled on the question of how an emergency should be defined have ranged from a very stringent definition, such as the medical care needed to preserve life or limb,[37] to a very broad one, such as the medical care needed simply to alleviate suffering or pain.[38] The definition of an emergency used in determining when the requirements of informed consent should be suspended must consider the extent to which their abandonment or relaxation undermines the values that the doctrine promotes.

If informed consent is suspended in an emergency, it should be suspended only if the time required to make disclosure and/or to obtain the patient's decision might be very disadvantageous to the patient's personal health. To permit treatment without obtaining informed consent in these situations allows health to be restored or possibly a life to be saved. Such a practice promotes the social value in health at minimal cost to the interest in individualism. If the patient in such a situation is having severe enough pain that there is no interest in the physician's disclosure, the right to it may be waived, as is discussed below.

THE INCOMPETENCY EXCEPTION

Closely related to the emergency situation is the exception granted for incompetent patients. Certain individuals recognized as incompetent to consent to treatment may be treated without their consent. Like the emergency exception, the only thing certain about the incompetency exception is its existence. There is no single or even well-accepted definition of "incompetency." However, there are several general ways in which the determination of incompetency can be approached, each of which has been utilized or its appropriateness suggested in court decisions, statutes, administrative regulations, or scholarly commentary.

Incompetency may be of two different types—general or specific. The individual who is intoxicated, actively psychotic, severely mentally retarded, unconscious, or senile may fall into the category of general incompetency. Since such individuals bear so little resemblance to the rational decisionmaker, they may be considered incompetent to make important decisions about their lives, including decisions about medical care. In contrast, incompetency may be specific, in that one may be incompetent to make certain kinds of important decisions and yet competent to make others. What is relevant to a determination of specific incompetency is not the individual's general qualities of intellect, affect, and reasoning, but his or her actual ability to make a specific decision. Specific incompetency may be determined by reference to (1) the person's mere ability to manifest a decision; (2) the manner in which the person makes a decision (e.g., whether it is rationally made); (3) the nature of the decision itself (e.g., whether it is a rational one); or (4) the person's understanding of the information disclosed by the doctor.[39]

In addition, it is necessary to distinguish between *de jure* (or legal) and *de facto* (or actual) incompetency. One is *de jure* incompetent either by being a minor or by being determined to be incompetent by a court. Minors are legally generally incompetent. An adult may be adjudged either generally or specifically incompetent. Some persons who are legally competent may in fact be incompetent. Therefore, their assent to treatment is not a valid authorization for it, nor is their dissent a valid refusal. In contrast, individuals adjudicated as generally incompetent may in fact be specifically competent to make a medical decision, or persons adjudicated incompetent in the past may in fact have regained their competency. In summary, although the incompetency exception exists, what it involves is quite unclear.

THE WAIVER EXCEPTION

Several cases and recent statutes have acknowledged that a patient may relinquish or waive the right to give an informed consent to treatment. However, the cases and statutes do little more than recognize the existence of waiver, and do not address several important problems relating to its definition and application.

Although the notion of waiving one's right to give an informed consent is relatively new, the waiver of other rights has long been recognized and thus provides substantial guidance in determining what a waiver of informed consent should look like. To be valid, a waiver must be an intentional and voluntary relinquishment of a known right.[40] Therefore, in order to relinquish the right to be informed or the right to decide or both validly, the patient must know that he or she possesses these rights; he or she must intend to give them up; and there must be no undue pressure on the patient to do so.

It is unlikely that the average patient will possess this knowledge. Therefore, it is incumbent upon the physician to tell the patient of the right to waive informed consent when the patient expresses a desire not to participate in the decisionmaking process by indicating a lack of interest in information, in decisionmaking, or in both. Such statements as "Please don't tell me about that, it will only upset me" (the functional equivalent of a relinquishment of the right to be informed) and/or "Doctor, you decide what is best for me" (the functional equivalent of a relinquishment of the right to decide) should activate the physician's duty to tell the patient that an individual has both a right to the information and a right to decide. However, the patient should also be informed of a right not to hear and a right not to decide (i.e., a right to waive).

A properly obtained waiver is in keeping with the individualistic values promoted by the doctrine of informed consent. The patient remains the ultimate decisionmaker, but the content of the decision is shifted from the decisional level to the metadecisional level—from the equivalent of "I want this treatment or that treatment or no treatment" to "I don't want any information about the treatment" or "I don't want to decide, you make the decision as to what should be done." Waiver permits taking care of a patient's health without the patient's full participation in the process of medical decisionmaking.

THE THERAPEUTIC PRIVILEGE

It is well established in the case law and commentary that the physician, in appropriate circumstances, may be excused from compliance with the requirement of informed consent by the "therapeutic privilege," which permits the physician to withhold information that would otherwise have to be disclosed if disclosure would be "harmful." Of all the exceptions to the informed consent doctrine, the therapeutic privilege is the most well known and discussed, despite the fact that few cases turn on its application.

Although the contours of the privilege are unclear, the general purpose of the privilege is to free physicians from a legal requirement which would force them to violate their "primary duty" to do what is beneficial for the patient.[41]

In practice, however, the privilege may legitimize the physician's natural reluctance to disclose unpleasant information to the patient. Therefore, if the privilege is not severely circumscribed in its scope, it threatens to swallow the general obligation of disclosure. If the harm to the patient from disclosure is viewed broadly as including the risk that the patient may choose to reject medical care, the privilege would permit the physician to substitute his or her own judgment for that of the patient's in every instance of medical decisionmaking.

The most stringent formulation of the privilege permits information to be withheld from the patient only when its disclosure would be so upsetting that it would render the patient unable to engage rationally in decisionmaking. At the other extreme is a definition of the privilege that allows the withholding

of information regarding any untoward consequences of a treatment where full disclosure will be detrimental to the patient's total care and best interest.[42]

Although disclosure of treatment information and patient decisionmaking are important values, they should not be so singlemindedly pursued that they become self-defeating. When disclosure threatens to impede patient decisionmaking, consideration must be given to dispensing with it. Indeed, some authorities suggest that disclosure must be suspended when it poses a reasonable threat of harm to the patient.[43] However, a loose formulation of the privilege is inconsistent with the underlying values and the functions of the doctrine of informed consent.

In addition to these four exceptions, it is arguable that there are a few others. Some courts have spoken about an exception to the consent requirement for the unconscious patient.[44] However, the unconscious patient is viewed most adequately as a subcategory of the incompetency exception.

Courts have also suggested that there is an exception to the disclosure requirement for common risks (risks of which the reasonable person ought to be aware) and for known risks (risks of which the patient is actually aware).[45] However, these two situations should not be viewed as exceptions to the disclosure requirement, but should constitute an integral part of the definition of the degree of disclosure that is required of the physician.

PROXY DECISIONMAKING

When one of the four exceptions to informed consent is properly invoked, the consequence is that the decision about medical treatment will be made by someone other than the patient. The problem is that of who should make the decision when the patient is disqualified from doing so. This problem, referred to as either "proxy consent," "substituted consent," or "third-party consent"[46] has received only scant analysis by the courts and legislatures. One of the few generalizations that can be made is found in legal treatises suggesting that when the patient cannot give consent, the proper practice to follow is to obtain the consent of a close family member, if available[47]; most physicians and hospitals routinely follow this practice.

There are several general options available for making a medical decision when the patient is appropriately disqualified from participation. First, the physician could be legally empowered to make the medical decision in all cases in which an exception is invoked, as is now the case in an emergency. However, to do so may foreclose the interjection of personal values into the decision-making process, resulting in a decision made exclusively on the basis of technical considerations supplied by the physician.

A second method of proxy decisionmaking involves the use of a family member or a friend of the patient. In theory, this method permits the interjection of nonmedical values into the decisionmaking process by a party whose allegiance is not to the medical profession. However, the family member or friend may not have only the patient's best interest at heart, since that person may be motivated by self-interest.

A third general way of making medical decisions without the patient's participation is for the case to be brought to the attention of governmental authorities, either administrative or judicial. By either making the treatment decision itself or by reviewing the decision of the proxy, the governmental authority could provide a forum in which individualism as well as society's interest in the patient's health may be explicitly brought to bear in the decision-making process. However, such procedures take time and resources and should not be prescribed for small decisions.

In present practice, when the patient is disqualified from participation in medical decisionmaking, sometimes the physician makes the decision; sometimes a family member is called upon to do so; and sometimes judicial proceedings are instituted by the physician, hospital administrators, or family members. The only relatively clear situation is an emergency in which the physician makes the treatment decision out of necessity. Although there has been a great deal of discussion by courts of this problem in recent years[48] in the context of the administration or cessation of treatment to the terminally ill, no similar guidance has been offered for the large number of cases involving medical decisions in more ordinary contexts when an individual patient is unable to participate in the decisionmaking.

INFORMED CONSENT AND ITS APPLICATION TO PSYCHIATRY

Until the late 1960s, the law concerning the legal rights of psychiatric patients lay dormant. Gradually in the decade of the 1970s, first through lawsuits and later through legislative reform, the procedures by which individuals are involuntarily hospitalized for psychiatric care have been thoroughly revised in order to make them conform to the dictates of the U.S. Constitution. Among the most important of these reforms are procedural safeguards, including the right to counsel, to a court hearing, to examination and cross-examination of witnesses, and to adequate notice of the nature of the proceedings. In addition to stricter procedures for commitment, there has been a concurrent narrowing of the substantive grounds for commitment. Under these more stringent criteria, individuals may be committed only if they pose a clear and present danger of substantial harm either to themselves or to others as a result of mental illness.

For persons who are already hospitalized, litigation, legislation, and regulation have established an equally extensive panoply of rights. The right to receive adequate and effective treatment has been foremost among them. More recently, beginning in the late 1970s, a number of lawsuits have been initiated at both the trial and appellate court levels to establish the right of involuntarily committed psychiatric patients to refuse treatment. These suits have been relatively successful, in that the courts have held that involuntarily committed patients cannot ordinarily be administered treatment without their informed consent.[49] The United States Supreme Court, after recently reviewing one of these cases, declined to decide the issue, so that the final resolution of the matter is uncertain as of this writing. Under most state laws, informed consent must be obtained from voluntary psychiatric patients as well. At least one state, California, also requires that voluntary patients be specifically told of their right not to be treated without their informed consent.[50]

Thus, within a relatively short space of time, the assumption that psychiatric patients were obligated to accept the treatments recommended by their doctors has undergone a complete reversal. Now it seems increasingly clear that informed consent must be obtained from psychiatric patients as well as from medical patients before treatment may be administered. Although the same exceptions apply to psychiatric patients as to medical patients, no additional exception is clearly created by the fact that the patient has been involuntarily hospitalized.

A MODEL OF INFORMED CONSENT

The doctrine of informed consent, both in its legal and ethical manifestations, is not amenable to empirical scrutiny without some further analytical dissection and simplification. Thus we have constructed a model of informed consent that both reflects case law and serves as a basis for empirical study.

One of our research objectives has been to determine the extent to which, if at all, the doctrine of informed consent is currently operating in specific settings in a psychiatric hospital. In order to establish what to study, how to study it, what data to collect, and how to analyze it, it is necessary to describe how informed consent is supposed to operate.

Based upon a reading of the informed consent case law, we have developed a "model" of informed consent to facilitate empirical investigation by clarifying the components of informed consent and their relationship to each other. The model is an attempt to infer from the case law an operational definition of informed consent that would inform us as to what data we should collect and how we should analyze it. This model is to be understood as a broad, preliminary, and simplified statement of how informed consent should operate.

We have identified several components of informed consent. They are as follows:

1. Disclosure of information (I). Certain information must be provided by the doctor to the patient. Patients in general are presumed to know certain information, and a particular patient may be presumed to know additional information on the basis of personal experience.
2. Competency (C). There is a legal presumption that a patient has the capacity to comprehend the information that the doctor discloses. Exactly how competency is to be determined is not clear; but if a patient is not competent, any decision that he or she makes will not be considered legally valid or binding.
3. Understanding (U). The judicial decisions implicitly assume that a person who is competent when provided with information will understand it. Since competency involves the capacity to understand, competency and understanding are closely related components of informed consent.
4. Voluntariness (V). The decision that a patient makes must be freely arrived at without undue pressure or coercion.
5. Decision (D). The patient must actually decide whether to accept or refuse treatment.

Taken together, these five components comprise the doctrine of informed consent. We freely acknowledge that these components are useful largely for analytical purposes. In the actual medical decisionmaking process, it is not nearly so simple to separate the components. Indeed, even in theory, there is some overlap among the various components of informed consent.

The basic model of informed consent does little more than incorporate these components in a linear fashion.[51] Simply stated, the model is that the doctor discloses information to a patient who is competent; the patient understands the information and voluntarily renders a decision. In the absence of any of these elements, the patient's decision is not legally valid. The consequence of a decision that is not legally valid is, in general terms, either that the physician may not rely upon that decision or that he must not do so. Thus if there has been no disclosure or inadequate disclosure, the patient's decision is not valid; if the patient is not competent, the decision is not valid; if the patient does not understand the information, the decision may not be valid; if the decision is not rendered voluntarily, it is not valid; or if the patient, for some reason, does not manifest a decision, there is no authorization to the doctor to render treatment. To summarize, a competent patient (C), given information about treatment (I), understands that information (U), and voluntarily (V) renders a decision (D) either to be treated (consent) or not to be treated (refusal). We depict this model as follows:

$$C + I \Rightarrow U$$

$$U + V \Rightarrow D$$

3

A Review of the Empirical Literature

At the time that we began planning this study, very few other empirical studies of informed consent had been published. Since then, more than 100 such studies have appeared in the medical and social science literature. Although they provide significant amounts of data about informed consent, there are many limitations inherent in these studies that severely restrict the usefulness of their findings.

Our review of their findings are presented here in accordance with the components of the model of informed consent that we describe in the preceding chapter.[1]

DISCLOSURE OF INFORMATION

Although the disclosure requirement is at the heart of the informed consent doctrine, few if any studies of informed consent have set about to determine what doctors routinely tell patients in day-to-day practice, although a few studies of doctor–patient communication deal with this topic independently of the context of informed consent.[2,3] In many studies of what patients understand, a statement often appears that "informed consent was obtained," but that is all we know about what patients were told.[4] Such statements tell us very little if anything about what and how patients were actually told. Occasionally studies assume that patients were read and/or were allowed to read consent forms, but the investigators did not actually study the disclosure process, so what remains is only a presumption of disclosure but no actual findings about it.[5] Other studies indicate that patients signed consent forms, but we are not told the content of those forms. A typical study in this regard states that patients were given an "informed consent" sheet containing information developed according to legal guidelines, and that this was read to patients.[6]

There have been a substantial number of studies of patients' attitudes toward disclosure, although it is not apparent why this should be so when there have been so few investigations of actual disclosure. Alfidi's studies are interesting because they come to contradictory conclusions. In one study, he found that 89% of patients who were informed of the serious risks of angiography "appreciated" receiving the information.[7] However, in a later study, in which he made disclosure contingent upon patients' affirmative response to an inquiry as to whether or not they wished to be informed of risks, only about one-third of the patients wanted to be informed.[8] Not surprisingly, even when patients indicate that they appreciate disclosure, more than one-fourth report that they are made "less comfortable" by this information.[7]

One way of reconciling these results is that in the first study the patients had already been given the information when they were asked to indicate their attitude toward disclosure, whereas in the second study they had not yet been informed. Perhaps patients view a *fait accompli* as a good thing, because they find that their fears have been unwarranted and nothing can be done to erase the experience. An alternative explanation is that the first study is more likely to be valid because it measured patients' attitudes toward a real past event, whereas the second study is hypothetical in that patients are not asked whether they were grateful for information received, but rather whether they wanted information at all—information that was characterized as relating to "significant hazards," a phrase with negative connotations.

Despite the wide attention in the medical literature paid to the physician's "therapeutic privilege" to withhold seriously upsetting information from patients,[9] there are no studies that systematically examine the central issues—namely, whether disclosure of information about the risks of treatment causes "harm" to patients, and what the nature of that harm is. Faden and Beauchamp report in their study of patient decisionmaking about nonsurgical contraceptives that there was "no evidence that disclosed information actually produced . . . negative consequences."[10] One problem with this conclusion, which the authors forthrightly acknowledge, is that the results may not be generalizable to patients whose medical condition is more serious than that of the subjects of this study, who were essentially healthy persons. Another problem that needs to be recognized by anyone seeking to study the impact of disclosure on patients is the need to define as precisely as possible the nature of the negative consequences that disclosure produces. To say that there are no "negative consequences" without defining the term more precisely is of dubious value. Other investigators report, not surprisingly, that some patients suffer "apprehensiveness," "anger," and "anxiety" from disclosure.[11] However, there is also some evidence that patients who are better informed suffer less anxiety about impending surgical procedures.[12]

COMPETENCY AND UNDERSTANDING

We discuss studies of "competency" and "understanding" together, primarily because of the conceptual overlap between the two[1] and because of the extremely small number of studies of competency.

The threshold problem in any study of what patients understand is to specify what is meant by the term "understanding." An in-depth exploration of this concept is beyond the scope of this chapter.[9,13] What is important for present purposes is that most investigators of understanding have chosen to look at one particular kind of understanding—what we refer to as "recall"— without any apparent recognition that recall is merely one kind of under-standing and not the one most relevant to informed consent. Even those investigators who have employed more adequate notions of understanding have not specified what they mean by the term, although it is clear that they were studying something other than recall.[14]

One of the most widely known studies of recall is that conducted by Robinson and Merav,[15] and its methods and findings are typical. Both investi-gators are clinicians, and the subjects of their study of informed consent were patients upon whom they performed heart surgery. They made audiotape recordings of discussions they had with 20 patients 1 to 2 days before their operations. They again interviewed these patients 4 to 6 months after the operations and recorded the conversations. What they found, in summary, was that the patients had "generally poor retention in all categories of informed consent information."[15] Other studies using similar methods have turned up similar results—that patients do not remember very well what they have been told. One likely but uninvestigated explanation is that patients' poor recall may merely be part of the normal forgetting process.[4] Indeed, it is possible that the patients remember more than normal subjects would have remembered, but there is no way of knowing whether this is the case because of the failure to perform controlled studies. At any rate, patient recall after 4 months is of dubious value to the study of informed consent.

One of the studies that rather clearly recognizes that understanding and recall are not equivalent, however, also concludes that the level of understand-ing in patients to whom disclosure has been made is not very high. In their study of families who had received genetic counseling, Leonard et al. reported that with respect to

> the minimum knowledge that a genetic counselor might hope would be retained as a basis for informed family-planning decisions . . . about ½ of the parents had the kind of comprehension that could make the information helpful to them, whereas in about ¼ that understanding was flawed in some way and for about ¼ the genetic counseling had served little purpose.[14]

These investigators employed an operational definition based upon a patient's ability to use information to make the very decision for which it was initially provided. This is the focus most clearly relevant to informed consent. Other studies that have used concepts of understanding more sophisticated than recall have also found patients' understanding to be at a rather low level. [16-18]

Several studies shed some light on why patients seem to understand as little as they do. One conducted for the National Commission for the Protection of

Human Subjects found that the consent forms that subjects in research protocols were asked to sign contained language that was too complex for most people:

> [O]verall, no more than 15 percent of the consent forms were in language as simple as is found, for example, in *Time Magazine*. In more than three-fourths of the consent forms, fewer than 20 percent of the technical or medical terms were explained in lay language. . . .[19]

Two other studies of consent forms also came to the conclusion that the language is too complex to be understood by most patients, since it is at the advanced undergraduate level.[20,21] Other reasons suggested for lack of comprehension are the length of consent forms[22] and the lack of time in which to assimilate information.[2,23] There is conflicting evidence as to whether innovative methods of disclosure, such as videotape, pamphlets, structured discussion, or informal group discussion, affect the patients' level of understanding, but here too the data is sparse.[10,24,25] However, patients who were provided with an opportunity to discuss written forms understood the information better than did those who had merely obtained information in writing.[26]

The understanding level of psychiatric patients is not significantly worse than that of medical patients; in fact, Soskis reports that the schizophrenic patients he studied were significantly better informed about the side effects and risks of their medications than were a group of medical patients. However, only one of 25 schizophrenic patients knew that the medication was for schizophrenia, whereas six of the 15 medical patients mentioned their diagnosis as the reason for taking the medication.[27]

Patients' understanding of information given to them about voluntary admission to a psychiatric hospital is also low[28]; patients' ability to recall having their commitment status changed from involuntary to voluntary was 65%, but in the authors' judgment, only about one-third of the patients were able to appreciate the significance of this change in their status.[17] In another study, no patients were able to recall the content of the voluntary admission form; even after it was reread to them, 33% could not even repeat one provision of it.[29] In a frequently cited study, Pryce reports that only 12 of 50 schizophrenic patients gave "true consent" to participate in a double-blind crossover study of an antipsychotic drug and placebo.[30] The finding is of limited value, however, because we do not know what patients were told, how understanding was determined, or what was considered "true consent."

A deficiency in a large number of the empirical studies, nicely illustrated by the studies of psychiatric patients, is their lack of comparability and generalizability. They are studies in diverse populations with varying degrees of acuteness of illness, performed on relatively small numbers of subjects.

A fair number of investigators have studied the nature and extent of understanding of what it means to be a subject in a clinical research protocol. One important thing for research subjects to understand is that research is not undertaken solely for the well-being of subjects, as treatment is for patients. The only study designed principally to determine the meaning to research subjects of nonbeneficial clinical research found that 61 of 140 subjects

> thought the purpose of hospitalization [of their child] to be diagnostic and/or therapeutic. These parents had failed to understand why the medical care of their children would be undertaken in a research center.[16]

Indeed, only six of the 140 subjects properly understood the purpose of hospitalization as being pure research. Actually, the research subjects were children, and it was the meaning to their parents of "research" that was investigated.

Several descriptive clinical studies suggest that patients who were subjects in psychiatric research may have mistaken, delusional, or highly personalized ideas about research procedures.[31-34] Patients may not have understood whether research procedures were designed primarily (or were likely) to help them, or whether the purpose of the research was instead to acquire new knowledge. These studies suggest that the understanding of research procedures may have been more problematic for acutely ill patients. While useful, these studies were not addressed exclusively to problems in obtaining informed consent, nor did they indicate what had been disclosed to the patient/subject.

DECISION

A number of studies shed some light on the relationship between the nature and the extent of disclosure to patients and whether or not patients consented to or refused treatment.[7,35-37] One of the earliest of these found that "228 of 232 patients consented to angiography after a straightforward disclosure of possible complication."[7] However, other studies have reported contrary findings. In an experimental design in which 100 subjects were given the hypothetical case of a man with a suspected brain tumor who had to determine whether to undergo a cerebral arteriogram, 50% would have refused the procedure on account of the risks. "Sixty percent of those who would have refused did so only because of specific, detailed knowledge of stroke syndromes, and the highest rates of refusal were for the most sinister complications."[38] Perhaps the high rate of refusal is because the subjects in an experimental design are not actually suffering from the illness and may be more inclined to say that they would refuse a procedure because of its risks than are persons who actually suffer from that illness.

A few studies shed some light on the nexus between what patients understand and the decisions that they ultimately make[22,39,40]; but, as in the case of the relationship between disclosure and understanding, the findings are not clear-cut. These studies are also experimental in design, and there is a strong need for clinical studies that examine the relationship not merely between disclosure and decision and not merely between understanding and decision, but also the complex relationship among what patients are told, what they understand about this information, how and whether they use it in making a decision, and whether they consent to or refuse treatment.

Both the empirical literature and the anecdotal literature on informed consent hint at another significant issue that has not received any direct study— the timing of obtaining informed consent. Occasionally studies indicate that informed consent was obtained not far in advance of surgery. [11,41] It is important to investigate the relationship between the proximity of informed consent to the performance of a procedure and the patient's decision about the procedure. If patients decide to undergo procedures and are only informed of risks just prior to their performance, we would anticipate that the patients are psychologically committed to the procedures and that the disclosure of risks is unlikely to change their minds. [4] However, if patients receive the information before the decision is made, it may be more likely that risk disclosure will induce them to refuse treatment. There is, however, no empirical data on this important issue.

A 1980 study by Faden and Beauchamp is one of the few that has systematically investigated the impact of disclosed information. [10] They found that this information was "the most important factor" in determining the patient's decision for only 12% of study subjects who were given information about nonsurgical contraceptive techniques. Previous patient experiences with contraception, as well as personal feelings, were important influences upon the patients' decisionmaking process. The disclosed information did not, however, impair or confuse decisionmaking and seemed to have made the decision easier for many patients. One recent study points the way for further research of this issue in psychiatry. Appelbaum and Gutheil report that a significant proportion of psychiatric patients who refused antipsychotic medications did not cite the risks or side effects of the medication as their reasons for refusal. [42]

Although informed consent is based upon the supposition that when provided with relevant information about treatment, patients will weigh the risks against the benefits of the proposed treatment and compare the risk-benefit ratios of alternative treatments, the evidence that exists suggests otherwise. The consensus is that doctors make recommendations and give patients some information about the recommended procedures, and then that patients go along with the recommendation. [17,43] Fellner and Marshall, in one of their two studies of kidney donations, report that "not one of the donors weighed alternatives and decided rationally." [43]

Despite the importance of proxy decisionmaking, [9] there has been little empirical investigation of the many facets of the subject—for example, (1) the frequency of the use of proxy decisionmakers, (2) the conditions under which proxies are used, (3) the identity of the proxy, and (4) the willingness of doctors to rely upon proxy decisions that do not concur with the doctors' own recommendations. The only study we have found deals with the frequency of proxy consent as opposed to proxy refusal. In the case of 17 presumptively incompetent psychiatric patients, consent was obtained from 15 relatives, and only two refused to permit the patients' inclusion in a study of the value of a drug for the treatment of schizophrenia.[30]

VOLUNTARINESS

Only a minuscule number of studies of informed consent look at the problem of voluntariness and the kinds of pressures that come to bear on patients in the process of medical decisionmaking. Voluntariness is the aspect of informed consent least amenable to empirical inquiry, because of the complex conceptual and methodological difficulties.

In a study of mothers who admitted their children to a hospital to be subjects in a research protocol that held out no benefits to the children, McCollum and Schwartz, in explaining that only three of 140 mothers refused to admit their children, speculate that "[a] clue to their conscious motivation is contained in the recurrent statement, 'I have no choice.'"[16] The only empirical evidence about pressure from other persons is Fellner and Marshall's conclusion that in making decisions about kidney donations, "there appears to be a . . . family system, which also tends to influence [decisionmaking] but which is very difficult to demonstrate."[44]

GENERAL METHODOLOGICAL PROBLEMS

The paucity of meaningful empirical studies of informed consent may be testimony both to the elusive nature of certain elements of informed consent, especially understanding and voluntariness, and to the pragmatic difficulties of undertaking empirical studies of informed consent. The pragmatic difficulties are in part consequent to the elusive nature of the concepts, but they also arise from problems in observing doctor-patient interactions, especially observing them in such a way as to minimize the influence on the informed consent process.

On balance, although there are some notable exceptions, the empirical studies of informed consent are marred by one or more serious deficiencies:

1. None of the studies is comprehensive. Each looks at a particular aspect of informed consent but ignores the totality of the decisionmaking process. By contrast, we have attempted to study each of the components of the medical decisionmaking process separately—voluntariness, information, competency, understanding, and decision—as well as the process as a whole.

2. Many of the studies are rather primitive in design, execution, and/or goals. While there is value in an incremental method of gaining knowledge about a problem, and studies should not necessarily be faulted merely because

they are modest in their approach, many investigators continually repeat past mistakes rather than learn from them. This is most apparent in the enormous number of studies of patients' recall. Even here none of the investigators attempt to replicate the work of others, let alone to improve upon it by more sophisticated conceptualization or methodology.

3. Most of the studies involve some serious intervention by the investigator into the normal course of medical practice and patient decisionmaking, often by prescribing what disclosure is to be made to patients or by asking questions of patients about the information that has been disclosed. However, at least these studies gather information about clinical practice; that is, they study real patients. Other studies are not done with patients, but rather with ordinary people, who are sometimes asked to place themselves in the position of persons having to make medical decisions for themselves or for others. Although both clinical research studies and purely experimental designs can yield important information, they are most useful once one knows about actual practices. The use of normal subjects or even the use of real patients faced with hypothetical decisions may not yield true results, since the emotional aspects of actual decisionmaking are absent. To the extent that in the clinic the affective aspects of medical decisionmaking take precedence over the cognitive, these issues require considerably more systematic study in relation to informed consent disclosure.

4. Many of the pertinent studies were not designed as studies of informed consent and hence cannot be faulted for shedding only piecemeal or unsophisticated light on informed consent. In our review, we have included studies on topics such as patient education, patients' compliance with doctors' recommendations, doctors' attitudes toward communicating with patients, and patients' attitudes toward receiving information and making decisions, because they shed light on aspects of informed consent to treatment.

5. One of the most serious deficiencies of the studies is the failure to investigate or to report what doctors actually tell their patients. Unless such studies are performed, questions of what patients understand and how their decisions are made cannot be answered properly.

6. Another major deficiency is a conceptual one. Those investigators who have sought to study understanding have, for the most part, looked at a concept—recall—that is only marginally relevant to the legal doctrine of informed consent.

7. It is difficult to know whether investigator bias is actually present in the studies, but in the ones where the "informed consent" investigator is also the physician (or medical researcher) for the subjects of the informed consent study, this possibility cannot be overlooked.

8. Finally, generalizability from any particular study must be undertaken with extreme caution, and comparability of studies is quite difficult. These problems result from the small number of subjects in the studies, the diversity of illnesses from which subjects of clinical studies suffer and hypothetical illnesses from which subjects of experimental studies must imagine they are suffering, and the variety of treatments involved (and thus the variety of information given to subjects).

In summary, what is reported as fact about informed consent may not be, despite the best of intentions on the part of those who have unearthed it. A high proportion of the studies are troubling because their conclusions are too sweeping in the light of the reported findings. Although some authors acknowledge the limitations of their findings,[11,32] more frequently they do not recognize them.

Neither the supporters nor the detractors of the informed consent requirement should find much comfort in the empirical literature. Whether informed consent is feasible is still an open question. Whether informed consent in a variety of psychiatric settings is feasible is the subject of our inquiry.

4

The Setting and Method of the Research

We emphasize in Chapter 3 that previous research on informed consent has focused almost completely on patients' understanding. Where the actual disclosure process has been recorded, it has almost invariably been limited to hypothetical studies or to studies in which the consent form was taken as the entire disclosure. Few studies have even considered the issue of voluntariness, and the decisionmaking process has been almost entirely ignored. We therefore decided that it was essential to study the actual process of disclosure and decision in a real-life setting. In other words, we were interested in getting as close as possible to the phenomenon of disclosure and decision. We were interested in documenting what actually takes place between clinicians and patients in regard to treatment decisions.

We chose to collect our data by means of participant observation, which, we believed, would bring us as close to the phenomenon of disclosure and decisionmaking as we could get. However, before we can describe our research methods, it is important to know the setting of the research.

"THE HOSPITAL": THE SETTING OF THE RESEARCH

The research was conducted in an institution we call "the Hospital," which housed both the inpatient and outpatient services of the Department of Psychiatry of a major university. The Hospital had 120 inpatient beds divided among five different inpatient units. These included a Child Psychiatry Unit, a Brief Hospitalization Program, a Research Ward, and two general psychiatric wards. In one recent year, the Hospital admitted 1465 patients to its inpatient services. These patients had an average length of stay of 20.4 days. The Hospital also had diverse outpatient facilities, including specialty clinics for a large number of specific disorders and treatments. Our study focused on the Research Ward; on one of the specialty clinics, which we call the Outpatient Clinic; and on the Evaluation Center (the admission unit). These units are described in more detail below.

Of particular interest in our research was that the Hospital was one of the few psychiatric institutions in the United States having a Legal Consultation

Service for the staff. This program provided consultation service to all units of the Hospital concerning legal problems that arose in the treatment of particular patients. It also participated in the education of psychiatric residents and other students. Because of the activities of this program, one might expect the Hospital to be more likely to have legally valid informed consent procedures than other hospitals without such a program would be.

Another aspect of the research setting was that it occurred within the legal jurisdiction of the Commonwealth of Pennsylvania. In 1976, just before our research began, the Pennsylvania Legislature passed the Mental Health Procedures Act,[1] which gained national attention because of its requirement that patients manifest danger to self or others before being eligible for involuntary commitment to a hospital. More important for our purposes, the Act and its implementing regulations also required that patients give informed consent for voluntary admissions to a hospital. The implementing regulations specified certain information that had to be disclosed to patients prior to their voluntary admission, and also mandated that patients play a role in developing their treatment plan once admitted to a hospital.[2] Finally, the Act contained an extensive section on patients' rights, which detailed patients' rights to confidentiality, to freedom from mistreatment or abuse by hospital staff, and to information about various aspects of their hospital care.

RESEARCH STRATEGY

Participant observation is usually thought of as a method of sociological or anthropological research. We prefer to characterize it as a general research strategy, employing a number of different methods that are used when the research goal is to gain new knowledge about the real world. Because we were concerned with events in the real world, we chose procedures for gathering data that interfered as little as possible with the ongoing, instantaneous interaction. For us, participant observation meant that we always chose the particular method that least affected the interaction and still provided the necessary data. This is the core of the research strategy that we pursued. Thus we sat and observed unobtrusively before participating in what we observed; we listened to others talk in preference to asking questions; we asked questions in conversational contexts before doing a structured interview; and we memorized incidents in preference to taking notes. However, when the passive procedure would not yield the necessary data, we did not hesitate to use a more active one. Of course, for some data we sacrificed our passivity. Because we believed that the conversational context of informed consent was important, we took notes except where it would have seemed very out of place, such as during informal talks among patients on the ward. If it was important to know someone's background, and if the subject did not volunteer the information, the researcher asked. When questions that needed to be answered were too complicated to ask in casual conversation, we felt it perfectly appropriate for the observer to say, "Hey, you got a minute? I want to ask you about something."

There were only two limitations in the pursuit of information. The first was the continuous need to maintain good rapport with staff and patients. In certain circumstances, questions could be embarrassing to the person to whom they were addressed. We were the guests of the staff and the patients, and we were acutely aware that it is bad manners to ask embarrassing questions in the wrong way. We found, like any house guest who stays longer than a few days, that good appearances can be maintained for only so long, and our observers were soon treated as part of the household.

The second limit on questioning was imposed by not wanting to influence the staff's or the patients' behavior. When questioning patients, our observer tried to stay away from questions that suggested new lines of thought to patients about treatment decisions. And in many ways, our discussions of cases with staff members were similar; we tried to encourage staff members to elaborate on their statements about treatment without suggesting new lines of thought. Sometimes this meant that we had to avoid asking questions we would have liked to have answered, because staff and patients seemed unconcerned with the topic. For example, we would have liked to have had a staff assessment of the competency of each patient each time a decision was made. However, the concept of competency as such did not seem to be part of the staff's way of thinking about decisionmaking. We felt that even to introduce the concept in a casual conversation risked changing the staff's behavior.

In spite of these limits, participant observation seemed to be the only viable research strategy, for a number of reasons. First, participant observation, more than any other method of data collection, gives the researcher a good "feel" for the phenomenon that is being studied. After all, we were interested not only in what forms were presented to patients and whether patients signed them, but also how they were presented, whether patients took the forms seriously, and so on. We were not just interested in whether patients could answer a list of questions about the treatment, but also whether they could put each piece of knowledge together in a rational way to make sense of the decision that they faced. No other method of data gathering would have provided us with access to as many subtleties of the phenomenon as participant observation did. As becomes quite evident, much of what we learned could not have been learned in any other way.

Observing the actual decisionmaking process allowed us to collect vital data not only on the more formalized dialogues between clinicians and patients but also on the unprovoked, spontaneous remarks that were made both before and after the procedure.

No adequate naturalistic description of informed consent was provided in the literature; this fact not only suggested that we should provide one but also limited our use of other methods of study. Experimental research and highly structured interview procedures are useful and appropriate only when the researcher is familiar with the fundamental dimensions of the problem or phenomenon to be studied. We, however, had only clinical impressions of the relevant parameters of the phenomenon. At that stage, any rigorous experimental or interview design would have forced us to focus our intellectual concerns very narrowly. A rather open-ended, naturalistic study based on participant observation seemed to be a far more viable strategy. Since we did not know what informed consent looked like in reality, committing ourselves to naturalistic observations was the most obvious avenue to take.

The study we designed was an unusual participant observation study. The typical product of participant observation studies is what anthropologists call an "ethnography." It is highly descriptive and aims at encompassing the totality of a society, social community, social group, or social setting. Had we done a typical participant observation study, we would have ended up producing an ethnography of various clinical settings of a psychiatric hospital. This would hardly have suited our research goals. After all, we did not want to study a psychiatric hospital; we wanted to study the natural process of informed consent in psychiatric hospitals.

In order to accomplish our research goals, we began our observations only after having established a particular analytical concern, which was provided by our model of informed consent as presented in Chapter 2. It was focused on the particular concepts of information disclosure, understanding, voluntariness, competency, and decision. When conducting their observations, our observers kept these concepts in mind. While they were hardly "operationalizable," these concepts functioned as what Blumer calls "sensitizing concepts."[3] They "sensitized" our observers to what was worth recording and pursuing in their observations. Only by using these concepts could the observers isolate from the concrete contexts of behavior the patterns that were relevant to informed consent. In other words, it was our analytical focus on informed consent that enabled us to observe what we report in this volume.

All this meant that during their observations our observers had to commit themselves deliberately to selectivity. They did not strive to produce an exhaustive ethnography of certain settings within a psychiatric hospital. Rather, they selectively recorded only what seemed to pertain to our primary analytical focus and concern—informed consent.

Another unusual feature of our research, compared to most other participant observation research, was our use of two observers to study all relevant decisions. Since our study essentially revolved around the relationship between two roles—clinician and patient—it seemed that the best way to gain an adequate understanding of what took place between the two types of role incumbents would be to capture the perspectives of both parties involved in the information process. We felt that any single observer would tend to adopt one of the two perspectives involved, especially when they conflicted with each other. To circumvent this problem, we made the decision to use two different observers—a "staff-observer" and a "patient-observer." Each of these two observers was assigned to describe the events that he or she viewed from only one of the two perspectives.[4]

While this was the theoretical rationale for using two observers rather than one, there were several other advantages to this decision. Using two observers enabled us to "cover" several events simultaneously. This was particularly useful in the Research Ward, where we were observing several staff members interacting with almost two dozen patients (all of whom were our research subjects) at the same time but not necessarily in the same room.

Some of the observations, however, did involve both observers' "covering" the very same event. On those occasions, especially in the Evaluation Center and the Outpatient Clinic, the two sets of notes that they produced were used for evaluating the reliability of their observations.[5] Yet even on these occasions, there was often a fundamental division of labor between the two observers.

Our patient-observer learned speed writing and could record full conversations almost verbatim. In most settings, we relied on this observer to record nearly everything that the patients and clinicians said to each other. Since in many settings the clinicians were also taking notes, our observer's note taking was not intrusive. The staff-observer, on the other hand, was instructed to be somewhat more selective in his observations and to be especially alert to certain analytically defined problems. This was necessary when several things took place together rather rapidly. It was also his role to observe and comment upon the nonverbal features of the interactions.

There were several fundamental differences between the two observers' relations with their research subjects. For example, the patient-observer was instructed to conduct relatively structured interviews with patients she observed at the end of the period of observation (for the interview schedules, see the Appendix). This was necessary because, with the exception of patients in the Research Ward and several patients in the Outpatient Clinic, her contacts with patients occurred only once.

In contrast to these "episodic" relations, the staff-observer's contact with staff members in each setting was continuous. Thus the data could be obtained in the seemingly looser structure of "casual conversation" over a long period of time. Furthermore, this relationship involved an entirely different problem of rapport. It precluded his asking clinicians questions that were too invasive or intrusive. Because of the continuous nature of his contact with the staff, the staff-observer also had to be especially careful not to sensitize his subjects about what he was interested in observing. He did this so as to minimize as much as possible the "observer's effect," which we discuss below.

During our observation period on the Research Ward, there was a total segregation between the two observers, so as to keep the clinicians' and patients' perspectives as separate as possible. Neither of the two observers was allowed access to the other observer's notes. Talk between them about the ward was also strongly discouraged. However, this raised the danger that the two observers would fail to collect comparable data or would not work on parallel analytical problems. To avoid this and to prevent "contamination" of the two perspectives, a delicate system of coordination was essential. We solved this problem by having each observer meet separately on a daily basis with both the principal investigator and the project director to review what was happening on the ward and what information to gather. This prevented possible contamination of the two observers' perspectives and assured that both would collect parallel data and work on comparable analytical problems.

Doing naturalistic research based on participant observation entails a serious validity problem. Collecting data by means of participant observation typically involves a methodological problem known as the "observer's effect." The very process of observing people may bring about some degree of modification of behavior on their part.

A problem inherent in the very nature of our study was that our research subjects, particularly the clinicians, might adjust their behavior toward what they perceived as "desirable" by the observers. We publicly described our project as a study of informed consent; as such, we appeared to be studying the sensitive phenomenon of compliance with the law. Furthermore, because our observers were known by the Hospital's staff (which included many of our research subjects) to be a part of a "Law and Psychiatry Program," it seemed possible that the observer would be concerned with law enforcement.

Admittedly, this must have affected some of the results of our study and might have led us to identify more compliance with the law than we probably would have identified otherwise. Yet there are several reasons that led us to believe the distortion was not so significant that it substantially detracted from the basic validity of our findings.

Because social scientists tend to view the social world primarily from their own professional perspectives and therefore tend to overemphasize their own significance for their research subjects, they have traditionally exaggerated the entire phenomenon of the "observer's effect" and have blown it out of proportion. Take, for example, the clinicians we observed. While they were in the midst of working and performing their tasks as demanded by their jobs, they did their jobs in a way that seemed to them to be for "good reasons." This meant that it would have been impractical for them to make substantial changes in their routine behaviors. This was the way they knew to deal with their work problems. Moreover, since they had "good reasons" for what they did, they assumed that our observers, if they were reasonable people, would be able to see and appreciate their reasons. They tried to assure themselves that our observers were reasonable and fair, and then they stopped worrying about them.

Likewise, the patients were usually too involved with their own problems, or with what someone else thought were their problems, to be very concerned by two peripheral people making a study of some law. We should also add that many of the cases we observed were quite long, stretching over several very intensive hours in the Evaluation Center and over several weeks and even months in the Research Ward. It is quite difficult to "fake" one's behavior for a period of several weeks when one is being observed almost constantly.

We tried our best to "desensitize" the patients and the staff members to our presence. Our observers were instructed to be as passive and unobtrusive as possible. As a part of that effort in two of the sites, the Outpatient Clinic and the Evaluation Center, our observers were instructed not to take notes or to ask questions during their first few days in the setting. On the Research Ward, the patient-observer did not take notes in the presence of either patients or staff.

Finally, we should also note that only in the first few cases in each setting did we notice any conspicuous signs that our research subjects' behavior was substantially different from what one would expect to be their spontaneous and "natural" behavior. In other words, if there was any detectable "observer's effect," it was primarily in the first few days in the setting only, after which it tended to disappear.

Probably the most important evidence that the "observer's effect" was substantial would be an increase in compliance with the law. Yet even during the first few days, we did not see a very high compliance with the law. In other words, the level of the staff's compliance was not very high, despite our observers' presence. We decided after some thought to include in our sample those cases in which we suspected some unusual effort by the staff to comply with the law, because these cases seemed to be especially strong indications of the problems inherent in efforts to comply with the law.

Another problem with our methods concerns the sample of cases we observed. How we obtained our sample differed, depending on the setting, but in no setting was our sample randomly chosen. Rather, they were "opportunity samples." In the Evaluation Center, for example, we observed the first case that we could at any particular observation session. Aside from one clinician who seemed hesitant about allowing us to observe, we witnessed a rather large and fairly representative sample of cases seen at the Evaluation Center. (More details on our sample in the Evaluation Center are contained in Chapter 5.) On the Research Ward, all patients who spent any time on the ward during the 7 weeks of our observations were included in our sample in some way.

In the Outpatient Clinic, we also selected an "opportunity sample." The observers tried to observe the first possible case of every observation session. The only exceptions were 10 patients who were selected deliberately because they were new to the clinic. Because we were interested in observing the establishment of the initial contact between clinicians and patients, the over-sampling seemed important.

Did these procedures produce substantial bias in our sample? And what sort of generalization was possible? Clearly, our data cannot be statistically treated as a random sample. Some combinations of cases are more likely to enter the sample than are others. For example, on the Research Ward, all cases during the 7-week period of observation were part of our sample, but no other cases were. This is not a statistically valid sample of anything except those particular cases that were observed. However, even if a statistically valid sample was drawn, it could only represent one hospital. The relationship of that hospital's practices to other hospitals is, statistically speaking, unknown.

However, this question misses the point. It would make no sense to claim that if 54% of our sample would have understood the benefits of ECT, a similar percentage elsewhere would have understood the same thing. Rather, what we have tried to look at were the basic patterns of decisionmaking—what sorts of information patients considered, what purposes staff members envisioned in disclosure, and so on. We were concerned with the universals of informed consent, not the distribution of particulars. To the degree that this is true, the problem of bias can be reduced to these questions: (1) Was there anything that systematically made these patients different? (2) Was there anything about the settings that led one to expect that the behavior was radically different in these settings than it would have been in other mental health settings?

We believe that by always taking the "next patient available," we reduced the first of these problems to insignificance. The reader will see, as we describe the settings of the research in succeeding chapters, that they are similar in a general way to most mental health treatment settings.

DATA ORGANIZATION AND ANALYSIS

Perhaps the greatest trouble with participant observation as a methodology is the difficulty in reducing the information generated to a coherent set of findings. The complexity of each incident is such that it is inevitably difficult to decide which parts of the event are essential and which parts are trivial. Moreover, there is such a large quantity of data that it becomes difficult to review it systematically when one wants to know, for example, how often the staff members in the various services told patients the names of the drugs they were taking. Since the field work generated over 4000 pages of field notes, it became essential to develop some way of summarizing the notes so that the relevant material could be easily drawn upon.

We tried two methods—one that worked and one that did not. The first method was essentially an indexing system. Over 100 different categories were developed (e.g., "patient's understanding of alternatives" and "staff view of patient's problems"). Two members of our staff then proceeded to index notes from the first two settings. This seemed to us an innovative way of providing the analyst with all of the relevant data necessary to write about the topics we thought would be of interest.

The result was a disaster. First, many of the topics we thought would be important were not important. However, a more critical problem was that what we got were statements and observations unconnected to the case in which they were imbedded. We could not judge what a patient's statement meant except in the context of the other aspects of the case. Thus the indexing system was abandoned.

The second system for gaining access to our data was less ambitious but more effective. It involved simply developing summaries of each case that we observed. While some of these case summaries on the Research Ward ran over a dozen pages in length, it allowed us to review the case quickly and to find where in the original notes the relevant information was to be found.

The analysis could then proceed. Four members of the project's professional staff each chose an analytical category (voluntariness, understanding and competency, disclosure, or decision) and began to analyze the settings. Each setting was worked on one at a time by all of the staff at the same time. In general, the notes for each setting received three systematic readings: once when the observation was going on, once to determine the issues to be analyzed, and once to make systematic notes on each issue. After this the analysts tended to refer more to the case summaries, although another two or three readings of the notes were not uncommon.

The result of these analyses were draft papers on each analytical topic for each setting. As each was completed, a meeting was held among all the project's professional staff members, at which time the papers were subjected to severe criticism, both theoretical and empirical. Several first drafts were simply thrown away, and all underwent at least one major revision. We believe that this type of mutual critique did much to increase both the reliability and the validity of the analyses.

The Evaluation Center

5

Introduction to the Evaluation Center

The first contact with the Hospital for a person seeking treatment took place in the Evaluation Center, which functioned as both an emergency room and an admission unit. Potential patients came for evaluation, on the basis of which either admission or outpatient treatment might be recommended. Other patients, whose admissions had been prearranged by their private psychiatrists, came to complete the necessary paperwork and other formalities necessary for admission. Still other patients were brought by their families or the police for examination; if found to meet certain legal criteria, they might be "involuntarily" admitted.

While all patients scheduled for admission and most of those seeking evaluation came to the Evaluation Center by appointment, others came with no prior notice. There was always the possibility that a staff-patient contact might erupt into violence or that other emergencies, such as a patient's experiencing an epileptic seizure or making a suicide attempt, might occur. Thus staff members were never sure what to expect on a given day, and they worked in a state of uncertainty, which engendered at times almost a "siege mentality."

This chapter is designed to provide a background understanding of the organization of the Evaluation Center and its routine procedures. By describing in detail several different types of cases, we also try to familiarize the reader with the type of data that is the basis for the next three chapters on informed consent in the Evaluation Center. We also describe the administrative regulations and common law specifically relevant to the Evaluation Center.

The waiting area of the Evaluation Center was described by one patient as looking like an airline waiting room. It was a large, rectangular, brightly lit, white room, dominated by a white reception counter. It was here that patients spent the bulk of their time waiting to be called by staff members for their interviews. In contrast, the staff lounge, where the staff members spent most of their time, was informal and cluttered. The walls were the same stark white as the patients' waiting area, but were partly concealed behind two large bulletin boards. The wall clock, which usually ran several minutes fast, and the pot of hot coffee always ready on the table lent an air of frenetic activity in keeping with the usual bustle of staff members' discussing cases, making phone calls, and writing in patients' charts. The Evaluation Center also housed private offices for supervisory personnel; a financial office where patients were interviewed regarding insurance coverage; and small interview rooms, each equipped with a desk and chairs, where most staff-patient contact occurred.

The professional staff we observed was composed of "clinicians"—six nurses, one social worker, and five medical students doing temporary clerkships in psychiatry, who conducted the initial interviews with patients and led them through the evaluation process. The clinicians were also responsible for presenting their findings to the other major professional participants in the process, the doctors. We observed seven psychiatrists and seven psychiatric residents. A doctor conducted a second interview with each patient, recommended a disposition, and in certain cases recorded initial findings and treatment plans on the appropriate forms.

The formal procedures by which decisions were made in the Evaluation Center were dictated by a curious mixture of professional, custom, and legal regulation. The Pennsylvania Mental Health Procedures Act[1] was the basic source of law governing admission to psychiatric hospitals and was supplemented by extensive regulations and forms issued by the Department of Public Welfare.[2] The regulations prescribe detailed procedures for obtaining informed consent from patients who are admitted *voluntarily*, and they define "informed consent" as including the following elements:

1. An understanding that the treatment proposed will involve outpatient, partial hospitalization, or inpatient status.
2. A willingness to be admitted to a designated facility for the purpose of examination and treatment as prescribed.
3. Consent given to the proposed treatment voluntarily and without coercion or duress.
4. Provision of the patient with a full explanation of the proposed treatment and rights and responsibilities of persons in voluntary treatment.

Detailed procedures are also prescribed for involuntary examinations and admissions; these are aimed not at obtaining informed consent, but at protecting patients from unwarranted commitment. Nevertheless, the procedures for involuntary examination do require that certain disclosures be made to patients, some of which are analogous to those required for informed consent to voluntary admission. The regulations do not prescribe any procedures for referral of patients to outpatient treatment, leaving whatever legal regulation there is to be inferred from common-law principles.

RESEARCH PROCEDURES

In order to document the admission procedure, our two observers placed themselves in the unit at different times of the day and night for a period of 7 weeks. These 7 weeks consisted of two blocks of time extending over a

3-month period. The first 3-week period began 2 weeks after the Mental Health Procedures Act went into effect. We expected that compliance with the law would be at a maximum, because staff members had recently been bombarded with explanations of the Act and the required procedures, and we expected that they would be attempting to follow its dictates. The second 4-week period began 10 weeks after the Act went into effect. By this time, we expected that the Act's requirements would be fully incorporated into the routine admission procedure.

Patients who entered the unit were approached by the researchers and/or by the Hospital staff, and the nature of the study was explained to them. Only those patients who consented were observed. Two patients refused any observations whatsoever. Staff members refused to allow any observations of one patient. For four other patients, only partial (but largely complete) observations could be made because either the patients, the patients' relatives, or the staff objected to the presence of observers during some phase of the admission procedure.

As noted in Chapter 4, one observer spent time with staff members while the other spent time with patients, so that the perspective of each group could be obtained. The observers took detailed notes while each patient was seen by a clinician. The staff-observer then observed while the clinician summarized the information for a psychiatrist. Both observers were again present when the psychiatrist talked with the patient. The psychiatrist then left to discuss the case in the staff room and was accompanied by the staff-observer. Meanwhile, the patient-observer remained with the patient and conducted an open-ended interview to tap the patient's perception of what had just occurred.

Because we wanted our observations to interfere minimally with the Evaluation Center's routine, the sample had some features of an opportunity sample. The researchers observed the first full transactions available during the hours of watching, and when observations were completed, the next patient was approached. However, since the study protocol was fully explained to the staff and posted in the staff room, the staff members knew that we were especially interested in observing voluntary admissions, and they sometimes shared with our observers their preliminary estimates about who might be admitted. When choices were possible as to which patient to observe, the observers chose the ones the staff said were more likely to be admitted, so that the total sample is a stratified one with an overrepresentation of admitted patients. The numbers and the eventual dispositions of patients are given in Table 5-1.

A VOLUNTARY ADMISSION

Two broad groups of patients were voluntarily admitted to the Hospital through the Evaluation Center: those whose admissions were prearranged, and those who came for evaluation on the basis of which admission was recommended. Both groups underwent the same basic procedure: an initial interview, a psy-

TABLE 5-1. Disposition from the Evaluation Center

Category	Our sample		Evaluation Center norm[3]	
	n	%	n	%
Voluntary admission	22	46	395	25
Involuntary admission	3	6	71	4
Involuntary admission (other)	1	2	3	0
Referral to Hospital clinics	15	31	858	52
Referrals outside Hospital	2	4	98	12
Refusal of treatment	2	4	20	1
No treatment recommended	0	0	35	2
Other	3	7	58	4
TOTALS	48	100	1538	100

chiatric interview, a financial interview, a physical examination, and the signing of admission forms. However, admissions that were not prearranged were invariably more complex and took significantly more time.

There was a tremendous variation among cases in terms of who did what, and when specific things took place in relation to each other. For example, we observed cases in which no initial interview was conducted, its functions being incorporated into the psychiatric interview. We also saw cases in which physical examinations were given and admission papers were signed before the psychiatric interview. For this reason, the following case should be regarded as exemplifying, rather than defining, the voluntary-admission procedure in the Evaluation Center. The case is intended to give some idea of the procedures and dialogues that we observed, and also to introduce the reader to the forms and required disclosures by which the Mental Health Procedures Act and regulations attempt to operationalize informed consent.

Delucia E was a short, fat woman with shoulder-length hair and dark brown eyes who came to the Evaluation Center dressed casually in dark pink trousers and a blue shirt bearing the name of her employer. She had gone to work as usual that morning but had been "behaving strangely" (i.e., staring fixedly at the ceiling); this prompted her boss to send her to the emergency room of the university-affiliated Medical Hospital. There she was given an injection of Benadryl, a drug used to counteract the muscle spasms associated with the use of antipsychotic drugs also known as "major tranquilizers." Then, at her own request, she was taken to the Hospital, where she was an outpatient. As is standard procedure when sending a patient from one university-affiliated hospital to another, Ms. E was accompanied by a campus security guard. Upon arrival in the Evaluation Center, she registered at the reception desk and was told to remain in the waiting area until called. There she was approached by our observers, who explained our study and obtained her permission to observe her case.

While the patient waited, the staff obtained her chart. This was always done when a person who had had prior contact with the Hospital entered the Evaluation Center, because the chart oriented the staff to the patient's psychiatric history and provided demographic data on the patient that was needed for filling out the new forms. Ms. E's chart indicated that she was a 26-year-old single woman who had been undergoing outpatient treatment for schizophrenia for approximately 3 years. For the past year, Ms. E had been a patient at the Outpatient Clinic of the Hospital. (For further information, see the entry for Ms. E in Table 5-2.)

Ms. E stared at the ceiling while in the waiting room, and when called by the clinician, she entered the interview room still looking upward. The following interview then took place:

CLINICIAN: Do you feel better now?

Ms. E: (*No reply.*)

CLINICIAN: Excuse me, would you mind telling me why you are looking up at the ceiling?

Ms. E: The voices tell me to look there?

CLINICIAN: Why?

Ms. E: I don't know.

CLINICIAN: What else do the voices tell you?

Ms. E: They tell me to commit suicide, to jump out the window.

CLINICIAN: Are they telling you to do that now?

Ms. E: Yes.

CLINICIAN: How long has this been going on?

Ms. E: For months—for 2½ years.

At this point the clinician asked Ms. E some detailed questions about her employment. Throughout the interview, Ms. E smoked and moved restlessly in her chair. Occasionally, she lowered her eyes, then raised them to the ceiling.

CLINICIAN: Besides hearing voices, do you have any other problems?

Ms. E: Yeah, my legs are sore.

CLINICIAN: Is your neck getting stiff?

Ms. E: No.

CLINICIAN: OK, Ms. E. Is there anything you think we can do?

Ms. E: I've been coming to the Hospital for 2 years.

CLINICIAN: Would you like to come in and stay in the Hospital?

Ms. E: Yes.

CLINICIAN: Are you willing to sign in?

Ms. E: Yes.

CLINICIAN: You've been coming to the Outpatient Clinic, right? Whom did you see there?

TABLE 5-2. Evaluation Center Patients

Patient	Age	Race	Marital status	Education	Occupation	EC diagnosis	EC entry status	EC disposition	Number of prior admissions
Adelle E	70	W	D	—	Homemaker	Schizo-affective disease	Invol	Invol adm	Multiple
Elsie H	72	B	W	7G	—	Senility	Vol	OP refer	0
Gwen X	58	B	S	10G	—	Alcoholism	Invol	OP refer	0
Nelson P	24	W	S	HS	Machinist	Schizophrenia	Invol	Invol adm	2
Irma O	35	W	D	5G	Maid	Schizophrenia	Invol	Invol adm	3
Tracey D	19	W	S	Coll	Student	Depression	Vol	OP refer	0
Cynthia M	30	W	M	Coll	Homemaker	Depression	Vol	Vol adm	2
Kate M	17	W	S	11G	Student	Anorexia nervosa	Vol	Vol adm	0
Hortense T	64	W	W	8G	—	Depression: dyskinesia	Vol	Vol adm	1
Gustav A	29	W	Sep	Coll	Engineer	Bipolar affective illness	Invol	Refusal; released	10
Julian G	55	B	S	12G	—	Alcoholism; schizophrenia	Invol	Already OP; released	13
Sara E	51	W	W	4G	Homemaker	Depression	Vol	Vol adm	1
Harrison T	41	W	M	PhD	Consultant	Manic depression	Vol	Vol adm	Unknown
Ina Q	38	W	M	HS	Homemaker	Depression (grief reaction)	Invol	Vol adm	0
Reavis C	23	B	M	Coll	Steel worker	Schizophrenia	Vol	Vol adm	11
Walter K	46	B	M	10G	Car washer	Organic brain syndrome	Vol	Vol adm	0
Doris X	24	W	D	HS	Homemaker	Depression; anxiety	Vol	Vol adm	2
Holly E	47	W	D	HS	Unemployed	Schizophrenia; organic brain syndrome	Vol	OP refer	0
Manuel C	14	W	S	9G	Student	Schizophrenia; organic brain syndrome	Vol	Invol adm	2
Jason X	59	W	S	6G	Upholsterer	Alcohol abuse; psychosis	Vol	Vol adm	7
Delucia E	26	W	S	Coll	Maid	Schizophrenia	Vol	Vol adm	0
Rosella D	51	W	M	Coll	Homemaker	Depression	Vol	Vol adm	1
Lori C	14	W	S	9G	Student	Depression	Vol	OP refer	0

Name	Age	Race	Sex	Educ	Occupation	Diagnosis	Adm	Disposition	No.
Wesley G	31	B	M	Coll	Tax examiner	No diagnosis	Vol	OP refer	0
Naomi G	34	B	M	11G	Cafeteria worker	Depression; anxiety	Vol	OP refer	0
Chester T	20	W	M	Coll	Never worked	Heroin abuse; depression; antisocial personality	Vol	Vol adm	0
Meyer I	31	W	M	Coll	Photographer	Depression	Vol	Vol adm	0
Maureen A	30	W	M	HS	Homemaker	Depression	Vol	Vol adm	0
Christopher N	28	W	S	Coll	Postal clerk	Heroin addiction	Vol	OP refer	3
Linda T	25	B	S	8G	Homemaker	Alcoholism; drug abuse	Invol	OP refer	0
Marcus I	55	W	M	—	Pharmacist	Drug abuse; affective disease	Vol	Vol adm	1
Minnie A	24	W	S	Coll	Typist	Depression; anxiety; alcoholism	Vol	OP refer	0
Rudolph D	34	W	D	Coll	Machinist	No diagnosis	Vol	OP refer	0
Jerome D	34	B	D	10G	Computer operator	Alcoholism; organic brain syndrome	Vol	OP refer	6
Brenda E	23	W	S	10G		Alcohol abuse	Vol	OP refer	2
Mitzie Q	22	W	S	10G		Schizophrenia; low IQ	Vol	Vol adm	4
Natania Z	28	W	M	BS	Chemical engineer	Depression; anxiety	Vol	OP refer	0
Eldred C	41	W	M	11G	Factory worker	Drug abuse; obsessive personality	Vol	Vol adm	1
Joseph W	16	W	S	11G	Student	No diagnosis	Vol	Refer to another hosp	0
Jim N	52	W	M	8G	Mechanic	Anxiety neurosis	Vol	Vol adm	Unknown
Jacob N	28	W	S	Coll	Military	Drug abuse; schizophrenia	Vol	OP refer	3
Arnold N	27	W	S	Coll	Film maker	Depression	Vol	Refusal	0
Peggy G	20	W	M	10G	Homemaker	Schizophrenia; drug abuse; psychosis	Vol	Vol adm	0
Wendel B	24	W	D	8G	Restaurant worker	Violent behavior	Invol	Vol adm	0
Jessica G	31	W	M	HS	Homemaker	Depression	Vol	OP refer	0
Niles X	38	B	D	7G	Unemployed	Depression; alcoholism	Vol	Refer to another hosp	3
Sally N	18	W	S	Coll	Student	Schizophrenia	Vol	Vol adm	0
Klara N	26	W	S	HS	—	Schizophrenia; drug side effect (Haldol)	Vol	OP refer	6

Ms. E: Ms. X.

CLINICIAN: When is your next appointment?

Ms. E: October 18. [This interview took place on October 8.]

CLINICIAN: When you were here to see her a few days ago, were you hearing the voices?

Ms. E: Yes, I've been hearing them for 2 years.

CLINICIAN: Does the therapist know that you are hearing the voices?

Ms. E: No, because I didn't talk to her. I didn't say anything about the voices.

CLINICIAN: Did you tell anybody?

Ms. E: Yeah, I told my boyfriend.

CLINICIAN: When?

Ms. E: When he kicked me out.

CLINICIAN: Tell me a little more about what you did today.

Ms. E: I went to work.

CLINICIAN: This morning?

Ms. E: Yes.

CLINICIAN: Until what time?

Ms. E: Until 6 A.M.

CLINICIAN: Can you tell me what day it is?

Ms. E: Friday.

CLINICIAN: Month?

Ms. E: October.

CLINICIAN: Date?

Ms. E: No.

CLINICIAN: Where are you now?

Ms. E: The Hospital.

CLINICIAN: Besides the voices, do you also see anything up there on the ceiling?

Ms. E: No.

CLINICIAN: Why are you looking at the ceiling?

Ms. E: The voices tell me to.

CLINICIAN: What do you see?

Ms. E: I see fine.

CLINICIAN: Do you see anything up there that I can't see?

Ms. E: No.

CLINICIAN: Are you feeling better?

Ms. E: No.

CLINICIAN: Which hospital did you go to?

Ms. E: I was in Medical Hospital.

CLINICIAN: And the shot hasn't helped you?

Ms. E: No.

CLINICIAN: What medications are you taking? You had a shot of Prolixin. Have you also been taking Cogentin? [The clinician was asking about medications she had received in the Outpatient Clinic, not about the shot she just received at Medical Hospital. Prolixin is an antipsychotic drug; Cogentin is a drug that combats the side effects associated with drugs like Prolixin.]

Ms. E: I've been taking new medicines, but they didn't help.

CLINICIAN: Since when did you take them?

Ms. E: Monday.

CLINICIAN: Do you take Cogentin?

Ms. E: No, not 'til 11:30.

CLINICIAN: Did you take any yesterday?

Ms. E: Yes.

CLINICIAN: Did they seem to help you?

Ms. E: No, I've got steadily worse.

CLINICIAN: Are you married?

Ms. E: No, single.

CLINICIAN: So you don't have to worry about anybody to take care of?

Ms. E: Well, there is my boyfriend.

CLINICIAN: But he's old enough to take care of himself. Are you depressed?

Ms. E: No.

CLINICIAN: Are you having problems with your boyfriend?

Ms. E: No. He knows I have problems, and he's going to help me fight my problems.

CLINICIAN: Do you have a medical problem?

Ms. E: Just this one. In my ear; it keeps talking.

CLINICIAN: So you're just taking Cogentin? [At this point, both the clinician and the patient were somewhat uncertain whether the patient was taking Cogentin.]

Ms. E: I have the pills in my purse. (*She opened her purse and began looking for the pills.*)

CLINICIAN: That's OK. It's OK.

Ms. E: I want you to see that it's not Cogentin.

CLINICIAN: It is Cogentin.

Ms. E: My doctor told me he was taking me off it.

CLINICIAN: How many are you taking?

Ms. E: Three.

CLINICIAN: When do you take them?

Ms. E: 8:30, 4:00, and 12:00. (*She handed the bottle of pills to the clinician.*)

CLINICIAN: This is Cogentin. Put the lid on so it won't get lost.

Ms. E: I don't have a lid.

CLINICIAN: Who is your next of kin?

Ms. E: (*She gave her boyfriend's name.*)

CLINICIAN: Do you know his phone number?

Ms. E: (*She gave a phone number.*)

CLINICIAN: That's your phone number.

Ms. E: Yes, he's staying with me.

CLINICIAN: All right. I'll tell you what: Would you like to sign here to give us your consent to treat you?

Ms. E: All right.

CLINICIAN: Would you like to give us permission to send information to the insurance company?

Ms. E: All right.

The clinician showed Ms. E the back of the Evaluation Center intake sheet:

I CONSENT to receive psychiatric and related medical treatment from the faculty and staff of the Hospital and the Clinical Practice Plan of the School of Medicine. I further agree to assume full financial responsibility for my treatment, and I authorize this hospital to release necessary financial and other information to insurance carriers, federal agencies, and the County of O'Hara as required.
Signed ——————— Date ———

Ms. E signed the form without reading it and wrote October 8, 1966, as the date.

CLINICIAN: Did the voice tell you it's that year?

Ms. E: No, I made a mistake. (*She corrected it to read 1976.*)

CLINICIAN: Do you have any other allergies besides penicillin?

Ms. E: No, that's all.

CLINICIAN: Will you come with me, Ms. E? I will take you to the financial office, and after that they will give you a physical exam, and the doctor will see you after that.

A trip to the financial office is part of every voluntary admission. Once there, the patient is requested to sign a large number of forms, including another longer form granting the Hospital permission to release information to the patient's insurer for reimbursement purposes; an assignment of insurance benefits to the Hospital; several statements of income, assets, and liabilities; and forms specific to particular insurers, such as Medicaid or Blue Cross/Blue Shield.

While Ms. E was in the financial office, the clinician went to the staff lounge and remarked to another clinician that she had a patient who she thought would be admitted. She repeated this to the doctor when he entered. She then demonstrated the way in which Ms. E was looking at the ceiling, and she told him Ms. E heard voices telling her to commit suicide. He immediately said Ms. E should be admitted, adding that he would have no time to interview her until later. The clinician then asked the doctor to fill out his sections of the admission forms because "I don't want her to change her mind in the mean-time," and stressed the importance of the patient's signing for admission "before she really goes off." After hearing some further information about her but before seeing the patient, the doctor agreed to prepare the admission forms.

The admission forms that are signed by any patient consenting to voluntary admission were designed by the Department of Public Welfare to incorporate certain elements of information that the Mental Health Procedures Act requires to be disclosed to voluntary-admission patients.[4] There are three sections on the state-promulgated standard forms that the examining psychiatrist is required to complete: (1) Initial Findings, (2) Description of Proposed Treatment, and (3) Description of Proposed Restrictions and Restraints. All of these sections appear on a single page that must be signed by both the doctor and the patient. In the space labeled "Initial Findings," the doctor wrote: "Responding to hallucinations of an imperative self-destructive nature." In the space provided for the "Description of Proposed Treatment," he wrote: "Hospitalize to prevent suicide. Begin treatment with sufficient antipsychotic medications."[5] In the space labeled "Description of Proposed Restrictions and Restraints," he wrote: "Ward routine."[6]

Meanwhile, Ms. E returned to the waiting area. When these forms were completed, the clinician called her to come to the interview room, cautioning her to look down while she was walking so she wouldn't fall.

CLINICIAN: I'm just going to ask you to sign in. I talked with Dr. Y, OK?
Ms. E: OK.
CLINICIAN: And he wanted you to come and be hospitalized for a few days.
Ms. E: Are you going to keep me?
CLINICIAN: If you would sign. Would you like to? OK?
Ms. E: OK.
CLINICIAN: (*Showing her the form that the doctor had filled out.*) Here are the reasons. The doctor says that you are listening to voices, and he wants to keep you here so that he can evaluate you. You are hallucinating and hearing voices, and they're telling you to do some harm to yourself, and we want to keep you to help protect you from getting hurt.[7]
Ms. E: OK.
CLINICIAN: Do you agree to that?
Ms. E: Yes.
CLINICIAN: I also want to tell you about your rights and the type of treatment you're going to get. You will go to the 10th floor, and Dr. X will probably keep you on medication and change your medication if necessary.

The clinician showed Ms. E a form entitled "Explanation of Voluntary Admission Rights," which is required by the regulations and issued by the Department of Public Welfare[8]:

Before your voluntary admission to this hospital, you have the right to:

1. An explanation of the type of treatment in which you may be involved.
2. An explanation of any restraints or restrictions to which you may be subject.

Upon your admission, you will have the following rights:

1. Within 72 hours after your admission, a plan of treatment will be developed. You may participate in the development of this plan.
2. You may withdraw from treatment at any time by giving written notice to the director of this facility; however,
3. You may be asked to agree to remain in the facility for a specific period of time up to 72 hours after you request discharge. If when you request discharge you are asked to remain for this period of time, someone will immediately explain why to you. The facility may institute involuntary commitment proceedings during this period.
4. You may not be transferred from this facility to another facility without your consent.

In addition to the above rights, the Bill of Rights attached applies to you upon admission. You will receive a longer, more detailed version of these rights within 72 hours after your admission. If you do not understand any of these rights, [name of mental health worker] would be pleased to discuss them further with you.

Ms. E: OK.

CLINICIAN: And if you have any questions about it, you ask Dr. Y. And if any time you want to leave the Hospital before you are discharged, you must notify them in writing. Would you agree to this and sign?

Ms. E: (*Signed the form.*)

CLINICIAN: There's one more place. I told you we would keep you here at least for 2 days, but we would like to keep you here longer, if they think you need it. But if you decide to leave before that time, we would like you to give us a few days' notice. OK?

Ms. E: OK.

As the clinician was speaking, she was showing Ms. E the admission form depicted in Figure 5-1.

CLINICIAN: You can see here that you voluntarily gave your consent.

Ms. E immediately began signing the blank form on the line marked "Name of Facility."

CLINICIAN: No, not yet. Will you sign here?
Ms. E: OK. (*She signed on the proper line.*)

PART II
VOLUNTARY CONSENT TO INPATIENT TREATMENT
(Adult)   (Date)

I voluntarily give my consent, without any coercion or duress, to receive inpatient treatment at _____ .

(Name of Facility)

I confirm that this treatment has been explained to me, including the types of medications which I may be given and the types of restraints or restrictions to which I may be subjected. I understand that I may: (Check and complete A or B)

A. ☐ Leave this hospital upon written request with _____ hours' notice.

    The reasons for giving notice before I leave have been explained to me.

B. ☐ Leave at any time I express my desire to leave in writing.

I confirm that my rights and responsibilities as a client as described in DPW Form #MH 781-B or #MH 781-C have been fully explained to me.

ANY PERSON WHO PROVIDES ANY FALSE INFORMATION ON PURPOSE WHEN HE COMPLETES THIS FORM MAY BE SUBJECT TO CRIMINAL PROSECUTION AND MAY FACE CRIMINAL PENALTIES INCLUDING CONVICTION OF A MISDEMEANOR.

_____
(Signature of Client)

Fig. 5-1. Form for voluntary consent to inpatient treatment.

CLINICIAN: The county would like us to send information about people who consent. Do you mind if we send information to the county?[9]
Ms. E: No, I don't mind.

The clinician then escorted Ms. E back to the waiting room and went to the staff lounge, where she filled out the blank sections of the "Voluntary Consent to Inpatient Treatment" form. She checked Box A and wrote "72" hours, signifying that Ms. E agreed to give 72 hours' written notice if she decided to leave the Hospital against medical advice.[10] She also called the inpatient ward to notify the nurse that a patient would be admitted. While on the phone, she wrote additional information on the hospital intake sheet. Her evaluation of the patient read:

This 26 Y[ear] O[ld] W[hite] S[ingle] F[emale] was brought to the Evaluation Center by Campus Police from Medical Hospital emergency room for evaluation. She had been behaving strangely at work this morning, and her boss sent her to Medical Hospital emergency room for evaluation, and she had Benadryl 50 mg at 8 AM at Medical Hospital and then was sent here. [Patient] appears sloppily dressed and her eyes are looking up at the ceiling because she says "Voices are telling me to look at the ceiling and jump out the window." She states she has been having active auditory hallucinations for past 2 years and has been coming to the Outpatient Clinic for followup care. She was seen at the Outpatient Clinic by Dr. A 10-4-76 and had Prolixin D 40 I.M. She is also taking Cogentin 2 mg T.I.D. She is too preoccupied c̄ her "voices" to give me any concrete information at this time. She states she is allergic to penicillin but has no other medical problems at this time.

Her next appt. at the Outpatient Clinic is scheduled for 10-18-76 at 3:30 p.m. Pt. was seen by Dr. Y and signed voluntarily to be admitted to 10th floor. Imp[ression]: Schizophrenia.

Meanwhile, the patient-observer was talking to Ms. E in the waiting area. When asked how long she expected to be in the Hospital, she said about 10 days. (She was subsequently released 13 days after admission.) She said she had come to the Hospital because her boss had noticed that she had had a "spasm," and he sent her to the Medical Hospital. She also said that she wanted to stay in the Hospital; but when asked how she had reached that decision, she replied, "They decided for me."

OBSERVER: Why?
Ms. E: To protect me from harm.
OBSERVER: Do you think that's a good idea?
Ms. E: Yes, because I might hurt myself.
OBSERVER: What kind of treatment might they give you?
Ms. E: They might give me electric shock.
OBSERVER: Do you think that's a good idea?
Ms. E: Yes, because it would put the voice in my ear back where it belongs.

The doctor then entered the waiting area and introduced himself to the patient.

DOCTOR: How are you feeling?
Ms. E: Lousy.
DOCTOR: Why are you looking up at the ceiling? Are you seeing things there?
Ms. E: No, the voices are telling me to.
DOCTOR: Well, we'll get you taken care of very quickly, OK?
Ms. E: OK.

The doctor then returned to the staff lounge, where he notified the clinician that he had seen the patient. After asking the clinician for more information about the medications Ms. E had been receiving, he wrote "as above" on the intake form below the evaluation written by the clinician. Meanwhile, at the patient's request, the clinician had notified the boyfriend about her admission and also had notified the Outpatient Clinic.

The patient-observer asked Ms. E the doctor's name, and she answered correctly.

> OBSERVER: Have you ever seen him before?
> Ms. E: No.

Ms. E then had a physical examination, after which she was escorted to the 10th-floor ward.

AN INVOLUNTARY EVALUATION

During the course of the observations in the Evaluation Center, we observed nine patients who were brought to the Hospital involuntarily. Although only three of these patients were subsequently involuntarily admitted, all nine were subjected to involuntary evaluation procedures mandated by law.

The Mental Health Procedures Act requires that, in order for a patient to be admitted for involuntary emergency examination, the person bringing the patient to the hospital must write a statement detailing the "grounds" under which the commitment is sought, and the patient must be given a copy of this statement immediately upon arrival at the hospital. This requires a showing that the patient has, within the past 30 days, engaged in conduct showing that he or she is a "clear and present danger" to self or others, including at least one of the following four acts[11]:

1. Inflicted or attempted to inflict serious bodily harm to another.
2. Acted in such a manner as to evidence that he would be unable, without care, supervision, and the continued assistance of others, to satisfy his need for nourishment, personal or medical care, shelter, self-protection or safety.
3. Attempted suicide.
4. Severely mutilated himself or attempted to mutilate himself severely.

The case we chose to exemplify involuntary admission is that of Nelson P, who was brought to the Hospital by his father and two brothers around 8 P.M. When we first saw Mr. P, a tall, thin young man with long dark blond hair, wearing blue jeans and a plaid flannel shirt, he was kneeling in the reception area flanked by his seated brothers. From time to time he would raise his head to the ceiling and utter prayers. At one point he said, "If there is sin in this world, let me die."

In filling out the petition for involuntary admission, his father had written that Mr. P was unable to care for himself:

Nelson is refusing to eat, sleep. He has not gone to work for the past 5 days. He refuses to put on his clothes. Someone has to be with him all the time and assist him in every way and also to prevent an injury to himself.

The clinician described him as "psychotic, schizophrenic, and he has a psychiatric history," and told the doctor, "I'm going to read him his rights, but I know that he won't understand."

The clinician then went to the waiting room and led the patient and one of his brothers to an interview room. The doctor was also present, as well as our observers. When the clinician asked the brother what had happened, Mr. P interrupted to say, "You are not my psychiatrist." He began to walk around the room with his eyes closed and arms outstretched saying, "I want to leave the room. I want to see Jean [his girlfriend]." At the clinician's suggestion, the doctor and the brother left the room. The clinician then introduced herself to the patient and asked, "Do you know where you are?"

MR. P: Yes. Take all the glasses out of here. (*He continued to walk around the room very slowly with his arms outstretched.*)
CLINICIAN: I would like you to sit down, Mr. P, because I don't want you to hurt yourself.
MR. P: I'm not going to hurt myself. (*He then knelt.*)
CLINICIAN: We want to take care of you. Before you see a doctor, you have to listen to your rights.
MR. P: I'm not committing myself.

Mr. P then raised his right hand and stood up as if to take an oath. The clinician began to read the sheet containing the patient's involuntary-admission rights. Keeping his eyes closed, Mr. P moved his arms onto the desk and began to move his hands toward the form, then raised them to the clinician's shoulders. She put his hands back on the desk and continued to read the rights without pausing.

CLINICIAN: You have been brought to the Hospital because a responsible person has observed your conduct and feels that you present a clear danger to yourself or to other people. Within 2 hours after you were brought here, you will be examined by a physician. If you are not admitted here, you will be returned to whatever place you desire within reason. If he agrees that you are clearly in danger of harming yourself or someone else, you will be admitted to this facility for a period of treatment of up to 72 hours. While you are here, you have the following rights:

1. You must be told specifically why you were brought here for emergency examination.
2. You may make up to three completed phone calls immediately.
3. You have the right to communicate with others.

4. You may give the facility the names of three people whom you want contacted, and they will contact them and keep them informed of your progress while here.

5. The County Mental Health Administrator must take reasonable steps to assure that while you are detained, the health and safety needs of any of your dependents are met and that your personal property and your premises where you live are looked after.

6. You need not consent to any treatment other than treatment necessary to protect your life or health or prevent you from physically injuring others.

7. When you are no longer in need of treatment or in 72 hours, whichever comes sooner, you will be discharged unless you agree to remain here voluntarily or unless the director of the facility asks the court to extend your treatment here.

In addition to the above rights, while you are a client at this facility . . .

MR. P: I am not a client.

CLINICIAN: . . . The attached Bill of Rights applies to you.

MR. P: Stop!

CLINICIAN: I'm almost done. You will receive a longer, more detailed version of the Department of Public Welfare regulations on rights within 72 hours after your commitment.[12] If you do not understand these rights, Ms. X will be pleased to explain them further to you.

The clinician then attempted to push Mr. P gently toward a chair and conduct an interview.

MR. P: You are forcing me.
CLINICIAN: Why are you here?
MR. P: Because I don't see good enough to spell.
CLINICIAN: Please sit down.
MR. P: I don't need a psychiatrist.
CLINICIAN: How long have you felt like this?
MR. P: Six.
CLINICIAN: Six what?
MR. P: (*No response.*)
CLINICIAN: Are you taking any medicine?
MR. P: I take my medicine—Stelazine.
CLINICIAN: How much?
MR. P: (*No response.*)
CLINICIAN: Do you take anything else?
MR. P: Shhh. Woman, leave me alone! Show me the door.
CLINICIAN: I want you to stay here until the doctor comes.
MR. P: Doctor?
CLINICIAN: Yes, Dr. M.

I affirm that when the patient arrived at this facility I explained his rights to him. These rights are described in Form MH783-A. I believe that he:

☐ does understand these rights.
☐ does not understand these rights.

Fig. 5-2. Form indicating involuntary-admission patients' understanding of rights.

Mr. P walked to the window and tried to open it, and the clinician turned him away.

Mr. P: Mary, do you love me? (*He began to pray aloud.*)
Clinician: Do you hear someone talking to you? Do you hear voices?

The doctor reentered the room.

Mr. P: I hear you speaking still. (*He put his hands over his ears.*) Can I drink?
Doctor: Do you hear voices?
Mr. P: No, but I smell.
Doctor: Do you smell things that are there or not there?
Mr. P: (*No reply.*)
Clinician: When I was reading the paper in which I told you what you were doing in the Hospital, did you understand what I was telling you?

At this point, some of Mr. P's family entered the room. He embraced his brothers, and they led him back to the waiting area. The clinician turned to the involuntary-admission form depicted in Figure 5-2 and checked the second box.

The clinician described Mr. P's behavior to the doctor, who concluded that he was a "classic case of acute schizophrenia" and that the patient would require Stelazine (an antipsychotic drug). In the eyes of the Evaluation Center staff, admission was a foregone conclusion, and arrangements were made for Mr. P to have a physical examination.

The clinician then interviewed one of Mr. P's brothers and learned that Mr. P was Catholic; that he worked as a machinist; that he had been hospitalized for psychiatric problems before; and that, although he had discontinued outpatient treatment 10 months ago, his family and friends had noticed a change in him only over the last several days.

This information was recorded on the Hospital's "Initial Contact" form, where the clinician had already written:

Mr. P came to the Hospital accompanied by ambulance and family members. He is casually dressed, ambulatory c̄ assistance, walks with his eyes closed, responses are brief, bizarre, affect is inappropriate, halluc. are apparent, and he is verbally but not physically resistive. Pt. was unable to give hx. or cooperate for this exam. Family states pt. has refused to eat or take medication since last Thursday 9/16. Mr. P was brought to Hospital on 9/24/76 and has become increasingly agitated and nonverbal except for incoherent responses. He is known to the Hospital having been an inpatient 6/4/75-7/17/75.

Family hx. includes parents—fa 55, mo 48, four brothers (27, 25, 22, 20), younger sisters (21, 19 & 18). All are living & well c̄ no psych hx except for 20 yr. old brother who is on meds for fainting spells.

Pt. left school after completing high school, has been working in the mill, and according to family, functioning well until one week ago.

To be seen by Dr. M.

[signed by clinician]

The doctor later added the following note to this:

Agree. Brother states pt. lives c̄ friends, works in mill. D/C'ed meds (refused to return) at Thanksgiving. Precipitants for exacerbation seem to be change of work schedule, fight c̄ good friend, trouble with car.

Brother states pt. has no insight and refuses to admit he is ill.

Exam as above.

Imp[ression]—acute schizophrenia.

Plan—admit to 9. Medicate c̄ Stealazine, Cogentin.

[signed by doctor]

One of the requirements for involuntary admission is that a person must be found to be "in need of treatment." To establish this need, the Mental Health Procedures Act requires that a patient brought to a hospital for involuntary emergency admission be examined by a physician within 2 hours of arrival. Although Mr. P was not extensively examined, he was seen by the doctor within 15 minutes of arrival.[13] To document the need for treatment, the examining physician is required to complete a form similar to that used in voluntary admissions. In the space provided for "Findings of the Examination," the doctor wrote:

Pt. has eyes closed. Either stands or kneels c̄ hands in praying position. Is unable to answer any questions. Needs physical assistance to find chair. Calls out to people who are not in the room or the building. Preoccupied with eye glasses.

In the space provided for "Treatment Needed," she wrote:

Hospitalization, medication with phenothiazines & Cogentin. Attempt to convince him of need for followup treatment.

When Mr. P came out of the physical examination, his family gathered around him, and he protested that he did not want to stay in the Hospital. His father said they would leave him here for a while and discuss it later. Then the family left. The clinician sat with Mr. P in the lounge until another staff member arrived to escort him to an inpatient unit.

AN OUTPATIENT REFERRAL

Unlike the situation in regard to voluntary and involuntary admission, the Mental Health Procedures Act and regulations mandate no specific forms or procedures to refer for outpatient treatment someone who has come to the Evaluation Center. We observed 15 cases involving referral to outpatient clinics. The following case illustrates one key difference evident between admission and referral cases. The referral patients were often subjected to a more lengthy evaluation than were either voluntary- or involuntary-admission patients, whose dispositions were decided upon within the first few minutes of contact with the Evaluation Center.

Jessica G was a stylishly dressed young woman who came to the Evaluation Center accompanied by a friend, who remained with her in the waiting area. Because she had previously been an outpatient at the Hospital, the clinician obtained Ms. G's chart before conducting the initial interview. The chart described her as a 31-year-old white married woman, mother of two children, who complained of feeling hopeless and depressed but who had previously refused to take antidepressant medication.

Having read portions of the chart, the clinician then called the patient into an interview room.

CLINICIAN: You were here last year, right?

Ms. G: No, this year.

CLINICIAN: (*Mumbled something under her breath about having to "do a whole new contact form," which the patient probably did not hear.*) Did any information change? Are you living at the same place? I have to ask a lot of questions. You've not been to a clinic, not since last August? (*While she was asking these questions, the clinician was transferring information from the previous "contact sheet" to the present one.*)

Ms. G: No.

CLINICIAN: You were never an inpatient here?

Ms. G: No.

The clinician hesitated and then checked with the patient whether specific items of information on the old contact sheet were correct, such as her social security number and the highest grade of education completed. While filling out the form, she asked:

CLINICIAN: Are you working?

Ms. G: No.

CLINICIAN: What made you come here today?

Ms. G: I was feeling depressed and upset.

CLINICIAN: About what?

Ms. G: A lot of things.

CLINICIAN: I have to ask you to sign here to give authorization for us to send the bills to Medical Assistance.

The clinician then began to question her about her problems.

CLINICIAN: Are you taking any medicine?

Ms. G: No.

CLINICIAN: You don't like medicine?

Ms. G: No, I just don't take them.

CLINICIAN: So you have no medical problems?

Ms. G: No.

CLINICIAN: Do you drink?

Ms. G: No.

CLINICIAN: Do you smoke reefers?

Ms. G: Yeah.

CLINICIAN: Do you use other drugs?

Ms. G: No, I just like reefers.

CLINICIAN: What do they do for you?

Ms. G: They help me get rid of my problem, relax.

CLINICIAN: Do you have problems sleeping?

Ms. G: Yeah.

CLINICIAN: Do you have trouble falling asleep?

Ms. G: Yeah.

CLINICIAN: Even with reefers?

Ms. G: Yeah.

CLINICIAN: How much do you sleep?

Ms. G: Five or six hours.

CLINICIAN: Do you have problems falling asleep?

Ms. G: Yeah.

CLINICIAN: How about eating?

Ms. G: I have no appetite.

CLINICIAN: Have you lost a lot of weight?

Ms. G: Yeah, about 5 pounds the last couple of weeks.

CLINICIAN: Is there anything special bothering you?

Ms. G: No.

CLINICIAN: Do you feel confused?

Ms. G: Yes, in a way.

CLINICIAN: What's confusing you?

Ms. G: A lot of different things. Like myself.

CLINICIAN: But you're not confused about the date and things like that?

Ms. G: I don't know it every day.

CLINICIAN: But you know where you are?

Ms. G: Yes.

CLINICIAN: Do you have problems doing things?

Ms. G: Yeah, I can't seem to get things done. Just like today, I couldn't get things done.

CLINICIAN: Are you neglecting your house and your children?

Ms. G: Yes.

CLINICIAN: Do you have a problem with your kids?

Ms. G: No. The oldest is in school.

CLINICIAN: So the kids are not a problem.

Ms. G: No.

CLINICIAN: How about your husband? Are you getting along with him?

Ms. G: No.

CLINICIAN: Does he smoke marijuana?

Ms. G: No.

CLINICIAN: Does your husband drink a lot?

Ms. G: Yeah.

CLINICIAN: Does he think that he's an alcoholic?

Ms. G: No, he doesn't think he's an alcoholic.

CLINICIAN: Do you think he's an alcoholic?

Ms. G: Yeah, I think he is. He came [to the Hospital] 3 years ago, but he didn't have any results. He didn't keep it up.

CLINICIAN: How often does he drink?

Ms. G: Every night.

CLINICIAN: What happens when he drinks?

Ms. G: Oh, we fight.

CLINICIAN: Is he bad with the kids or just you?

Ms. G: Sometimes he takes it out on the kids.

CLINICIAN: Are they afraid of him? Do they hide?

Ms. G: Yeah, they want to leave.

CLINICIAN: Does he beat them?

Ms. G: No.

CLINICIAN: So he's angry when he drinks. Some people are happy. Does he hurt you?

Ms. G: Yes.

CLINICIAN: Does he ever hurt you bad enough that you come to the hospital?

Ms. G: No.

CLINICIAN: Are you afraid of him?

Ms. G: No.

CLINICIAN: Do you always fight about the same things?

Ms. G: Yeah.

CLINICIAN: What kind of things, financial things?

Ms. G: No, more the people I've been with.

CLINICIAN: So he doesn't approve of your friends?

Ms. G: No.

CLINICIAN: And what about his? Do you approve of them?

Ms. G: He never brings anybody to the house.

CLINICIAN: Where does he work?

Ms. G: He's a security guard for the Ajax Company. A couple of nights he works in the evenings and then he works about 2:00 to 10:00.

CLINICIAN: So he hardly ever sees the kids, right? What do you do all day?

Ms. G: Nothing.

CLINICIAN: Are you lonesome?

Ms. G: Yeah, I just sit at home.

CLINICIAN: Is that part of your depression?

Ms. G: Yeah, just sitting at home by myself.

CLINICIAN: So you're just by yourself with the kids? How many miles is it from Los Angeles to New York?

Ms. G: I don't know.

CLINICIAN: Are you good in geography?

Ms. G: No.

CLINICIAN: Where is the Middle East?

Ms. G: Somewhere in South America.

CLINICIAN: No, it's near Europe. Let's see how good you are at math. (*She asked Ms. G to do some subtraction, which she did correctly.*) There's a proverb: "People in glass houses shouldn't throw stones." What does that mean to you?

Ms. G: If a person is doing something and another person is doing something in the same situation, why should you talk about the other person?

CLINICIAN: How long have you been depressed and not eating and sleeping well?

Ms. G: One month.

CLINICIAN: How long has it been so bad that you're not able to take care of the house?

Ms. G: It's not that bad.

CLINICIAN: I was wondering why you came today. What can we do for you? Can you explain what you think we can do for you?

Ms. G: I want something to calm down my nerves—like I got last year—some pills.

CLINICIAN: Did they help you? Do you want the same kind of meds? Did they make you feel better?

Ms. G: Yeah.

CLINICIAN: OK, you have no other medical problems? Nothing has changed since last year, and you want a similar kind of medicine, more or less?

Ms. G: Yes.

CLINICIAN: But I understand that you refused to take it last time.

Ms. G: I took it. I did take it.

CLINICIAN: But I think they wanted you to continue the medicine and you stopped.

Ms. G: It's not true. I was seeing a doctor on the eighth floor. I got depressed and I called him.

CLINICIAN: Do you know what the medication is?

Ms. G: No, I was taking two different kinds.

CLINICIAN: (*After consulting the chart.*) What kind of medicine have you been taking?

Ms. G: A pink pill and a red and white capsule.

CLINICIAN: So you don't know the name of them?

Ms. G: No.

CLINICIAN: I'll tell you what: Dr. R will see you today. He's with a patient, and there is one more patient before you, but he will see you after that. Thank you for waiting.

The patient returned to the waiting area, and the clinician went to the staff lounge. When the doctor came in, he was told that Ms. G just wanted medication and would probably not need to be admitted. When the doctor left to examine another patient, the clinician wrote her note on the initial contact sheet.

> Jessica G is a 31 y[ear] o[ld] married, white female, mother of two children, came to Evaluation Center requesting some relief from Depression, possibly by some medication. She was here at Evaluation Center in 7/14/75 and again 8/13/75 for intake, but was never admitted.
>
> Ms. G appears very depressed, states her problems are same situational problems c̄ her husband. Her husband and mother-in-law drink, and both are alcoholic but is not being treated. Please read notes from 8/13/75 for past history and further information. She is oriented in all spheres and had no problem subtracting numbers. She is well oriented; not suicidal.
>
> She says we can look at the old chart for records because there are no new problems but same problems only got worse. She was placed on Sinequan, then changed to Tofranil 50 mg BID last year which she stated did give her relief from depression. To be seen by Dr. R.

[signed by clinician]

When the doctor returned, the clinician presented Ms. G's case to him. She gave him the chart to read and told him that Ms. G was "very, very depressed"; that she seemed very sad; that she had the same problems as she had had the previous year; and that she had never been hospitalized, but had been referred to the Mood Clinic, where she had refused to take medication.

DOCTOR: So she was referred to the Mood Clinic and refused to go there?

CLINICIAN: She took antidepressants, and that's all she wants now.

DOCTOR: Did you tell her that it could take 10 days?

CLINICIAN: Well, she just doesn't want to take the medication all the time and be a "patient."

She then explained again that Ms. G had the same problems—that she was very depressed and had an alcoholic husband.

CLINICIAN: His mother is also an alcoholic, and he and his mother drink together. The problem is how . . .

DOCTOR: Does she drink?

CLINICIAN: No. She smokes marijuana, and she says that it helps her with her sleep. She doesn't have any appetite, and recently she lost 5 pounds. She has three children.

DOCTOR: Does she have problems getting to sleep or waking up?

Approximately 40 minutes after the interview between the clinician and Ms. G had ended, the doctor entered the waiting area and introduced himself to Ms. G. He asked her to wait another 10 minutes while he read the chart and went into an interview room to do this. Then Ms. G was called to the interview room.

DOCTOR: I understand that things have been getting bad and that's why you're here today, and it's the same thing as it was before when you were here a year ago. It's the same situation.

Ms. G: Yes.

DOCTOR: How have you been handling things in the meantime? I understand that you're thinking of leaving your husband?

Ms. G: We talked about it, and we're trying again.

DOCTOR: I understand it's been getting worse in the last couple of days.

Ms. G: I just feel depressed and all smothered up.

DOCTOR: What's he done?

Ms. G: He's been drinking, and I've been getting nervous, and I can't stand it any more.

DOCTOR: Why are you here today, as opposed to last month?

Ms. G: I got to the point where I can't hold on on my own no longer.

DOCTOR: So you're thinking of doing yourself in?

Ms. G: No, I'm thinking of running off and leaving everything.

DOCTOR: Where would you go if you left?

Ms. G: I'd go to New York.

DOCTOR: Have you any children?

Ms. G: Yes.

DOCTOR: So you thought you'd run off?

Ms. G: Yeah, I thought I'd do that.

DOCTOR: Do you think it would be any benefit for you, being in the Hospital?

Ms. G: No, I don't think so.

DOCTOR: I understand you've had difficulty sleeping, you're not hungry, and you don't look forward to doing much.

Ms. G: Yes.

DOCTOR: Do you have crying spells?

Ms. G: No. I have been crying some about my problems.

DOCTOR: So you have been crying. Do you have trouble concentrating on things?

Ms. G: No.

DOCTOR: Do you look forward to anything?

Ms. G: No.

DOCTOR: Do you see any way out?

Ms. G: No.

DOCTOR: Would you like some help in trying to find a solution and trying to straighten it out? It's been going on for a long time.

Ms. G: Yes.

DOCTOR: I understand that you were on medication for a short period of time. Did that help?

Ms. G: Yes, I was on two kinds of pills.

DOCTOR: Which one helped?

Ms. G: Both helped. I got some pink pills at first, then I got some red.

DOCTOR: We have a clinic which regulates that medication, and we send people to the clinic where they get medication and are followed through the clinic.[14] I understand that, before, you didn't want to do this.

Ms. G: (*No response.*)

DOCTOR: Was this because the pills didn't help you?

Ms. G: Yes, they did.

DOCTOR: I understand that you were drowsy all the time.

Ms. G: Well, they helped me sleep.

DOCTOR: Well, I think that even with medication, you still have to face some problems, don't you? Do you think there's nothing you can do about that?

Ms. G: It's so difficult.

DOCTOR: Physically difficult?

Ms. G: No.

DOCTOR: Does he know that you're down?

Ms. G: Yes.

DOCTOR: What does he think about that?

Ms. G: He thinks it's ridiculous.

DOCTOR: Have you ever thought of suicide?

Ms. G: Yeah, a couple of years ago.

DOCTOR: So it was actually worse a couple of years ago?

Ms. G: Yes.

DOCTOR: How long have you been feeling this bad—not eating and sleeping?

Ms. G: About a month.

DOCTOR: What can we do for you today, and what did you expect in coming here?

Ms. G: I just expected that you would give me something to help me get some rest.

DOCTOR: OK, would you be willing or interested in seeing a therapist?

Ms. G: (*Nodded.*) Uh-huh.

DOCTOR: You would? Would your husband come?

Ms. G: No, he wouldn't come.

DOCTOR: You're sure of that?

Ms. G: Yeah.

DOCTOR: Well, I think it would be a good idea. Let's see, I'm going to schedule you for clinic. The trouble with this clinic is that it doesn't like people to be premedicated. They like to give people the medicine themselves, but let me see. I'll contact them and find out when you can have your appointment. If it's too long—say, more than a day or so—we can give you something.

The doctor went to the staff lounge and told the clinician, "We want psychotherapy. The question is what to do with the Mood Clinic, about her being premedicated."

CLINICIAN: Is she willing to come into the clinic?

DOCTOR: Yes, what's the schedule?

They looked at the clinic schedule for a few minutes in silence.

CLINICIAN: Maybe she should go to the Aftercare Clinic?

DOCTOR: Yeah, but then again she sees me. Isn't it possible to schedule her for this week?

CLINICIAN: Everything is full.

DOCTOR: Well, I'll give her something for now and schedule her for next Wednesday.

CLINICIAN: When someone is referred to the Mood Clinic, Dr. N wants a very long note.

DOCTOR: I'll write only the reason for the referral. It's clear—she's depressed. Should she go for tests?

CLINICIAN: What do you want to do? Schedule her for tests and an EEG and to refer her to the Mood Clinic and psychotherapy?

DOCTOR: Yes. Is she on Medical Assistance?

CLINICIAN: Yes.

The doctor then wrote a prescription for Tofranil. The clinician took the prescription and appointment slips to the waiting area and explained to Ms. G that she would have a physical examination[15]; if she had any problems, she should come back to the Evaluation Center. She cautioned her not to be late for any appointments.

The patient-observer then interviewed Ms. G. When asked if she knew what kind of treatment she was going to receive, Ms. G replied that she didn't know exactly but didn't feel she needed any more information. Ms. G said she was going to talk to some people about her problems and that she thought it would help her. She had come back because she had been helped here before.

The clinician then interrupted the interview to tell Ms. G that the people from the Mood Clinic would call her if there was any change in her appointments and that it might also be possible for her to have some home visits.

Meanwhile, the doctor had written his note on the initial contact sheet.

31 Y[ear] O[ld] W[hite] F[emale] c̄ chaotic marital situation which she has been unable to effectively deal with. There is considerable fighting and arguing between her and her husband. In the past she has responded to both Tofranil and Sinequan c̄ improved sleep. Marital situation has deteriorated again to the point of her wanting help. She says she has been "depressed" 1 month. Today complains of DFA anorexia, 5# wt. loss. Her mood is depressed, affect is flat. Denies suicidal intent. No psychotic ideation. Judgment & insight OK. No ideas of reference or paranoid thoughts. States that she feels "lonesome" & neglected. Could not do serial 7's. Knew the past 5 presidents. Oriented × 3.

Impression: Pt. c̄ a chaotic marital situation well described in intake interview of 8/13/75. Problems described then remain. Impression is Affective disorder, depression, probably situational.

Plan:

1. ADC Screening Clinic 12/22/76
2. Have started her on Tofranil 50 mg. po h.s. M.S. #10
3. Community Intervention Team

Although it was obvious that Ms. G consented to the referral, there was no clear point at which her decision was manifest.

6

Information and Understanding
in the Evaluation Center

In this chapter, we discuss the "informed" part of the informed consent doctrine as it applies to decisionmaking in the Evaluation Center. The data on which this chapter is based are identical to the data used in both the previous and following chapters. However, this chapter discusses the data only as they pertain to the associated issues of disclosure and understanding. We do not restrict ourselves to information required by state regulation; we also consider some of the disclosures that seem to be mandated by common law and the ways in which the staff and the patients dealt with them. Put another way, this chapter discusses the staff's view of treatment, the patients' view of treatment, and the ways in which what staff members and patients said to each other affected the patients' view.

WHAT PATIENTS WERE TOLD AND WHAT THEY UNDERSTOOD

Of all the factual data that the Evaluation Center staff could possibly have provided to patients, there is some information the informed consent doctrine requires, since it is, in theory, directly material to patients' decisionmaking. Presumably, the patients also ought to have understood it. It includes the following:

1. The nature of the treatment (e.g., whether it would be outpatient or inpatient, how long it would take, and who would treat a particular patient).
2. The purpose of treatment (in this case, the nature of a particular patient's disorder, since the purpose of treatment was relief of the problem).
3. The risks and benefits of the treatment.
4. The special risk of the 72-hours rule.
5. Any possible alternative treatments.

Let us now consider each of these topics, one at a time.

THE NATURE OF THE PROPOSED TREATMENT

The informed consent doctrine bases its model of the doctor-patient relationship on the traditional economic model of buyer and seller. As a buyer, the patient is supposed to weigh the advantages and disadvantages of the treatment (the product). Even more basically—just as an ordinary automobile buyer expects at least to know whether the car is a Ford or a Plymouth, a small sedan or a large station wagon—the patient should want to know what sort of treatment he or she can expect.

Probably the first thing a patient should have understood about the nature of a treatment proposed in the Evaluation Center was whether it was to be done on an outpatient or an inpatient basis. The results here are uniformly positive. We saw no cases of patients being admitted to the hospital without being told and understanding that they were being admitted. Likewise, all patients referred to outpatient treatment understood that they were not being hospitalized, but were being referred to outpatient treatment.

Beyond this knowledge, however, staff disclosures about, and patients' understanding of, the particulars of treatment were not very extensive. For example, at the time at which they were considering whether or not to sign themselves into the Hospital, patients usually lacked even the faintest clues as to the length of the period to which they were committing themselves. On the few occasions that patients asked, they were typically told they ought to come into the hospital "for a while." In 22 cases where admission to the hospital was considered, we observed only four instances in which staff members on their own initiative made some reference to the expected length of stay in the Hospital, and all of them were quite vague. One patient was told it would take "a few days"; the second, that the tests he would undergo would require "more than one day" in the hospital; the third was told that this was a "short-term" hospital; and the fourth was assured that she was not going to stay in the Hospital for the rest of her life. This limited disclosure in part reflected the fact that the Evaluation Center staff was not responsible for how long the patient stayed in treatment, and they did not want to commit the treatment staff to anything definite.

Another type of information about treatment that a rational patient/consumer might be expected to want is to which ward he or she is going. The inpatient units of the Hospital varied considerably, both in terms of their attitude toward length of hospitalization (short-term vs. medium-term) and their general therapeutic orientation (behavior modification vs. medication). However, patients were rarely informed of even the name of the ward to which they were going. Most patients, of course, had no reason to ask about which ward they would be on, since they knew nothing about the differences and the staff never mentioned that there were any such differences. Only the two patients who were potential research subjects and were admitted to the Research Ward were told or had any idea that there were any substantial differences among wards.

There are also other types of information that patients might have wanted if they were going to make informed decisions. This includes what types of treatment they might receive (medication, psychotherapy, group therapy, etc.). There was little disclosure of this information to most patients.

Given an almost complete lack of disclosure of the details of possible treatment, it is not surprising that patients did not understand very much. Their spontaneous statements, as well as their responses to our patient-observer's questions, revealed very little grasp of the type of treatment they might receive.

One group (10 of the 41 patients about whom we had substantial data) could not or would not indicate anything concerning what they expected their treatment to consist of, beyond reiterating the purpose of the treatment. Thus, when asked what they expected from the treatment, this group responded either with goals ("It will help me control my anger") or a statement that they didn't know. This should not, however, be taken too literally. Several of these patients were quite articulate and had had previous experiences with psychiatric treatment. It seems, therefore, that some of them meant only that they had no specific knowledge about what would be done for them, beyond what they knew about psychiatry in general.

A second group (19 patients) expressed more specific ideas about what would happen to them, although not necessarily more realistic ones. Although they thought they had a grasp on what the experience of hospitalization would be like, their understanding was not very detailed. Five patients in this group, all of whom were to be admitted as inpatients, saw the hospital and treatment as focused on rest and a chance to get away from their problems. They did not express any knowledge of or interest in chemotherapy, group therapy, milieu therapy, or anything else that the staff viewed as treatment. Two patients in this group, both involuntarily committed, saw the hospital as a snake pit set up to destroy patients. One mentioned prefrontal lobotomies, shock, and torture in discussing what he expected. Likewise, two voluntary patients expected that their treatment would be shock treatment. Although the diagnoses in both cases (organic brain syndrome and schizophrenia) made ECT an unlikely choice of treatment, both patients seemed to approve of receiving ECT.

In the last subgroup of this second group of patients were 10 patients whose responses cannot easily be categorized but whose understanding was poor. All indicated some understanding of what would happen, but their ideas tended to be highly general glosses for very complex processes. Thus Harrison T, a wealthy, eccentric man in his 30s with mystical ideas, said that he expected he would "learn" and that the hospital would make him "feel." Rudolph D readily reported that he would have extensive tests and talk to the doctors, but what the tests would be like and what he would talk about he did not know. Natania Z, a recent immigrant who was referred to an outpatient clinic, thought (incorrectly) that she was going to get psychoanalysis, which she believed would help "to persuade [her] to think the right way"; but her difficulties with English raised the question of whether she did not understand what she would be receiving or simply could not explain it.

The patients who best understood the nature of the treatment proposed for them (11 in number) tended to describe what was going to happen to them in a manner similar to the staff's description. These patients fall into three distinct subgroups. Three were addicted to some sort of drug and were coming in for withdrawal. They all knew in some detail the specifics of the procedure for withdrawal and the length of time it would take. A second group was composed of five patients who were applying for outpatient counseling. While none of them knew how the counseling would work, all were told and understood they would be seen individually, and those who would be receiving drugs understood that too. The two patients noted above were admitted to the Research Ward and understood some of the details of what made that a special ward (see Chapter 9). Finally, one patient (Holly E) was being seen in the Outpatient Clinic (see Chapters 13-16). Her medicine was going to run out before her next appointment, and she wanted a refill. Her understanding of the benefits and purpose of the drug was clear, full, and technically correct, although she was apparently not aware of any long-term risks.

In general, we can say that beyond the knowledge of whether the treatment would be inpatient or outpatient, few patients were told very much about the details of their likely treatment. What they did understand came mostly from previous experience with the treatment or from what was told to them before they came to the Hospital.

THE PURPOSES OF THE PROPOSED TREATMENT

According to the informed consent doctrine, the staff ought to disclose and patients ought to understand the purposes of treatment. Since treatment is directed toward the alleviation of the patient's problems, this means that patients must be told about and understand their problems. In the Evaluation Center, therefore, the critical issue concerning the purposes of treatment was what the doctor found wrong with a particular patient. As we describe in Chapter 5, disclosure of the doctor's findings was part of the official forms that all patients should have received.

One of the most remarkable findings of our study has been that patients rarely were explicitly informed about the findings of the initial evaluation; that is, about "what was wrong with them." The information that the evaluating physicians wrote on the admission form, for example, was usually minimal and often vague. For example, the verbal description given by the clinician to Delucia E, whom we discuss in Chapter 5, was quite brief:

> "Here are the reasons. The doctor says that you are listening to voices, and he wants to keep you here so that he can evaluate you. You are hallucinating and

hearing voices, and they're telling you to do some harm to yourself, and we want to keep you to help protect you from getting hurt."

However, this was based on an even briefer written statement by the doctor. Even so, this was atypically elaborate. In 15 of the cases, the patient was told nothing beyond what was written on the form or a slight paraphrase of it, and these findings were usually extremely brief. Evaluations such as "Depressed lady on Librium," "Patient not sleeping well and is hyperactive," and "24-year-old lady with depression and difficulty ordering her thoughts" were by no means atypical. Occasionally the descriptions were incomprehensible for patients. One patient was shown this list:

1. B.P.
2. Periph Vasc Disease
3. ASCVD w/CHF (treated)
4. 1° AD—unipolar
5. Paresis L ulnar distribution

Information was often conveyed in technical terms, such as "Korsakoff synd." or "Wilson's disease." Finally, we must note that in two cases the patients signed blank forms and received no information whatsoever as to why they were being treated.

However, this is a deceptive way of describing what staff members disclosed about the patients' problems. All of the patients who came to the Hospital voluntarily, and many of those who did not, knew why they came and had a clear idea of the purpose of treatment. In two-thirds of the cases, the staff and the patients established a tacit agreement about the purpose of treatment quite early in the discussion. The clinicians often began interviews by asking, "Why are you here?" or "What is your problem?," and patients typically responded by presenting problems that the staff reformulated into technical terms as the diagnostic problems. In these cases, the written description of the problems was understood by both patients and clinicians simply to stand for the problems that they had discussed. However, in about one-third of the cases, the matter was not so simple.

The staff, as mental health specialists, saw the patients' essential problems as located primarily in the patients, rather than in the patients' environment, in what the patients had done, or in their intentions or lack of skills or education, although these were often recognized as subsidiary problems. They saw the patients as needing psychiatric treatment, not education, modified living arrangements, moral reform, or punishment. The staff often agreed that the patients had difficulty in their home lives, had broken the law, needed vocational training, or even needed moral guidance; but they saw difficulties in these areas as derivative of psychiatric or neurological deficits. Patients did not always agree. Although disagreement occurred in less than half of the cases, it systematically undercut the entire dialogue between staff and patient when it did occur.

The largest group of patients who did not accept the psychiatric model saw themselves as being brought to the Hospital for doing something bad or something that someone else did not like; that is, they saw their difficulties as based on a particular act. Thus Manuel C, when asked why he was brought to the Evaluation Center, responded, "For hitting a nurse, I guess." He viewed the Hospital as a jail; that is, as a place to which one is sent for doing a bad thing. Likewise, Gwen X saw herself as in the Hospital for something she did—for "jumping on [her] niece." She remained steadfast in that view, and no real effort was made to persuade her otherwise, because she willingly accepted outpatient treatment anyway—not because she had changed her view of the problem, but because it provided someone to talk to and alleviated her loneliness. Manuel C, Gwen X, and six other patients all maintained the view that they were brought to the Hospital because they did something bad, not because they had basic psychiatric or neurological difficulties.

Another divergent way in which some patients understood their problems was that the problems were the result of difficulties in their environment that were not primarily their responsibility. Mitzie Q, a 22-year-old white woman who was brought to the hospital by her father, exemplified this type of divergent understanding. Although this was not her first hospitalization for schizophrenia, Ms. Q did not accept the view that schizophrenia was the core of her problem; instead, she insisted that the problem was primarily the way her family treated her and secondarily the way her boyfriend and friends treated her. She emphatically rejected the notion that she provoked their hostile behaviors. She felt the Hospital was an alternative environment in which the people were nicer to her than her family was. She saw coming to the Hospital as the next best thing to getting her own apartment, which she could not afford. If she had any problem, she thought it was the practical one of not having the skills to get a job. By contrast, the staff saw her as schizophrenic, with basic difficulties in her mode of relating to others. Consequently, her understanding of the purpose of treatment was radically different from the staff's view. Ms. Q did not enter the Hospital seeking treatment in an ordinary sense of the word. Her specific disagreement with the staff was an unusual one. Only three of our 48 patients saw their problems as amenable to relief by manipulation of the environment.

Another view held by some patients was that their difficulties were primarily technical ones, and they lacked only a technique or a means for dealing with specific environmental situations. Minnie A was one of two cases of this type that we saw. Both Ms. A and the staff agreed that she was having difficulties with her parents. However, the staff saw these difficulties as a reflection of her "inadequate personality," whereas Ms. A did not think that the difficulties were a part of her personality or even necessarily caused by her parents. Instead, she wanted the Hospital to provide her with "advice"; that is, she wanted an education in how to deal with her parents. She did not see a need to change anything about her personality.

All of the above cases—the eight who saw their problems as act-focused, the three who saw their problems as environmentally based, and the two who saw themselves as lacking appropriate means—were exceptions to the rule. Of the 37 patients on whom we had adequate data to ascertain their understanding of the purpose of treatment, 24 clearly manifested the belief that there was something wrong with them, that their problems were essentially located within themselves, and that treatment of some psychological or neurological sort would be the proper remedy. Typically, they came complaining about being depressed, hearing things, or presenting some other problem located within themselves and requesting needed treatment.

This is a very significant breakdown, because, with only one exception, the 24 patients who believed that their difficulty was within themselves were the most cooperative patients. They tended to accept the staff's recommendations and to volunteer information freely. Moreover, the staff, perhaps reacting to these patients' presentations of their problems, tended to be more open about their thoughts on the cases. The patient–staff communication in these cases was much better than in the others, although even here it left much to be desired. Thus we found, paradoxically, that understanding determined information rather than the other way around. Most patients arrived with their own "understanding" of the purpose of treatment, and this sharply affected the information given to them. In the cases where the patients' views did not correspond to the staff's views, the patients were not told the staff's formulation of their problems. Mitzie Q, for example, wanted to come into the Hospital in order to get some rest, to get away from her family, and to visit her friends on the ward. At no time was she told that the staff wanted to hospitalize her in order to treat her schizophrenia. Instead, the staff, by failing to comment, allowed her to believe that they accepted her version of what the Hospital would do for her.

From the staff's point of view, these cases were very problematic, precisely because they believed that the patients "lacked insight" and stubbornly held to an unrealistic view of their problems. The prospect of confronting the patients with the staff's view of the problems seemed likely to mean "losing" the patients. Thus they were inclined to allow the patients' view of their problems to go unchallenged.

RISKS AND BENEFITS

The dimension of informed consent that has probably gained the most attention from theorists and lawmakers is that of the risks of treatment. Most of the common law of informed consent has evolved from cases in which the court found insufficient risk disclosures. Commentators as well as judicial dicta have often emphasized that disclosure should permit the patient to balance the risks against the benefits and to consent to treatment only if in his or her judgment the benefits of the treatment outweigh its risks.

Doctors are not always certain what the risks and benefits of treatment are. Inpatient treatment, we might argue, offers as a major benefit the relief of symptoms and clarification of diagnosis; its major risks are the stigma of being a mental patient, the regimentation of the hospital, the lost time away from home and work, the possible loss of income, and the possibility of being committed. Outpatient treatment seems to offer many of the same benefits (although not necessarily for the same patients), and its only major risk is probably the potential stigma.

The Evaluation Center staff nearly always failed to inform patients about the benefits of treatment. With few exceptions, the only statements of benefits we observed were merely brief indications that the patient would "feel better" or be "helped" or "evaluated." This, however, did not necessarily derive from any desire to hide information from the patients. Rather, the staff assumed that patients, who came to them for some relief from their suffering, would take it for granted that the recommended treatment would make them feel better.

The staff rarely expressed doubts as to the successful outcome of the treatment. When they did display some hesitation about the prospects of improvement, it was usually in the form of skepticism about a fast recovery, not in terms of any general doubt. Thus three patients were warned not to expect immediate recovery, since the treatment could possibly take several months.

In three other instances, the staff either communicated to patients some degree of uncertainty or provided them with some information that was meant to destroy unwarranted illusions about treatment. For example, a resident told this to Maureen A:

> "I don't pretend that by coming into the hospital we can help you with your [marital] problems. What we can do is get you in better shape physically so that you can cope better with your problems. It will probably improve your sleep and make your mind clearer, *but it won't solve all your problems*." (emphasis added)

The most extreme example we saw was when the psychiatrist warned Wesley and Naomi G that couples therapy would not help if either of them would not cooperate fully, and that they might end up separating from each other. However, these are isolated exceptions to a general pattern of recommending treatments as though their positive outcome was highly likely.

The staff usually did not inform patients about possible failure or about possible risks of the proposed treatment. We never observed a clinician discussing with patients the possible negative consequences of hospitalization— employment problems, the stigma of being a mental patient, relations with friends, and so on. Nor did we ever see clinicians spontaneously mention to patients the possibility that they might be involuntarily committed during their stay in the hospital. Since staff members did not disclose very much about the risks and benefits of treatment, we cannot report whether or not the patients understood the risks and benefits that were disclosed. Instead, we describe what the patients themselves saw as risks and benefits.

First, we found that more than half (25) the patients neither expressed in any way nor indicated by questions any concern that the procedure being contemplated had any disadvantages. Eleven of these patients had been referred to outpatient treatment and hence were not committing themselves to anything at that point. It seemed that several of these patients did not argue about the referral because they knew they did not have to go to their appointments. Thus perhaps the absence of any expressed appreciation of risks in these cases was only a matter of the patients' not expressing it. The fact that almost one-third of these patients did not follow up on these referrals partially supports this interpretation.

However, 14 of the patients who expressed no feeling that there were any disadvantages associated with treatment were prospective inpatients. These patients, even when asked about disadvantages, expressed no concern about the stigma of hospitalization, the loss of liberty, the company they could expect on the ward, or the separation from their families. As a group, they tended to be either very upset and desperate about their symptoms, very dependent upon someone who was deciding for them, or very psychotic. They had made up their minds to come in and did not want to consider reasons to the contrary.

However, 18 patients felt that treatment did have risks.[1] Of these 18 patients, only two had been referred to outpatient treatment. One case involved Lori C, a 14-year-old girl who was frightened by the neurological tests planned for her. The other was Wesley G, a man who came for marital counseling, who expected the experience to be unpleasant and was afraid it might make the problem even worse.

The disadvantages cited by the 16 patients who were going to be admitted to the Hospital were diverse. Seven mentioned that they would be locked up and didn't like that; but only Cynthia M expressed the classic fear that she would be "put away forever," and even she commented that she knew it wouldn't happen. For the others, this concern seemed to be primarily that they would not be free to move around while in the Hospital.

A second group of disadvantages that patients mentioned had to do with the effect of hospitalization on the patients' outside personal affairs and relationships. Christopher N was worried that his parents would discover he was a heroin addict, and Sally N was worried that her father would be upset by the suggestion that she needed psychiatric care. For other patients, problems with child care, missed school time, an unfaithful girlfriend, and the cost of hospitalization were major disadvantages. In all, eight patients had some concern with this kind of problem.

A rather large group of problems related to skepticism about or fear of treatment procedures in the hospital. Three patients mentioned "shock treatment" in a negative way, and one of them, Gustav A, also expressed fear that the hospital would lobotomize and torture him. At a more mundane level, one patient was afraid of having blood taken; another patient was afraid that a medical problem would be mismanaged as he claimed it had been during a previous hospitalization. Chester T, a heroin addict, saw the Hospital's policy of not giving methadone to patients as the major risk in admitting himself for withdrawal. Only one patient mentioned a concern that the "cure" might not be permanent. Finally, two patients mentioned as risks their discomfort with the social life expected on the ward and their having to associate with people with whom they would be uncomfortable.

In brief, although there was little discussion between staff and patients about the risks of treatment, some patients had their own ideas about risks. Nonetheless, the fact that more than half the patients, including many who were to receive inpatient care, saw no risks in treatment is surprising.

The benefits of treatment were rarely mentioned explicitly by patients and often had to be inferred from the discussion. In 16 cases, the patients cited the purpose of the treatment as its benefit and nothing else. Thus, patients said they hoped "I will feel better" or "I will feel less depressed."

In another seven cases, patients expressed the belief that there were no benefits at all or did not mention any benefits even when asked. All of these patients were brought to the hospital by someone else and were pressured to accept treatment. Four of them came under court order, and the others were pressured by relatives or by the police.

Other benefits expressed by three patients (and perhaps the most important for the doctrine of informed consent) were benefits not directly related to personality change, but rather to the patients' environment. Minnie A hoped that the treatment would allow her to change her relationship with her parents so that they would not fight so much, and Wesley G expected that counseling would help him get his wife back.

Another group of eight patients saw treatment as beneficial both in its fulfillment of its stated purposes and in its effect on some environmental problems. Natania Z, a recent immigrant, expected that treatment would alleviate her depression and would help her adjust to America; Tracey D, a college student, thought he would feel better and would be able to do better school work; Eldred C expected that he would be withdrawn from his Percodan addiction and in so doing would be able to prove to his insurance company that his chronic pain was not caused by taking too many prescribed drugs.

Finally, five patients saw the benefits of hospitalization not as consequences of treatment, but as intrinsic to the mechanism of treatment itself. Three patients viewed admission to the Hospital as an opportunity to get some rest and as a beneficial development, independent of its effect on their personalities. Gwen X saw her counseling session as a chance to talk to someone and not feel so lonely. And Mitzie Q, the most dramatic example of this group, envisioned the prospect of hospitalization as fun. Having been in the Hospital before, she wanted to see her friends among the patients and staff and to enjoy the jukebox.

These findings provide some support for the idea implicit in the doctrine of informed consent that patients must be entitled to make their own decisions on the basis of technical information supplied by doctors and on personal preferences they supply themselves. Sixteen patients saw personal benefits to treatment that the staff could not have predicted simply from knowing that the individuals were patients and thus ought to want to get better. These findings support the notion that patients have private reasons for wanting treatment, just as some patients have different views from those of the staff about the risks of treatment.

THE 72-HOURS RULE: A SPECIAL RISK

It can be argued that the common-law doctrine of informed consent requires the disclosure of many different risks of psychiatric hospitalization. However, the disclosure of only one has been specifically mandated by legislative action. The analysis of the disclosure of this particular piece of information highlights some of the general characteristics of the disclosure process in the Evaluation Center, particularly disclosure on legislatively mandated forms.

The regulation about withdrawal from voluntary treatment derived from the Mental Health Procedures Act specifies:

> If the proposed treatment includes inpatient status, informed consent may include the applicant's voluntary agreement to remain in treatment for a specified period not to exceed 72 hours after having given written notice of intent to withdraw from voluntary treatment. (§7100.2.2.2(c))

Since disclosure of information concerning withdrawal from voluntary treatment is required by law, one might expect that it would be standard and not vary substantially across staff members or patients. This was far from being the case. The stipulation itself is quite tricky, and it seems that any way of disclosing information regarding it, other than simply reciting the text, would be misleading in one way or another.

Some basic confusion was introduced by the way in which these principles were operationalized by the State Department of Public Welfare, which produced a form that was to be read and signed by patients before admission to a hospital. The form contains the following choice for patients to make:

I understand that I may: (Check and complete A or B)

    A. Leave this hospital upon written request with _____ hours' notice.
          up to 72

       The reasons for giving notice before I leave have been explained to me.

    B. Leave at any time I express my desire to leave in writing.

The structure of this form may have unnecessarily complicated matters. B is essentially redundant, since patients can simply write down "0" where the number of hours was to be entered in A. The bifurcation between A and B makes it look as if patients have only two and not an infinite number of possible choices. This may have accounted for some of the difficulties in explaining this particular piece of information in the Evaluation Center.

What "72 hours" referred to also confused Evaluation Center patients, partly because several patients were told explicitly they would have to agree to stay in the Hospital for at least 72 hours, while others were told they would have to give 72 hours' notice before leaving. Thus some patients understood they could leave the Hospital only 3 days after notification in writing that they intended to do so, while others understood they could simply leave the hospital after being there 3 days.

The case of Mitzie Q highlights not only the difficulties that even the most conscientious staff members had in explaining the regulations concerning withdrawal from voluntary treatment, but also the problems patients had in understanding them. When Ms. Q's rights as a patient were explained to her by the nurse/clinician, they included the following:

> "Now, you will be able to leave if you want to, but you will have to tell us, and we may ask you to stay 3 days after you say you want to withdraw."

When Ms. Q, who did not fully understand, asked, "Three days from now?" the nurse/clinician repeated, "No, when you decide to leave the Hospital." Soon afterwards, however, Ms. Q made it clear that she had not yet fully comprehended the stipulation. When the nurse/clinician presented her with the consent form she was supposed to sign, the following interchange took place:

CLINICIAN: We would like you to give us 72 hours' notice and request in writing that you want to leave.

Ms. Q: 72 hours from now?

CLINICIAN: No, from whenever. It means that you tell us that you want to leave, and then 72 hours later is when you can leave.

Ms. Q: What's today? Monday. That means I can go by Friday. Can I leave then?

At this point the clinician gave up, and rather than try again, he gave Ms. Q the following misleading information: "I can't tell you that. It depends on your doctor." Faced with this new information that contradicted what she had been told before, Ms. Q insisted, "But you said up to 3 days. You told me." The clinician's response was this:

> "Well, it means that if you are not getting better, the doctors can keep you for awhile longer. . . . This part is very hard to understand, I know. It's just that we don't want you to leave right away. We'd like you to give us some notice before you leave."

The explanations concerning withdrawal from voluntary treatment were specified quite explicitly on the Patients' Rights form that the patients did receive:

> You may withdraw from treatment at any time by giving written notice to the director of this facility; however,
>
> You may be asked to agree to remain in the facility for a specified period of time up to 72 hours after you request discharge. If, when you request discharge you are asked to remain for this period of time, someone will immediately explain why to you. The facility may institute involuntary commitment proceedings during this period.

Presumably this information was supposed to be given to patients before they had to choose whether to check A or B and consent to treatment. Only thus would the statement "The reasons for giving notice before I leave have been explained to me" included in the consent form make sense.

In about half the cases, however, such an oral explanation was not given to patients until *after* they signed the form. This undoubtedly diminished their chances of checking B. Of the 22 admissions we observed, only three patients actually did check B. This is not surprising, since the possible advantages of checking B were usually not communicated to patients. In almost half the cases we observed, the option to choose between A and B was, however, rather clearly communicated orally to the patient. For example, the clinician told Jim N:

> "You have a choice to check either of these blocks. If you check the lower one, you can leave the hospital any time. If you check the top block, you can put in any number of hours up to 72; and if you decide you want to leave the hospital, we can keep you for that number of hours. That will allow us and you time to think it over. . . . Whatever you sign, this is your own business. It's up to you."

And Eldred C was told:

> "You have two options. You can check either A or B. The first one you can leave the hospital by giving up to 72 hours' notice, and the second one you can leave at any time."

It should be noted, however, that although half the patients were given the option to choose between A and B, only a few of them were told, as Jim N was, that checking A actually involved a range of possibilities and that they could write any number of hours up to 72. This is reflected in the fact that most of the patients who checked A wrote down "72" without any apparent reflection. The only patient who deviated from this pattern was Eldred C, who, after having done the same thing, asked the nurse/clinician, "I can put 8 hours here or any number, can't I?" When the clinician confirmed that indeed this was the case, he wrote "8," since he expected it would take 8 hours for his wife to travel from their home to the hospital to pick him up.

The remaining patients were not orally informed that they had the option to choose between A and B, and were in fact sometimes even told the contrary, as in these examples:

"If we admit you, we have a rule. You have to stay here at least 72 hours."[2]

"You can stay for an indefinite period of time, but you must let us know 72 hours before you leave."

"You can leave at any time if you'll just give us 72 hours' notice."

"This says you're able to leave the hospital upon written request with 72 hours' notice. So you write '72' here."

Chester T's wife, who asked the nurse/clinician if her husband would be able to sign himself out, was told that "he has to stay 3 days at least." At least in this case, the staff understood that this was deceptive. When the clinician later told the psychiatrist what she had said, he laughed and remarked that if Mr. T had read the form, he would have seen that he did not have to do as she requested.

The Evaluation Center staff's general tendency to encourage patients to check A was, in part, a response to pressures from the inpatient units of the Hospital, which were reluctant to admit patients who might withdraw from treatment right away.[3] As a result, several patients were simply given a form on which A had already been checked and the number "72" filled in by the staff. Only Sally N gave even a mild protest. While reading the forms before signing them, she realized the resident had already checked A and had written down "72," and she asked him, "Why has A been checked instead of B?" The resident replied,

"Because frequently when persons are not evaluated and only need one test, they come in for one day and leave. But this doesn't apply to you."

Ms. N accepted this explanation, and their dialogue shifted to another topic.

We should also note that while the form stated that patients who wanted to withdraw from voluntary treatment had to notify the ward staff in writing, only a third of the patients were actually told this by the staff.

While external pressures in part accounted for the frequency with which staff members misinformed patients about their options regarding withdrawal from voluntary treatment, their behavior also probably reflected a basic alienation from this particular law. From the staff's point of view, many of these patients needed treatment and could not be trusted to make reasonable judgments.

ALTERNATIVES

As we have said, the presentation of alternatives is central to the free choice that informed consent is supposed to promote. The spirit of the informed consent doctrine seems to require that several types of information be presented about alternatives. The "procedures" about which the patients in the Evaluation Center had to make decisions were admission to the Hospital or referral to some form of outpatient therapy. In some cases, each of these procedures was an "alternative" to the other, but in all cases another alternative was *not* to receive any treatment at all (see Chapter 2). In the case of outpatient treatment, there were different kinds of outpatient treatment available in the hospital, including three different chemotherapy clinics, three types of psychotherapy clinics, and some combination of these treatments; of course, not all of these were appropriate for a particular patient (e.g., family therapy for a single adult). When inpatient care was indicated, different units in the hospital were oriented toward providing different forms of treatment.

The presentation of alternatives was one of the most problematic areas in the Evaluation Center. Generally, the only choice presented to patients was whether or not to undergo treatment, and even this was communicated more implicitly than explicitly. The staff usually proposed only one particular treatment to patients; the patient could either consent to this or refuse it. When staff members did present patients with a variety of alternative courses of action, it was nearly always done as if the alternatives were not important. Jessica G, for example, was casually asked in the course of negotiating for outpatient treatment, "Do you think it would be any benefit for you, being in the hospital?" When she said "No," the subject was dropped. Only Naomi and Wesley G, of all the patients we observed, were presented with two alternative modes of treatment (individual and family therapy) between which they were expected to choose.

None of the above should be taken to mean that patients never had decisions to make about treatment; it means only that the decisions were rarely between alternative forms of treatment. Instead, they tended to focus on the time and place of treatment and on whether they should get treatment at all. It is true that 17 patients never mentioned or had mentioned to them by the staff any options about treatment. The patients felt they needed to be treated and either told the staff what type of treatment they needed or accepted the staff's suggestion. Another 14 patients considered only whether or not they needed to be treated. Formally, this can be thought of as involving the alternative of "no treatment"; however, these decisions did not involve any questions except how to maximize the patients' mental health and/or whether the patients were sick at all. They did not involve the private values or personal concerns upon which a patient might legitimately base a decision different from that of the technical expert, the doctor.

Five other patients mentioned or considered an alternative to treatment that would apply if the preferred treatment could not be obtained or failed. Linda T planned to go to a hotel if the Hospital would not admit her. Another patient planned to go to a bar and "get drunk" if he could not get treatment. In only one of these five cases was there the alternative of what would ordinarily be called "treatment." In this case, Wesley G considered and agreed to individual counseling if his wife refused marital counseling. Only Mr. G can be said to have weighed treatment alternatives, while the other four cases manifest an active decision that treatment was better than a nontreatment alternative.

Finally, six patients can genuinely be said to have considered alternatives to at least some aspect of treatment. However, most of these cases did not focus on treatment alternatives, nor did the decisions actually resemble informed consent. Jerome D had to decide whether he wanted to be hospitalized immediately or to come back and be seen the next day, but he was almost passive, while his mother actively participated in the decision. Jacob N considered two alternative places for treatment, although apparently merely as a pretext to satisfy his mother's desire that he go through with the interview. Jessica G did consider the options of admission or family therapy as well as the outpatient treatment she eventually received, but only long enough to explain to the clinician that her husband wouldn't have come to family therapy and that inpatient treatment was unnecessary. However, Wendel B, a man who had to decide whether to sign himself in or risk the chance that a court would commit him; Rudolph D, a man who chose to receive treatment at the Hospital rather than in his own catchment area, even though he had to pay for it; and Chester T, a heroin addict whose alternatives involved withdrawing without methadone in the Hospital or going to another hospital at the risk of losing his wife, who wanted him to withdraw immediately, all seemed to have understood their situations as containing alternatives about which they could choose. It should be noted, however, that none of these alternatives concerned which treatment the patients should receive within the confines of the hospital.

HOW INFORMATION WAS PRESENTED

We have reviewed what was disclosed and what patients understood. However central these facts may seem to the question of whether or not informed consent took place in the Evaluation Center, they are no more critical to our understanding of the problem of informed consent than is the question of how information was given to patients. The manner of disclosure directly affects what a patient learns. We start by discussing the problem of vagueness in oral communication.

VAGUENESS

One of the most obvious difficulties with oral disclosure is that spontaneous talk is often vague. What patients were told about what would happen to them, while perhaps clear to the staff, was often very vague to patients who understood little about the Hospital's routine practices. The descriptions of the treatments that the staff recommended were a good example. Patients were typically told they ought to be admitted in order "to be treated" or that the staff would see what they could do in order to "help" them. For example, the resident who admitted Sally N told her father over the telephone, "We think she needs something, and also we are willing to do something for her." When inpatient treatment was proposed, patients were typically informed they were to come into the Hospital for "evaluation," an expression that had a fairly concrete meaning to the staff but provided very little information to a patient who did not have their background knowledge. Descriptions such as "some testing" or "some medications" were routinely used by the Evaluation Center staff to describe the nature of treatment. Only rarely did the staff specify which particular tests and which medications the patient might get. One patient who asked what kinds of treatments were available was told, "Medications and therapy." When outpatient treatment was recommended, patients were usually told only that they would be referred to "a clinic," even though the Hospital ran a substantial number of quite different outpatient clinics. Sometimes patients were told, as Natania Z was, that the clinic dealt with "situations like yours."

We should bear in mind, however, that vague formulations are characteristic of everyday oral communication in general. As Garfinkel has demonstrated quite convincingly, all speakers inevitably take for granted many details about which they expect their listeners to have some previous knowledge, and therefore they omit these details from what they communicate.[4] Since psychiatric treatment was fairly routine to the Evaluation Center staff, they tended to forget that patients are often not familiar with what the staff takes for granted. In this light, the staff's use of such expressions as "things" in "You can stay and you'll just have to sign things" or in "We can bring you in and see what is going on—give you some tests and things" was not necessarily evasive or indicative of a deliberate intention to conceal facts from patients.

While it is possible to understand the reasons why staff comments to patients were not clearer, expressions like "whatever" in "I would like you to read this and see if you agree; it's for the interview and treatment and whatever" were simply not very helpful to patients trying to understand what was happening. A statement such as "I want you to wait here and I'll go and talk with some other people" was not very informative either. Nor was the statement "I have to talk over some stuff with some guys in the staff room," which was made by a resident to Maureen A, very clear about just what the resident was going to say to whom. Such vague expressions were routine parts of the staff's communication with patients in the Evaluation Center.

Walter K was the only patient admitted whom we observed being given even a somewhat specific description of the test he would have to undergo ("I think you should come in for some tests so we can check your memory and concentration") before making a decision about treatment. Manuel C received a lot of very clear and specific information—namely, that aside from several tests, he would also have to undergo head X-rays and brain wave tests; and that they might consider changing his medication to one that might control his outbursts better than the one he was now taking. But the information was given to him only after the decision concerning his treatment had already been made.

(The significance of the temporal location of the information disclosure is discussed later.) Wesley G was the only other patient who was informed extensively about the tests he would undergo, but that was only after he insisted vehemently that he wanted more information.

PATIENTS' QUESTIONS

Wesley G's demand for more information raises another aspect of the process of disclosure: patients' questions. Given that the staff disclosed little information and that much of it was vague, what did the patients do in response? The question is, after all, the linguistic procedure existing in all languages that allows one to get more information and to clarify vague statements. However, it was not a mechanism that patients used very much. Patients' questions were, statistically speaking, extremely rare phenomena. Twenty patients asked no questions at all pertaining to treatment.

Although 21 patients did question the staff, the pattern of their questions did not indicate that they were trying to gain information to use in making a decision. Two patterns of questions overwhelmed all other types of questions asked by patients. First, many patients' questions indicated that they were looking for reassurance that everything would be all right and that they had made the right decision. This was more prominent in some patients than in others, and all patients showed some need for reassurance even when no questions were asked. However, eight patients showed it prominently in their questions. One example was Cynthia M, who asked the clinician about the procedures for leaving the Hospital because she was "afraid that I'll be put away forever." Similarly, Sally N asked "You're not going to put me in a straitjacket; you're not gonna put me in a cell?" However, Sally N exhibited a need for less dramatic assurance—that the Hospital was a pleasant place, that the treatment would work, and that it would not take too much time. That it was the reassurance that was critical, rather than the substantive information (at least in Sally N's case), was shown by the fact that she frequently received vague or noncommittal answers to her questions and continued to ask these questions anyway. Doris X asked for reassurance that, "You're not going to send me to [the state hospital], are you?" And, like Sally N, she also asked for assurance of other sorts—for instance, "Will my [ex-]husband know?"

The mild reassurances that some patients wanted are closely related to the second major motivation for questions: to obtain an idea of what the future would hold. Questions were asked about the Hospital and its procedures, but they did not seem to be directed at making decisions about whether or not to receive treatment. Rather, they were focused on the information necessary to anticipate the patient's future in the Hospital. The patients seemed to be preparing themselves cognitively for hospitalization. Thus, for example, Mitzie Q asked, "What kind of tests?," "Will I be able to go swimming?," and "Will I be able to have a radio in my room?" And Eldred C asked, "How long will it take [to get off the drugs I have been taking]?" *These questions could have been directed at deciding whether or not to be admitted, but they were asked after the patients had agreed to admission.*

In these and many other questions, we saw patients asking questions for reassurance or for information with which to adjust to the situation, but not questions designed to help them decide whether or not to receive the treatment.

WRITTEN COMMUNICATION

We have seen that oral disclosure was typically vague and that patients did not ask questions in order to gain information on which to base their decisions. Perhaps in part because of these problems, the Department of Public Welfare mandated that some information must be presented on written forms and that many of these forms should be prepared by the Department of Public Welfare and not written by the staff. Much, perhaps most, of the information concerning patients' rights and recommended treatment plans was communicated to patients in a written form.

From a legal-bureaucratic point of view, written forms have two advantages. First, they apparently allow the regulators more control over what information the patient receives. By requiring that a signed form become a part of the patient's record, the government officials concerned with protecting patients' rights can assume that the patient gets a chance to see the information. Second, hospital administrators find it useful to have written records as a protection against lawsuits. This interest in written material has been encouraged by several studies. Robinson and Merav, for example, found that

> The patients, all of whom underwent open heart surgery, not only forgot extensive portions of preoperative taperecorded conversations with their surgeons, but often fabricated details, and some even denied having had an informed consent discussion.[5]

And Sharpe describes the function of the form:

> The use of a form is an attempt to codify the patient's understanding and agreement, and to provide evidence of both the fact and the nature of the authority granted his physician.[6]

Those who advocate written information argue that it is far more advantageous from the patients' standpoint, since they can follow the information at their own pace; can reread particularly difficult or confusing sections; and are far less likely to be distracted by "external" factors, such as the presenter's looks, gestures, accent, and so on. In the case of the Patients' Rights form in the Evaluation Center, patients who were admitted to the Hospital were also supposed to be given a copy of the form to keep so that they could always refer to the information as a whole or to particular parts of it, even if they had not fully comprehended it in their first reading.

In actuality, however, not all patients who signed themselves into the hospital were given the Patients' Rights forms to keep.[7] When we interviewed patients on the Research Ward about their rights as patients, most remembered that such forms existed, and several commented that they had kept them. Several commented how pleased they were that they did indeed have rights, in spite of being in the hospital. However, most of those patients could not remember any of the specific rights.

We also noticed that patients frequently did not read the forms they were signing. There were probably many reasons for this, including difficulty in reading complex forms, a sense that actually reading the forms indicated distrust of the staff, and a sense on the part of the patients who had been in the Hospital before that they knew what it was like. Perhaps most important, though, was that they had a lot of forms to sign, and many seemed to be *pro forma* decisions.

It should also be added that forms were not always actually shown to patients. Very often the staff read the forms to patients; while the staff members read them conscientiously and usually only when they were skeptical about a patient's ability to read, it is important to realize that the existence of the forms did not always guarantee that patients would see them. In many other instances, although patients read the forms themselves, they were "coached" by the staff as to what portions they ought to read. A staff member presented a patient with an entire page of printed information and said, "I want you to read this first paragraph." Likewise, Doris X was told by the nurse/clinician, "It's these points—one, two, three, and four—which are the ones you should be reading." And Cynthia M was told, "It's not necessary to read to the end. We want you to look at this top part." On several other occasions, patients who started to read a form were told by the staff members who had given it to them that they did not have to read it. In most instances, the information that staff suggested patients not read was indeed quite irrelevant. However, we ought to remember that, in general, patients had no idea what was relevant and what was not relevant, and yet they took the staff's word for it. The existence of the signed form does not guarantee informed consent.[8]

The standardization of information by presenting it in a written form presupposes some standardization of the category "patient." This is very much in line with the universalistic standards of American civil liberties, according to which any patient has the right to information, for the very reason that he or she is a patient. However, this universalization entails some major disadvantages, since it discourages any differentiation among individual patients according to their idiosyncratic needs. Written communication is often inadequate for meeting the particular needs or levels of understanding of particular patients. When clinicians present information orally, they can get some feedback from patients (from their questions, comments, perplexed looks, and so on) as to how much patients understand, but the standard form is deaf to any such feedback.

This problem applied not only to information such as patients' rights, which were legally supposed to be disclosed in a standard form, but also to several of those forms that contain blank spaces for the staff to provide particular information, such as specifications of the proposed restrictions and restraints on the initial evaluation sheet. Each psychiatrist in the Evaluation Center filled in this seven-line space differently, but the statements did not differ according to patients. One psychiatrist always wrote the phrase "Ward routine," and another always entered, "Ward door is usually locked." The residents who trained in the Evaluation Center adopted, without any exception, one of these formulas for their use. Of course, the lack of individuality here is part of the entire process of treating the forms as routine paperwork, and the staff members did not go out of their way to inquire what the current restrictions on each ward were or to make judgments about which patients might receive chemical or physical restraints. However, there is no question that this would have taken more time and might have upset some patients.

DISTANCING

The fact that a considerable amount of information that patients received was presented to them in written form is suggestive of the impersonalization of the duty to inform. Documents are therefore effective mechanisms of depersonalizing bureaucratic processes. Presenting information as a standard written formula allows an almost total separation and dissociation of the information and the particular person who presents it to the patient. Clinicians may be held responsible for reading or for showing patients the explanation of their rights, but they are not held responsible for what those forms say. Everyone understands that the forms were designed independently of the clinicians, and the clinicians do not necessarily personally endorse what is contained in the forms.

This could be seen very clearly in the way the Evaluation Center clinicians used first-person pronouns when presenting patients with information. Not having been held personally responsible and accountable for the information they conveyed, they very often tended to use the plural pronoun "we" instead of the singular "I."

The responsibility of the staff for informing patients was bureaucratized; that is, it was primarily associated not so much with them as particular persons, but rather with their roles as "mental health professionals." When they provided patients with certain information, they did not do so primarily because they personally believed patients ought to be informed, but rather because it was an official obligation involved in the positions they occupied. The impersonalization of the staff's responsibility for informing patients implies that what was actually involved was not a personal commitment of one particular person to inform another particular person, but rather an act whereby a "clinician" informed a "patient."

The bureaucratization of the duty to inform patients is clearly manifested in the way some staff members managed to distance themselves from the information they disclosed to patients. As Goffman has suggested in his discussion of "role distance,"[9] a person can perform a certain procedure while discounting it at the same time. This is obviously facilitated when communication between the informer and the informed is mediated by a standard written form. We observed in the Evaluation Center many instances whereby the staff disclaimed the information they themselves provided. Consider, for example, the following "disclaimer" made by psychiatrists to Meyer I:

> "This form is very preliminary, and by no means explains all the treatment that you are going to get. I need you to sign some forms which I have filled out here for admission. They don't say too much. . . ."

In a number of cases, staff members managed to dissociate themselves from the information they provided to patients by saying they were informing them primarily because they had to. One clear-cut evidence of this was the clinicians' frequent use of "have to" in communicating with patients:

> "There is something I have to give you. I have to give you your rights."

> "We have to give you some idea of the treatment you will be getting."

> "At admission we have to tell the patient the general treatment plan and what the restrictions are."

> "This is Dr. _____'s initial findings. He has to tell you how he plans to treat you."

The clinician who informed Maureen A about her right to refuse having information about her sent to the county, began by saying, "There is something else I have to let you know." Another nurse/clinician, who was asked by Rosella D what she thought about the same right, replied, "I, as a clinician, have to give you this choice."

In one extreme instance described in Chapter 5, a clinician told Nelson P that before he could see a doctor he had to listen to his rights. At a certain point while she was reading them, Mr. P forcefully interrupted her: "Stop!" The clinician said, "I am almost done," and continued reading. This instance suggests that the duty to inform patients was so bureaucratized that even when the patient did not wish to hear his rights, the staff members felt it was their duty to go through the procedure anyway. As Jay Katz (personal communication) has commented, "What was originally intended as a right has become a rite."

STAFF'S ATTITUDE TOWARD DISCLOSURE

We have generally refrained from reporting the staff's statements about how they felt about informed consent procedures. Like many behavioral researchers, we have found that expressed attitudes and behaviors do not necessarily correlate. The Evaluation Center staff mostly expressed skepticism about the particular informed consent procedures that were required by state regulations, but they expressed some support for the general values of informed consent. However, their behavior in several critical areas indicated that even this general support for the concept was more rhetorical than practical. Let us look at several specific aspects of staff behavior.

Temporal Aspects of Disclosure

The information most often disclosed to Evaluation Center patients was that information whose disclosure was officially mandated by statute. However, a closer look at the temporal location of the disclosure of this information also shows that the staff regarded information disclosure as a rite that had to be performed as part of their official role, rather than as a matter of great personal consequence, and that they had little commitment to informed consent as an ethical doctrine.

According to the logic of informed consent, a certain sequential arrangement of activities is essential. Patients must be presented with the relevant information *prior* to their making decisions. If this is not done, it is hard to see how they can use the information to make their decisions. The staff's behavior reflected the belief that patients did not need to consider the information before they made their decisions, and the staff typically presented patients with parts of the information only *after* the decisions had been made. Probably most suggestive of the significance of the information disclosure within the decision-making procedure is the fact that inpatients never changed their decisions after having received the formal written disclosures.

It is most interesting to note that in most of the cases, the information concerning the 72-hours rule was given to patients along with the signing of the consent form while reading their rights or immediately before they were asked to sign the initial evaluation sheet. Its disclosure was temporally juxtaposed to the signing of the forms, not by accident, but because it was regarded by the Evaluation Center staff as part of the bureaucratic routine of signing forms. As a result, such information was only rarely included among patients' basic considerations as to whether or not to undergo inpatient treatment.

To appreciate the bureaucratization of the duty to inform patients, we should also note that twice, in response to our questions, staff members told us that they did not have to read the patients their rights because the particular patients in question were committed involuntarily. This was legally incorrect, but, more important for our present point, it reflected a belief that informing patients of their rights was a legal duty that involved the official roles they occupied, rather than a moral obligation to which they were personally committed. They saw no reason to inform patients when they did not have to.

All of this reflects a more general expectation on the part of both staff and patients (if we are to judge by the lack of patients' questions) that intake was a process whereby the staff received information from the patients, not the patients from the staff. That the formal disclosure of information usually took less than 5 minutes of a procedure that typically lasted several hours is indicative of the general attitude about its importance.

It was symbolically significant that, with only one exception, it was always nurse/clinicians rather than psychiatrists who read patients their rights. Informing patients about their rights was not regarded as a duty of enough importance to justify the use of the most highly trained and highest-status professionals. Legal imperatives do not necessarily parallel professional morals, and the staff did not consider information disclosure to be at the same level of importance as proper diagnosis and referral. It is not that they necessarily viewed disclosure as detrimental to their practice of psychiatry (although occasionally we heard arguments that it was); it is just that they did not regard it as essential.

Concern with Patient Understanding

Staff attitudes about informed consent were also reflected in their level of interest in whether or not patients understood what was told to them. As mentioned in Chapter 2, it is arguable that the informed consent doctrine obliges the doctor to determine whether the patient understands the information that has been disclosed. Attempting to ascertain whether the staff undertook this effort is almost as difficult as trying to determine whether the patients themselves understood. One way of ascertaining the extent to which staff members tested patients' understanding is to examine how often the staff indicated a concern about what a patient had understood. We found that this rarely occurred.

On eight occasions, the staff asked patients whether they understood something about which they had to make a decision. Four of these instances came at the end of the reading of the Patients' Rights form for involuntary admissions. Since state law required this, and since the form contains a box to check whether or not the patient understood, this was not surprising. Another such question came after a patient signed a Release of Information form. Two cases related to explanations of the point at which the patients could leave the hospital after they had been admitted. The final case involved a clinician's asking the son of a patient who could not speak English whether the patient understood what the clinician was telling her through the son's translation.

Given the large number of opportunities to ask such questions, these eight instances are tantamount to "almost never" and clearly do not constitute planned efforts to ascertain whether the patients understood. No effort was ever made to get patients to repeat in their own words what they understood. Rather, except for the four instances that were mandated by law, these questions seemed to be similar to the conversational devices used by all speakers to assure themselves that their listeners are actually listening to what is being said and to try to get the listeners' attention.

We noted earlier that patients did not ask questions. Perhaps this was in part because the staff was seldom receptive to questions. Sally N, for example, who was the most inquisitive patient that we saw in the Evaluation Center and who questioned almost everything the staff told her, was diagnosed as a paranoid schizophrenic. The resident who evaluated her commented, "There is nothing like a paranoid patient to get a good informed consent from." Her having asked so many questions was taken as contributory evidence of her paranoia.

Although staff members usually answered patients' questions, they did not always do so. For example, when Natania Z, a foreigner whose English was poor, managed to ask, "Could I have my health again or not?" the resident replied: "I have a few questions. Have you been in contact with chemicals over the past 6 months? Have you even been in a chemical lab?" Even when directly questioned by Natania Z, this resident kept collecting rather than giving information. On another occasion, Rudolph D asked the psychiatrist, "Do I need help?" The "reply" was "That is a good question," after which the psychiatrist went on collecting information from the patient. We observed only three instances in which patients complained to the staff that they had not been informed as to what their treatment might consist of and what medications they might get, and of those cases, only Wesley G got more information as a direct result of having complained. Doris X, for example, who repeatedly complained that she had not been told what her treatment would be, was told by the psychiatrist that this was what she had read in the initial evaluation sheet. The initial evaluation sheet read:

> Patient will be further evaluated, and further treatment will be discussed with the attending physician and may include medication and/or adjunctive therapies.

Staff Motivation to Disclose Information

Nevertheless, the patients who got the most information were usually those who asked the most questions. Patients such as Doris X, Sally N, and Chester T, who were quite persistent in their questioning, received much more information than did other patients.

All this suggests that staff members informed patients best when the law required it or when disclosure was necessary in order to induce patients' compliance with the staff's recommendations. When patients balked, giving them information was often used to keep the evaluation process going. Wesley G, for example, was given information about the physical tests only because he objected to undergoing them. Rudolph D and Lori C were the only other patients to get an explanation of what the physical exam would be like. Lori C was told by the psychiatrist:

PSYCHIATRIST: We're going to find out if we can control your temper outbursts. We're going to do some lab tests, and we'll do some brain wave tests.

MOTHER: This won't hurt, Lori.

PSYCHIATRIST: They'll paste some buttons on your head and then you think of something pleasant . . .

Later Lori was told again that it would not hurt and that there would be no pelvic exam. However, this information was given only after Lori's mother told the psychiatrist that "the idea of a physical might scare her . . . I'm not sure she's going to like this." Similarly, all of the "information" Niles X got was part of the staff's efforts to convince him to go to the general emergency room across the street. In these and many other cases, the staff informed patients not in order to facilitate their independent decisionmaking, but rather in order to overcome their resistance to cooperating.

Of course, part of the reason that the staff provided patients with so little information was not that they did not believe it was the right thing to do. Rather, they themselves had very little idea of what would happen to patients once they got to an inpatient ward or an outpatient clinic. For example, in spite of what the law required, there was no way a psychiatrist could tell patients what medications they would actually get, since that was someone else's responsibility and not under the control of the admitting psychiatrist. However, this is not an adequate general explanation. There were a number of cases where the staff provided the patients' relatives or friends who accompanied them to the Evaluation Center with more information than they did the patients. In the case of Doris X, for example, her boyfriend was told by the clinician why the staff recommended hospitalizing Ms. X, how they planned to treat her, and for how long, but Ms. X was not told. The same applies to Walter K, whose wife was told her husband's drinking might have affected his brain; to Joseph W, whose mother was told that her son might have schizophrenia; and to Adelle E, whose daughter was told her mother was there for admission (Ms. E herself was told only that she was there "to be treated"). These did not necessarily stem from a deliberate effort to conceal information from patients, but they do show clearly that some of the failure to inform patients cannot simply be explained on the basis of the staff's lack of information. Furthermore, based on their preliminary formulation of patients' problems, the Evaluation Center staff did have some idea about the overall class or classes of medications that patients were likely to receive once hospitalized, and thus they could have disclosed this information.

Finally, we ought to remember that it was on the basis of the information they received in the Evaluation Center that patients were supposed to decide whether or not to undergo the proposed treatment. As becomes clear later, once patients were admitted, they usually saw themselves as bound to accept the proposed treatment. If they left the Hospital after learning about their proposed treatment, they would be labeled as having left treatment "against medical advice." Nonetheless, the Hospital staff generally believed that patients could be better informed of the specifics of treatment once they got to the ward. This seemed to reflect a general belief that patients need information to get along on the ward and to comply with treatment, but not to decide about it.

Effects of Staff Judgments of Patients' Capabilities on Disclosing Behavior

Part of the staff members' resistance to disclosure came from their perception that patients did not understand. Like most speakers, the clinicians adjusted what they said to what they perceived to be the patients' ability to understand in order to facilitate understanding. Staff members in the Evaluation Center routinely made judgments about patients that functioned as judgments of their ability to understand the treatment issues before them. These judgments were tacit and not explicit, but they nonetheless deeply affected the staff's behavior toward patients.

The core of this judgment was based upon the severity of the patient's psychiatric symptoms. The staff used the common-sense assumption that the sicker the patient was in terms of his or her symptomatology, the less likely it was that the patient was able to understand and make rational and voluntary decisions.

In order to test the hypothesis that the staff based its judgments of the ability of patients to understand on their symptomatology, two members of our research staff, after thoroughly reviewing all the relevant data, ranked each patient on a 1-to-5 scale according to how the Evaluation Center staff treated them as capable of participating in the decision about their treatment. The two raters' judgments correlated .91 with each other. The patients were then also coded as to whether their predominant symptoms were those of acute psychosis, organic brain syndrome, acute intoxication, or another problem (including all depression, neurosis, drug addiction, and schizophrenia without acute psychotic symptoms). Using the statistic η^2 (a statistic for this level of measurement comparable to r^2), these four categories accounted for 51.2% of the variance in the degree to which patients were treated as competent. This clearly indicates that the patients' perceived symptoms directly reflected whether or not the staff treated patients as capable of understanding. The more serious the symptoms that the patients presented were, the less likely the staff was to treat the patients as able to understand.

The staff's decision about whether or not the patients were capable of understanding had profound effects on the way in which the patients were treated. One way in which the staff responded to patients whom they viewed as incompetent was by excluding them from participation in the decisionmaking process. This is not to say that their wishes were necessarily overridden, although in about half the cases they were. Rather, it is that the staff made no effort to engage them in open, detailed, and reasoned discussion about what was wrong and what should be done. The staff pronounced what was to be done *ex cathedra*, and the patients then might or might not be given a chance to say no.

Elsie H, a 72-year-old patient diagnosed as senile, is a good example. The doctor first discussed the patient with her daughter in private and only then interviewed the patient, but with her daughter present. He began the interview by asking the patient why she was in the Hospital, and the patient said that her daughter brought her. He then asked her several questions to determine whether she was disoriented. He also asked her how she felt, to which she responded that she was all right. He asked about pains in her head and her seeming slowness in getting around. She denied anything was wrong; when she refused to be admitted, the doctor explained to her daughter that she could not be forced, but that he would prescribe sleeping pills and an outpatient visit. The point is not that the doctor did not make the right decision or had too little evidence upon which to decide. Rather, the discussion (both the questioning about the nature of the problem and the explanation of what should be done) was conducted with the daughter, not the patient. Only the right to say no was reserved for the patient.

Another patient thought to be incapable of understanding was Peggy G, who was diagnosed as having an acute schizophrenic episode. Most of the information about her came from her husband, because the clinician did not think her reliable or clear. The doctor decided that even though she wanted to go home, she should be admitted, and he simply ordered her to be taken to the ward. Although she did not protest, it was clear to both the observers and to the doctor that she did not want to go but thought she had no choice. Reavis C, a patient who was ordered to sign by a policeman standing over him, was also judged by the staff to be incapable of understanding the issues in the treatment decision.

In contrast, the patients whom the staff viewed as capable of understanding were always included to some extent in the decisionmaking process. Whereas interviews with the other patients were typically very brief, interviews with patients perceived as capable of understanding were much longer. These patients were typically allowed to present and to develop their problems at great length and with minimal interference from the staff. Moreover, the staff tended much more to share their doubts with these patients than to present their decision as a *fait accompli*.

Tracey D, a depressed college student, is a good illustration. The clinician interviewed him without his mother, who had accompanied him to the hospital. When the clinician wanted to clarify some points with the patient's mother, she asked his permission to bring the mother into the interview room. When the doctor was actually considering what to do, he did it in the presence of the patient and out loud: "I guess the thing on my mind now is what to make of it. Is coming here what you wanted?" This quality of tentativeness about what should be done and openness to the patient's suggestions was entirely absent when the staff dealt with patients they saw as not capable of understanding.

Another way in which the sicker patients were restricted from participating in the decisionmaking is the manner in which patients were asked questions. Part of an interview with Jason X, a patient whom the staff judged as almost completely incapable of understanding, went this way:

CLINICIAN: You have a lot of bruises here. It looks like you ran into something. Is this where you got the chest pains?
PATIENT: Yes.
CLINICIAN: What happened? Did you run into something?
PATIENT: I don't know.
CLINICIAN: Did you have an accident?
PATIENT: Yes, ma'am.
CLINICIAN: What kind of accident? Was it an auto accident? Were you walking?
PATIENT: Yes.
CLINICIAN: What happened to you? Did you get scared? Did you fall down?
PATIENT: Yes.
CLINICIAN: Do you remember what happened? Were you hurt?
PATIENT: Yes.

By contrast, what follows are a series of questions (without the patient's lengthy answers) asked of a mildly depressed patient whom the staff saw as quite capable of understanding:

"You said sometimes you are manic? Can you be more specific about what it is like?"

"How often does this feeling come?"

"As far as the last time you had a high period, when was that? Is there a pattern to your high periods?"

The questions to the first patient were formulated so that information could be obtained from a mere yes or no. As in a game of "Twenty Questions," the clinician guessed about the problem and asked for confirmation or refutation. In the second case, even though we deliberately picked a part of an interview in which the issue at hand was a relatively concrete one of describing symptoms, the questions were more open-ended, allowing the patient to structure the problem as she felt appropriate.

Who Disclosed the Information

One major difficulty with the communication of information in the Evaluation Center had to do with who had the responsibility to do it. As we have seen in the case of the information concerning the patient's right to withdraw from voluntary treatment, the very same type of information that was disclosed on some occasions by the psychiatrist or resident was disclosed at other times by the nurse/clinician. As a general rule, there was very little clear-cut division of labor among the staff members with regard to the allocation of the responsibility to inform patients.

We found only two consistent patterns of allocating the responsibility for information disclosure. The first one is discussed earlier in this chapter—namely, the fact that, with the exception of one case, nurse/clinicians always presented patients with their rights, since the presentation of rights was generally seen as a low-priority, low-skill task that did not require a doctor's attention.[10] Second, the staff person who showed the patient the form with the initial evaluation, the proposed treatment, and the proposed restrictions and restraints was also the person who provided information concerning the 72-hours rule, since those information "forms" were almost always presented together. That person could be either a physician or a clinician. Even the evaluation form itself, which was always filled out by the physician as mandated by law, was sometimes presented to the patient by the psychiatrist and sometimes by a clinician.

The law, of course, does not specify how the responsibility for informing patients ought to be allocated. With the sole exception of the responsibility for filling out the form that includes the initial findings of the evaluation, the proposed treatment, and the proposed restrictions and restraints, which is assigned specifically to the admitting physician, the law is indifferent concerning who ought to inform the patient about what. This is not surprising, since the division between clinicians and psychiatrists in admission units is not universal.

When dealing with the issue of who is responsible for informing patients, we must remember that in modern psychiatric hospitals, large numbers of people are typically involved in some part of patient care. Information disclosure is imbedded in this phenomenon. Responsibility for information disclosure, like general responsibility for clinical care, belongs to several clinicians rather than to one. In some instances, responsibility for patient care is shared collectively by the entire staff of a unit; in others, it is split among staff members so that each one is responsible for only one part of patient care (for ordering medications, for administering them, and so on). In both cases, however, the full responsibility for hospitalized patients is "located" in a collective entity, so that no individual staff member is exclusively responsible for them.[11]

When patients go to a private psychiatrist, there is little question as to who is responsible for informing them. Only one person is fully and exclusively responsible for everything that relates to their patienthood. The psychiatrist in private practice can never claim that he or she did not inform the patient about something because somebody else should have done it or had already done it. Informing the patient is the psychiatrist's responsibility, no one else's.

In a hospital, however, patients are cared for by more than one person. Thus the question of who is responsible for providing them with information does arise. It is within such a therapeutic context that the phenomenon of "floating responsibility" for informing patients emerges.

The situation of multiple care-givers often involves "gaps" in the responsibility for informing patients. In the Evaluation Center, some pieces of information were rarely presented to the patients. The responsibility for disclosure "floated" among the Evaluation Center staff members. With the absence of any clear-cut functional differentiation along professional lines with regard to the responsibility for informing patients, a psychiatrist could always assume that a clinician had already disclosed a particular piece of information to a patient, and the clinician could always assume that the psychiatrist was going to do it. With each of them leaving it for the other to do, it was often not done at all.

The phenomenon of "floating responsibility" with regard to information disclosure also occurred on the level of interunit communication. Many Evaluation Center patients who were admitted to the Hospital, for example, were told that they would be further informed on the ward and that they should address further questions to the staff there. Our evidence indicates that this did not happen. The ward staff assumed that the patient had been informed in the Evaluation Center. This was true especially with respect to the Patients' Bill of Rights, which was supposed to be given to all patients along with their voluntary- or involuntary-admission rights. Since it was supposed to be given to patients as an integral part of their decisionmaking process *before* they made the decision as to whether or not to come into the Hospital, it is hard to blame the ward staff for having assumed that the information had already been given to patients in the Evaluation Center.

THE UNDERSTANDING OF THE BEST INFORMED

Before we can conclude this chapter, we must make one more attempt to determine the cause of the failure of patient understanding. Our findings, as we have reported them so far, show that patients in the Evaluation Center did not typically have a detailed idea of what they were agreeing to when they were admitted. However, there are at least two possible interpretations of this fact. First, it might be argued that these patients were inherently incapable of understanding the complex issues involved in the decisions. Second, it might be argued that, given the poverty of explanation that they received from the staff, no one could have possibly understood what the prospective treatment was all about. Although the lack of patients' questions does not indicate a great interest on the part of the patients, this may not mean that they might not have understood the issues if they had been properly informed.

In order to resolve these issues partially, we decided to try to isolate the patients whom the staff had most fully informed. Unfortunately, with a single exception, the five patients who were best informed were also highly competent ones. This reflects the fact, as we noted above, that staff disclosure was usually based in part on the staff's perception of a patient's ability to understand the disclosure. Thus we can only test here whether, given adequate disclosure, reasonably intelligent and nonpsychotic patients are capable of understanding.

The evidence from these five patients is encouraging as to the ability of some patients to understand some essential aspects of treatment decision in the Evaluation Center. Although all the patients failed to understand some important component of the decision, this does not seem to be due in most cases to their inability to do so. Only Mitzie Q, a young woman whose difficult relationship with her family and disorganized thought pattern undermined her ability to participate in the treatment decision, failed to grasp most of the information.

All five patients understood that the staff proposed to admit them to a psychiatric facility and that they had a legal right to refuse. Only Mitzie Q failed to appreciate the fact that it was a psychiatric facility. She treated it as though it were a resort and as though the critical issues in her decision concerned the entertainment and recreation facilities in the hospital. In all cases except that of Ms. Q, the patients had a reasonable grasp of some important risks and benefits. Chester T, a heroin addict, for example, clearly appreciated that the Hospital's withdrawal program did not involve the use of methadone, which he wanted, but that the risk of not admitting himself was that his wife would probably leave him. Sally N also understood that there were risks involved in entering the Hospital, primarily the stigma of being a patient and the length of time she might have to spend in the Hospital. She saw the benefits as getting treatment for her disease. Here, however, she misunderstood what was going on, primarily because the staff did not tell her that they saw her as paranoid and planned to treat her for that as well as for the troubles she had described to them. However, it must be pointed out that although these patients had some reasonable understanding of risks and benefits of treatment, in no case did they have the sort of general list of risks and benefits that the informed consent doctrine seems to envision. In all five cases, the patients' views of the risks and benefits seemed to have been largely internally generated.

Although this group of patients was relatively well informed, two of them did not really understand the purpose of treatment. The staff felt that Doris X needed hospitalization because her medications had to be closely monitored and adjusted and because she had not done well in outpatient therapy. However, Ms. X was convinced that she had been brought by the nurse from an outpatient clinic to the Evaluation Center because she had shown up too early for her appointment. She did not see her current troubles as a personality trait, but rather as situational. Thus hospitalization for her was just a time to escape some of the pressures temporarily. Likewise, Mitzie Q's descriptions of herself were positive. For example, she said, "They [her parents] order me around all the time, but I can take care of myself." While her ideas shifted back and forth, in general she did not see the hospital as a place to help her with her internal problems, but rather as a refuge from the troubles with her family and her friends. While neither patient was explicitly told, "We think you are mentally ill, and we think that you need to be in the Hospital for treatment," such a statement seemed to be implied by the dialogue. Given the implied criticism of each patient's self, it was probably hard for them to understand this implicit statement.

Unlike the majority of patients, all five patients in this group mentioned some alternative to the doctors' proposed treatment, although not all of the alternatives were treatment. Thus Chester T considered another hospital as well as self-withdrawal from heroin; Mitzie Q considered going to a bar and getting her own apartment as an alternative to admission; and Sally N and Doris X both mentioned going home and not admitting themselves. Only Maureen A seemed to assume that the choice was entirely up to the doctor. While she mentioned outpatient treatment as a possibility, she made it clear that she would do whatever the doctor recommended.

In summary, this group of patients was much better informed and understood much more than the patient group as a whole. However, like the other patients, much of their understanding of the issues was self-generated, not generated by the staff's disclosures. There is reason to believe that had disclosure been full and careful, at least some of these patients would have understood what the informed consent doctrine envisions.

Voluntariness and Decision
in the Evaluation Center

With its emphasis on information and understanding, the ethical model of informed consent seems to imply that, unless there are strong pressures to the contrary, a patient who is properly informed and understands what is disclosed will make a rational, autonomous decision. In Chapter 6, we note that many of the admissions and referrals in the Evaluation Center involved little information and less understanding. It might thus seem difficult to determine whether or not an autonomous, rational decisionmaking process is possible in such a setting. Perhaps this is so, but a close look at the details of the patterns of interaction is very suggestive.

In this chapter, we try to describe the patterns of decisionmaking in the Evaluation Center; we consider their ramifications for the model of informed consent; and we then take up a number of systemic structures present in that setting that influenced those patterns. In particular, we ask these questions:

1. How free is the patient to decide?
2. Who makes the decision?
3. In what ways is the disclosed and understood information used in the decisionmaking process?

PATTERNS OF DECISIONMAKING

In what follows, we try to exemplify some of the patterns of decisionmaking that we saw in the Evaluation Center. Many of these patterns were markedly divergent from the ideals embodied in the doctrine of informed consent, but let us begin with those that were not.

MUTUAL PARTICIPATION

With a few exceptions, we did not see patients in the Evaluation Center acting as informed decisionmakers according to the doctrine of informed consent. In only two cases that we observed did a patient ultimately reach a decision after considering both the risks and benefits of different options that the doctor disclosed to the patient prior to the decision, and did the outcome of the case correspond to what the patient chose. Our findings demonstrate many barriers to the ideal of mutual participation between patients and doctors in reaching medical decisions.

However, it is interesting to look briefly at one of those two cases of mutual participation in decisionmaking.

Wesley G, a black man in his early 30s who worked as an accountant, managed his entire interview with extreme seriousness. His face betrayed hardly a trace of emotion. He initially described his problems as being marital difficulties with his wife, although in further discussion he reported that he was also having difficulties at work. He said he wanted marital counseling but that he was not sure his wife, from whom he was currently separated, would agree. He initially objected to the routine physical that the Hospital wanted but agreed after it was explained. Shortly after his first interview, he picked up Ms. G at work and brought her in for an interview. She told the clinician that she no longer loved her husband but could not say definitely that she wanted a divorce either. Both agreed that her family's hostility to him was a major source of difficulty.

The staff members presented Mr. G with a recommendation of individual therapy for both him and his wife, followed by family therapy. They told him that neither type of therapy would assure that they would not get a divorce. He asked whether it was possible to get both at the same time and was assured that it was. The doctor presented Ms. G with the same options and also told her that there was no guarantee it would work. While Ms. G acquiesced to marital and individual therapy, Mr. G called the next day to cancel the marital therapy, presumably because Ms. G was no longer agreeable.

Mr. G's decision seemed to be based on an understanding of the risks of the alternatives to treatment. The staff presented him with the choice without any coercion or undue influence and left the choice up to him. Mr. G's case was a rarity in the Evaluation Center.

WAIVER

A pattern of decisionmaking that is permissible, if not desirable, in the informed consent model is what may be called a "waiver" of the right to decide. Legally, a waiver is an acceptable mode of decisionmaking, but the staff did not formally treat it that way and continued to get signed consents where it would otherwise be appropriate. Let us consider an example.

Rudolph D was a 34-year-old machinist who presented himself to the staff as charming, intelligent, and "cool." He reported that he was insecure, anxious, and fighting frequently with his fiancée. He had previously been in therapy for depression following a divorce but found that he could not pay the $35 an hour that the private psychiatrist charged. His major complaint was that he needed some help with the deteriorating relationship with his fiancée. He was quite determined that he should be treated at the Hospital or in one of its outpatient clinics, rather than at the clinic which served his catchment area. He based this on the Hospital's reputation and the experiences of some of his friends. When told of the clinic in his catchment area, he said, "I went there once, and . . . the guy I talked to was an English major, and I thought, "Now how in hell can he help me?"

In general, Mr. D presented a picture of a highly competent, intelligent individual with a clear-cut idea of what he needed; but when asked about what type of treatment he wanted, he responded, "On that I have nothing to say. I think I'll leave it up to somebody who knows what they're doing."

While Mr. D's explicit waiver was unusual, many patients indicated through their comments that they felt the staff should decide what was best. In general, patients did not act as if they believed they should be making decisions. Although in most cases it was difficult to decide just where the patients located decisional responsibility, there is substantial evidence that many patients felt the doctor was the proper decisionmaking authority. They were engaging in a "waiver of decision," even if it was not an explicit and legally adequate one.

This type of waiver was quite common, even typical, although the staff did not generally treat it as a waiver. Klara N, after admitting herself, justified her decision to the patient-observer by the statement, "You've got to trust the doctors." Likewise, Marcus I said that he had argued with his wife as to whether or not he should come into the Hospital, but he finally decided to "give Dr. S a chance"; since he thought it was best that he come into the Hospital, "I figured I would. . . . You gotta trust somebody in this, and he's the one in charge, so I guess I gotta trust him." Although Mr. I was well educated about medical problems and knew enormous amounts about his problem, in the end he too relied on the doctor's advice. Even Sally N, perhaps the patient most actively engaged in questioning and challenging the staff, demonstrated trust of the doctor to the extent that when Dr. R told her that the 72-hours option "does not apply to [her]," she accepted his statement without question. She also trusted both her therapist from another clinic and the Hospital staff, in that she followed their treatment recommendations without having been given an explanation of how they would help.

Although no case was explicitly treated by the staff as a waiver of decision, there were a number that could have been so treated. Harrison T was the most interesting example. A wealthy, eccentric, 35-year-old man, Mr. T had been living the life of an itinerant hippie in a slightly bizarre manner. Despite a disinclination to think of himself as sick, he cooperated with the staff and his brothers, who had brought him to the hospital, saying, "I'm just a babe. I believe whatever I'm told." Similarly, Maureen A, a neurotically depressed, middle-aged woman, relinquished her right to decide when she agreed, "I will try and do anything." She based her decision on her feeling that she didn't know what was the underlying problem in her life, and that only the doctor's technical expertise could settle this question. What is puzzling is that as a group these patients were among the most knowledgeable, most competent, and least cognitively disturbed patients. They had detailed understanding of the medical model and of their problems, yet they were the ones who gave up their right to decide. It may be that waiver is based on a self-perception of incompetence to decide, but it does not seem to be objectively true that those who waive are less competent than those who do not.

Patients also showed their trust in the staff by the manner in which they dealt with the consent forms. Although the Department of Public Welfare has tried, through the phrasing of the consent forms, to alert patients that the forms deal with important decisions and implicitly to warn that the staff cannot always be trusted, their efforts were thwarted by the frequent failure of patients to read the forms. Of the 48 consent forms that our observers saw, 21 were not read at all, and another five were only skimmed or glanced at before they were signed.

PRIOR DECISION

One difficulty we found with the implementation of informed consent is that for many patients the decision was a "process" that occurred prior to, and not after, the formal information disclosure. Of course in all the cases we saw, the decisions had complex histories that were deeply imbedded in the life histories of all the participants. Their decisions were not picked out of the air, but depended on past experience, knowledge, and ideas. The idea of informed consent is not incompatible with this. It simply specifies that the disclosure will provide both the opportunity for and an occasion to put together all of the information and to weigh it against personal values.

However, in 10 cases that we observed, this did not happen. The decisions about hospitalization were made prior to coming to the Evaluation Center; the patients sought or had already agreed to admission to the Evaluation Center. Informed consent in the Evaluation Center was at best "a last chance to say no" and more often was simply a legal formality. In none of these 10 cases did it appear that the disclosed information was in any way "material" to the patients' decision as to whether or not to come into the Hospital. Consider the case of Jim N:

Jim N, a 52-year-old auto mechanic, told the staff that he had been severely anxious for 17 years. He also said that he drank too much beer and in the past had had suicidal ideas. Hospitalization elsewhere, medication, and even ECT had failed to help him. He was referred for admission by his cousin, who told him that this hospital had helped him greatly, and by his private psychiatrist. After signing out of another hospital the previous day, Mr. N and his wife traveled

120 miles by bus to the Hospital. Mrs. N returned home by bus before Mr. N was ever seen in the Evaluation Center.

Mr. N's physical examination and financial interview were completed prior to his being seen by the Evaluation Center clinician who took his history. Since these procedures were only done for patients who would receive treatment, this procedural irregularity indicated that the staff never had any question about admission. After the clinician's interview and before the patient was seen by the admitting doctor, the clinician told Mr. N, "What I want to do next is have you sign the admission form."

About half an hour later, Mr. N was seen by the admitting doctor, whom he told, "I need some type of help. I was recommended to come here, and I'm seeking to ease my anxiety, to live normal, to act normal, to talk normal, and not to do dumb things." After questioning Mr. N about this illness and its past treatment, the doctor showed him the evaluation form, and Mr. N signed immediately while commenting that this was his "last resort."

In the interview conducted with the patient observer immediately following the interchange, Mr. N said he had no idea what type of treatment he might receive in the Hospital and that it was up to the doctors to decide. He also said that he couldn't remember what was in all the papers he had just signed because there were "so many of them."

Mr. N made no decision in the Evaluation Center. His decision was made before he entered the door.

THE PASSIVE PATIENT

In some instances we saw, there seemed to be no decisions on the part of the patients at all, despite the fact that the patients were hospitalized or referrals were made. What these patients "decided" (if anything) was not to protest while others made the decisions. There was no review of alternatives with these patients, or even an explicit consent. This does not seem to have been the result of the seriousness of the patients' pathology, since the phenomenon was more common among patients referred for outpatient treatment. More important was the fact that written consent for inpatient hospitalization was required by law, and inpatients were thus forced to decide something, while no such formality was required for the patients who were not hospitalized. Many outpatient decisions were somewhat like chemical residues: Outpatient treatment was what remained after the staff or patient had made a decision against hospitalization. The staff then made an outpatient referral because there did not seem to be much else to do. Patients sometimes did not participate in the outpatient decision at all. The decision was made by the staff alone or by the staff in conjunction with the patients' relatives or friends. Several of these cases involved proxy consents, which we discuss in detail below. Joseph W, a

16-year-old boy with a possible psychosis, was eventually referred to a private psychiatrist in his home town, but the negotiation was carried on almost exclusively with his mother. However, in several instances such as that of Naomi G, who was simply referred to family therapy, the referral was made without any agreement on the part of the patient.

Another group of passive patients was composed of chronic patients who seemed to have given up attempting to control most aspects of their lives, not just psychiatric decisionmaking. Control had been relinquished to events in general and to the treatment staff in particular.

The following interaction between the clinician and Violet M, a patient who had been hospitalized many times (and whom we observed during our preliminary studies), is exemplary:

CLINICIAN: What do you think about coming in here?

Ms. M: Do you think I should?

CLINICIAN: We have our own thoughts about it, but we would like to know what you think.

Ms. M: Oh, I guess that would be all right.

The resident then entered, and the clinician told him, "She thinks it would be a good idea to come in," and then said to the patient, "Dr. D and I both think it would be a good idea if you came in."

Ms. M: Yeah.

DOCTOR: You think it would be a good idea?

Ms. M: Well, I thought maybe.

DOCTOR: Well, we think it would be a good idea. Would you sign yourself in?

Ms. M: Maybe.

The clinician gave her the form.

CLINICIAN: This is for you to come in. You're coming in voluntarily. (*Ms. M looked puzzled.*) Do you need glasses?

Ms. M: (*Signing.*) No, I can see without them. I can't read but I can see.

Throughout this interaction, the patient indicated by her passivity that she did not think her decision was very important, even when the clinician explicitly asked for it. The clinician and the doctor then demonstrated that she was right by ignoring her expressed hesitance and letting her sign without reading the form. For Violet M, as for eight patients in our full study of the Evaluation Center, the decision to be hospitalized was routine and not a matter to be deeply considered.

PROXY CONSENTS AND THE PATIENTS' FAMILIES

Unless a court appoints someone as a guardian for an incompetent patient, the law provides no place for third parties in the informed consent model of decisionmaking. Yet here, once again, theory and practice diverge. Persons other than the patients and the staff played a prominent role in the negotiation about treatment and/or in obtaining the patients' consent in 10 of 22 of the cases in our sample of voluntary admissions and in 12 of the 22 cases who were not admitted. While the staff members did not always accede to the wishes of the relatives or friends, they often based their decisions on information given by relatives or friends and on the requests of these third parties. Since both the information and the demands for service were often divergent from what the patients themselves said, this is a significant departure from the model.

In general, there were two basic roles that third parties played in negotiating treatment decisions. First, they participated as the representatives of patients who, for one reason or another, could not or would not participate in the decision themselves. Second, they participated as partisans for their own points of view. Let us consider an example of both types. Sara E's son exemplifies the most extreme example of the first type of third party, although inevitably there are elements of his own interests that are reflected in his actions.

Sara E was a 51-year-old woman who had come to the United States from Italy 10 years earlier. She spoke almost no English, and all communication between the patient and the staff went through the son's translations. Mrs. E's husband had died 5 years earlier, and she seemed never to have recovered from the grief. Her son described her as lying in bed all day and telling him that she was dying and that that was what should happen. He also told the clinician that he and his wife had been able to take care of his mother up to this point only because he was in school. He expected to graduate soon and get a job, which would preclude his being able to care for her. Through the son's translation, the clinician learned from Mrs. E that she had thoughts of suicide. The son also said that it was Mrs. E's idea to come to the Hospital. However, the son answered almost all of the clinician's questions himself and only translated for his mother when the clinician asked him to. The son summed up the problem:

SON: I don't know what it is, Doctor. For the longest time now she won't get up, she won't eat, she won't talk, she won't do nothing. We have to give her medicine three times a day.

After a few more details about her depressed state, including that she talked about suicide, the doctor told the son that they would get her into the ward very soon. The clinician brought the forms to sign.

CLINICIAN: Tell her that this is the form which she needs to sign to come into the Hospital.

The son translated and Mrs. E nodded.

CLINICIAN: Tell her I want her to check the first block agreeing to stay at least 72 hours.

The son translated and Mrs. E did so. The son then drew her name for her and she copied it on the form. The rest of the forms were filled in in a similar manner, and the son translated the Patients' Bill of Rights for her.

Although Mr. E had some personal interest in the outcome of the case, since caring for his mother placed an enormous burden on both him and his wife, he seemed mostly to act as her agent. He was apparently trying to implement her wishes. Closer to the other end of the continuum was Lori C's mother, who, although she clearly cared about Lori, was trying to arrange treatment for Lori that she suggested Lori would not like.

Lori C, a 14-year-old girl who lived at home with her three sisters and her mother, was brought to the Evaluation Center by her mother. Lori had not wanted to come to the Hospital for evaluation, but she was persuaded to do so on the previous evening by a doctor at the emergency room of another hospital and by her mother. She thought that she and her mother were coming to see how they could stop fighting. Lori's mother reported that her behavior had changed recently. She quarreled frequently with her sisters and her mother, hit her mother, and threw things. On the day prior to our observing in the Evaluation Center, she had overturned a television set and had threatened to take an overdose of aspirin. Lori, however, saw her sisters and herself as fighting a lot and her mother as picking her out for special punishment.

The clinician interviewed Lori alone. When asked why she got angry and teased her sisters, she said she didn't know. "We tease and hit and get into a fight, and then my mother comes and she hits me." Lori told the clinician that her mother had told her that the Hospital would be able to help all of them. "She told me you could do some things that would help us." In response to the clinician's suggestion, Lori agreed it would be advisable for the whole family to come once a week to talk about their problems.

The clinician then interviewed Lori's mother and told her that Lori had agreed to be treated here. Lori's mother expressed relief. The clinician asked the mother, "Do you want family therapy or to admit her, or what do you want us to do with her?" The mother replied that she wanted Lori to be seen here as an outpatient because she knew that Lori wouldn't want to stay. The clinician indicated that all the family would need to come together for therapy, and the mother agreed to this.

The clinician then presented her findings to the doctor, indicating that the family agreed to family therapy. The doctor, however, noted that something in Lori had changed abruptly over the last year and wanted first to schedule a physical examination and an electroencephalogram (EEG).

The doctor then interviewed first Lori and after that her mother; he recommended a physical and an EEG. He told the mother he was worried about Lori because she didn't know why the anger began. The mother was concerned that the physical would frighten Lori, but she readily agreed.

The doctor then explained his plan to Lori. Her mother assured her that the test would not hurt her. The doctor asked Lori, "Is that OK?," and Lori said, "OK"; but as she walked out of the room, she was shaking her head. Lori's mother said, "She doesn't want to have the tests done." The staff clinician began to explain future appointments for Lori to the mother, who said, "I don't know if Lori is going to cooperate with this," and Lori said, "I don't want it." The mother and the clinician attempted to reassure Lori, but she continued to object. The clinician told the mother, while Lori was present, "Well, I don't want to push you; I want you to have some time to talk it over; you can let us know if she changes her mind because it is helpful for Lori to do these things." The clinician told the mother, "I'd try talking with her at home; we can't force her." The clinician asked Lori whether she would come if the doctor wanted to see her again, and Lori nodded yes. Lori's mother tried to reassure her about the physical exam, but there was no final resolution in the Evaluation Center as to whether or not Lori would consent. Her mother said she would continue to talk with Lori about the tests. Four days later Lori was admitted to the Hospital involuntarily after she apparently attempted to cut herself with a razor, tried to pull her hair out, and tried to tear her clothes.

The case of Lori and her mother involved a substantial element of proxy negotiation. Her mother acted in part as a negotiator for Lori and in part as a negotiator for her own desires. Lori clearly did not see her simply as an ally.

In each of the above cases, the family member, while quite actively involved, was not very coercive. In seven other cases, however, the pressures on the patient were more apparent. In three cases, family members attempted to renegotiate with the treating staff after the disposition had been settled by the patients and the staff, and in three other cases family members pressed for treatment of the patients against the patients' will.

Perhaps the most oppressive case of family involvement we saw was that of a drug addict, Chester T, who arrived at the Hospital accompanied by his wife. He told the nurse/clinician, "My wife won't see me any more if I'm not in the Hospital today." Upon learning that he would not be given methadone during the course of his withdrawal from heroin, Mr. T wavered in his decision concerning admission. He maintained that he couldn't afford to be in the

Hospital and could withdraw from drugs at home. His wife urged him to stay in the Hospital, saying that he would get specialized treatment and also reminding him that he had never been short of money and had always been able to acquire it before. Finally she urged him to sign the consent form, saying that unless he did so he would "have been wasting all these people's time." After eventually signing, he said he did so "because I have no choice." His wife agreed, saying, "I have influence over my husband."

In the case of Klara N, whose father and grandmother accompanied her to the Evaluation Center carrying her suitcase, both relatives told the doctor that she should be hospitalized. They appeared disappointed when outpatient treatment was recommended. The grandmother again stressed, "She's very sick." Similarly, in the cases of Jerome D and Walter K, when staff members decided not to admit the patients, the relatives who accompanied them tried to change the decision. The relatives used similar tactics, describing the potential dangers of the patients and the possible harm that could come from their being sent home. Jerome D's mother maintained that he was on the verge of buying a gun. Walter K's wife expressed fears that he would harm her mother if he returned home. As Mr. K was about to sign the consent form, his wife encouraged him to do so, stressing the emergency nature of the circumstances surrounding their coming to the hospital. She said, "The doctor walked us here; he knows that you should stay." The patient seemed to hesitate in his decision and said, "Do me a favor, I'm going home." At this point the wife said, "But Doctor [their family doctor] wants you to stay, Walter."

Thus we see that, despite the absence of a legal role for a patient's family in the model of informed consent, patients' families did play a large role in the Evaluation Center. In some cases, this role approximated the role of proxy for incompetent patients. In other cases, the relatives acted as advocates for their own position. In some cases, relatives put substantial pressure on patients and/or staff members to make decisions in the way the relatives wanted. In the case of Walter K and his wife, which we discuss next as an illustration of another empirical difficulty with informed consent as a model of decision-making, family pressure was very pronounced. Mrs. K was very emphatic in trying to persuade the doctor that Mr. K needed hospitalization.

MUTUAL VACILLATION

The model of informed consent implies that both the patient and the doctor have stable ideas of what they want. The doctor should have a relatively clear-cut notion of the choice of viable treatments and of which ones are best. The patient should have a clear-cut idea of his or her own value preferences and goals. Given these ideas, the doctor and the patient can discuss and negotiate an optimum treatment.

However, we saw many cases in which either the patients or the doctors did not have a clear-cut idea of what was best. The case of Walter K is interesting because neither the doctor nor the patient had a consistent, clear-cut idea of what he wanted, and the decisionmaking process seemed to take on a character that we call "mutual vacillation."

Walter K, a 46-year-old, temporarily unemployed man, was brought to the Evaluation Center by his wife, who said that he was falsely accusing her of trying to poison him and that she was afraid of him. During the initial evaluation, the clinician learned that Mr. K had fears of dying, was hearing voices, was somewhat confused, and had been drinking for 20 years, although he had stopped drinking 1 month previously.

Mr. K changed his mind frequently about hospitalization. At one point he asked, "Are you going to put me up for the night?," while at another time he indicated that he felt good, that he would not hurt his wife, and that he did not want to come into the Hospital. Mrs. K, whose presence in the room Mr. K had requested, constantly contradicted him and repeatedly pressed for his immediate admission.

She carried on the bulk of the dialogue with the staff, repeatedly emphasized her fear of Mr. K, and repeated a series of stories about his psychotic behavior. She frequently reminded Mr. K that his admission was what the doctor who had referred them to the Evaluation Center had recommended.

The admitting doctor was initially reluctant to admit Mr. K, because his problem appeared to be chronic and not an emergency. The doctor believed it was "unfair" to the ward to admit a routine case at 10:30 P.M. when the ward had very few staff members. He also noted to Mr. and Mrs. K that the Hospital was very overcrowded.

After some discussion with Mr. and Mrs. K and after a physical examination, the doctor tentatively acquiesced to Mrs. K's request and decided to admit Mr. K, depending upon his willingness to be admitted. At this point, however, Mr. K refused hospitalization, although Mrs. K continued to press for it. The doctor then invited them to decide between them, saying, "Look at each other and decide." Mrs. K again expressed her fears, and the doctor immediately asked Mr. K again about hospitalization; this time, he said, "OK, yeah." After two more brief changes of mind, Mr. K finally consented to admission. Mr. K signed the doctor's evaluation page without reading it, and he quickly signed the admission form as well.

The doctor and the clinician then made two calls to the ward to explain the admission. During the first call the ward doctor agreed to accept the patient, but after the second discussion, the admitting doctor again changed his mind about the necessity for immediate admission. He decided that since this was not an emergency and since the ward was short of staff members and busy preparing for a special review the next day, it would be best to postpone the admission. He, therefore, told Mr. and Mrs. K that there were no beds available and that they should return the next day but that, in an emergency, they could return the same evening. In fact, the patient did return and was admitted at 1:30 that morning.

As we note above, Mrs. K is an example of an aggressive third-party participant in decisionmaking. However, what interests us more is that she was the only participant in the decisionmaking process who did not change her mind at least twice. If Mr. K had a consistent, clear desire about whether or not and under what circumstances to be hospitalized, we were unable to discover it. Rather, it seems that his opinion shifted from moment to moment, based on "irrational" factors. Perhaps it was related to the organic impairment that the admitting doctor diagnosed. However, the admitting doctor was not much clearer about what should be done. Since he saw the case as a chronic one for which treatment could do little except improve symptom management, he was influenced by the competing pressure of Mrs. K and the ward staff. Obviously, the decisionmaking process here was not the rational evaluation of risks and benefits that the doctrine of informed consent proposes.

REFUSALS

Another evidence of the staff's power in decisionmaking was the infrequency of outright refusals. Only two patients successfully objected to a treatment that the staff proposed. Gustav A, a patient brought to the Hospital by the police for disturbing the peace and for being psychotic, was released when he loudly and determinedly refused to consent to admission. Elsie H refused an admission that her daughter wanted. The staff did not push this very hard and referred her to an outpatient clinic. Two other patients might be said to have refused treatment when they walked out of the Evaluation Center after waiting for long periods of time.

Three other patients refused admission but were eventually admitted. These objections were overcome by the staff and/or the patient's relatives or were simply ignored. Walter K wavered back and forth and finally did what the doctor wanted. Reavis C, a 23-year-old, unemployed man brought to the Hospital by a policeman, consented only after being ordered to sign by the policeman who, he believed, was his ally in breaking up a crime ring. Peggy G, a 20-year-old housewife, reported hearing voices "screaming at me in my head" and was viewed as incompetent by the admitting doctor, who informed the medical students, "As you can see, she is psychotic, and there is no use relying on what she says for any kind of information." She was persuaded to sign by her husband. When at a later time she wanted to leave the Hospital, the doctor said to the staff, "She wants to leave; let's get her up to the floor."

The articulated "no's" or refusals to the doctor's recommendations were equally infrequent among the 20 outpatient cases. Only one patient ever explicitly refused an outpatient referral.

The low frequency of clear-cut refusal of staff recommendations was also true for the many decisions we observed concerning patients' release of information to third parties. We observed a total of 25 instances in which the staff requested that patients sign forms to release information, but we saw only one example in which the patient refused to consent to release the information. Christopher N, a 28-year-old employed heroin addict, refused to release information to third-party payers because he feared his family would learn of his addiction.

In summary, while there were other patterns of decisionmaking, by and large the staff's view of the best prospective treatment prevailed, whether or not the patients were inclined to agree.

STAFF DECISION

The doctrine of informed consent makes no real provision for staff decisions about treatment. However, since the staff and not the patients had the power to admit, to refuse to admit, to refer, or not to refer, the staff always made the decisions. This decision may or may not have been synonymous with the patients' decision. When the staff refused to go along with a patient's treatment request, then the "outcome" of the case resembled neither the initial patient request nor the initial staff recommendation. Often, however, the staff was able to persuade, cajole, or coerce such a patient into the preferred treatment.

Niles X, a 30-year-old black man, came to the Evaluation Center very drunk. He wandered around the waiting room and occasionally entered the staff room saying, "Please, ma'am, help me; I want somebody to talk to." The nurse and the resident who interviewed him learned that, besides consuming "half a dozen, maybe more" bottles of wine, he had taken four "sleeping pills," which turned out to be Trilafon. The residents quickly decided that Mr. X should go to the emergency room of Medical Hospital across the street.

The doctor said, "If you've taken pills and have drunk all that wine, you should be checked out physically. This is a psychiatric hospital. We can call and get somebody to take you over." When Mr. X seemed reluctant to go, the resident continued, "I'm a psychiatrist. OK? And you don't look too good to me. I'm a doctor, and I think you should be checked out medically." Mr. X did not seem to agree. As the resident and the nurse walked out of the room, he said, "I know what's wrong with me; I have a mental problem, suicide." Four minutes later the nurse returned.

NURSE: Someone is on their way over to pick you up and take you to Medical Hospital. They'll check you out to see if what you have taken has hurt you.
MR. X: But I have delusions.
NURSE: We have to find out if what you drank has hurt you in any way.
MR. X: I'm thinking of killing myself.
NURSE: I know, but first of all we have to check you out physically.

Mr. X was escorted to Medical Hospital by two policemen, apparently still unconvinced but unresisting.

The staff seemed to treat this and four other cases as "quasi-emergencies." They considered the consequences of the wrong decision to be too important to be left to the patients. The patients' views of their cases were overridden by the staff, who felt that something needed to be done immediately. In these cases, the patients' participation in the decisions was severely limited.

Just as frequently, patients were persuaded to accept the staff's point of view rather than simply being overruled. For example, the staff in six cases tried to persuade the patients or relatives that admission was *not* necessary; the staff failed in only two of these attempts. In these cases, the staff's decision was ultimately more powerful than the patients'.

This was also true for the outpatient referrals. We saw only one case in which the patient was eventually referred to the type of outpatient treatment that he or she desired when the staff disagreed, and even this referral was in addition to the type of therapy the staff preferred. Two other outpatients also changed the staff's mind. The doctor wanted to admit Elsie H, a 72-year-old woman with a diagnosis of mild dementia, who said very little. Mrs. H, however, refused hospitalization, and after that the staff negotiated with Elsie H's daughter to have Mrs. H evaluated as an outpatient and to start her on sleeping medication. Mrs. H did not participate at all in this decision. Jacob N's mother convinced the staff to accept Mr. N for outpatient evaluation and treatment at the Hospital, although the staff's initial preference was to refer him to the Veterans Hospital where he had been treated before.

BARRIERS TO MUTUAL PARTICIPATION IN THE EVALUATION CENTER

As we have seen, there were a number of patterns of decisionmaking in the Evaluation Center that were nothing like those envisioned by the informed consent doctrine. Behind this fact are a number of systematic difficulties that we now explore. Let us begin with the behavior of the staff.

STAFF BEHAVIOR

One reason why patients might allow the staff to make decisions for them is that considerable pressures are put on them. The law considers these pressures under the rubric of "force" and "undue influence." Let us consider the role of force first.

Force

On any continuum of pressures that might be brought to bear on patients in the decisionmaking process, one extreme is the use of physical force. Physical force itself occupies more than one point on the continuum, ranging from deadly force at one extreme to mere touching at the other (a touch might be beneficial rather than harmful, but it still utilizes physical force). Another point on the spectrum of force involves threats to use physical force. As long as they remain unconsummated, the law does not consider them as problematic as the use of force itself.

Physical Force. We observed three cases in which physical force was used to get patients to do what the staff wanted. Adelle E and Wendel B were brought to the Hospital against their wishes by police officers for involuntary examination. When each attempted to leave, he or she was restrained by a policeman: When Adelle E registered her displeasure at being in the Hospital by walking out of the Evaluation Center, a policeman grabbed her by the arm and propelled her back into the center, as a policeman also did with Wendel B. In another situation a more trivial example of the use of force occurred. Nelson P was reluctant to step off the elevator into the inpatient unit to which he had been committed, and an aide from the unit took him forcibly by the arm and led him into the ward. All in all, force does not seem to have played a major role in the decision process directly. However, the use of force of law is another type of force we must consider.

Force of Law. One of the most interesting and difficult problems of voluntariness concerned the way in which the staff attempted to persuade unwilling patients to sign into the Hospital voluntarily. These were primarily patients who had been brought to the Hospital involuntarily and who might have qualified for involuntary commitment. Whether they did, in fact, qualify for temporary involuntary commitment depends upon the interpretation the doctor placed in each case on the statutory phrase "dangerous to self or others," as well as the way in which the doctor characterized certain facts about each patient's immediate past.

Wendel B came to the Evaluation Center under an emergency commitment order that his woman friend obtained after he had attacked her the previous evening. He was brought to the Hospital by police and was accompanied to the Evaluation Center by his woman friend and another man. Staff members attempted to persuade him to admit himself to the Hospital. One clinician said to him, "It might be worthwhile to find out why you get into tempers like that. Have you ever been in the hospital?" The psychiatrist asked him how he felt about signing in voluntarily and stressed that the patient's best interest would be served by allowing the staff to take care of him. He told Mr. B that a lot of his difficulties were associated with his temper, and that these might be difficulties that "we can help you with if you come to the Hospital." The doctor's use of the conditional tense connoted that the patient had some degree of choice in the matter.

Mr. B agreed that it was a good idea to get rid of his temper, but he was reluctant to enter the Hospital because he believed that his woman friend would enter into a relationship with the man who had accompanied them. The psychiatrist was sympathetic and, at the patient's request, agreed to talk to the woman friend; however, he added, "I would recommend that you come in . . . What you should be thinking about now is how you are going to get some help." The patient was still unsure; the psychiatrist said, "Well, this is ultimately your decision." Yet as he was about to sign the admission papers, Mr. B asked, "If I don't sign the papers, you can't keep me?" The nurse's response was that "It would be better for you if you sign yourself in."

The constraints were even greater than Mr. B suspected. His woman friend had made it clear to the psychiatrist that should he be let go from the Hospital, she intended to get another warrant to have him returned. Later, in a discussion with the patient-observer, Mr. B acknowledged that he felt forced by the way in which he was brought to the Hospital. "She got a warrant to bring me in here without me knowing it. If that ain't pressure, boy, I don't know what is."

Threat of Force. The final way in which force was used in the Evaluation Center was in the form of a threat. Although the case of Reavis C contains many elements, for the moment we look only at the use of a threat of force persuading Mr. C to sign himself into the Hospital.

Reavis C was a young man who believed that he was trying to break up a plot focused in the Hospital itself. When presented with the staff's suggestion that he should enter the Hospital, Mr. C had trouble making up his mind. This was especially discernible when he was asked to sign the form consenting to in-patient treatment. Present were the psychiatrist, a social worker, and a police-man—all of whom exerted some influence during the signing-in procedure. The psychiatrist showed the patient the first part of the consent form and said, "I want you to sign this." Mr. C said he did not want to sign, at which point the policeman interjected, "Mr. C, sign it!" The patient then signed. The psychiatrist then turned to the next page and requested that the patient sign that too. He refused once more, and the social worker said, "Mr. C, we would like you to sign." The patient looked to the policeman, who responded with, "Sign!" and he did so.

This case presents an extreme illustration of the complexities involved in determining whether a person is coerced into doing something against his or her will. A set of conditions that appear constraining to an observer may not appear so from the perspective of the participant. In signing into the Hospital, for instance, Mr. C believed himself to be collaborating with the policeman, with whom he thought he was working to uncover a vice ring in the Hospital.

While force, particularly the force of law, did explain some patient behavior in accepting staff recommendations in the Evaluation Center, it was a small factor. We see some of the others at work as we observe other patterns of decisionmaking there.

Staff Use of Family Pressures

The staff dealt with family pressure on patients in several ways. In some cases, the staff acted as a buffer for patients and persuaded the families to go along with the decision that patients made or acquiesced in. This occurred in the case of Klara N, whose father and grandmother had brought her to the Hospital and had urged the staff to admit her. The patient herself did not have any clear preference in the matter. When the psychiatrist asked if she would be willing to come into the Hospital, Ms. N replied, "I don't care," and she was agreeable to the final staff recommendation for outpatient treatment. Both the father and grandmother were dissatisfied with this outcome but were eventually persuaded by staff members to accept it. Likewise, in the case of Elsie H, whose daughter asked to have her admitted, the psychiatrist informed the daughter that unless her mother agreed to admission, the law forbade the Hospital to admit her. In the case of Gwen X, it appeared that the staff, on the basis of past interaction with the patient, had developed a personal liking for her and were loath to admit her merely for hitting her niece.

Another example of the staff's stressing the independence of the patient vis-à-vis family members is the case of Lori C, which is described above. When she began the interview, the clinician first made sure that she saw the patient alone and asked her why she was at the Evaluation Center. When the patient responded, "My mother brought me here because she told me you could do some things that would help us," the staff member then tried to elicit the patient's own opinion on the matter. She asked the patient, "Do you think that's a good idea, or do you have another idea?," suggesting that there could be a choice.

However, this case also illustrates the complexity of the dynamics among staff, patients, and relatives. The clinician initially appeared willing to support the patient's right to decide whether to be in the Hospital; at a later stage, however, when the patient refused to go along with the psychiatrist's recommendation, the clinician made an alliance with the mother in order to get her to influence the daughter. The clinician acknowledged that the patient could refuse the tests but nevertheless urged the mother in the patient's presence to talk with her daughter at home and to call the Hospital should the patient change her mind.

Another instance of staff members' using significant people to exert influence over patients occurred in the case of Doris X, a patient who wavered about coming into the Hospital. The clinician suggested to Ms. X's boyfriend that perhaps she would be willing to hand over the decision to him, saying, "She seems to have trouble making decisions. It's as if she wants someone else to make the decisions. Perhaps she wants you to make it." In general, the staff interposed themselves between the relatives and the patients when they thought that the relatives were demanding the wrong treatment, and they tried to use the relatives to influence the patients when the patients were resisting proper treatment.

STAFF ETHICS AND THE PROBLEM OF SERIOUS CONSEQUENCES

When considering staff behavior that went counter to the ethics of informed consent, we must remember that staff members were concerned with other ethical obligations besides informed consent. It is our impression that they felt their first obligation was to the patients' health and that they took the protection of others very seriously. Thus, when staff members believed that a patient was dangerous or might have suffered harm, they were less willing to let the patient make a decision that they believed to be the wrong one. Niles X and Reavis C, both discussed above, represent cases in which patients intermittently objected to their treatment disposition; the one, to being referred to a medical hospital for medical evaluation, and the other, to being admitted for inpatient care. Both eventually submitted to the decisions of their clinicians. In both cases, the staff put unusual pressure on the patients. They were unwilling to let either patient make up his mind by himself, because they saw Mr. C as potentially homicidal and Mr. X as a potentially serious medical case. The possibly serious consequences of the wrong decision overwhelmed their willingness to listen to the patients.

FORMS

The process of presenting consent forms to patients is an important aspect of staff behavior in the Evaluation Center, because the forms developed by the Department of Public Welfare were intended to assure that there would actually be a free, voluntary decision in the admission process. Yet the ways in which the forms were presented to patients undercut this effort. Let us consider several aspects of the presentation of the forms.

Lack of Privacy

The physical structure of the Evaluation Center and the routine organization practices made much of the activity in the center—activity that was personal and hence deserving a modicum of privacy—take place in a public setting. Thus patients were sometimes presented with forms to be signed in the common areas of the center, rather than in the comparative privacy of the interviewing rooms. Marcus I was approached to sign papers in the reception room, where there were at least five other patients present. Eldred C was also approached in the reception area, asked to come to the counter, and told that he was not officially admitted until he had signed the forms.

Timing and Distractions

A related problem involved the obtaining of consent at inappropriate times. For instance, patients were sometimes asked to sign forms when distractions were present. When Maureen A was signing the consent forms, she was simultaneously being questioned about her husband. Many patients signed consent forms while being told what they were signing. Mitzie Q was presented with the consent forms when she was upset that her father had left the Hospital without saying goodbye. She seemed unable to concentrate on the forms and asked continually about her father.

Routinization

One of the admission forms that patients signed was meant to document their provisional treatment plan. The tone and manner in which the material was sometimes presented to the patient during the signing-in procedure conveyed the impression that to engage in any kind of discussion on the issue would have been peculiar or unusual. Specifically, when presenting the forms to patients, clinicians would say, "I need you to sign this," or "I have to ask you to sign this." The formulation and tone of the sentence implied that this was a routine event and that numerous patients had previously signed this paper without so much as a second thought.

That patients also considered this to be a routine event is clear from the fact that, when asked to sign a form stating "I confirm that this treatment has been explained to me, including the types of medications which I may be given and the types of restraints and restrictions to which I may be subjected," only two patients questioned this statement or expressed dissatisfaction at the amount of information given. This even held true when a patient was asked to sign this confirmatory statement before being shown the treatment plan. Patients were either insufficiently interested in reading the form or felt that they could not question the statements.

Quantity

Far from creating the conditions necessary for an open and free dialogue between staff and patients, the sheer number of forms to be signed by patients often inhibited them. The patient signed one form upon first contact with the clinician and then, depending upon his or her financial status, had to sign up to nine more forms in the financial office. If admitted, the patient was exposed to three more forms—the consent to voluntary admission, the Patients' Rights form, and the treatment plan. The fact that these came at the end of a long series contributed to the feeling that the signing of forms was merely routine and tended to discourage scrutiny of the forms. Thus in a follow-up interview, when asked what he had signed, Eldred C told the observer, "That's all paperwork; I guess it has to be done, but I don't try to remember all that stuff."

ORGANIZATIONAL FEATURES OF THE EVALUATION CENTER

A number of subtle pressures on voluntariness arose out of the structure and routine procedures of the Evaluation Center. Let us look at a few of these.

Hospital Records

A strong reliance on the Hospital's records of patients' past hospitalizations might, in subtle ways, have impinged upon such patients' autonomy. As soon as a patient arrived at the Evaluation Center, the staff sent for the record, and if one existed it was perused by the staff. This is, of course, a routine medical practice. The staff maintained that reading such a patient's record beforehand reduced the uncertainty of meeting a new patient under stressful conditions, and that this procedure aided in effectively diagnosing and referring the patient. Yet, *in every instance that we observed, when there was a conflict between the record and what a patient said, clinicians believed the record.* That the record was considered fundamental was echoed by one psychiatrist, who asked rhetorically, "How can you diagnose without the record?" With patients who had past records, diagnoses were based on the written notes of clinical personnel who had prior contact with these patients. For such patients, the interview with the clinician was a formality as far as the diagnosis went. For instance, Irma O was not asked to supply information regarding her situation. By merely looking at her chart and knowing that she had been brought in by the police, the doctor decided that she should be admitted without interviewing her. In the case of Mitzie Q, a patient seen only by a medical student, the supervising psychiatrist advised the student to admit her solely on the basis of reading her records. Because the Hospital's records were so important in determining how the staff viewed problems, it was very hard for a patients' perspective to be heard. If the decision about treatment was primarily up to a patient, the role of the record would not be so important in structuring the decision. But since, as we have seen, the most common decisionmaking pattern was for the staff to decide, the importance of the records was a major constraint on the patients' ability to get the desired treatment decision.

Delay

From the point of view of some patients, one of the most critical characteristics of the organization of the Evaluation Center was the amount of time that it took to evaluate, refer, or admit patients. Patients spent long periods of time in the center both waiting for various aspects of the procedure and actually being processed. Incoming patients were seen by a clinician and a physician and then given a physical exam and a financial interview. The average amount of time that patients spent in the Evaluation Center was about 4 hours. Even this was exceeded when new residents began their periods of rotation in the Evaluation Center, because they typically took a lot of time to reach a diagnosis and were required to discuss their findings with a supervising psychiatrist. This created a backlog of patients, so that the amount of time spent in the waiting room was increased. The case of Maureen A illustrates the way in which the length of time taken to reach a diagnosis and disposition could compromise the options available for patients. The patient arrived at the Evaluation Center at 12:25 P.M.

At 2:40, she saw a clinician for 20 minutes and discussed her symptoms. It was not until 6:20 that she was seen by a psychiatrist for a period of 30 minutes. During the interim she sat in the waiting room. She was in a great deal of physical pain from shingles. At her first interview she was willing to consider outpatient treatment, but after her long wait she felt that she could not face the prolonged journey home alone on several buses and just wanted to lie down. At 9 P.M., 8½ hours after she had entered the center, she was taken to an inpatient ward.

Time

Another organizational constraint was the staff's perception of being pressed for time. Staff members were sometimes willing to support the patients' right to make a choice about whether to admit themselves; but when a patient took several hours to make the decision, the staff appeared impatient and sometimes presented patients with an ultimatum. Chester T and Doris X were told that, unless they decided within a specified period of time, the available beds in the Hospital might be filled by other patients. That the staff seemed to think that giving a patient a great deal of time to decide about treatment could be counterproductive was clear from the case of Sally N, who took longer than any other patient to arrive at a decision to come into the Hospital. As the psychiatrist commented when returning to the staff room with the admission form that Ms. N had just signed, "The more leeway you give people, the longer it takes them, and the more problems they get into about deciding."

Catchment Areas and Free Choice

The fact that public psychiatric hospitals have the power to restrict their treatment to those who fall within a designated catchment area places further restrictions on patients. Chester T came to the Hospital to withdraw from heroin and requested that he be allowed methadone during the detoxification. When told that it was not Hospital policy to give methadone, he said that he would go to another hospital. He was then told that it was unlikely that he would be accepted for treatment there, since he lived outside the catchment area of that hospital. In economic terms, this is a monopoly.

PATIENTS' EXPECTATIONS AND BEHAVIOR

Patients' Lack of Background Information

Another impediment to informed patient decisionmaking concerns two types of background knowledge that the doctrine presumes patients have but that the patients we observed did not have. One of these may be clarified by looking at the case of Sally N.

Sally N, an 18-year-old student, was the most questioning patient that we observed. Yet while she asked many questions, Ms. N lacked both the technical background and the practical experience to understand many of the answers. She jumped from question to question and failed to distinguish complete from incomplete staff answers. Thus after saying, "I think I'll decide to stay," she was then given the description of the proposed treatment:

DOCTOR: You'll be here for observation and pharmacotherapy.

PATIENT: What's that?

DOCTOR: Well, it's a type of medication used to slow down thoughts. It's used for two things: one, to slow down thoughts . . .

PATIENT: I don't like that idea at all.

DOCTOR: It will make you less tremulous and anxious.

PATIENT: I'm not really anxious. I'm just anxious today because I'm in a strange place.

DOCTOR: . . . And, two, it will make your voices decrease. Not all of a sudden, but gradually.

PATIENT: But I'm not hearing voices; it's kind of a transition from one experience to another, experiences in which we are of a different opinion.

DOCTOR: Well, you may not be put on those kinds of medications right away; but after the evaluation we'll put you on medications, probably within a certain spectrum.

PATIENT: Called . . . ? What are the names of some of those?

DOCTOR: Well, you can refuse drug treatment. But the names of some of them might be Thorazine, Mellaril, Prolixin . . .

PATIENT: Librium?

DOCTOR: No. But I can't promise that you will get them anyway.

And when Ms. N discovered that Box A and not Box B had already been checked for her by the staff (the 72-hour hold provision of the law) and that she would not be able to leave the Hospital when she wanted to, she asked, "Why is Box A checked and not Box B?" She was told, "Because usually when a person doesn't come to be evaluated and ccmes only to have tests or just for a day—but this doesn't apply to you." Ms. N accepted this. When our patient-observer asked Ms. N what led her to decide in favor of admission, she replied, "Well, nothing specifically, except when I was talking to the doctor, I knew that I had come here for help, and then when I was telling him about my writing[1] it reinforced how disturbed I am; and then that, coupled with his understanding attitude, convinced me to stay."

Thus even the most suspicious and questioning patient did not have the ability to distinguish truth from half-truth and relied primarily on the doctor's attitude and the manner in which he related to her as a basis for decision.

Perhaps even more serious was the fact that patients often lacked the value context within which to respond as citizens protecting their rights. The most interesting example was the decision that some patients encountered as to whether or not to permit their names and some information about the hospitalization to be released to a county agency that was keeping track of the use of mental health facilities. The Hospital administration felt that routine reporting of such information would violate the patients' privacy and therefore decided to give patients the right to forbid the forwarding of the information. Although the way in which this issue was presented to the patients varied, depending upon which nurse or doctor was involved, most often the patients were told it was completely the patients' decision and that the Hospital was "indifferent."

How the patients managed this decision is of particular interest in the study of how decisions were made. We observed only nine examples of this decision, since staff members typically forgot to raise this issue with patients. Three patients seemed to have decided purely on the basis of a mild suggestion from a staff member. Thus when told, "The county likes us to send information about the patient, but we think that is unfair . . . and you can write that you don't want this sent," a patient responded, "What do you want me to write?" Likewise, when told that "The county likes us to send information about people who consent; do you mind?," another patient readily agreed. In the three cases in which the patients were given moderately explicit directions on what to do, their decisions seemed to be quite simple. On the other hand, when patients were given no guidance, they sometimes became confused. Consider the case of Cynthia M:

CLINICIAN: Now one more thing. We send the county information about the patients for statistics. If you don't want us to, you have the right to refuse to permit us to send any information about you. Write here OK or not.

The patient didn't seem to understand.

CLINICIAN: If you don't want to, you can say no. It is up to you.
PATIENT: (*Hesitating.*) I don't see any reason why I wouldn't want the county to know.
CLINICIAN: If you don't want to, you can write that there.
PATIENT: I don't understand.
CLINICIAN: What don't you understand?
PATIENT: You want me to choose whether you will send this information to the county?
CLINICIAN: Yes.
PATIENT: Will that benefit the Hospital?
CLINICIAN: Don't worry about the Hospital. I don't want to influence you. This is your own decision. . . .

The patient eventually refused to release the information, and a few minutes later told the patient-observer:

> "Did you see me? I was so confused about the thing about the county. I thought, 'Now if I don't let them release the information, will they make me an involuntary patient, or is it that if you want a job with them they won't have records on it?' I was getting confused. . . ."

Other patients showed similar confusion. One patient decided that it might help her get the county to pay for her treatment if the information was released, since, being indigent, she was worried about paying for treatment. Another patient, somewhat bewildered, asked the clinician if releasing the information would interfere with her getting a county job later. When the clinician responded that she didn't want to influence the patient, the patient's spouse suggested that the county might hold it against her future job application if she did not release the information, and that maybe it would interfere with other future financial benefits. The patient released the information. Still another patient consulted his lawyer, who was present, after failing to get any guidance from the clinician. In summary, for some decisions patients felt that they needed the staff's advice on how to proceed in areas they did not understand. Lacking this advice, they became confused.[2]

Weighing Risks and Benefits

Another difficulty of the decisionmaking process in the Evaluation Center, from the point of view of the informed consent doctrine, was an almost total lack of patients' weighing of the comparative risks and benefits of alternative treatments. Instead, the patients acted as though the issue was one of whether or not they needed to be treated (i.e., whether or not they were sick). They seemed to take it for granted that if they were sick they should seek treatment. This type of reasoning is markedly different from the utilitarian calculus that is implied when the law of informed consent specifies that patients must be told the risks and benefits of alternative treatments. While it might be argued that patients were implicitly weighing risks of treatment against the benefits of care, we saw no evidence of this. At no point did any patient say or indicate by his or her behavior, "I know I'm sick, but I don't want treatment because it involves too many risks [disadvantages, hassles, etc.]." Rather, all arguments against treatment took the form of denials of any substantial psychiatric problem.

Moreover, with few exceptions, once patients agreed that they were in need of treatment, they seemed to leave the decision as to the specific kind of treatment to the doctors. The exceptions to this were the patients who had pragmatic problems about one type of treatment or another. For example, Doris X hesitated for a long time before agreeing to come in, but she was concerned about arranging for the care of her child and securing her fiancé's support, not about whether treatment would help or hurt her.

This does not mean that these were not legitimate concerns. Indeed, these were concerns of which the patients were the best judges. It is precisely because such factors are legitimate aspects of decisions about treatment that patients must have substantial input into treatment decisions. However, none of these were related to the risks and benefits that the staff members were supposed to disclose. By and large, patients seemed content to leave the weighing of risks and benefits of various treatment plans up to the staff.

Another important type of evidence showing that patients were not balancing risks and benefits in order to decide whether or not to accept treatment is that the advantages and disadvantages were not considered, or at least not mentioned, by patients concurrently. For instance, Cynthia M, a housewife who complained that she was anxious and depressed, spent by far the largest part of her time in the Evaluation Center presenting her problem and assuring herself that the treatment would benefit her. She was quite concerned about risks, but she discussed them and apparently considered the risks and benefits of hospitalization at two different times in different contexts. Sally N was also concerned about the disadvantages of hospitalization, but she asked about them *after* deciding to admit herself. Another piece of evidence is that many patients expressed the feeling that they didn't know what would happen to them, either positively or negatively, except that they would get "treatment." Eldred C, an intelligent and well-informed patient, when asked what he expected from treatment answered, "Only the Lord knows."

Although our findings show that many decisions do not involve very much weighing of risks and benefits, two things must be said in qualification of this finding. First, it is methodologically difficult to see such decisionmaking procedures, and we have often relied on indirect evidence. It is possible that more "rational" decisionmaking actually occurs but is not accessible through these methods.[3] The second qualification concerns the logical structure of utilitarian decisionmaking. To weigh the risks against the benefits of a single procedure requires that they at least be put on a single ordinal scale. That is, one must be able to say, for example, that ECT is less bad than more depression. However, to decide which is the best choice between two alternatives with risks of different magnitude and probability requires an interval scale. Likewise, the construction of a risk-benefit ratio for comparison of alternatives requires such a scale. It is likely that the information presented to patients is inherently too vague to use in that manner, and that the patients' failure to do so reflects in part the great cognitive difficulty of the task.

THE DOCTOR-PATIENT RELATIONSHIP

Another difficulty for informed consent in the Evaluation Center was the views of patients and staff about their respective roles. Patients' perceptions of their role in the doctor-patient relationship constrained them from making forceful statements as to their treatment preference in the presence of the psychiatrist.

For example, Naomi G's husband came to the Evaluation Center seeking marital counseling. Immediately after his interview at the Evaluation Center, he went to her place of work and brought her to the center. Ms. G was not interviewed by the psychiatrist, but was merely brought into the interview room where the psychiatrist was discussing marital therapy with Mr. G; Ms. G was then told that she should participate. She made a number of negative comments about her feeling for her husband, to the effect that the marriage was over. The psychiatrist identified these as problems that ought to be looked at more deeply in the context of marital counseling, and he made an appointment for them for couples therapy. A day later the husband called the Hospital to inform them that his wife would prefer individual therapy. It seems that only outside the presence of the psychiatrist, where it was not necessary to argue with him, could Ms. G express her treatment preference.

Staff members frequently used persuasive techniques that relied on the prestige associated with the medical profession. They invariably used the plural "we" when recommending treatment, and thus located themselves within the professional community and involved the authority of medicine. One staff member talked to Doris X about coming into the Hospital, stating, "*We* need to get you started on medicine today." Similarly, the nurse/clinician said to Manuel C, "*We* are going to begin a new medication which may work better." When taking down information on a patient, the clinician maintained, "It is to help *us* find how we can help you."

At other times, the clinician invoked the doctor's prestige. For instance, when the clinician told Delucia E, "I talked to Dr. Y, . . . and he wanted you to come and be hospitalized for a few days," she was using Dr. Y's status as a persuasive technique. Sometimes the doctor did the same. Niles X, discussed above, was told, "I'm a psychiatrist . . . and you don't look too good to me. I'm a doctor, and I think you should be checked out medically." The influence associated with professional expertise was also invoked when trying to convince relatives of a certain course of action. Thus Dr. R said to the father of Sally N, "This is my recommendation, that she should come in as quickly as possible. There is no useful purpose in delay. All my training and judgment tells me that this should be done."

STAFF-PATIENT COMMUNICATION GAPS

One of the major difficulties with the idea of informed consent in the Evaluation Center was that patients and staff often saw the issues in radically different lights. Often these differences were so great that the staff did not feel it was possible to compromise. From their perspective, such patients were crazy, and there was no reason to expect that they could be made to understand the issues at hand. For example, when 70-year-old Adelle E boisterously told the staff that she was pregnant and wanted to go to a general hospital, and that she planned to go to Hawaii that week although she had little money, the staff largely ignored her ideas and focused their views of her problem on her history of threats to the police, her unusual ideas, and her overactivity. Likewise, although Elsie H sat passively and expressed no desire for any help from the Hospital, the staff focused on her dementia and suicidal history and wondered whether she would have problems taking care of herself. Irma O complained that she didn't "know why they keep bringing me over here" and denied what her family said. The staff believed her family's and the police's assertions that she frequently set fires and struck out at others. Gustav A accused the staff of planning torture and lobotomy, but the staff believed that although he did not meet the commitment criteria, he was severely manic. When Harrison T was asked, "Do you think you should be in the Hospital?" he replied, "Yes . . . the question is whether I should run it." While the staff viewed Mr. T as an intriguing person, they did not think that he would be a good replacement for the Hospital's director. Reavis C believed that he was breaking up a crime ring centered in the Hospital, but the staff noted his chronic psychotic episodes and worried about assaultive behavior. Linda T came to the Hospital "wanting a rest," but the staff worried about child neglect and the possibility of an overdose. Mitzie Q wanted to get away from her family for a rest and for fun in the Hospital, but the staff saw her as schizophrenic and worried about her impact on her family. While Peggy G worried about her house trailer being bugged, the staff saw her worries as a symptom of her psychosis.

Such basic disparities between the way the patients formulated their problems and the way the staff formulated them were present for 3 of the 4 patients who were hospitalized involuntarily, for 5 of the 21 patients who were hospitalized voluntarily, and for 8 of the 19 patients who were not admitted. The problem for joint decisionmaking in these cases was not only that the patients' and the staff's formulations of the problems were initially different, but that, for a variety of reasons, neither patients nor staff educated the other about their respective points of view. In some of these cases, the patients were irrational by almost any everyday standard. In other instances, the patients gave histories or had complaints that were inconsistent with what the staff had learned from others about the patients, and the staff believed the third parties. Other patients, while cooperative, had concerns that were difficult for the staff to take seriously. Still other patients' disorientation, alcohol toxicity, or psychosis led the staff to view them as incompetent. Whatever the reason, the outcome was the same in each case. The information exchange was abbreviated, and/or despite limited information exchange, the staff did not explain its view of a patient's problem to the patient. Instead, the staff pretended to accept the patient's idiosyncratic views when the patient was cooperative and willing to go along with the disposition favored by the staff, or else it relied upon others or upon the law to ensure the proper treatment disposition. Thus while the extent of legal incompetency among the patients was arguably not great, one-third of the patients spoke or acted in ways that led the staff to dismiss them as reasonable decisionmakers.

8

Summary of the Evaluation Center Findings

The findings from the Evaluation Center are complex, and the data have taken many pages to describe and evaluate. Thus this chapter clarifies the basic findings, so that the reader can grasp the overall picture that might occasionally have been lost in the detailed analyses presented in Chapters 5-7. Let us begin by describing the general patterns of decisionmaking.

PATTERNS OF DECISIONMAKING

The predominant pattern of decisionmaking in the Evaluation Center was that the staff made the decisions. This was seen in staff members' occasional behavior in ignoring what a patient wanted when they felt the matter was very serious, in their ability to persuade patients to accept their point of view, and in the infrequency with which staff preferences were overridden in the end.

Another group of patients was almost totally uninvolved in the decision because of their own passivity. In these cases, the patient was almost completely passive. To our surprise, this was more true for outpatients, and the patients' pathology was only one of several causes for the behavior.

The decisionmaking process sometimes involved friends and relatives of the patients, who played a substantial role in the decisionmaking. In these cases, which often overlapped those in which the staff was the predominant decisionmaker, one or more family members became significant actors in the decisionmaking, often overshadowing the patients completely. Sometimes the family members seemed to be acting as agents for the patients, while at other times they argued against what the patients seemed to want. In some cases they used strong pressures to try to persuade the patients and/or the staff members to go along with their desires.

As noted in Chapter 7, we came to call another form of decisionmaking "mutual vacillation." In this pattern, neither the patients nor the staff members seemed to have a clear-cut idea about what should be done, and the preferences of both patients and staff vacillated as new information or new situational factors came into play.

We also observed what can be called "prior decisions," in which the decisions were already made when the patients arrived at the Hospital; the admitting process was often substantially abbreviated, and disclosure seemed to have no impact on the decisions whatsoever.

We also saw a number of patient "waivers" of the right to decide. This has some relationship to the decisionmaking pattern we called the "passive patient," since once again the patients seemed to be leaving the decision almost entirely up to the staff. In these cases, the patients involved were explicit in their desire to leave the decision up to the doctors. Typically, these patients were better educated and more articulate. They expressed feelings that they could not make an adequate decision themselves and that the decision had to be made by the staff members, who understood the problem and the way in which to deal with it.

Our sample of Evaluation Center decisions also contained a small number of patient refusals. Two patients refused inpatient admission; one patient refused an outpatient referral (although several did not show up for their appointments); and two patients left the Evaluation Center before receiving a formal treatment plan. However, some of the patients who refused admission were persuaded to accept it or had their objections ignored and were simply hospitalized. None of the refusals involved any sort of sustained dialogue with the staff.

The final decisionmaking pattern is what can be called "mutual participation," which is what informed consent is supposed to involve. We saw only one case that could be adequately described as primarily a mutually made decision, although several other cases had some elements thereof.

In summary, we did not see a great deal of decisionmaking that actually resembled informed consent. The question, then, is how to account for this. There were certainly many things in the Evaluation Center that went into the failure of decisions to approximate informed consent. These can be divided into four parts. The first of these is the question of how much disclosure and understanding there was. The second involves basic troubles with the Evaluation Center as the setting for informed consent. The third concerns the staff's and the patients' expectations. Finally, there seemed to be certain difficulties that are inherent in the doctrine of informed consent as currently formulated. Let us begin with a review of what patients were told and what they understood.

DISCLOSURE AND UNDERSTANDING
IN THE EVALUATION CENTER

Although the doctrine of informed consent specifies that patients should be told about the treatment they are going to receive—in this case, the nature, purpose, risks and benefits of, and alternatives to various types of inpatient and outpatient treatment programs—the only thing that patients were systematically told about the nature of the treatment was whether they were going to receive inpatient or outpatient treatment. Invariably, the patients knew at least that much about the proposed treatment. However, they were typically told and understood little or nothing about such issues as the length of their treatment and the special nature of the ward or outpatient clinic in which they were going to receive treatment.

Patients' understanding of the purpose of treatment was usually that it would remedy their "problems." In most cases, patients came in and presented their problems to the clinicians, who then agreed that the Hospital would treat them for those problems. In these cases, it seems the patients understood the purpose of treatment, even though it was the patients themselves who disclosed it. However, in a number of cases, the clinicians did not accept the patients' definition of their problems and prescribed on the basis of their own professional definition of the patients' problems without disclosing this fact to the patients. The patients were thus left implicitly with the idea that the clinicians had accepted their definition of the purpose of treatment.

Patients' understanding of the risks and benefits of treatment was definitely limited, because there was very little disclosure of either risks or benefits. Patients were typically told that treatment would help them to "get better," and they tended not to ask much more. Patients were almost never told that there was a risk that the treatment would not produce the intended result, nor were any other risks disclosed. Thus it is not surprising that about half the patients saw no risk whatsoever in receiving treatment, and the other half saw risks that were mostly idiosyncratically involved with their personal lives.

Disclosure about alternative treatments was no better. Staff members presented no alternative treatments unless a patient refused the recommended treatment. Perhaps it is not surprising, then, that when asked about alternative treatments, patients discussed only possibilities that did not involve the Hospital, such as going to another hospital, going to a motel, or some change in their environmental circumstances.

THE EVALUATION CENTER AS A SETTING
FOR INFORMED CONSENT

If we have learned anything from our studies, it is that informed consent problems differ in different types of settings. The Evaluation Center seemed to have some difficulties that were different from any of the other settings we studied. These included the following:

1. The level of pressures from family members who accompanied the patient was intense. While the specific goals of the family members differed substantially from one case to another, in over half of the cases we observed, family members played a significant role in the decisionmaking. This is clearly not envisioned as a part of the decisionmaking process of competent patients in the doctrine of informed consent.

2. Another difficulty was what Egon Bittner (personal communication) has called "the problem of seeing around the corner." The basic problem was that the staff had to describe to the patients something with which the patients had no experience. Whereas on the Research Ward or in the Outpatient Clinic patients were making decisions about things with which they had direct experience, this was usually not true in the Evaluation Center. Moreover, the staff seemed frequently to forget this fact. They tended to talk in jargon and to use concepts with which the patients had little experience. Staff disclosures often presumed knowledge of reasonably complex background information that the patient often did not have.

3. The third problem can be called "floating responsibility." Because there were multiple care-givers involved, and because no staff member had clear-cut primary responsibility for the disclosure of information, disclosure often seemed "to fall between the cracks." Just who was supposed to provide the information was not exactly clear, and the result was that often no one did.[1]

PATIENTS' AND STAFF'S EXPECTATIONS

Perhaps the most basic difficulty that we found facing the implementation of the doctrine of informed consent was a consistent pattern on the part of both the Evaluation Center staff and the patients to act as though the decision was properly the responsibility of the staff. This is perhaps not so surprising on the part of the staff. Cynics will not be surprised at the finding that staff disclosure with either done to persuade a patient to accept the staff's recommendations or was simply the filling out of the required forms in the most ritualized and minimal manner. However, the patients' behavior shows evidence that the staff's behavior was also in accordance with the expectations of the patients. For example, patients were typically willing to accept treatment while knowing almost nothing about the treatment except the goals. Likewise, the only alternatives patients considered were extrahospital alternatives; it was as though they believed the staff would not provide them with any in-hospital alternatives if they so asked.

Another indication of patient expectations that staff members would make the decisions is the fact that patients rarely asked questions. Those questions they did ask focused exclusively on gaining reassurance that the decisions already made were correct and on gaining some idea of what the future would hold for them. The questions were asked after, not before, the decisions were made. It does not seem that patients, at least as indicated by their questions, expected to have a major role in making treatment decisions. It is also interesting that the attitude that the decision should be made by the staff was at least as common among the more competent patients as it was among the more psychiatrically impaired.

The staff's pattern of disclosure also seems to indicate a fairly paternalistic view of what the patients' role in decisionmaking should be. For example, we repeatedly found that staff members told the patients' relatives more about the treatment than they told the patients themselves. This indicates that the limits of the disclosure to patients were a matter not only of not knowing the details of possible treatments that the patients might receive, but also of a reluctance to disclose something to the patients. Similarly, although staff members were occasionally willing to accept patients' decisions that ran contrary to their own judgments of what would be best for the patients, they never did so where they considered that the outcome of a bad treatment decision would be serious in its consequences either to the patients or to others. Thus what we saw was a basic pattern of paternalism on the part of the staff and waiver on the part of the patients. While there were certainly marked exceptions to both of these patterns, this seemed to be the general expectation.

BASIC PROBLEMS WITH THE DOCTRINE OF INFORMED CONSENT AS APPLIED TO THE EVALUATION CENTER

Even if the staff and patients had been more receptive to the informed consent model of decisionmaking, there would still have been some basic difficulties in applying the doctrine of informed consent as it is generally understood to the Evaluation Center. These include the following:

1. What should be disclosed about psychiatric treatment at the time of hospitalization is not clear. This partially explains why the staff disclosed far more about such special treatments as withdrawal from heroin and admission to the Research Ward than they did about routine treatment.

2. Independent of whether or not there is adequate disclosure, if a patient does not accept the psychiatrist's view of the nature of his or her problem—that is, that it is located in the patient and not in the setting or in a particular act or series of acts that the patient has performed—communication between the staff and the patient seems destined to fail. About one-third of the patients we saw did not see their problems as being psychiatric, and they were the ones to whom staff communication was most deceptive. This seems to be a serious problem.

3. The general notion of the doctrine of informed consent has been that a patient will base his or her decision in a large part on the doctor's disclosures. In this context, it is more than casually interesting that approximately half the patients saw the benefits in completely nonmedical or nonpsychiatric terms.

4. Our study of the 72-hours requirement shows that when the staff wished to get around legal restrictions built into the forms, it was quite easy for them to do so.

5. In general, written disclosures seem to have been a failure. Forms were frequently not read and, even when read, seemed to be poorly understood. Staff members successfully discounted the forms' contents when they wanted to and usually presented forms only after they had reached verbal agreement with the patients about what their decisions should be. Formal disclosure contained in the forms provided by the Department of Public Welfare did not, in any case we observed, cause a patient to change his or her mind about a treatment decision. On the other hand, forms did apparently increase the amount of disclosure for a particular issue.

6. Staff members seemed to be inclined to give information only if they felt that patients were capable of understanding. This could be justified under the incompetency exception. However, the determination of whether or not a patient was competent was made on psychiatric grounds and did not follow either legal standards or legal procedure.

7. Patients typically lacked the background knowledge necessary to understand the disclosures made by the staff. It is unclear whether or not staff disclosures could be sufficiently simplified that the patients would be able to understand their ramifications.

8. As far as we were able to determine using our methods, patients apparently did not decide about psychiatric treatment by weighing risks and benefits, but rather by deciding whether or not they were in need of treatment and then accepting the proposed treatment within a very broad range of limits.

POSITIVE FEATURES OF INFORMED CONSENT IN THE EVALUATION CENTER

Our review of the findings has emphasized the deficits of informed consent in the Evaluation Center. We believe this is appropriate, given the data; however, it is possible that this emphasis can overshadow a description of the role that the patients played in making their own decisions in the Evaluation Center.

To begin with, patients whom the staff saw as capable of understanding were generally told a good deal more than other patients were. In general, this group of patients was referred for treatment for the complaints they presented. While these patients did not determine (nor did they try to determine) what their specific treatment would be, they indirectly determined their treatment when they presented complaints that the clinicians could reformulate in psychiatric terms and treat with psychiatric procedures. In general, those patients viewed as capable of understanding played a substantial role in the decisionmaking process, although not the one envisioned in the informed consent doctrine.

The second positive thing that can be said for decisionmaking in the Evaluation Center is that, with few exceptions, there was very little overt coercion of patients into treatment.

Finally, although no patient understood enough of the ramifications of the decision to satisfy the aspirations embodied in the doctrine of informed consent, the most competent and well-informed patients did seem to understand a substantial amount of what they were getting into. Even though there were some blind spots in their knowledge, they went into the decision with their eyes open.

The Research Ward

9

Introduction to the Research Ward

The Evaluation Center, as we have seen in Section Two, was the place where the overwhelming majority of patients had their first contact with the Hospital. One of its major functions was to refer patients to inpatient units in the Hospital. Another large group of patients was referred to outpatient treatment. Outpatient treatment is discussed in Section Four. In this part, we present the findings of our study of informed consent on the Research Ward, one of the four inpatient units in the Hospital.

The Research Ward was somewhat different from a conventional psychiatric inpatient unit, in that it had a dual purpose. Like conventional units, it sought to provide treatment for patients' psychiatric disorders. But in addition, as its name suggests, it also served as a location for research. Thus, patients on the Research Ward underwent procedures that had two different purposes: Treatment was undertaken primarily, if not exclusively, for the benefit of the patients, whereas research was performed primarily to extend knowledge about the safety and efficacy of a procedure.[1]

In addition to the fact that research was performed, another characteristic of the Research Ward that distinguished it from conventional psychiatric wards was that the ward was organized as a "therapeutic community." Although this is perhaps not as unusual as its being a research ward, still most psychiatric inpatient units do not function as therapeutic communities, let alone as therapeutic communities that are also research wards. On the traditional psychiatric ward, the staff takes a very active role in deciding what sorts of treatment patients are to have and dispensing it to patients, who are viewed as occupying a relatively passive role. In contrast, the concept of the therapeutic community demands that patients involve themselves in the life of a ward, openly discussing problems and assuming responsibility for their own behavior and the well-being of other patients.[2]

WARD MEETINGS

To accomplish this, the patients' daily activities on the Research Ward were structured around a wide variety of meetings, in which patients were expected not only to participate but also to assume some of the responsibility for the supervision of other patients. Each patient's primary therapeutic relationship was conceived as being with the community as a whole, which consisted of both staff and patients, rather than with one particular staff member. Both patients and staff shared a joint schedule of activities, which included the following:

1. Walking Rounds (Tuesday-Sunday mornings). Patients sat in a large circle, and either a ward psychiatrist or a physician's assistant, accompanied by the head nurse, walked from patient to patient and engaged each in a largely public discussion of symptoms, treatment, discharge plans, community involvement, and so forth.

2. Weekend Report (Monday morning). The Weekend Report replaced Walking Rounds on Monday. Staff members and certain responsible patients reported on the weekend activities of each patient to the entire staff and patient group.

3. Weekend Meeting (Saturday-Sunday). Staff members and certain responsible patients reported on the weekend activities of individual patients.

4. Group Therapy (Monday and Thursday mornings). Patients were divided into four groups, each led by a nurse or social worker, for traditional group therapy.

5. Rehash (Tuesday and Friday mornings). This was a "staff-only" meeting to discuss patients' requests for passes outside the Hospital and for promotions in the stepladder system of privileges and duties before these requests were presented to the patient community.

6. Advisory Board Meeting (Tuesday and Friday mornings). The Advisory Board was composed of five representatives elected by the patients. One of its functions was to vote on the patient requests that the staff discussed at Rehash. All patients and some staff members attended the Advisory Board Meeting to discuss the patients' requests, but only board members voted on them. Patients not on the Advisory Board participated in the meeting by discussing pass and status requests, thereby helping the board to reach its decision. As a rule, a patient whose request was under discussion was not permitted to participate in this discussion; this forced patients to discuss their requests with others before the meeting. In theory, the staff members participated in the meeting in the same capacity as the patients who were not board members. However, because they were seen as presenting the official views of the staff, their opinions were usually given greater weight.

7. Staff Review (Tuesday and Friday afternoons). The staff met to discuss the Advisory Board's decisions.

8. Patient–Staff Meeting (Tuesday and Friday afternoons). The staff discussed Advisory Board decisions with patients. Patients were notified which decisions of the Advisory Board would be allowed to stand and which would be vetoed. New patients were formally introduced to the community at this meeting; general announcements were made; and problems that affected the community as a whole were discussed.

9. Nurses' Team Meetings (Thursday). This meeting was designed to keep the nursing staff, which was divided into two groups, Team A and Team B, apprised of developments of each patient's case.

10. Staff Rounds (Monday–Friday). Each patient was discussed, and decisions about proposed treatments were made; these decisions were usually presented to the patients involved during the next day's Walking Rounds.

11. Nurses' Report (daily). The departing day shift of nurses informed nurses on the next shift of particular issues involving patients and kept them abreast of specific case developments.

12. Little Leaderless Groups (Monday–Wednesday and Friday afternoons). These were "patient-only" meetings in which small groups discussed individual problems, community issues, and gripes about staff and other patients. These were sometimes replaced by a "Big Leaderless Group" meeting, in which the entire patient community met for the same purposes without staff members.

13. Task Group. Meetings were organized around particular problems facing patients generally, such as obtaining a job or preparing for discharge. A staff member was present to assist.

14. Couples Group Therapy; Family Group Therapy (Tuesday and Thursday evenings). Groups of patients met with staff and family members to discuss marital and family issues and the problems faced by spouses and families of patients.

15. Wrap-Up (daily). This was the final meeting of each day, in which patients were called upon by the Advisory Board chairperson to discuss how their day had gone and to receive critiques from other patients and from staff members. Community issues were also discussed at this meeting, and general announcements made.

STEPLADDER STATUS SYSTEM

Another facet of the therapeutic community, alluded to above, was the stepladder status system. When patients entered the community, they were assigned the "bottom rung" status of "staff special" until the staff decided that they were ready to begin assuming some responsibility for their own behavior. At that point, the patients were promoted to "10-minute check" status. Future promotions were then largely in the hands of the patient community. Patients could earn promotions by behaving "appropriately" (i.e., keeping emotions in control, participating in meetings, discussing problems) and by evidencing an ability to assume responsibility for other patients. As status increased, responsibility in the community increased also. Those patients who attained "monitor" status or above were expected to supervise lower-status patients and to write reports on other patients' weekends and passes. Privileges also increased with status. While patients on "staff special" status were restricted to the floor, those on "10-minute check" status were permitted to go to the cafeteria for meals and to recreational activities. Those patients who attained the highest status, "4-hour open," were permitted to leave the Hospital unaccompanied for up to 4 hours daily and, with the approval of the staff and the Advisory Board, to take 12-hour passes on weekends and holidays.

TREATMENT ON THE RESEARCH WARD

Standard procedures included both those of a diagnostic and therapeutic nature. Diagnostic testing included routine physical examinations, psychological testing, the determination of the level of certain drugs in patients' blood, and "sleep studies."

Treatment on the Research Ward was of three general kinds: milieu therapy, psychotherapy, and somatic therapies.

MILIEU THERAPY

"Milieu therapy" is a term used to refer to the therapeutic aspects of the hospital environment itself. On the Research Ward, the two most important aspects of the milieu were the therapeutic community and the stepladder status system.

PSYCHOTHERAPY

In addition to the various kinds of group therapy that occurred in the context of patient meetings, each patient was assigned to a social worker who was supposed to be that patient's primary staff contact. Patients met individually with their social workers so that the social workers could obtain information about the patients and their families, discuss present problems that the patients were having, and help make plans for the future. The social workers also conducted marital or family therapy, involving family members as well as the patients.

SOMATIC THERAPIES

Medications

Almost all patients on the Research Ward received some sort of medication during their hospitalization. The most frequently used medications were tricyclic antidepressants, such as Elavil, Aventyl, Tofranil, and Sinequan; phenothiazines (antipsychotic drugs), such as Trilafon, Prolixin, Mellaril, and Thorazine;

other antipsychotic drugs, such as Haldol; and lithium carbonate (a mood stabilizer).[3]

Electroconvulsive Therapy

ECT, or "shock treatment," was used to treat some seriously depressed patients on the ward.[4]

"RESEARCH" PROCEDURES ON THE RESEARCH WARD

A wide variety of research projects was being undertaken at all times on the Research Ward. Our observations focused on only one of these projects, which we refer to here as the "Protocol." This was a study investigating the relationship between a patient's EEG taken while sleeping ("sleep-EEG") and the efficacy of Elavil, a tricyclic antidepressant drug, in the treatment of that patient's depression. Patients participating in the Protocol underwent the following procedures:

1. Two weeks without any drug treatment ("drug-free").
2. One week of treatment with placebo.
3. During the next 28 days, approximately 50% of the patients received increasing doses of Elavil, while the remainder continued to receive a placebo.

In addition to medication, research patients had nightly sleep-EEGs, thrice-weekly self-ratings of their mood, and psychological testing three times during the 28-day period.

The consent form that research patients signed read in part:

Consent Form: EEG Sleep in Affective Disease

Purpose: We are trying to assess the effectiveness of the antidepressant drug, amitriptyline (Elavil) in the treatment of depression. While there is considerable evidence that this drug may be helpful in some patients with depression, many people get better with no medication at all. Furthermore, the side effects of this antidepressant drug (blurred vision, weight gain, constipation, and irregular heart rate) may be troublesome. Therefore, we are conducting electroencephalographic (EEG) sleep studies in the hopes of developing a set of objective predictors identifying those people who require this drug specifically, in addition to the usual psychological and social treatments provided by the Hospital, to recover from their depressive episodes. . . .

For variable lengths of time during the study, you will be given inactive medication (placebo). Some patients will also be given the antidepressant drug, amitriptyline (Elavil) during this period of time. . . .

You must realize that while psychological and social treatments on the Research Ward are generally very beneficial to the treatment of depression, the study itself may provide no direct benefit to you. However, consent to participate is a requirement for admission to the Research Ward.

The primary risk of the Protocol for its participants was that if a patient was receiving inactive medication or was not responding to Elavil, treatment was delayed for the duration of the study. This was particularly risky in dealing with patients who were seriously depressed, because of the possibility that they might attempt suicide during the period in which they were not being treated. This risk did not materialize during the study, possibly because untreated or unresponding patients were concomitantly receiving milieu therapy. Some patients, the most severely depressed, were also withdrawn from the research when the need for additional treatment was deemed urgent. An additional risk for subjects lay in the side effects of Elavil, which are dizziness, weight gain, and dryness of the mouth.

Benefits of being a Protocol patient included extensive diagnostic studies, which, according to the principal investigator, uncovered previously undiagnosed physical and neurological conditions in approximately 10 to 15% of the persons studied. These patients were then dropped from the Protocol. The sleep studies also provided additional information on each patient's diagnosis and, in the case of those who received Elavil, offered some predictive data on future response to treatment. The reason most often cited by patients for participating in the research was the financial benefit. All costs of subsequent treatment for the duration of the hospitalization not covered by insurance were paid for by the research grant at no cost to the patients, even if patients were dropped from the Protocol before its completion.

INFORMED CONSENT ON THE RESEARCH WARD

The common law of informed consent was more clearly applicable in the Research Ward than in the Evaluation Center or the Outpatient Clinic. Procedures performed on the Research Ward, especially ECT and medications that involve significant risks, have been held by courts to require informed consent for their administration. But quite apart from the common law, there is a body of statutory and regulatory law—both state and federal—that is also relevant.

The Mental Health Procedures Act mandates that an "individualized treatment plan" be drawn up for each patient (§106). To the greatest extent possible, this plan is to be made with the cooperation, understanding, and consent of the patient (§107). Although the term "informed consent" is not used, these requirements mirror three elements of informed consent: voluntariness, understanding, and decision. The regulations echo the Act's mandate requiring that the treatment plan be formulated with the consultation of the patient or his or her family or legal guardian to the extent feasible, and that it be written in terms easily understood by the patient, to whom it is to be made available for review. The Patients' Bill of Rights, with which all patients are supposed to be furnished upon admission, informs patients that "You have the right to participate in the development and review of your treatment plan." Despite this assurance, however, no direct participation of patients in either the formulation or review of their treatment plans was observed, nor were any instances seen in which patients were shown their written treatment plans.

The treatment plans were much more extensive than were those in the Evaluation Center. Clyde Z's initial treatment plan, for example, read:

> Clyde Z is a 42 Y[ear] O[ld] W[hite] S[ingle] M[ale] $\bar{c}$ chief c/o [complaint of] depression and anxiety. R/O [rule out] (1) 1° affective disorder (2) Alcohol Abuse $\bar{c}$ 2° depression (3) Situational depression. There are as yet no signs or symptoms inconsistent $\bar{c}$ above diagnoses.
>
> Diagnostic procedures will include routine lab W/U [workup], EEG, EKG, Psych testing, [Vitamin] B_{12} level & Folate level. Observe for signs of D.T.'s [delirium tremens]. Place on Librium withdrawal schedule.
>
> Target symptoms include energy, irritability, concentration & memory (recent), interest in usual activities, morbid thoughts, death wish (fleeting) & sleep disorder.
>
> Non-psychiatric problems include peripheral neuropathy secondary to alcoholism, post operative TUR 1974 (removal of prostate gland) post op rt herniorrhaphy 1975, chronic obstructive pulmonary disease.
>
> Recommendations for drug rx [treatment] deferred until W/U is complete.
>
> Patient is a staff-special status & will be restricted to unit. Environmental supports will be investigated. Estimated length of stay 30-45 days.

While it is not clear whether this plan was ever shown to Mr. Z—nor, indeed, whether he could have understood the symbols and technical jargon if it had been—some of the information contained in it was conveyed to him orally.

In addition to the general requirement of consent to the treatment plan, one type of treatment in use on the Research Ward, ECT, may also have been subject to specific regulation. In any event, the common-law precedents were rather clear that informed consent had to be obtained either from the patient or from a relative to administer ECT.

The Mental Health Procedures Act does not specifically require informed consent to "research" procedures, as opposed to "accepted" procedures; nor does the initial regulations designed to implement it require such consent. However, regulations that were proposed shortly before the observations began and that went into effect shortly after they ended required that informed consent be obtained for all research procedures undertaken in psychiatric hospitals. Moreover, they required that all research be conducted in "strict compliance" with federal regulations for the protection of human research subjects, even when federal law would not so require.[5] These federal regulations required, among other protections for human research subjects, that informed consent be obtained.

A HYPOTHETICAL DAY ON THE RESEARCH WARD

Research Ward cases, unlike those of the Evaluation Center and the Outpatient Clinic, do not easily lend themselves to presentation as sample cases. Each individual case, involving anywhere from one to 20 major treatment decisions (e.g., the instituting of a new treatment, the modifying or discontinuing of an existing treatment, the scheduling of discharge, or the extending or revoking of privileges) that took place during an observation period ranging from 3 to 39 days was much too complex to summarize here. This complexity was exacerbated by the therapeutic community's requirement that every patient involve himself or herself in discussion with other patients, which resulted in each treatment decision being the product not only of the individual patient and the staff, but also of the community as well. For these reasons, the material we present to exemplify activity on the Research Ward is a conglomerate of several cases. The format is that of a day on the ward, although for reasons of clarity the day focuses only on a few patients rather than on the entire community. This is a hypothetical day, not any particular day that was observed, and it is not necessarily typical. Rather, it is a collection of bits and pieces of idiosyncratic data chosen from several days, interwoven to give a sense of informed consent issues on the Research Ward.

Janice Q's day began when another patient, a member of the "wake-up" committee, knocked on her door. She washed in the sink in her room, dressed, and then accompanied several other patients and the patient-observer to the cafeteria for breakfast. Over breakfast, the conversation revolved around Ms. Q and Brenda N. Ms. Q had completed her participation in the research Protocol the evening before and was eager to discover whether she had been receiving Elavil or placebo. She told the other patients that she had mixed feelings about which she preferred, saying that on the one hand she didn't want to be on any medication at all; but on the other, she felt that she needed some type of medications to cope with the world outside the Hospital.

Ms. N was sympathetic to Ms. Q's situation. She too had participated in the Protocol and, although she had been receiving the active medication, Ms. N had not significantly improved. Now after having tried several drug combinations without success, the staff was urging her to consent to ECT. She told her companions that, although she did not want to have ECT, she saw no other choice and repeatedly said, "If ECT doesn't work, then I'll go to the bridge." For approximately a week, as she struggled with the decision of whether or not to have ECT, Ms. N had been given extensive information about it by staff members. Thus when Lila C, another patient seated at the table, asked what ECT is like, Ms. N was able to describe it fairly thoroughly:

> "Well, you lie down and they give you an anesthetic and that relaxes you and then they put a little disc on one side of your head. It's unilateral, not bilateral, and you go into a convulsion. I don't like the idea and I'm scared of it. I'm scared because

the doctors don't know a great deal about how it works and I'm scared because I don't want to lose my memory. I saw how Renato [a former patient] was after ECT. He didn't know me and he got confused at meetings."

The other patients urged Ms. N to consent to ECT, telling her that it would help her and that the memory loss was only temporary. Ms. Q added, "You know it's best."

After breakfast, everyone returned to the ward and joined the rest of the community in the lounge for Walking Rounds. All of the patients sat in a circle, and two staff members—one of the psychiatrists or the physician's assistant, accompanied by the head nurse—walked from patient to patient engaging each in a discussion. The staff-observer walked with them, taking notes, while the patient-observer sat in the circle and recorded her observations only after the meeting had ended. Since Walking Rounds normally lasted from 45 minutes to 2 hours, and since each discussion took place within earshot of every other patient, it was not unusual for patients to obtain a great deal of information at this time just by listening to the staff's discussions with other patients.

Ms. Q listened to the staff's discussion with Lloyd G, who was seated to her right. Mr. G began the conversation by questioning one of the basic rules of the community:

PATIENT: I want to have a private conference with you.

DOCTOR: About what?

PATIENT: About my problems.

HEAD NURSE: This is why the other patients are here. I doubt very much if your problems are very different from theirs.

PATIENT: So okay. I'll forget it.

HEAD NURSE: That sounds like a kid who says he won't play any more.

PATIENT: I mean I will withdraw my request. I didn't know how it works here.

DOCTOR: In general, we don't encourage such things, both for practical reasons and because that's the way this place is set up, unless there's an unusual reason.

PATIENT: I think I have a lot of unusual reasons, even though they may not look so unusual to you.

HEAD NURSE: You should know that if the staff gets information about you, it goes back to the community. We are sharing information here, and we don't have secrets. And we don't want to be in the bind of giving certain patients special treatment. Maybe when you feel more comfortable you will be able to talk more freely.

PATIENT: Maybe.

HEAD NURSE: Are you as tense inside as you appear to be?

PATIENT: Yes. I'm on "constant observation" and I don't think I should be.

HEAD NURSE: Do you understand why?

PATIENT: Because you think I'm going to hurt myself.

HEAD NURSE: Did you try to commit suicide in the past?

PATIENT: No.

HEAD NURSE: But you've talked about it here.

PATIENT: I had tendencies, but they went away.

HEAD NURSE: Were these only thoughts?

PATIENT: Yes. I'm not going to hurt myself.

HEAD NURSE: When you thought about it, how did you think you would do it?

PATIENT: I thought about it not actively as I used to, but in a very passive way.

HEAD NURSE: But let's say you will have an active thought. Would you feel comfortable to tell someone?

PATIENT: Yes. I'm not going to hurt myself.

HEAD NURSE: But let's say that you did, who would you tell?

PATIENT: Someone in the staff. I'm talking with Brenda and Janice, but they will be leaving soon.

HEAD NURSE: Janice will still be here. Who do you know on the staff?

PATIENT: I don't remember names.

HEAD NURSE: (*After informally polling the staff members who were present.*) I've asked the staff members here, and they don't feel comfortable taking you off constant observation. We don't know you well enough. You talked about suicide.

PATIENT: I was misunderstood because I was thinking about it passively and not actively. I have humanistic rights that were taken away from me.

HEAD NURSE: Our duty towards you is to keep you alive.

PATIENT: I can't convince you that I'm not going to hurt myself.

HEAD NURSE: Not now. Not at this moment. Usually we are wrong, but we prefer to be this way rather than too lax.

PATIENT: But it hurts me. There are very few rights that I had, and they were taken away from me, and they mean much to me.

HEAD NURSE: That was the decision of the staff.

PATIENT: Well, I think the staff was wrong.

HEAD NURSE: I told you that's possible.

Dr. J and the Head Nurse moved on to Janice Q, who was the next patient in the circle. The Head Nurse began the discussion by making reference to this being the day that Ms. Q would discover whether she had been on active medication or placebo.

HEAD NURSE: Today's the day. What do you think?

PATIENT: I really don't know. I'm not certain about it at all.

DOCTOR: If it turns out that you are on placebo, I want to put you on Aventyl. That's what Elavil turns into in your body after it's been metabolized, and I prefer to give you Aventyl. (*Patient smiles.*) The reason is because it's easier to measure your blood level. We're sure of the therapeutic level of Aventyl, but we're not sure about the Elavil. In fact, part of our research is about trying to establish that. That's why we take the blood samples. So if you're on placebo, I'd like to start you on Aventyl.

HEAD NURSE: We are going to open the capsules today.

PATIENT: What if I was on Elavil?

DOCTOR: So then we'll need to think. I also want to see your sleep studies before I make a decision. In the near future I'll go over them with you.

PATIENT: I feel a little better, but I don't know if it's because of medication or because of the group therapy and couples therapy.

DOCTOR: Do you know how many symptoms are from you and how many are from your husband?

PATIENT: My husband called me last night, and he was in very bad shape. He drank a lot. He feels threatened that he gets worse as I get better.

HEAD NURSE: What will he do if you leave?

PATIENT: I don't know. Maybe it will make him a new person.

DOCTOR: He doesn't consider himself an alcoholic, but according to you he is. There gets to be a point where they hit bottom. Also, he's talking about suicide, and he's a higher risk for that.

PATIENT: Yes, the social worker we see for couples therapy mentioned that.

DOCTOR: Everything predicts it: white, male, alcoholic, with depression, problems with his job. Do you know if he's trying to blackmail you?

PATIENT: I don't know.

DOCTOR: Be aware that it's possible that one day he will kill himself.

Ms. Q buried her face in her hands and began to sob.

PATIENT: I don't know anything that will work. I can't handle it.

HEAD NURSE: Because of all the binds.

DOCTOR: I know that it upsets you, but we want you to be aware of that, so you can start dealing with it and talking about it. Also, you should be aware that, as she told you, he puts you in a bind. He makes you responsible for his problems.

PATIENT: I don't know whether to stick around or get out. I can't handle it. Everything becomes worse. I thought I could handle it before and I couldn't. If I couldn't before, I won't be able to now.

HEAD NURSE: To leave or to stay?

PATIENT: To get him to stop drinking. It's getting worse, and it will only continue to get worse.

HEAD NURSE: I don't think that you can help that. But it's difficult not to feel responsible. I understand.

PATIENT: I'm not sure where the responsibility stops. I also have a responsibility to the children and myself. I don't want to get down. (*She clenched her fists.*) He's very angry that I'm not home, that I don't have a discharge date.

HEAD NURSE: That will probably continue as you get better and stronger.

DOCTOR: As for a discharge date, we want things to get more straightened out. You have a number of major problems.

PATIENT: Yes. They are biggies.

DOCTOR: They sure are. I wish I didn't have to tell you about the suicide, but it's important that you be aware of the potential realities.

PATIENT: I'd rather know.

The doctor and nurse then moved on to the next patient, and Ms. Q continued to sob intermittently throughout the remainder of Walking Rounds. Each patient had at least a brief discussion with the doctor and the nurse. After the rounds had ended, Dr. J asked the Head Nurse if she thought this had been "too much" for Ms. Q, and she said that she thought it had been "OK." Dr. J then went into the hall and talked to Ms. Q privately for a few moments. This discussion was not observed, but it is clear that he told her that she had been receiving placebo in Protocol. She then joined a group of other patients for group therapy.

The staff then had a Rehash meeting to discuss pass and status requests. There was some discussion of the wisdom of permitting Cora T to attain "monitor" status, which would give her access to areas of the building from which egress was possible. This was a particularly crucial question at this time, as her 20-day commitment was due to expire, and the staff planned to seek recommitment for 60 days because she refused to remain in the Hospital voluntarily.

NURSE A: If she's going to be court-committed, she'll stay here and she probably won't try to leave.

NURSE B: She'll leave.

DR. M: If she wanted to be court-committed, she'd probably sign herself in.

The issue was discussed for some time, some staff members favoring the status increase and others opposing it. The matter was not resolved.

The staff was also hesitant to approve Clyde Z's pass request, because they feared that he would drink. Dr. M settled this issue by fiat, ordering the staff to "[t]ell him that if he's going to drink while on weekend pass, he'll be kicked out."

It was also at this staff meeting that Dr. J informed the staff that Janice Q had been receiving placebo. They responded with silence, and he continued:

DR. J: I also saw her sleep [studies] and it looked much worse than I thought. The REM latency [time from falling asleep to onset of dreaming] was about 30 or 40 minutes. I want to start her on Aventyl in order to know her therapeutic blood level.

HEAD NURSE: She's such a nice lady.

The staff-observer noted an air of sadness among the staff members, many of whom made comments to the effect that they really liked her.

After briefly discussing the other pass and status requests that had been submitted, the nurses who normally attended the Advisory Board Meeting went to the lounge where the patients had already assembled.

The meeting was called to order by the chairperson of the Advisory Board, Brenda N. The secretary, Janice Q, read each pass or status request before it came up for discussion. The first request brought up was that of Noelle H, who had requested a weekend pass. Initially, the discussion was in favor of granting it. Two patients praised Ms. H's self-control and expressed confidence that she would return to the Hospital if she encountered any problems. Another stressed the importance of Ms. H's having the opportunity to readjust to her home and maintain social contacts outside the therapeutic community. A nurse raised her hand and addressed her comments directly to Ms. H, telling her that she did not look as if she were doing well and adding:

NURSE: I don't see the logic of sending you out on pass to a stressful situation. We've tried such things in the past and failed. Again, what's the logic? Passes for two days—one of your complaints is that you find it stressful to be with your daughter. (*She turned to the Advisory Board members.*) I don't want you to give a pass to someone who isn't ready, because it will just hurt her.

Ms. N: I think I'm going to make an enemy of someone.

Ms. H: It's OK.

Ms. N: Yesterday Noelle talked on the phone and she was shaken up. She was also complaining a lot of anxiety, a feeling of being inadequate with her daughter. She was also concerned about her dizziness [a side effect of her medication]. Two days is a little too much. It would be better if her husband would just take her to Mapleton as a "Buddy."

Ms. H: Is it possible to take a shorter pass, like only 2 hours?

NURSE: We'll have to vote on the pass as it is. In a situation like this, it had to be planned and discussed outside these meetings. Vote on the passes as they are now.

The request was brought to a vote and defeated 5-0, although one board member then said that she had changed her mind, and the vote was revised to 4-1.

Clyde Z's pass request came up next.

Ms. E: I know that he wants to get out and just walk out in the nice weather.

Ms. C: It will add a lot to his confidence.

NURSE: (*After a pause.*) Why is everyone so quiet? It seems that many patients don't know much about Clyde's passes.

Ms. Q: Does Clyde intend to see people?

MR. Z: I always see my friends.

Ms. Q: Well, usually it's mentioned on the pass.

Ms. E: Clyde mentioned to me that he's going to see friends.

Ms. H: It's very important that he will be with someone because he's a loner.

Ms. D: It will be good for him to be with his nephews.

Ms. Q: Do you have definite plans to go and visit your nephews?

MR. Z: Yes.

Ms. Q: (*To the nurse.*) His anger has calmed down, and also the fact that he doesn't shake now adds to his confidence. Also, it sounds as though his pass is more planned.

The request was brought to a vote and passed 4-0. Although he was a member of the Advisory Board, Mr. Z was not permitted to vote on his own request.

Cora T was not present when her status increase was discussed, because she had been sent to Medical Hospital for treatment of a physical problem. Discussion was negative, and several patients expressed fear that she would not be capable of handling the responsibilities of "monitor" status—in particular, that she would not be able to escort lower-ranking patients to the cafeteria and be responsible for their well-being. There was also some discussion of whether she would use the increased status to escape, and when the vote was taken, her request was unanimously denied.

Later in the meeting, Ms. T returned. When all of the requests had been voted on, she asked what had happened to hers:

BRENDA N: It was turned down.

FAYE C: I talked against you because as a monitor it would be very difficult to keep you from leaving the building.

BRAD C: I voted against you.

BRENDA N: I did too, because I don't think that you are capable of handling yourself.

MILDRED L: I didn't think you would be able to be responsible for others.

JANICE Q: You said that no one is going to keep you here and that you'll leave. We still don't know what will happen [with the extended commitment], but if you do have to stay here, and you're a monitor, you'll probably leave, which will be detrimental to you.

FELICIA E: I voted against you for the same reasons. As a monitor you'll leave the building without anyone and just stay out.

CORA T: You haven't tried it yet.

STANLEY G: Even as a 10-minute check, you wouldn't stay with your monitor in the cafeteria.

CORA T: (*Angrily.*) Next week I'll be out anyway. I don't care why you voted. I'm just sorry I came here in the first place and I'm leaving next week.

Ms. T then stood up and walked out of the meeting, something that was almost never done.

The Advisory Board Meeting adjourned, and the patients went to lunch. Over lunch, the conversation centered on the drug Aventyl, which Noelle H, Phyllis D, and now Janice Q were receiving. Ms. Q asked Ms. H whether she felt any better.

Ms. H: Yeah, I can dance around now. No, really, I feel dizzy. I don't know why they gave me Aventyl because that's an antidepressant, and I was on it before, and I got dizzy, and I think that I need a sedative, and there's no sedative in that. I'd just give my right arm for a tranquilizer.

Ms. D: I don't feel any more relaxed on it. My sleep has improved a little bit, but a couple of evenings ago I was really hyped up, and I just had to go out for a walk, and I walked all the way to the park and back just to get myself calmed down. I'm going to give this 4 weeks . . . no . . . maybe 5 weeks and then I'll hit the Old GrandDad again.

Ms. H: Well, I don't really want anything that isn't going to calm me down because I'm really anxious, but I guess I will go with this program because I have a history of stubbornness with medicines, so I will give it a try to the end.

Ms. Q: Who said that?

Ms. H: He did. Dr. J said it at the last meeting that I had with him. I guess he's right and I should try this stuff out to the end.

The patients returned from lunch and lined up for their 12:30 medications. Meanwhile, the staff members were in Staff Review, considering the votes of the Advisory Board.

DR. J: It must be explained to [Clyde Z] that he just shouldn't drink. In the future, when someone is scheduled for diagnostic studies, he shouldn't be allowed to go on pass, because it's just a waste of time and money.

PHYSICIAN'S ASSISTANT: Do you want me to give him a urine test when he comes back from the pass?

DR. J: No, I'll just tell him that if he's going to drink, I'll discharge him.

They were pleased with the vote on Ms. T's request, but several expressed surprise that Ms. H's pass had been denied.

NURSE A: Probably they would have given it to her if I didn't interfere. The pass didn't sound too well planned.

HEAD NURSE: She probably just wanted to go home to take pills.

NURSE A: I agree, but I didn't want to bring that up, because I'd already brought up other things.

NURSE B: Ms. H understands and seems relieved that it was denied.

After discussing the other Advisory Board votes and deciding that Lloyd G should continue on constant observation, the Staff Review dispersed, and staff members joined patients in the lounge for the Patient-Staff Meeting. Dr. M chaired this meeting. A nurse began by announcing the staff's decisions as to which patients could be promoted to "10-minute check" status, and other staff members began to bring up the other issues for the meeting. A psychiatric aide brought up Clyde Z, asking if community members knew his plans for his pass. After several patients had spoken, two nurses entered the discussion:

NURSE A: Remember, Mr. Z, that you can come back if you feel bad.

NURSE B: What about drinking?

MR. Z: I don't have any intentions of drinking. I came here to be cured. If I drink I'll just be wasting my time. I want to give it a chance, give it a try.

PSYCHIATRIC AIDE: I'm very glad to hear that the community feels you are responsible, because drinking will just corrupt your sleep studies next week. Why was Ms. T's status request denied?

Various patients explained that she hadn't behaved in a responsible manner as a "10-minute check."

Ms. T: Can I say a word? I was responsible. All those stories about me aren't true.

A PATIENT: She isn't really a big problem.

DR. M: Anyway, the fact is that it was denied. Apply again. In the future, one day, it will pass.

After this meeting staff members returned to the conference room for Staff Rounds, a daily meeting in which staff members kept one another apprised of each patient's treatment and progress. Dr. J began the meeting by notifying the staff that he had taken steps to extend Ms. T's commitment, and that the hearing would be held the following week:

DR. J: I told Ms. T that, and she didn't have much to say.

PSYCHIATRIC AIDE: Do you want her mother to be at the hearing?

DR. J: I don't know. It won't hurt. My thesis is that she is psychiatrically sick, and that I don't think she will cooperate on an outpatient basis. I'm not at all sure that the court won't just discharge her.

DR. M: She looks better.

DR. J: She's in a grey area.

The discussion then turned to Noelle H's treatment with Aventyl.

NURSE: Today she told her husband she's going to kill him if he won't come here and bug Dr. J to give her something. She still wants the Sinequan[6] and not the Aventyl. I told her to forget that. Noelle says that everything is worse—her sleep and everything.

DR. J: I told her that on Friday she can choose and try anything she wants to try. I talked with her a number of times.

The discussion then turned to Clyde Z.

SOCIAL WORKER: Whatever he's on, he's much, much better.

HEAD NURSE: He's only on Dalmane [sleeping medicine] now.

NURSE: There's so much change in him—he isn't irritable any more.

PSYCHIATRIC AIDE: Is he definitely leaving on the 18th?

DR. J: Yes. I suggest he be referred to the alcohol clinic for follow-up.

SOCIAL WORKER: He's going to be offended because he doesn't think of himself as an alcoholic.

DR. J: We can try [the] General Psychiatry or Mood [Clinics]. I really don't care where he goes. Anything that Mr. Z would want, like General Psychiatry or the Alcohol Clinic, would be fine with me.

PSYCHIATRIC AIDE: Dr. J, what will the discharge diagnosis be? Do we write him up as an alcoholic or as depressed?

DR. J: It depends on what clinic we're sending him to.

There was also some discussion of the suicide threats of Janice Q's husband.

HEAD NURSE: Ms. Q's husband told her that he may shoot himself or hang himself on the basement pipes. He was drunk.

PHYSICIAN'S ASSISTANT: She's afraid to talk with him about their marriage.

HEAD NURSE: Nick [the physician's assistant] and I suggested to Ms. Q to wait until the session with you before she discusses divorce with him.

SOCIAL WORKER: How did Ms. Q respond?

PHYSICIAN'S ASSISTANT: She was angry.

HEAD NURSE: She felt that she was in a bind.

NURSE: Her husband apparently doesn't want her to get off the medicine. It's a projection, because he needs the medicine himself.

DR. J: From what I hear about her alcoholic husband, he is a prime candidate for suicide.

SOCIAL WORKER: The situation with his job has deteriorated.

At the same time that the staff members were meeting for Staff Rounds, the patients had organized themselves into Little Leaderless Groups, one of the few meetings in the therapeutic community at which staff members were not present. The topic of discussion was medication, and Cora T expressed curiosity as to whether she could drink any alcohol while on Trilafon and Prolixin.

Ms. N: I suggest that you talk to Dr. J or [the physician's assistant] about it, but its probably better to err on the side of sobriety and not to take too much to drink. I've been told that the effects of alcohol are increased due to drug intake.

Ms. T: The thing is the holidays, like Christmas time. Do you think it would be best to do what they do here [i.e., before Protocol] and go 2 weeks drug-free?

Ms. Q: No. Definitely not. You should never go off the medication without discussing it with a doctor.

Ms. N: I think it would be best if you talk to [one of the nurses]. He knows an awful lot about medicines, and he'll tell you as much if not more than any of the doctors could.

Ms. Q: Yeah. He's a mine of information. I agree that you should do that.

After this meeting, the patients had a few hours of free time, which was used by those on requisite status to go to other areas of the Hospital (such as the patient library or the recreation room) or to leave the Hospital for a walk or shopping. The patient-observer often accompanied such patients, engaging them in informal discussions of treatment and the therapeutic community. Meanwhile, the day-shift staff was preparing to leave, and the evening shift was arriving. Information was exchanged between these two groups at another meeting, the Nurses' Report. The nurse who led this meeting brought up each patient briefly, detailing treatment changes and notifying the evening shift of particular situations, such as Cora T's pending recommitment and Janice Q's having been on placebo (as well as her husband's threats of suicide).

At 5 P.M., the patients returned to the ward for medications, and those on requisite status went to the cafeteria for dinner. The patient-observer sat down with Ms. T and attempted to discuss her pending commitment hearing.

OBSERVER: Did you talk to Dr. J in his office recently?

Ms. T: Yes.

OBSERVER: What went on?

Ms. T: He gave me the Bill of Rights or something.

OBSERVER: What was on that?

Ms. T: Oh, it says I can have a lawyer.

OBSERVER: Are you going to get one?

Ms. T: They said they are going to get me one. I don't want to talk about it.

At this point, the patient-observer broke off the discussion, and other patients began to chide Ms. T about walking out of the Advisory Board Meeting.

MR. Z: You should think about controlling your emotions. Like what you did, just getting up and walking out, that ain't natural. You know, I think you should just grin and bear it no matter what they say.

Ms. N: That's right. If you're upset with the treatment they're giving you here, you should ask to be transferred to another floor.

Ms. T then returned to the topic of her commitment, mentioning that she had talked about it with a social worker.

Ms. T: [The social worker] wants me to sign in if they don't commit me.

OBSERVER: Why?

Ms. T: So they can regulate the medicine. I'm taking Trilafon and Prolixin to calm my thoughts.

OBSERVER: Are they doing you any good?

Ms. T: I think they're calming my thoughts, but my arms get stiff, my tongue gets thick, and I have blurred vision. In any case, I think I can get my medicine regulated in a community mental health center, and it's not necessary for me to be in a hospital for that.

OBSERVER: Are you going to the hearing?

Ms. T: Probably.

OBSERVER: Why?

Ms. T: I want to hear what they say about me.

OBSERVER: Why don't you want to stay in the Hospital?

Ms. T: I want to get back to my apartment and get involved in volunteer work and get involved with the church again.

After dinner, the patients had free time for visitors, although most of the married patients were required to attend a Couples Therapy meeting with their spouses.

The patient community reconvened at 9 P.M. for Wrap-Up, the final meeting of the day. Discussion focused on Noelle H, who told the others that Dr. J had told her that he would go over the results of her sleep studies that had been completed several days before sometime the following day.

Ms. H: He told me that my sleep studies are equivocal. I know that means they are open to interpretation, but I don't really know what that means here. I was standing at the desk earlier today with my head down and Dr. J came by and did a loving thing. He put his hand on the back of my neck and said, "Friday, OK?" I said, "What?" and he said he was going to give me medication until Friday. He's a kind, sweet man, even though he doesn't say much.

TABLE 9-1. Research Ward Patients

Patient	Age	Race	Marital status	Education	Occupation	Discharge diagnosis	Number of prior admissions
Mack S	48	W	D	5G	Dishwasher	Depression	1
Brenda N	36	W	M	—	Homemaker	Depression	1
Mildred L	15	W	S	9G	Student	Anorexia nervosa	1
Bruce T	39	W	M	TS	Bridge inspector	Depression	1
Renato I	41	W	M	TS	Cable splicer	Depression	1
Chet H	57	W	M	8G	Core maker	Depression	1
Martin T	20	W	S	HS	Stock clerk	Drug abuse; secondary depression	1
Alphonse S	41	W	M	DDS	Dentist	Depression	1
Max I	28	W	D	Coll	Sales clerk	Paranoid schizophrenia	2
Jodie T	29	W	M	BA	Counselor	Schizo-affective disease; schizo-depression	1
Dwayne T	29	W	M	BA	CPA	Probable dystonia musculorum deformans	0
Priscilla C	39	W	M	HS	Homemaker	Unipolar depression	4
Lila C	18	W	S	Coll	Stock clerk	Paranoid schizophrenia; drug abuse	1
Cora T	33	W	D	10G	Companion	Paranoid schizophrenia	7
Timothy M	37	W	M	11G	Garage owner	Psychotic depression	1
Samantha M	26	W	M	Coll	Homemaker	Depression associated with epilepsy	6
Rosali I	46	W	S	HS	Housekeeper	Schizo-affective disease; schizo-depression	1
Felicia E	36	B	Sep	HS	Sales clerk	Depression; alcohol abuse	0
Harriet L	52	W	S	8G	Housekeeper	Depression; overdose with Valium	0

Name	Age	Race	Marital	Education	Occupation	Diagnosis	
Lucy T	66	W	M	—	Sales clerk	Chronic schizophrenia; possible brain syndrome	29
Justin M	35	W	D	TS	Surveyor	Chronic alcoholism; secondary depression	3
Clyde Z	42	W	S	HS	Chef	Chronic alcohol abuse, acute episode; secondary depression	0
Brad C	49	W	M	Coll	Draftsman	Depression	2
Faye C	43	W	M	TS	Homemaker	Drug reaction; chronic alcoholism; depression	7
Christine E	25	W	S	TS	Cashier	Depression	2
Werner G	55	W	M	Coll	Postal clerk	Psychotic depression (chronic)	5
Janice Q	38	W	M	Coll	Homemaker	Depression, status post overdose; secondary to depression	0
Stanley G	21	W	S	Coll	Short-order cook	Adjustment reaction of adolescence	0
Phyllis D	35	W	M	HS	Homemaker	Manic depression	0
Velma B	62	W	W	8G	Laundress	Manic depression	7
Karen H	19	W	S	HS	Waitress	Primary affective disorder	2
Leonard T	28	W	S	DDS	Dentist	Depression, post suicide attempt by hanging	1
Noelle H	28	W	M	Coll	Homemaker	Depression	1
Graham X	64	W	M	9G	Maintenance worker	Psychotic depression	2
Edward M	38	W	Sep	PhD	College professor	None	Multiple
Lloyd G	50	W	M	BS	Business owner	Manic depression	4
Stella L	56	W	M	—	Homemaker	Depression	5
Eloise T	22	W	D	Coll	—	Polydrug abuse; affective disorder probably secondary	3
Molly X	42	W	M	MS	Homemaker	Manic depression	0
Jeremy D	31	W	D	MS	High school teacher	Unipolar depression; borderline personality	4
Pearl M	22	W	M	Coll	Telephone operator	Adult adjustment reaction; drug abuse	0

ELOISE T: I agree.

Ms. H: I had a meeting with [my social worker], though, and she said that if I didn't agree with the treatment plan by Friday, I should leave. My husband said, "What do you mean? Noelle is either sick here or she's sick outside where she can kill herself." I think if I didn't have a history of a bad attitude towards drugs before, then they wouldn't be doing this. They would be looking at me and knowing that I was a sick girl and I needed to be taken off this Aventyl before now because it is making me sick. It's making me feel real ill, and Dr. J gave it to me before.

KAREN H: Did you have it before for this length of time?

Ms. H: Yes.

Ms. Q: Pat also is on Aventyl and is getting better after awhile.

Ms. D: Yeah. I was real cranky in the beginning. In fact this last week I was, and I've been on it over 2 weeks now. It was just on Friday that I began to feel better.

Ms. H: Well, drugs act differently on different people. You just think because it worked for Phyllis that it's going to work for me. All I know is that I didn't expect that I would feel worse than I did before I came in here, and I do.

PSYCHIATRIC AIDE: Well, not everybody who comes here is at the lowest point of their illness, and it could be that your illness is just running its normal course here in the Hospital.

Ms. H: Yes, I know, but the options are running out for me. I've tried almost every antidepressant drug and that's what really worries me.

Ms. Q: Well, perhaps if we all wish really hard, then tomorrow will be the time when you'll begin to feel better. Let's hope so.

Ms. H smiled weakly, and the discussion turned to other topics. Brenda N kept the discussion going by asking different patients how their days had gone.

After Wrap-Up, Lloyd G was sitting in the lounge with the staff member who was observing him, and Janice Q and the patient-observer joined them.

MR. G: I'm just wondering what are the alternatives to Protocol. I'm thinking of getting off it because some people here I know get treated in 3 weeks.

Ms. Q: Well, why do you want to do that?

MR. G: Well, it seems like a long time. It's going to be more than 6 weeks and I want to get home and get things taken care of.

Ms. Q: Well, first off, what's your insurance like?

MR. G: I don't have any at all.

Ms. Q: Oh, well, one of the good things for [my husband and me] was that with the Protocol, they pick up the tab. All that your insurance doesn't cover, they cover. Also, if you're on Protocol, you get to talk to more people, and they give you more tests.

MR. G: I think I have more problems than anyone here.

Ms. Q: Well, have you discussed these problems with your wife?

Mr. G: No. She doesn't know everything. I have a lot of financial problems. I have two lawsuits pending against me, and I think that's what's led me in here, and I've been sick for 9 years.

The discussion continued for a few minutes, until another patient told Janice Q that she had a phone call, and she left to take it. Shortly afterwards, the patients got their last medication of the day. Those who were undergoing diagnostic or research sleep studies went to the sleep study lab.

CONCLUSION

The above is not a statistically adequate description of the Research Ward. However, it should give the reader some picture of the routine and how issues were handled on the ward. In order to provide a more detailed picture of each patient, basic information about each patient is included in Table 9-1.

Among the 41 patients that we studied on the Research Ward during our 7 weeks of observation, eight participated in the Protocol at some time during these observations, while five others had previously participated during this hospitalization prior to the beginning of our observations.

This information should facilitate comprehension of the next two chapters, in which we describe the disclosure, understanding, and decisionmaking process in more detail.

Information Flow on the Research Ward

THE COLLECTIVE NATURE OF INFORMATION

A central feature of the information on the Research Ward was that most disclosure was done during the daily Walking Rounds. In these rounds, as noted in Chapter 9, two staff members—usually one of the psychiatrists and the head nurse—slowly walked around a circle in which all of the patients were seated. While each patient was addressed individually, the discussion was public and usually could be heard by everyone in the room. As a result, who constituted the "audience" of any particular piece of information was unclear. While in the Evaluation Center (and, as we see later, in the Outpatient Clinic) information was given to one patient at a time (with an occasional friend or family member present), on the Research Ward patients were informed primarily collectively, as a community. The audience for staff disclosure was typically not only the patient but also the entire community.

The Research Ward based its treatment philosophy in part on the concepts of "milieu therapy" and "therapeutic community." The staff emphasized time and again that the idea of a therapeutic community meant that they should not meet with patients in private. Thus, as much as possible, they tried to avoid private disclosures.

No type of information was ever communicated to patients solely on an individual basis and in private. Although a few types of information were often communicated in private, they were the exceptions to the rule of public disclosure. Some types of information were conveyed to patients by staff members only on a collective basis. New admissions, conclusive discharge dates, staff endorsements or vetoes of the patients' Advisory Board decisions concerning weekend passes and status requests, and special announcements (e.g., a prospective visit by an inspection team, changes made in the daily or weekly ward schedule, a suicide of an ex-patient, and the pending departure of the chief of the unit) were communicated only to the community at large at the Tuesday and Friday Patient–Staff Meetings. Most other types of information—in particular, information regarding treatment, general information about research, and most information about diagnostic tests—were almost always disclosed to all patients as a group.

The Research Ward staff knew very well that they were communicating with the whole group of patients when they talked to a specific patient in group meetings. They often did this quite deliberately. The chief of the unit told our staff-observer that often a piece of information addressed to one patient in particular was meant to be "overheard" by other patients as well. Thus, before telling Eloise T that she would be kicked out of the unit if she brought any drugs onto the ward, the other psychiatrist told our staff-observer that he wanted to emphasize this not only for Ms. T, but also for all the other patients as well. Even when the staff did not have such deliberate intentions, the public nature of the Walking Rounds meant that most of the information they conveyed was public anyway.

Daily rounds may be viewed as having had the latent function of being educational sessions for the entire community. Thus when the risks involved in ECT (shock therapy) were discussed several times during Walking Rounds with Brenda N, not only Ms. N but also the other patients could hear what they were. Patients could and did use such information when they themselves were supposed to consider that treatment. Likewise, when the psychiatrist discussed a discharge date with Mildred L, the rest of the community had access to and could make use of information about the way staff arrived at their decisions concerning discharge.

While we never observed that staff members held patients accountable for information that was given to other patients during Walking Rounds, patients could and did learn much more about treatment than simply what the staff told them personally. Evaluation Center patients (and, as we see later, Outpatient Clinic patients) did not have such educational opportunities.

The structure of information disclosure affected the way we came to analyze patients' understanding on the ward. Patients in a real sense shared their knowledge collectively, both because it was addressed to them as a group and because they continually discussed treatment with one another, preserving in the process a body of patient knowledge that existed independent of any specific patient's knowledge. We refer to this knowledge as the "collective understanding" of the patients. In our analysis of understanding on the Research Ward, we outline the "collective understanding" of the patients about treatment and only then discuss why particular patients' understanding differed from the group's. This collective understanding was the belief of every patient without being anyone's in particular. This is not to say that these were beliefs that every patient agreed with in all situations. Rather, by "collective understanding," we mean beliefs and assumptions that were routinely stated without challenge by members of the group in the presence of any random collection of group members as being generally true.

SOURCES OF COLLECTIVE UNDERSTANDING

The doctrine of informed consent implies that the information provided by the doctor is the core of technical information that the patient needs to understand in order to make a decision. Our observations on the Research Ward indicate that, while patients did obtain information about treatment from doctors and other staff members, there were other, more significant, sources of explicit information.

PAST EXPERIENCE AS INFORMATION

In discussing treatment among themselves, the primary source of information that patients referred to was their own past experience with psychiatric treatment, which for the majority of patients had been considerable. Consider a few typical uses of the patients' past experiences:

1. In Wrap-Up, Karen H asked Lloyd G whether he had any hope that this place would help him, and he said that, yes, he did have some hope. He said that he had been taking lithium before, and this had helped him to curb his highs . . . so that his manic episodes were not so extended, but the lithium didn't seem to help him in the times when he got depressed, and he was depressed right now. He said it seemed that every couple of years he needed to be hospitalized because he just got to the point where he couldn't function at all.

2.   PHYSICIAN'S ASSISTANT: Do you think any of your problems will be resolved by medicine?

     MILDRED L: I don't have much faith in medicine. It never helped me. I was on Prolixin, and it didn't help me, and also aspirin doesn't solve my headaches. They just don't help. I just don't understand how pills can make you feel happier.

OTHER PATIENTS AS SOURCES OF INFORMATION

A close second in importance as a source of information was the treatment experience of other patients. Patients learned from the stories that others told them and from watching what happened to others. Patients who had been on the ward for a substantial period of time had a fairly large sample of experiences of others to draw upon. Brenda N, who was being encouraged by the staff to get ECT, told the staff in Walking Rounds, "Well, I've seen a number of people in the unit get it, and I just don't want it." Later the same day she told the patient observer, "Look at Martin. I don't think it did him any good, and he's had a few of them." Five days later, when she was leaning toward ECT, Ms. N said in Wrap-Up that Ethel, a patient who had been discharged weeks before and who had received ECT, had written her to say she was doing very well. An aide asked, "Has all this had any effect on your decision about ECT?" and Ms. N responded, "Yes, it has given me hope because I know what she went through, and I know she was on Protocol, and I know all the stages of treatment and how ECT helped in the end."

Nor were other patients hesitant to offer their own experiences and other information about treatment. They often volunteered information on their own initiative. Thus, when Harriet L expressed worries about the cost of hospitalization, Brenda N and Janice Q, who had both been on Protocol, carefully explained that as a Protocol patient the cost of her hospitalization would be paid by the research grant. Similarly, when Bruce T complained about not knowing the purpose of the Cogentin prescribed for him, Martin T, who had taken it for some time, explained that it was supposed to take care of the side effects caused by the other medications.

OTHER SOURCES OF INFORMATION

While it is not possible with our methods to provide exact measures of the extent to which various sources of information were used by patients, references to staff statements were less than one-third as frequent as references to either the patients' own experience or the experiences of others. Staff statements were referred to slightly more than any other remaining sources individually, however. Even then, staff-provided information was not always referred to with confidence. For instance, Lloyd G sought reassurance from the patient-observer that what the staff told him about the Protocol was correct. He asked, "This is a 6-week deal, huh? That's what they say," and then asked if they would give him Elavil after that. This is not to say that patients never used what staff members told them in making decisions. For example, Leonard T did decide to take ECT largely because his doctor told him it would get him better faster.

Interestingly, other sources of official information were referred to by patients almost as much as the staff's overt communications were. Information posted on ward bulletin boards and material taken from magazines and newspapers were used with considerable frequency by patients when trying to evaluate treatment courses. Several patients learned of their proposed discharge dates when staff members wrote them on the blackboard in the staff meeting room, which was also used for weekly group therapy meetings. On one occasion, a patient checked the side effects of the drug Aventyl in the *Physicians' Desk Reference* because she was skeptical about what she thought her doctor had told her about the absence of risks associated with the drug (her account of what the doctor had said was different from what the staff-observer had recorded).

Direct staff communication to patients was not as significant a source of information as the doctrine of informed consent assumes that it will be, in part because patients' contact with the doctors was largely restricted to Walking Rounds. Although patients complained frequently among themselves about the difficulties of getting access to their doctors, they asked few detailed questions about their treatment even in Walking Rounds. Mostly they simply responded to the questions asked by doctors and nurses. In part, the reason lies in the patients' feelings about the doctors and about Walking Rounds, as this discussion illustrates:

> Priscilla C [a new patient] said, "How do you manage to say things in front of other people like that?" [referring to talking about personal matters in groups]; and Brenda N said, "Oh, you just ask someone and get them to tell you my story. It wasn't always that way. . . . All new patients feel like that." Mildred L said, "Yeah, everybody gets nervous before they go into those things. I know I do. And then doctors' rounds are the worst. My hands get really sweaty and it's really just awful. I get really nervous. . . ." Ms. N added, "Yeah, I used to get sweaty until they gave me Trilafon, and now I just don't have the physical capacity to get sweaty in my hands, but I still feel really nervous."

It was not just contact with the doctors during Walking Rounds that was difficult for the patients. Patients were anxious about approaching the doctors and other staff members in other situations as well. For example, the patient-observer noted:

> Brad C began to talk about the fact that he has some aches and pains. He said, "I don't know whether these are side effects or what. You don't really like to be running to them with every little thing."

Or, on another occassion:

> Phyllis D and Janice Q and [the patient-observer] were sitting in the lower lounge when [Ms. D's doctor] walked to the elevator from the staff room. Ms. D said, "If I had the courage I'd go up and ask him what was happening with my sleep studies." After some encouragement from Ms. Q, Ms. D did go and ask.

These and other comments from patients reflected a perception of a large status difference between themselves and the staff. Most patients found it hard to question the doctors in any detail, because they saw the doctors as being very busy and too important to be concerned with their troubles. However, this raises the question of why the patients did not question the lower-status staff members more about their treatment. The answer is not clear, but it is possible that there is a sort of "Catch-22" phenomenon here. The lower-level staff members were easier to approach because their status *was* lower; but *because* their status was lower, they were also seen as being less knowledgeable and therefore less worthy of being questioned. This was reflected in the way in which lower-level staff members gave patients advice. They tended to cite "research" and "studies" to support their advice, and they sometimes began with personal disclaimers about the limits of their knowledge. One patient suggested to another that they might ask a night nurse about a drug that the second patient was getting. However, the context makes clear that this nurse had an exceptional knowledge of drugs and their effects.

Thus the staff was only one of a series of information sources that patients on the ward had, and apparently not the most prominent.

THE STRUCTURES OF STAFF DISCLOSURES

PROBLEMS OF MULTIPLE INFORMERS

The fact that a number of staff members were responsible for discussing treatments with patients led to several types of problems. One obvious possible consequence was that patients could receive conflicting messages. For example, Cora T had a somewhat confusing series of communications with the two ward psychiatrists regarding the issue of whether or not they would commit her. On April 20, during Ward Rounds, the following conversation took place between Ms. T and Dr. M, the ward chief:

> Dr. M: Well, as far as the court proceeding is concerned, we got 22 days, unless you want to sign yourself in for longer. Has anyone talked to you about that?
> Ms. T: No.
> Dr. M: Well, these 22 days are going to expire in another 5 days.
> Head Nurse: 6 days.
> Ms. T: Well, I want to leave.
> Dr. M: Where are you going to get the medication that will help you to continue to improve?

There followed some discussion about aftercare plans, and it concluded when Dr. M said:

> Dr. M: Well, that's what I have to check. Anyway, your plan now is to be discharged in 5 or 6 days.
> Ms. T: Yes.

However, the next day in Walking Rounds Dr. J, who had predominant responsibility for Ms. T, saw the matter differently.

> Ms. T: Dr. M told me I can sign myself out.
> Dr. J: I'm not sure what he told you, but I am the doctor that takes care of you.
> Ms. T: I don't care about that. I'm leaving in 5 days.
> Dr. J: Well, we'll see.
> Ms. T: I'm getting out of here.
> Dr. J: We'll ask for an extension.

As the conversation proceeded, Ms. T got more and more angry and eventually walked out of the room, saying that she would leave the ward. Ms. T was eventually recommitted. The point is not whether Ms. T should have been committed or whether one psychiatrist is bound by his colleague's promise, but, rather, that the structure of communication in a complex system like the Research Ward made such contradictory information inevitable. There were a number of other examples of this problem.

The second result of multiple informers is the pattern of providing information that we have called "floating responsibility." The nature of organization on the ward was such that it was not clear to either staff or patients exactly who should tell a particular patient about any particular treatment decision. Thus, when Mildred L asked why she had not received the Dalmane (sleep medicine) that she was told she would get the previous day, the physician's assistant told her that he had no idea, since he had not attended the previous day's Walking Rounds.

On the other hand, because responsibility for informing patients was not clearly delegated among the staff members and because patients often did not see their own psychiatrists for 2 or 3 days, the staff would sometimes become concerned about whether patients had in fact been informed. Thus the staff member conducting Walking Rounds would check with the patients in question as to whether they had been informed. For example, during Walking Rounds one psychiatrist found it necessary to check with Noelle H whether she had been told about being drug-free for 2 weeks. Felicia E was asked whether she had been told what her medications were for. Another psychiatrist checked with Justin M whether a colleague had explained that the Elavil he had begun taking had a sedative effect as well as causing dryness in the mouth. Such incidents were common.

The multiplicity of staff informers also caused an interesting staff response to patients' questions—namely, referral. This entailed referring patients from one staff member to another staff member who might be more qualified to answer questions. On some occasions, the referral pattern was associated with the staff's status system. Lower-echelon staff members would refer patients to higher-echelon staff members for answers to professional questions. For example, when Justin M was given another patient's medication by mistake and asked a nurse how it would affect him, she suggested he ask the psychiatrist, since he was "the authority" about those matters.

However, the concept of role differentiation is far more useful than the idea of status in helping us understand referrals. The crucial factor was the particular staff member's area of expertise. A patient's psychiatrist was the "expert" on issues concerning discharge plans, sleep studies, or changes of medications[1]; a physician's assistant was the "expert" on all other tests; a nurse was the "expert" on ward status promotion; and so on. Thus, when Lila C asked a psychiatrist when she would be promoted, he referred her to a nurse. When Karen H asked a psychiatrist when she would be told about the results of her X-rays and EEG, he referred her to a physician's assistant. Even within these categories, there was some differentiation. When Harriet L was concerned about glasses that would correct her blurred vision, the head nurse referred her to one particular nurse who was known to be most knowledgeable about those matters.

PERSONAL STYLES OF INFORMATION DISCLOSURE

While our analysis has tried to emphasize the systematic and organized features of the structure of information flow, we must now consider another major variable in the structure of disclosure—personal style. Nowhere in all of our observations was this difference so marked as between Dr. J and Dr. M. Dr. J often displayed his doubts and uncertainty when informing patients. For example, he told Felicia E, "My problem is that honestly I don't know what I can do to help you." Moreover, he rarely promised the patients anything; rather, more than anyone else on the ward, he tended to inform patients about alternative treatments and possible risks they might be taking. Although Dr. J told us repeatedly that he was skeptical about the efficacy of informed consent, his disclosure style was much closer to the model of proper disclosure implied in the doctrine than was the style of Dr. M. Dr. J tended to act as if he believed that the final decision was the patient's. He was usually less personally involved in convincing patients that he was right and in trying to persuade them. At least in relation to Dr. M, he acted as though his role was to encourage patients to make decisions. He was also careful not to establish unrealistic expectations in the patient's mind. He was generally more informative, less personally involved, perhaps less comforting, but also less misleading. Dr. M's style as an information provider was almost the opposite. He was personal, always comforting, supportive, and reassuring, but he was also frequently misleading in his efforts to encourage the patients.

Following Weber's classic distinction[2] between charismatic and legal-rational bases of authority, we can contrast here the legal-rational manner of information disclosure of Dr. J with the charismatic manner of Dr. M. Though we are dealing only with the personal differences between the two psychiatrists, we nevertheless believe that these are manifested in two polar types of disclosure.

The legal-rational manner of disclosing information—which seems to be encouraged by the doctrine of informed consent—neutralizes the personal elements of the informing party and emphasizes the information itself. The doctor simply conveys the necessary information without any personal involvement. He also has no personal stake in whether or not the patient accepts the recommendation; thus avoidance of any personal promises and ease about displaying doubts or uncertainties are characteristic of this style. The extreme end of this mode of disclosure is disclosure through the written form—impersonal, detached, and legally adequate.

The contrast between legal-rational disclosure and charismatic disclosure is probably best seen in the way Dr. M presented to patients the benefits of the recommended treatment. He frequently made personal promises as to the benefits patients would experience from his recommended treatment. When he gave Mellaril to Velma B, he literally promised she would sleep that night. To Lila C, he said, "I promise that you'll get better." When he told Mildred L that he was increasing her Tofranil, he added, "I want to give you some insurance against sadness." The reader may note here not only the use of the singular pronoun "I" (the legal-rational manner of disclosing usually entails the use of the plural pronoun "we" in referring either to the staff or to the medical community as a collectivity), but also the use of the word "insurance," which implies certainty. Similarly, when Werner G was hesitant about the benefits of ECT, Dr. M told him, "I think that your thinking will be changed and you'll be a new person. Take my word." The best example of this style of "you can rely on me" is probably the following remark made to Leonard T: "I'll do something that I very rarely do. I'll guarantee you that you'll be cured. You probably never did that with patients." (Mr. T was a dentist.)

While the "legal-rational" psychiatrist tended to view treatment failure as a result of an objective process that he could not always control, the "charismatic" psychiatrist tended to view it as the staff's or his own failure. This was not just done to impress patients. At a staff meeting from which patients were excluded, Dr. M blamed himself and the staff for Mildred L's failure to get better. When Samantha M committed suicide, he told the patients that this showed that the staff members were not magicians and could fail.

The paradox of these two different ideal types of disclosure is that neither format really meets the goals of informed consent. Although the legal-rational form of disclosure leaves the treatment decision up to the patient, it does not promote the sense of communication and rapport that many advocates have hoped informed consent would produce. The formality and disinterestedness of legal-rational disclosure was at times perceived by the patients as uninterested and uncaring. Thus, although the patients saw Dr. J as a good, competent psychiatrist, it was Dr. M to whom they were more attached. The sometimes deceptive style that went with the personal charismatic approach to disclosure did not concern the patients. Dr. M, in their perception, cared about them. They felt he communicated with them more openly than did Dr. J.

THE ASSUMPTIONS UNDERLYING PATIENTS' UNDERSTANDING

Before we can discuss the substantive disclosures and the patients' understanding of them, we must first describe what patients took for granted when listening to the disclosures. Specifically, the patients and the staff, as collectivities, routinely took for granted that patients on the Research Ward had serious problems that the treatment was designed to help. All treatment discussions were based on this premise. Even introductory remarks between patients and staff members were based on this. For example, in everyday interaction when two people are introduced, each person usually locates himself or herself in terms of friendship, kinship, or occupational systems (e.g., "I'm a friend of Harry's," "I work with your wife," "I'm Susan's cousin") and then inquires about similarities in others he or she meets. On the Research Ward, however, patients typically asked one another, "How did you get here?" "What's your problem?" "Are you depressed?" Lloyd G introduced himself to the patients, "I'm Lloyd G; I am a manic-depressive, and I'm from _____."

This assumption that the existence of problems applied only to patients was made abundantly clear on the patient-observer's first day on the Research Ward, when a staff member approached her in a friendly manner and asked, "What brings you to the Hospital?" That the question formally made sense and could be answered in a simple fashion did not prevent the staff member from being very embarrassed by her mistaking the patient-observer for a patient.

This is not to say that every patient on the ward agreed that his or her problem was what the staff said it was. For example, for his first several weeks on the Ward, Dwayne T remained skeptical that his problem was fundamentally psychiatric and not physical.

However, the most interesting case was that of Christine E, a patient without a clear sense of a problem to be treated, who apparently persuaded the Evaluation Center to admit her. The admission diagnosis was "possible depression," but the staff was unable to elicit from her a distinct problem that could be treated psychiatrically. For several weeks, each Walking Round and most patient discussions about Ms. E focused on what her problem could possibly be. Ms. E finally learned to describe herself as depressed.

The ramifications of this perception that all patients had problems that required treatment are great. Both patients and staff members seemed to take it for granted that the appropriate response to having a psychiatric problem was to cooperate with the staff in the prescribed treatment. Indeed, this was so taken for granted that there were few explicit verbalizations of this norm by either patients or staff. The verbalizations that were offered were always directed to the very sickest patients, who were presumed to have difficulties in understanding what was going on. Thus the following conversation took place between Cora T and Janice Q when Ms. T's doctor was proposing to have her committed rather than allowing her to leave:

Ms. T: I don't think I'm getting anything out of being here.

Ms. Q: Well, at the same time I don't think you are putting too much into it.

Ms. T: But I don't think they are doing me no good here.

Ms. Q: That's just what people are here for, to do you good.

Werner G, another very sick patient, was the focus of the following conversation in Wrap-Up when he said he would not take ECT in spite of having previously signed a consent form.

MILDRED L: Well, you don't want to stay here the rest of your life, do you?

PRISCILLA C: Well, he won't spend the rest of his life in a place as nice as this.

MILDRED L: (*Ominously.*) Yeah, it will be some place that is not as nice as this at all.

KAREN H: (*To Mr. G.*) Why don't you try and show us by accepting the treatment the doctors are giving you?

Of course, this should not be misunderstood to mean that patients always cooperated with the treatment proposed by the staff. It simply reflected an assumption on the part of almost all patients that, unless there were contrary reasons, one should do what the doctor suggested. The result was that most patients made only a single decision—that treatment was needed. After that, almost any proposed treatment was accepted if it was recommended by a doctor. Thus patients did not object to being told in Walking Rounds, "We increased your medicine last night" or "We started you on Dalmane." Of course, this does not mean that patients never objected to a doctor's suggestions; they often had past experiences or knew the experiences of others that made them suggest to the doctor that another treatment would be preferable. However, even here the assumption was that the final decision was the doctor's.

THE RESEARCH WARD'S "SPECIAL" STATUS
AND THE COLLECTIVE SELF-CONCEPT

One reason that the patients were inclined to be particularly cooperative with the doctors' proposals for treatment was their view of the Research Ward as a very special place. They continually emphasized to each other that the Research Ward was very special, with an especially capable staff. The frequency with which they repeated these statements can only be understood in the context of another concern: the meaning of being psychiatric patients.

The special nature of the ward was emphasized frequently. Thus Brenda N told a new patient:

> "Well, no matter how you feel, you know they are going to do you some good. This hospital is a very good one, and it's very hard to get into this ward. I know, I had to go through three doctors to get here, so if they accept you, it must be because they can do you some good, so don't ever give up."

Or:

STANLEY G: I think they're doing a pretty good job of selecting people here. I think we must fit in with one another.

JANICE Q: Yeah, we're all pretty much the same. There is nobody here who is really terribly out of it.

It is interesting that in talking with Mr. G, to emphasize the patients' sanity as a group, Ms. Q used the suggestion that the Research Ward was a relatively pleasant place. In some instances the conclusion is even more explicit. For example, on the second day of her field work, the patient-observer noted:

> Somebody remarked to me later that I was lucky to be doing this study on this ward because they said, "We are just depressed here. But on the other floors, they're really crazy."

And later:

> After breakfast, coming up on the elevator with Justin and Phyllis, Stanley was fooling around and let out a big shout. Justin said, "Well, I think we should stop the elevator at 9 [another ward] and let you out."

The patients' concerns about being crazy were often expressed in jokes and play.

> There was a good deal of joking around the ward. After Wrap-Up, Janice and Stanley were having a conversation in which Janice mispronounced a word or stumbled on it. Stanley looked at her and said, "Ummm," and then pretended to give her a giant shot. Earlier in the day, a group of people visited the unit, leading one patient to comment that it was like a factory tour. Then a couple of people made an attempt to play crazy and moved around with their tongues hanging out, clawing the walls; they then laughed among themselves.

The import of this general pattern for informed consent is clear. In order to protect their sense of not being like the other patients in the Hospital and of not occupying a stigmatized role, the patients had to think of the ward and its staff as being especially good and competent and that the staff's reputation distinguished its patients as being more likely to be helped and less truly crazy. This could not help but color their perception of the staff's recommendations. Indeed, patients frequently told each other that a specific treatment must be right because the staff was so capable and competent. Of course, this is a difficulty for informed consent that is, at least to some degree, specific to a university hospital and is not likely to arise in a state hospital or other facility with a lesser reputation. However, we now turn to the issue of patients' understanding of the normative locus of decisionmaking.

WHO MAKES THE DECISION: THE PATIENTS' VIEW

In the next chapter, we discuss the problem of who really made decisions on the Ward and how the decisions were made, but now we must describe the patients' understanding of who was to decide. Our data do not make this appear to be a complicated issue. In spite of the doctrine of informed consent, the patients tended to view decisions as the responsibility of the doctors. The doctors' only obligation was to listen to their symptoms and to take their points of view seriously.

For example, some patients did not remember the names of all the drugs they were getting, including many patients who were probably capable of remembering. However, when they failed to remember or even when they felt they should have remembered, the patients did not show the embarrassment that one would suspect. Remembering the names of drugs was the business of the doctors.

Another incident reflecting the patients' deference to staff authority occurred when Martin T was being thrown off the ward for having too much sexual involvement with Lila C, a young schizophrenic girl. Partly because the staff told Mr. T's parents not to allow him to live at home, Mr. T found himself with nowhere to go that night. Mack S, another patient being discharged that day, offered to let Mr. T stay with him for a few days until Mr. T could find his own place. The head nurse, having overheard the story, lectured Mr. T, "No, you're not. Absolutely not. Number one, it's not his apartment; and second, you and Mack are mortal enemies. What else are you going to do?" Mr. T accepted this even though he was being thrown off the ward, and Mr. T was not a particularly docile person.

Or consider Justin M, who was given medicine by mistake on the last day of his drug-free period before his sleep studies. His account of the incident is interesting.

> "Brenda N came down and said they were calling me for medicine. I said, 'But I've already had mine.' [He was taking vitamin pills.] But she said, 'Well, they're still calling you.' So I went back up there, and the nurse was standing there with a cup with two tablets in it. So I look at them and I think, 'Well, I'm not going to tell her her job.'"

For Mr. M, deciding on what medicines to take was not his job, but the nurse's.

This general pattern is confirmed by the patient-observer's interviews with patients when they were discharged. When asked who should make decisions about treatment, slightly more than half said that the doctors should. Although the remainder used phrases such as "mutual decisionmaking" and "decide jointly," further exploration showed that about three-fourths of this group felt that the decision was ultimately up to the doctors. They simply wanted to know the reasons and to be listened to. Only one patient, one who had been committed to the ward, felt that ultimately the decision should be up to the patients. The only exception to this general pattern was the decision about ECT, which we discuss now.

SPECIFIC INFORMATION: DISCLOSURE AND UNDERSTANDING

Before we begin the specific discussion of the disclosure and understanding of information concerning treatments, we ought to make a general methodological remark. The very nature of a complex system like the Research Ward meant that we could not have access to all information disclosure. Hence we can rarely be absolutely certain that certain information that we did not observe being disclosed was in fact never disclosed. Thus the present discussion is focused primarily on what was disclosed, rather than on what was not. However, we are certain that we had access to all of the general types of situations in which disclosure occurred; and we feel free to conclude that if we never saw a type of information disclosed, it was certainly disclosed only rarely.

ELECTROCONVULSIVE TREATMENT

Of all the modes of treatment practiced on the Research Ward, ECT stood out as "special" for both patients and staff, perhaps because of the wide folklore of horror associated with ECT and because, generally speaking, the staff saw ECT as involving the greatest risk to patients. Perhaps this is the reason that ECT, unlike the introduction of new medications or changes made in old ones, was never given to patients before it was discussed with them. Of course, all patients getting ECT had to sign a consent form and thus had to be informed before the treatment was given. However, ECT was always discussed with patients at some length before they were given the form.

The consent form that patients signed prior to receiving ECT read in part:

Informed Consent: Electroconvulsive Therapy (ECT) for Inpatients

Your physician has recommended Electroconvulsive Therapy (ECT) for you because it is rapid, effective, and drug therapy has been ineffective or contraindicated. . . .

Like any other medical or surgical procedure using general anesthesia, ECT involves some risk. Complications are infrequent, the most common being fractures and dislocations of the extremities or back. . . .

After treatment your condition will be similar to that of a patient emerging from brief anesthesia. You will be mildly confused and sleepy. This will disappear during the next hour. You may also notice a mild memory loss, but this will be temporary. When you return to your room and familiar surroundings, your thoughts will again become organized, but you will not remember the treatment itself.

The consent form for ECT contained a substantial amount of information, but for the present it is only important to note that patients did not receive the consent form until after the decision to accept ECT had, in effect, already been made. Thus the patients' decision as to whether or not to get ECT was based on the information presented orally, which is the center of this discussion.

One result of the general agreement that ECT was a special and unpleasant treatment was that the staff usually presented it after other options had already been tried. There were only three exceptions among the patients to whom ECT was suggested. Leonard T received ECT because, in the staff's opinion, he was likely to attempt suicide a second time if they waited for antidepressants to work. The staff prescribed ECT for Velma B because of her history of failure with antidepressants and her success with ECT. ECT was suggested as a treatment in a speculative manner for Brad C, and the staff did not push it.

The "last-resort" nature of these recommendations more or less precluded any meaningful alternative. Although patients were told time and again that it was their choice, they were also given another message—namely, that they did not have a choice if they wished to get well. Brenda N, Werner G, and Velma B, all of whom refused ECT vehemently and were told numerous times that they did not have to undergo that treatment if they did not want to, eventually consented and received it. Ms. N, for example, was told specifically that the staff had "run out of options." Even the consent form itself stated in the first sentence that "Your physician has recommended Electroconvulsive Therapy (ECT) for you because it is rapid, effective, and *drug therapy has been ineffective or contraindicated*" (italics ours).

In all eight cases that we studied in which ECT was proposed to a patient, the staff disclosed the purpose of the treatment. In two instances, the staff provided the patients with a fairly full description. For example, the psychiatrist told Graham X that he probably now suffered from the same problem as he had during his previous hospitalization on the unit. Mr. X was reminded that 50 days of medication treatment had not helped him previously but that ECT had helped him. A few days later, another psychiatrist told Mr. X:

> "There is some risk in ECT, but in order to treat your depression, there is less risk there than in having you on medication for a long time. Also, last year you didn't seem to get better with medication."

Since Mr. X was to be given the treatment in Medical Hospital, the psychiatrist added:

> "The reason that you'll go to Medical Hospital is that if something should happen— a heart attack or something—they'll be quicker to treat you, though we have all the equipment. But they do it all the time. I don't think that will happen, but there's always a small chance, so that's why I want it there. Do you understand that?"

Another patient whose disclosure we observed thoroughly was Brenda N. When they first approached her about ECT, the staff reminded Ms. N that she was depressed and that antidepressants had not helped her in the past. Although she responded negatively to the suggestion, several days later the psychiatrist commented that half the patients who did not respond to Elavil, as Ms. N had not, did respond to ECT. He added that he was giving her those statistics so that she could use them when she made a decision. A few days later, during a long session in his office, he mentioned another reason why he preferred ECT to Elavil in her case—namely, that it does not involve gaining weight. (Ms. N had become quite fat while taking Elavil.)

Although staff members sometimes presented the benefits of ECT by predicting that it would relieve the patients' symptoms of depression or even that it would "cure" the patients, they often tried to demonstrate its success by example. With Graham X and Velma B, this example was the patients' own previous improvement with ECT. Patients who had not had previous personal experience with ECT were shown other patients who had done well with it. In general, the staff was not inclined to share with patients any doubts they might have had about the efficiency or safety of ECT. In two cases, the psychiatrist promised the patients that ECT would work. On the other hand, we observed two cases in which the staff expressed some hesitancy about ECT. Brad C was told that ECT might relieve his depression but not cure it, and Brenda N was told they could not guarantee that ECT would help her forever. Later Ms. N's psychiatrist again expressed some uncertainty, but his manner of presenting it was not calculated to induce skepticism: "I don't guarantee that the ECT will be more effective [than Elavil], but overall the chances are 80-90% that it will."

We did not observe the staff informing every ECT patient of the risks. However, it is our impression that they usually did. The cases we actually observed all involved roughly the same disclosure. The following detailed disclosure to Velma B was typical:

> "Now there may be some confusion and memory loss . . . Usually it clears up after the treatment, but some people still have it later. I want to mention the risks too. There is a chance of death for one in every 3000 patients, and also there is a chance of injury such as stroke or heart attack in every 3000 patients . . . I need to tell you the risks so you can know if you want it or not. I know that in the past you didn't have any problems. I think you won't have any now either, but I can't guarantee that. Anyway, if you weigh the risks versus the benefits, I think the benefits outweigh the risks."[3]

In other cases, the disclosure was a bit more discursive. When Brenda N's husband, during a meeting with the psychiatrist and Ms. N, asked about autopsy results on ECT patients to check for brain damage, he received this answer:

> "There were studies. Someone in Oregon has reviewed the literature from the '30s, and they did find particular hemorrhages in the brain. But at that time they were still without oxygen and IV, and only the lack of oxygen caused the damage. At that time they didn't give enough air because the blood gases weren't available. So I just don't know how to evaluate these statistics."

Mr. N asked about the current evidence, and the psychiatrist answered, "There is no evidence; otherwise we wouldn't do it." Although this disclosure was atypical in its detail, and although some persons might read the literature differently, the staff did not seem to be withholding information about ECT.

Thus we see that while the staff did not always fully respect a patient's initial refusal of ECT, the disclosure in general was quite thorough. This leads to these questions: What patients as a group knew about ECT, and how they viewed it? Let us begin with their perceptions of the risks and benefits. In general, patients saw ECT as a potential way of "getting better." All but the newest patients knew other patients whom ECT had helped or even "cured."

But the risks were also present. First they were told, and usually understood, that ECT did not always work. The patients on the Research Ward usually assigned ECT a 50% chance of success when numbers were given.

However, once again, the decision to have ECT does not seem to be a decision that was made by weighing risks and benefits. Most often patients accepted the advice of a doctor if ECT was suggested, but none of them expressed the desire for it. Rarely did they make clear and convincing cases against it, but they all seemed to dread it. Instead of explicitly stating the risks, patients usually took it for granted that everyone would understand why they didn't want ECT. The most consistently used word was "fear." As usual, Brenda N expressed it best: "I'm really scared of it. It seems kind of barbaric. It might be an unnatural fear, but I don't want it." Even Leonard T, who had a medical education (dentist) and who was convinced that ECT was the best treatment, ended his discussion by saying, "I suppose it seems rather strange, but I really have this fear that I'll go to sleep and never wake up."

The major risk that the patients named was temporary memory loss. Patients rarely acknowledged that some persons believed that the memory loss may occasionally be longer-lasting. Instead, the arguments about ECT seemed to balance what the patients perceived as a substantial but uncertain chance of improvement versus a fear of ECT. We could speculate about the source of that dread, but we only knew for sure that it existed.

Perhaps the most impressive thing about the patients' understanding of ECT was their belief that they had a right to make an independent decision about it. We never saw a patient simply agree to get ECT. Invariably, the decision had to be considered and pondered before it was accepted. As we see later, this contrasts sharply with the ways in which patients saw other treatments. For the patients, ECT was something that everyone knew about, everyone had an opinion about, and no one wanted for himself or herself prior to receiving the first treatment.

This leads us to a paradox. Why, given this fear of ECT and the freedom to refuse, did patients continually end up accepting ECT as a treatment? The answer is that patients generally accepted it only when convinced that it was "the last resort." Patients who accepted ECT typically saw themselves as having no other alternative except continued depression or possibly even eventual suicide. ECT was, in the patients' oft-repeated phrase, "a last resort." Of course, ECT was not the only treatment decision we saw justified in this manner. Patients occasionally spoke of the ward itself or of one of the drugs as a "last resort," but not with the consistency with which they used the term for ECT. These are the comments of a few patients:

BRENDA N: I'm afraid of it, but there doesn't seem to be much to do besides this.

LEONARD T: It's really a last resort for me.

BRAD C: (*Responding to why he would take ECT if it was offered.*) I've tried everything and nothing seems to work. I just may have to accept that this is something that I have to live with the rest of my life, but I don't know if I can bear it.

Similar views of ECT were expressed by patients in their discharge interviews with the patient-observer:

VELMA B: It's for people who haven't been helped by the medication.

NOELLE H: It's given when medication hasn't worked . . . [and] there is a great risk of suicide.

ELOISE T: That's the treatment for people in severe depression when medicine hasn't worked for them.

The "last-resort syndrome" was present to some degree in many decisions on the Research Ward and in the Evaluation Center. Many patients felt that, for social and emotional reasons, they had no choice but to do what the doctor suggested. However, nowhere was this as strong as in decisions to accept ECT.[4]

MEDICATIONS

Probably the most fundamental characteristic of information disclosure about medications was that it was usually done during or after the medication was being administered. This basic pattern of temporal relationship between treatment and information, which we also saw in the Evaluation Center and (as we indicate later) in the Outpatient Clinic, was sharply different from ECT disclosure. The information about medications often seemed to be provided as an afterthought or a casual observation, as the following examples illustrate:

> Dr. M then turned to Lila C. He checked her tremor and stiffness in her arms and told her that they had given her "a little extra" medicine. She looked at him as if to say that she hadn't known. Dr. M checked with the physician's assistant and told her that they gave her more Cogentin.

Likewise, Christine E learned new information about what was going on with her medications only in passing.

DR. M: What impresses me is that your symptoms don't worry you. You are the least distressed patient here. Is it misleading?

Ms. E: No, I feel good. I didn't do good on the 100 mg of Mellaril that I was on because I had problems getting up. The Elavil is OK. They gave me three pills yesterday [a dosage increase from two pills previously].

Dr. M: We are going to increase it slowly. Do you have any blurred vision?

Ms. E: No. . . .

In both these cases and in many others, the information about the change in medication was communicated only incidentally. Often the information was communicated in the process of asking the patient how he or she had responded to the medication. In part, this was because most of the staff's decisions were made at their own conferences during the early afternoon and were put into effect during the next administration of medications in the early evening. Usually the next time the psychiatrist met the patient was the following morning during Walking Rounds, after the change in treatment had already taken place.

However, many patients were told about the medication changes beforehand. Here again, the information seemed to be given in the form of a casual observation or a pronouncement, not something on the basis of which the staff expected a decision. This example is typical:

> First [during Walking Rounds] they talked with Faye C. Dr. M asked her how she slept and if she was "zonked" by the Tofranil and Dalmane that they gave her. Ms. C told him about her suicide attempt before she came to the Hospital and the events of the day before that had precipitated it. They talked about her interpretation versus her husband's interpretation as to whether or not she was suicidal. She also talked about the security of being in an institution and she commented that it frightened her. At the end of the conversation, Dr. M told her that he would continue to give her Dalmane, would increase the Tofranil, and would also give her something like Trilafon to decrease the anxiety. Then they moved on.

Dr. J told Chet H that he heard from his family that he was not back to his normal self.

Mr. H: I'm normal.

Nurse: Well, your family says that you're not like you used to be. . . .

Mr. H: You have to be discharged to prove that you are OK around here.

Nurse: You aren't aware of any change in your personality?

Mr. H: No.

Nurse: Well, why don't you ask your family [in family therapy] what they think is different in you, and you can help both you and us.

Mr. H agreed. Dr. J then told him that he had gotten a little Trilafon last night and that gradually they were going to increase the dose.

As far as we could tell, in many cases the patients were not explicitly informed of changes in medications. In none of these cases did the staff inform the patients so that the patients might decide, and this attitude seems to have been conveyed to the patients.

As we can see, the names of the medications were used in almost all cases. Rarely did the psychiatrists not go beyond such generic categories as "a medication," "an antidepressant," or "a medicine to help you organize your thoughts."

The purpose of treatment was explained more thoroughly on the Research Ward than in the Evaluation Center or the Outpatient Clinic. Thus, when the psychiatrist decided that Brenda N's troubles with urinary retention were too serious to ignore and that he had to reduce the dosage of Tofranil and Cogentin, he explained this to her. Some weeks later, while she was being treated with ECT, the staff explained to her that her Dalmane had been discontinued because of a possible anticonvulsive effect. The psychiatrist added that they were not certain about this, but that they would rather err on the conservative side. Staff members also routinely explained the reasons for a change in treatment. Thus they told Lucy T that she would get some medicine because she had some problems falling asleep, and Clyde Z was told that his antidepressants were increased because he looked more sad than usual. The staff even told Werner G that the reason he had not been given Cogentin was because he had bladder problems. Sometimes these explanations were fairly complex. Yet even Velma B, a patient whose ability to understand was questionable, received a substantial explanation of the purpose when the staff switched her from Trilafon to Mellaril.

> "We discontinued the Trilafon. The reason is that Mellaril is a little more sedative. Also with the Mellaril we don't need the Cogentin. The Cogentin gave you some troubles."

Sometimes the staff did not feel an explanation was necessary, since it was implicit from a related discussion. For example, when Mildred L complained that no one had explained to her why her Tofranil was discontinued, the head nurse reminded her that the day before she had insisted that it made her feel bad.

It should be reiterated that many of the explanations of purpose were given to patients only after the treatment decision had already been made. This may be why we found so few alternatives presented. As was also the case in the Evaluation Center, this was one of the weakest points in the information disclosure. In fact, we observed only one patient, Noelle H, with whom several alternative medications were discussed. Dr. J told Ms. H,

> "Then there are a number of alternatives that we can take. One is to switch you to Sinequan as you suggested. The other is that there are some drugs for treating anxiety that comes with depression. There is one called Dalmane; there is one called Clonopin, and that's reasonable to try. Also someone may suggest Trilafon, so we'll put that down on our list. The other alternative is to have ECT. . . . These are the alternatives we have. Think about them and see which you prefer."

Two days later, he reiterated,

"There are a number of options. One is to increase the Aventyl. Another is to switch to Sinequan. Another is to add to the Aventyl some drugs that will treat your anxiety. There is Dalmane. There is another one, Clonopin, which is similar to Librium or Valium, and we use them here with patients who have anxiety or depression."

Ms. H had a long history of having been on almost every possible antidepressant and/or antianxiety drug, and she seemed to complain about most of them. The fact that she was the only patient who was given an option to choose among various medications must be seen within this context.

However, patients were sometimes given the option to refuse the proposed medication. On a few occasions, a patient was asked whether or not he or she wanted to get the medication, but the option to choose between two or more treatments was limited to the above case.

Let us turn now to the information given to patients concerning the benefits of the medication recommended to them. Usually, when a certain medicine was recommended to a patient, the recommendation was accompanied by a statement of a possible expected benefit. Almost invariably, this benefit was the relief of some symptom about which the patient was complaining or from which the staff thought the patient suffered. Thus Molly X was told that Elavil should reduce her level of tension; when the doctor started her on lithium, he told her that it would balance her mood so that it would not go up or down any more. Likewise, the doctor told Lila C that the Prolixin would help get rid of her auditory hallucinations. There are almost endless examples of this type of disclosure during our observations of the Research Ward. There were only two exceptions to this focus on symptom relief as a benefit, both rather trivial. First, patients given antiparkinsonian drugs such as Cogentin were told that this drug would relieve side effects, not that it would relieve symptoms. The second exception was Christine E, a patient who did not present the staff with any clear-cut symptoms. She was told only that her antidepressant medication might help her "function better."

Of course, in this area as in others, staff did not always make the possible benefits of treatment explicit. They seemed to have felt that the benefits were implicit in the fact that a recommended treatment came as a response to a patient's complaint.

As with other information about medications, information about the benefits of the drugs was usually given after the drug therapy had begun. On one level, it can be argued that this violated the spirit of the doctrine of informed consent, since a benefit that is given after a decision has already been made is entirely irrelevant to the decisionmaking process. However, this is less clear when we remember that decisionmaking about medications is processual rather than located at one point in time; that is, every time a patient takes medication, it is as if he or she has made a decision not to discontinue that treatment. Thus information given while the patient is still on medication is relevant to his or her decisionmaking process.

When we look at the disclosure of the risks of the medications, we find that the staff concentrated on the side effects of the drugs. Thus they warned Justin M that before he would feel better, the Elavil they were prescribing would make him sedated and make his mouth dry. Likewise, the staff told Felicia E that her Cogentin would make her mouth dry. There are dozens of such examples. What is important is that the staff made no disclosures about possible long-term risks of the drugs. For example, no mention of tardive dyskinesia (a potentially irreversible disorder of movement usually secondary to long-term usage of antipsychotic drugs; see Chapter 13) was made to any of the patients who were taking antipsychotic drugs. (Dr. J subsequently explained that he does not consider tardive dyskinesia to be a risk since no patient he has ever treated has ever gotten permanent dyskinesia.)

As with the disclosure of benefits, patients often heard about the acute side effects of a certain medicine only after having suffered from them. Thus only when she noticed that her speech was slurred did the staff tell Velma B that this was a common side effect of most sedatives, and only after she had difficulty waking up was she told that Mellaril was probably responsible. Likewise, the staff informed Leonard T about the risk of getting blurred vision only after he had already been suffering from it. Typically, such explanations came as responses to patients' complaints. It was an explanation of what was happening, rather than the basis for a decision. Consider Molly X's interaction with Dr. J, who was doing Walking Rounds:

Ms. X: Do you want to know how I feel today? A little groggy. . . . Otherwise I think I'm what you would consider normal, but my eyes are out of focus.

Dr. J: Have you felt in the last couple days that your mood is high?

Ms. X: What day do you pick? On Monday and Tuesday I was very high [prior to starting Thorazine] until I slept. Yesterday and today, I'm not.

The conversation continued for a few minutes, focusing on the current status of Ms. X's symptoms. Suddenly she changed the topic.

Ms. X: Does the Thorazine cause my mouth to be dry?"

Dr. J: The Thorazine and the Cogentin cause the dry mouth and the blurred vision. It will go away sometime in the future; and also when we discharge you, you'll be on a lower dose.

Two things are clear from this interaction. First, Dr. J was not very interested in explaining the side effects, since he ignored the first mention of blurred vision. Second, he did not seem to be trying to hide the fact that there are side effects to the drugs, since even though Ms. X asked only about her dry mouth, he spontaneously discussed the vision difficulties as well. This seemed to be typical. Information disclosure was a second-level priority for the staff, but they did not seem to be trying to deceive the patients.

Let us now consider patients' understanding of the medications. The patients seemed to believe that decisions about medications were entirely up to the staff. This was reflected in what they said, even when they did not agree. Thus Noelle H said, "I don't see why they didn't put me on Sinequan. [She had just been prescribed Aventyl.] That's what I did good on." Another patient told the patient-observer that the doctor had changed his mind and decided not to start him on lithium. "[The doctor] says it will affect my hands and make them shaky, and that won't be any good for my work. I need to have steady hands." It should be noted that he described the decision as being entirely up to the doctor.

Perhaps the most impressive reflection of the patients' concept that the responsibility for medication resided with the doctors was in Felicia E's dialogue about whether or not to continue a medication that was causing severe side effects.

DOCTOR: Is it so bad as to warrant discontinuing the medicine?

Ms. E: Yes, the one that disturbs my vision.

DOCTOR: Well, both Elavil and Trilafon cause that. You put me in a bind. You complain about depression and anxiety. I give you the medicine and then you complain about the effects. I just can't win. . . . You are the one, not me, who has to decide what disturbs you most.

Ms. E: (*She seemed confused.*) Now you put me on the spot.

DOCTOR: That's the alternative.

Ms. E: I want to get rid of my depression and nervousness, but I also want to improve my vision.

DOCTOR: But you can't have both. . . .

Ms. E: Doctor, is my vision important? Because it is to me.

Although the doctor in this case tried to make the patient choose, she refused, believing that the responsibility for finding a solution to her dilemma lay with him. She wanted both her vision and her mental health, but when faced with a choice between the two, she asked the doctor to decide which was more important.

There were a few instances when patients objected overtly to the proposed drug treatment; even then, however, the way in which it was done indicated the exceptional nature of such objections. Mildred L, who had had a series of severe side effects from previous drug treatment that did her no apparent good, insisted to some other patients that she would not take any more medicine until she had talked with her doctor. Although she was not convinced by what he said, she took the medication anyway. This was a persistent theme with all patients who did not like taking the medications. Justin M was an example. After describing what medication he was getting and why, he said, "It sounds weird to me, but what do I know?"

Another reflection of the attitude that medication decisions were the doctors' responsibility was that many patients were unable to name new medications that had just been prescribed for them. Although after a few days all but the most confused patients knew what drugs they were taking, since this was a topic of continual discussion among the patients, many relatively intact patients told our patient-observer and/or other patients that the doctor had just changed their medicine, but that they were unable to name the new one.

Given that the patients did not treat medication as a matter that they should determine, the level of knowledge that some patients had and made available to other patients when necessary was very high. For example, after Harriet L was told she had been getting Elavil rather than a placebo while on the Protocol,

> Harriet came down to the lounge area where Noelle H, Karen H, and Phyllis D were sitting. The patient-observer asked her if she found out what she was taking, and she said it was Elavil. Karen and Noelle seemed excited. "Who told you?" "They just told me now," Harriet replied.
>
> Karen asked her how she felt about it, and Harriet just shrugged her shoulders. . . . Phyllis asked her how much she was taking, and she said, "I'm taking four 150 mg [tablets], so that's 600 mg." Both Phyllis and Noelle said that couldn't be the case, because the highest dosage allowed is 300 mg per day.
>
> "But I was taking one four times a day, and now they gave me four at once at night," Harriet said. "Well, probably the 150 is what all the four come to."

However, it must be emphasized that while such knowledge was collectively understood by the patients, most patients did not know their dosage levels or the permissible limits of dosage.

Finally, we should discuss the patients' collective understanding of the risks of the drugs they were taking. This was a reflection of what the staff told them. For example, we have no evidence that any of the patients taking antipsychotic drugs had any understanding of tardive dyskinesia. On the other hand, the patients' knowledge, both collectively and individually, of acute side effects seemed to be quite high. During Walking Rounds, patients often spontaneously reported to staff members that they had something that might be a side effect. These examples are typical:

> Faye C began by telling the physician's assistant and the head nurse [who were making Rounds] that it was very hard for her to wake up in the morning. She asked whether that was due to her increase in Trilafon.

> When asked in Rounds if she had any changes since she came in, Felicia E responded that she felt better, but the medication caused her mouth to be dry and her vision to be blurred.

Lila C approached the staff observer and asked whether she was shaking because of
the medicine or for some other reason. [At this point, Ms. C was quite psychotic.]

It is apparent that in these and in many other cases, the patients knew enough
about side effects to ask the right questions.

RESEARCH

In discussing participation in research with patients, the staff did not always
clearly distinguish among the concepts of research, treatment, and diagnostic
testing. Thus many patients did not understand that the research was not a
form of treatment.[5]

To begin with, the research was referred to as "the Protocol" or "the
Protocol study," and patients who were research subjects were referred to as
"being on Protocol." Although "protocol" is a familiar term to medical researchers, it is hardly popular jargon. Furthermore, in discussing the research
with patients, the staff frequently referred to diagnostic tests given both to
ordinary patients and to research subjects as being benefits of the research. The
following discussion took place between one of the psychiatrists and Lloyd G
about the advantages of being a research patient:

MR. G: I don't know. I'm not 100% convinced.
DOCTOR: Convinced of what?
MR. G: That the study will help me to select medicine for my treatment.
DOCTOR: It can help in that.
MR. G: But not necessarily.
DOCTOR: We think that it might help some. It can help some.
MR. G: So it's not a real 100% prognosis that you'll come up with from the
sleep studies for a particular individual.
DOCTOR: The sleep studies can answer fairly reliably whether a person is
depressed or not. As for the medicine, they give some indication. But it's not
like they answer the first question. We don't know what they say about
prognosis. Anyway, with your history of manic-depressive disease, the prognosis is good.

The doctor did not explain that diagnostic sleep studies, whatever their
value, were available to every patient on the ward and were thus not a specific
benefit of being a research subject,[6] although research patients did receive
further sleep studies after they received Elavil or placebos. Staff members also
told research patients that being on the ward longer (the Protocol required a
35-day stay before ordinary drug therapy could begin) could be an advantage.
Karen H got this explanation from her social worker:

"There are some advantages for you in staying here. This long stay gives people
more time to straighten out their heads and also, especially at your age, to plan

your future, school, and so on. It gives the staff more time to work with your family, and it's a reasonable amount of time. Also, you don't have any demands such as a job or children requiring you to go back home immediately."

The staff did not explain that nonresearch patients could also stay in the Hospital as long as necessary, nor that the 35 days for which the research patient agreed to stay was not the expected period of treatment but rather the period prior to the beginning of individualized pharmacotherapy. In general the staff did not systematically discuss on the ward the disadvantages of participation in the research; and their statements were consistent with, although not explicitly productive of, the patients' general belief that the Protocol was mainly an experimental treatment program. Patients' collective understanding of participation in the Protocol was partially a product of what they were told and partially a product of their own fabrication. While some patients entered the Research Ward believing that they had to be part of the Protocol to be on the ward (and, in fact, this is what the consent form for the research stated), they quickly learned otherwise. For example, Phyllis D, who was participating, asked another patient in the Protocol how many people were presently in the study and learned, to her surprise, that there were only three. After a few days on the ward, however, almost all the patients believed that "Protocol" was a special status with a special type of associated treatment.

This special status was seen as having special advantages and disadvantages. There were two main advantages. Karen H, unsure about whether or not she would be on the Protocol, stated one of the perceived advantages on her second day on the Ward: "Well, I could find out more about me and my depression. And that band [a method of measuring activity level] you wear sounds interesting. It sounds like a good program." More than a week later, after several changes in her decision, Ms. H consented to being a research subject. Her perception of the advantages had come to focus on the other major benefit: "I signed, but I didn't think I had much option, because I didn't have any insurance and I couldn't afford to pay." Many patients expressed the same feelings. They hoped that it would help their treatment, and they were convinced that it would relieve a major financial burden. The former hope was, at least occasionally, carried to extremes. Brad C, for example, seemed to believe that being on the Protocol was a special form of treatment. Talking to other patients, he said, "You know, you really get discouraged here. Like you, Brenda. You've been on Protocol, and you've been through the drug program, and you're still here." Ms. N responded, "That's right." Ms. N apparently did not find such a view of the Protocol too strange to accept. In independent interviews with a large sample of patients on the Protocol, we found that more than half the patients failed to see the Protocol as being primarily research, or that they understood "research" to be largely if not exclusively an effort to understand them as particular individuals better or to improve their individual treatment.[6]

This is not to say that patients saw nothing counterproductive to their treatment from being in the research. Patients knew and discussed among themselves the fact that being on Protocol might delay their getting an active drug. However, they did not seem to understand that even if they were getting Elavil rather than a placebo, they might get the wrong dose, or that Elavil might not be the right drug for them.

Another disadvantage seems to be entirely symbolic. Quite independent of the "objective" risk, some patients did not want to be researched. The expression "guinea pig" was frequently used. Thus Brad C, when recounting his admission, said that when he first talked to his doctor, "He wanted me to be on Protocol, but I didn't want to do that. I didn't want to be a guinea pig. I think that's exactly what you are." Of course, this objection was not limited to patients on the Protocol. One patient commented that the staff-observer's presence at a Patient-Staff Meeting was something you had to put up with in a university hospital. In this sense it was possible to argue, as Eloise T did, that Protocol patients were privileged because they had a choice.

NOELLE H: Sometimes I feel like a guinea pig, like they are testing all different kinds of medicines out on you.

KAREN H: [a Protocol patient] Well, I am one.

ELOISE T: Yeah, but you knew it. I mean you signed the form that said you were going to be in the research, right?

KAREN H: Yeah, but I would have been in debt for the rest of my life if I didn't.

SLEEP STUDIES

All patients on the Research Ward, regardless of whether or not they were Protocol patients, got "diagnostic" sleep studies for a 2-day period following 10 days without medication. Here again, the patients did not see this as a matter of choice, but rather as a part of the treatment on the ward. However, with the exception of one patient, who felt that the 10-day drug-free period was superfluous since she had not had any drugs before, there were no complaints. Patients typically saw the diagnostic sleep studies as one of the special benefits of being on the Ward. Indeed, Noelle H reported that the opportunity to get sleep studies was her major reason for coming to the ward. She expected that they would allow her "to find out the true nature of [her] depression."

In general, the patients were very interested and curious about what the sleep studies showed. In a number of cases, patients were annoyed or even angry with their doctors for failing to review with them the results of the sleep studies. This interest in the sleep studies was seen as so natural that at an Advisory Board Meeting, Brenda N commented that Christine E's failure to pursue the results of her sleep studies with her doctor when she didn't understand them was a sign that something was wrong with her.

Most patients eventually received the results of their studies, although sometimes only after several requests. Thus, although patients placed great stock in the findings of the studies, the staff did not make much use of them for clinical purposes and did not understand the patients' preoccupation with these findings. When they did disclose the findings, staff members provided the patients with considerable information. Consider the psychiatrist's detailed report to Harriet L about her sleep studies:

DOCTOR: I want to go over the sleep studies (*showing her the printouts*). Did they show you up on the 13th floor [referring to the place where the monitoring equipment for the studies are kept]?

Ms. L: Yes.

DOCTOR: Well, they go through this record, and they score every stage of your sleep. Here, for example, in Stage Two, you woke up. They go over all your sleep of the entire night, and then they add it up on this graph. Now, TRP here means "total recording period." That's how many minutes you were plugged in. SL is "sleep latency," and that's how long it took you to fall asleep. Here it's 22 minutes. EMA means "early morning awakening." It means how much time you lay in bed after you woke up before you were unplugged. Here it's 42 minutes. TS is the time from the first moment of the sleep until the last moment of the sleep. This is the time you actually slept and the time you were awake. Here you slept 358 minutes, and you woke up 6 times for a total of 11 minutes. RL means "REM latency." That's the time from the onset of your sleep to the first moment of the period of your dreaming. The rest is just a breakup of the other stages of your sleep. That's esoteric. All this is based on an average of two nights. There are some differences, but not great ones. Here, for example, it took you 2 hours to fall asleep, and on the second day 22 minutes, and averaged that's about an hour. At your age, it has to be about 30 minutes.

Ms. L: To fall asleep?

DOCTOR: Yeah. That's abnormal. Now, this early morning awakening—a normal person shouldn't have it, but you did lie down. Now, the percentage of time that you slept out of the time that you were plugged in is 82%. At your age, a normal person is supposed to have (*he opened a book and showed her a graph*) 94%. Now, the average of your two nights is 70%, so you should be here on the graph. That's what we see with depressed people. They don't sleep really well. Another thing we find with the time until dreaming. Now normally (*he showed her the book again*) it's about 84–88 minutes. You had 80 minutes. This is low but still within normal limits. This is unexpected, and I don't know why you had it. This isn't what we usually see in someone who's depressed.

Ms. L: So you say that I wasn't depressed?

DOCTOR: No. This is a research tool. We've already had such people in the past. We don't know what it means. Many things with you—like the low sleep efficiency, for example—are typical to depressed people, but this (*he showed her something on the printout*) is atypical. We don't know how to explain it.

Ms. L: Is it that I didn't get enough sleep, or I slept too much?

DOCTOR: Well, here it seems you slept like someone depressed. Now here (*he showed her the printout of the other night*) it took you only 6 minutes to fall asleep, and you woke up only 3 minutes. That's a lot. Here, for example, there was a big improvement. It took you 2 hours to fall asleep here, and here only 6 minutes. And here you slept only 55% of the night, and here about 90%. Your sleep has improved. Usually, when the mood improves, the sleep improves too.

Ms. L: So you say I improved as I went on?

DOCTOR: Yeah. Being on the medicine, you improved. This is about it.

Ms. L: So as I get better, my sleep gets better too?

DOCTOR: Yes.

The question this dialogue raises, as did many of the interactions in which the staff went into the technical detail necessary for a "rational" decision, is that of how much the patient understood. After a long, detailed explanation, Ms. L could only ask bewilderedly if she was getting too much or too little sleep. She did not understand the psychiatrist's idea that the pattern of a series of variables would provide a diagnosis. Given the technical jargon contained in the explanation, this is not surprising. However, it is important to remember that the material the psychiatrist was explaining was hardly simple.

DISCHARGE

Research Ward patients were generally very concerned about the duration of their stay on the ward. As Julius Roth[7] has demonstrated, patients find discharge dates indispensable for structuring their own ideas regarding their hospital "careers." Thus it is hardly surprising to find that many patients frequently asked when they would be discharged. Lila C and Harriet L, for example, asked every few days.

The staff was usually patient with such repetitive questions, since they were aware of the anxiety that produced them. However, with the best intentions, they were often quite vague about discharge dates. Staff members typically dated events in the patients' career not in calendar-time units, but rather in patient-time units.[8] Thus, when Lila C asked when she would be discharged, her psychiatrist could only tell her that it depended on her mood and on how she planned her postdischarge life. Nor could he be more precise in terms of calendar time when he told Molly X that before she could leave, he wanted to stabilize her sleep and to make sure that she was not depressed and prone to hurt herself.

As the discharge time for a patient approached, however, the staff usually was more definite about the date of discharge. Thus Faye C was informed that she would be kept for "another 7 to 10 days," Timothy M that he would stay for another 15 days, Christine E that she would be discharged "sometime next week," and Lucy T that she would be discharged "on Friday." On a few occasions, the staff members also provided the patients with the rationale for their decisions. When the psychiatrist recommended that Christine E should stay another 10 to 14 days, he explained,

> "The reason is that a part of your problem is how you can get along with people. You are very quiet and withdrawn, and here in the community it's possible that you'll talk and interact with other persons."

Patients were also sometimes told that these discharge dates were tentative. For example, Brenda N was told that she would be discharged in another week if she still felt the same, and Cora T, Timothy M, and Christine E were informed that their discharges the following week were contingent upon how their weekend passes went.

Yet these tentative discharge dates created serious communication problems between staff and patients. On the one hand, patients sometimes did not take them seriously. For example, although Dr. M told Lila C on April 15 that she would "probably be here another 2 or 3 weeks," she was shocked when, on April 25, he told her he wanted to discharge her in 2 days. On the other hand, patients sometimes took tentative discharge dates too seriously. On two occasions patients learned about their tentative discharge dates only by accident, because these dates were listed on a blackboard in a room where some group therapy meetings were held. The two patients were shocked to learn about the dates in this way and had to be reassured that these were only tentative dates. Nevertheless, the procedure of posting these dates on a blackboard accessible to some patients without mentioning the dates to the patients in question demonstrated that the staff did not consider informing patients about their discharge dates a top priority.

The patients' collective understanding of discharge was clearly that they wanted to leave the ward but ought to stay until they were better. Patients demonstrated this dual belief in two ways. First, with few exceptions, patients insisted that they wanted to go home and complained about having to stay on the ward and being separated from their loved ones. Second, they continually reminded others that they should "stick it out." Perhaps the most interesting version of this argument was Janice Q's when she was trying to persuade Lloyd G to stay.

> "When I was coming into the Hospital, I know that when they said 6 to 8 weeks it seemed an awfully long time, and I didn't think I could do that, that I could leave my family, and who would take care of the laundry and the cooking and seeing that the kids were all right, and I felt that more problems would be created by my absence. But then I decided that in relation to the whole rest of my life, 6 to 8 weeks wasn't really very much."

This is not to say that every patient on the ward actually wanted to go home when the doctor proposed it. Mack S, a slightly retarded man with a difficult interpersonal manner who was very dependent on the Hospital, described leaving the Hospital as "like giving up my right arm." Brenda N and Mildred L both quite effectively resisted leaving the Hospital before they felt ready to leave, in spite of the staff's giving them discharge dates. At the other extreme, Max I signed out Against Medical Advice (AMA), and Lloyd G stayed only after much persuasion.

These exceptions notwithstanding, the general idea was that patients should stay until the staff said they could leave. The legitimate desire to leave depended on being "well." Thus when patients decided it was time to leave, it was important for them to show that they were well. Faye C, as the patient-observer noted, was quite blunt about this.

> Faye had said that she has been hoping for a discharge this week (so she could be at a Parent's Weekend at her son's school), and today she was wearing a very nice pale burnt orange suit made of suede-like material and a scarf around her head. Brenda commented how nice she looked and Faye said, "Well, when I want something, I really make an effort; and I really want to get discharged by Friday so I'm trying to look good and get dressed up so [her doctor] can see how well I am." She mentioned that her husband had given a glowing report on her condition, which went into the Weekend Report. "I think [her doctor] may not take that as being exactly true, because he knows my husband wants me home." She said that it was necessary for her to demonstrate by her actions that she cared about herself.

In general, the patients believed that the ultimate decision about when to leave belonged to the doctors. It was not that they didn't know that they could leave. Justin M put it best when the patient-observer asked him if he could leave when he wanted to:

> MR. M: Oh yeah, I could leave.
> OBSERVER: How much notice would you have to give?
> MR. M: 72 hours, but, you know, if you're wishy-washy about leaving, then they'll enforce that and hope that you'll change your mind. But if you make a stink about it and say, "Let me leave; otherwise I'll break that chair," well, then they're going to really want to get you out and will get you along the way and say, "Certainly, here's your suitcase."

However, leaving AMA was not seen as a good idea, and not only because it would not solve the problem. What follows illustrates a common belief on the ward:

> Noelle H and her husband and Stanley G and Karen H were talking about leaving AMA. Noelle said she might even consider it, because she was feeling pretty bad now. [However,] Stanley said, "It only takes about half an hour for them to fill a bed when somebody leaves. Then they won't let you back to be treated here." Karen said, "Oh, well, I don't think I'll be doing that then."

INDIVIDUAL UNDERSTANDING
AND THE PROBLEM OF COMPETENCY

It needs to be reemphasized that our concern with understanding has not been with the understanding of individual patients, but rather with the beliefs that gained general acceptance among the patients when they were talking together. Therefore, the beliefs and ideas cited above tended to come from the most active, talkative patients and are not a random sample by any means.

This question thus arises: How much did the beliefs of individual patients correspond to this collective set of beliefs? For a number of reasons, which we discuss earlier, this is not easy to determine, but it is possible to make a number of general statements.

First, by the time they left the Research Ward, most patients had an understanding of their treatment that closely approximated the one we have described for the group as a whole. This is quite clear in their discharge interviews with the patient-observer. Indeed, most patients developed this understanding during the first week on the ward. The process seemed to be a rather simple matter of socialization. They learned about treatment, its risks, its benefits, and alternatives by talking to other patients, by listening to discussions in the Walking Rounds, and occasionally by talking with staff members. All of this took time, however. Patients frequently did not understand many elements of treatment early in their stay. This was true even of quite competent patients.

For example, consider Phyllis D, a reasonably intelligent woman on Protocol whom we watched being admitted and about whom there was no question of competency. To her surprise, on her second day she learned from Janice Q that only three patients on the ward were presently on Protocol. She apparently thought that this was a condition for being admitted to the Research Ward. She said, "How come they get off and we don't?" On her fourth day, she still did not understand that if she was on Protocol, she was required to stay a minimum of 7 weeks. On her sixth day, she learned for the first time that only Advisory Board Members and not the whole community voted on patients' passes. It is, of course, not surprising that it took time for patients to learn what was going on, but it was important because the formal consents to many aspects of treatment came very early in a patient's stay.

The other major factor that affected how much an individual patient's understanding reflected the collective understanding was the patient's cognitive capacity. This was, of course, closely associated with the severity of the patient's "illness" and was almost identical to the level of the patient's general competency.

Of the 41 patients we observed on the Research Ward, only 11 could possibly be said to have been even marginally legally incompetent during our observations. Probably only five would have been declared judicially incompetent for any of the treatment decisions that they made. However, as a group, these were the people who had understandings that were most divergent from those of the general patient group.[9] Many of their ideas were simply incorrect. For example, among the small group of five or more clearly incompetent patients, there was consistent failure in the ability to answer relatively simple questions about treatment. Thus Graham X was consistently unable to report to either staff or patients why he was taken to a medical hospital's operating room to be given ECT (he had a bad heart), in spite of having it explained to him at least three times. Werner G could not remember what drug he was getting a few minutes after being told. This group also held some beliefs for which the probability of being true closely approached zero. Cora T, for example, apparently believed that the female staff members were all lesbians and wanted to rape her. Molly X, an overbearing personality who was extremely difficult for both patients and staff to tolerate, apparently believed that her presence on the ward was making both the community as a whole and patients individually considerably better.

However, a number of their understandings of treatment were not incorrect but simply controversial. For example, both Werner G and Graham X believed that ECT had not been of any permanent help to them. Cora T, Harriet L, and Lucy T all believed that they would be better off going home instead of getting the treatment that the staff thought best. Nonetheless, as we note in our analysis of the interactions in the Evaluation Center, the opinions of these patients were continually overridden by the staff, and these patients were told least about their treatment. The staff members treated these patients as incompetent and, in effect, substituted themselves as decisionmakers. Thus Graham X and Werner G both eventually got ECT in spite of their initial objections; Cora T was eventually committed; and Lucy T and Harriet L were kept in the Hospital after they wanted to leave.

SHIFTING LEVELS OF COMPETENCY

Perhaps the most striking finding on the Research Ward was the variability in patients' competency over time. Several of the patients seemed completely incapable of understanding minimal facts about treatment at one point, but could give fairly detailed advice to other patients at a different point. Werner G is perhaps the best example.

Mr. G entered the Hospital almost unable to talk. Among his few words was the statement that he didn't want "treatment," which apparently referred to ECT. He was frightened that the EEG sleep studies were ECT. Despite his continuous insistence that he didn't want ECT, the staff decided to give it to him and brought in Mrs. G, who suggested that he should just be given the paper and told to sign. He did sign, but the next day refused to accept treatment. Following considerable pressure from the staff, patients, and Mrs. G, he did get ECT. Prior to ECT,

Mr. G talked almost not at all, was apparently unable to say what medicine he was getting, did not try to change his ward status beyond "10-minute check," sometimes failed to attend meetings, and so on. Other patients' opinions about Mr. G were best expressed when Stanley G was assigned to do a Weekend Report on him. After finishing another task, Mr. G announced, "Now I am going to see [interview] Werner." The patient-observer noted, "Everybody laughed because Mr. G had so far done very little except sit in his chair, walk to his room, and go down to meals. When spoken to, he just answered in monosyllables." Mr. G said, "Yes, I'll write a very concise, informative paragraph on Werner."

Yet following several ECTs, Mr. G began to go to meetings on his own initiative and initiated relatively complex interactions. Thus he told Velma B, then considering ECT, "I wish you a lot of luck; I hope you'll feel the same as I do after eight [ECTs]. I think you should be given a lot of encouragement." He began to ask about discharge dates and to discuss with the staff what job he might get.

In this context, it is also important to note that Mr. G's high level of competency did not continue; he "relapsed" soon thereafter.

While Mr. G was the most extreme example of fluctuating ability to understand treatment decisions, he was not the only one. From a theoretical point of view, it must be emphasized that competency, at least in psychiatric settings, is not a static property of the patient, and that its shifts are at least partially related to clinical course. If the competency of the patient is to determine the role of the patient in the decisionmaking process, this determination must be made and reviewed frequently. This clearly argues against reserving this determination for a formal court hearing.

STAFF ATTITUDES ABOUT DISCLOSURE TO PATIENTS

Finally, we want to discuss briefly how the staff behaved about information disclosure in general. Certainly, more than in the Evaluation Center, the Research Ward staff seemed genuinely concerned about patients' understanding. This involved not merely responding to patients' questions, but, more significantly, checking with patients on their own initiative as to whether the patients were clear about their therapeutic situation.

Staff members did not do this as mere lip service. In fact, on several occasions they were not satisfied when patients said that they understood, and they tried to make the patients explain things back to them. For example, when the psychiatrist asked Janice Q whether she understood what the "gadget" (the mobility band) on her arm was, and she replied that it measured her activities, the psychiatrist insisted that she explain how. Similarly, when giving Werner G his medication, the nurse not only asked him whether he knew its name but also told him, when realizing that he did not remember, that it was Elavil and gave him the dose as well. Mr. G was asked what the drug does and, when he did not know, was told that it was an antidepressant.

We even observed one instance when a patient was penalized for lacking information. A request for a status promotion was denied to Lila C on the grounds that she was not familiar with the duties and privileges associated with the higher status.

There were numerous other instances when staff members went out of their way to explain treatment. When Mildred L was taken off her medication, her psychiatrist asked whether she knew how he had arrived at that decision. The staff asked Felicia E on two occasions whether she knew what she was taking, why, how much, and what might be the side effects. When Graham X became somewhat blue (literally) and the staff decided to have him undergo some blood tests in order to check the amount of oxygen in his blood, the psychiatrist asked him whether he understood why they were drawing blood.

When staff members were capable of implementing decisions without a patient's consent, they were generally less concerned with the patient's accepting their decision than with the patient's understanding their motives. When Lloyd G, Molly X, and Leonard T were put on constant observation by the staff, they were all asked whether they understood why. When Molly X replied that it had to do with her having said that she would hurt herself, the head nurse corrected her by making a very slight but subtle change: "No, because you said yesterday that you would not guarantee that you wouldn't." She was clearly concerned that Ms. X get the staff's perspective on the situation as precisely as possible, even though she knew that Ms. X did not agree with the staff's action.

On several occasions, the staff was clearly concerned not only with a particular patient's understanding of the staff's intentions, but also with the understanding of the rest of the community as well. When Martin T was thrown off the unit after having made sexual advances to Lila C, the staff wanted the other patients to understand their reasons for having done so. The chief of the unit made it a point to ask the head nurse to explain to the rest of the community why this action was undertaken. When Graham X began ECT treatment, the psychiatrist checked with the other patients to see whether they understood why he was getting it. After explaining to them that during a previous hospitalization ECT had helped Mr. X whereas drugs had not, and that because of his heart condition medication would be more risky than ECT, he concluded, "I just want to make sure that everyone here understands that."

We do not mean to imply that the staff was always open to questions. When discussing Eloise T, for example, at least three staff members referred to the fact that asking "so many questions" was indicative of her "manipulative" habits. The head nurse complained that on Ms. T's first day on the unit, she already wanted to know all the ward's rules. Max I, a patient who eventually signed out of the Hospital AMA, commented several times to our observers that he believed the psychiatrist who admitted him was threatened by the fact that he asked many questions, and the psychiatrist was not very responsive.

Moreover, the staff was often preoccupied with its own concerns and thus ignored the concerns of the patients. A typical example occurred one morning when the physician's assistant and the head nurse were making Walking Rounds:

PATIENT: Is it unusual that you get such a dry mouth from Trilafon?
PHYSICIAN'S ASSISTANT: It is a side effect we can't control.
PATIENT: Will it go away?
PHYSICIAN'S ASSISTANT: Is that your main problem?
PATIENT: Yes.
NURSE: Do you think that you won't be able to work because of it?

In their anxiety to understand the severity of the side effect, the staff ignored the patient's concern about its duration.

Staff members also sometimes replied to a patient's questions by returning the questions to the patient to answer. When asked by Felicia E whether her crying was caused by her illness, the physician's assistant responded by asking her the same question. Similarly, when asked by Mildred L whether patients are sent home when they are cured or in order to cure them, her social worker replied, "How do you perceive that?" And when Lila C asked a nurse whether she was improving, the nurse merely returned the question to the other patients to answer. Of course this is a standard psychotherapeutic technique, but it does not make the communication any more like informed consent.

We observed only one instance in which a staff member made an explicit remark about the worthlessness of informing a patient. The psychiatrist who recommended ECT to Velma B told our staff-observer that he found it hopeless to discuss with her at length his rationale for making that recommendation, since her mood swings from mania to depression and back again made her opinions and decisions very unstable.

In general, the staff of the Research Ward worked hard to communicate with patients. What resulted was not what most ethicists would call informed consent, but it was human communication in a fairly open and reasonably honest manner.

11

Freedom and Constraint:
Decisions on the Research Ward

Decisionmaking on the Research Ward was much more complex than in the Evaluation Center, in part because there were more decisions to make, but mainly because there were many more people involved and the decisionmaking process usually lasted longer. In the Evaluation Center, the typical patient was asked to make the decision with two staff members and with any friends or family members who may have accompanied him or her; on the Research Ward, however, there were a large number of staff members, including three different shifts of nurses and psychiatric social workers, several doctors, a physician's assistant, and several volunteers. An even more important difference was that in the Evaluation Center the patient had almost no contact with other patients, whereas on the Research Ward other patients were extremely significant participants in the decisionmaking process. Likewise, in the Evaluation Center the duration of the contact between patients and staff never exceeded an 8-hour period. However, on the Research Ward, while some decisions seemed to take place in an instant, others dragged on for several weeks. A final complexity was the tremendous variety of decisions that had to be made on the Research Ward. Whereas in the Evaluation Center we found that patients typically made only the decisions whether to accept treatment and whether that treatment was to be inpatient or outpatient, Research Ward patients had to make decisions about a variety of different modalities of treatment; the restrictions to be placed on themselves and other patients; the types of drugs they would receive, and in what dosages; and participation in various research projects. All of these characteristics of the Research Ward contributed to the complexity of the decisionmaking process and to the problem of patients' voluntariness on that ward.

Yet within this chaos of people and decisions, certain general patterns of decisionmaking were quite clear. These patterns seemed to be based upon staff expectations and general traditions handed down within the patient community about how decisions ought to be made. While new patients coming onto the ward may have had their own ideas about how decisions should be made, and occasionally expressed these ideas to our patient-observer and/or to other patients, they were faced with the appearance of a general consensus and the routine procedure about how the decisions were in fact made. These general patterns were organized around the type of decision to be made.

Thus in our description of the problems of decisionmaking and voluntariness on the Research Ward, we first describe how each type of decision was typically made, and then describe the exceptions that occasionally caused either the staff or the patients (or sometimes both) to decide that the decision should be made differently in a particular case. Finally, we describe the sanctioning resources (inducements, pressures, and coercive forces) that enabled the staff and patients to enforce compliance with those general patterns, and the ways in which these sanctions were used.

GENERAL PATTERNS OF DECISIONMAKING

STAFF DECISIONS: TESTS AND MEDICATIONS

The general pattern in the decisions about medications and about the tests that patients were to get was that the staff decided these matters. Although patients' input was often considered, and patients were occasionally able to effect the final decision, the decisions were always primarily made by the staff.

In this context, it is worth considering a series of decisions made about the medication of Lila C.

Ms. C, an 18-year-old girl, was hospitalized after she began to hear communications from radios and television sets that were turned off; she was very frightened by her psychotic experiences. When we first observed her, she was having diagnostic sleep studies and was thus receiving no medications. The day before her first sleep study, she asked the doctor when she would begin to receive medication. She was told that medication would begin 2 days hence. The next day, during Walking Rounds, she was asked if she had any worries about the coming day. The patient responded that she was frightened about the shock treatment, apparently referring to the EEG sleep studies she was getting. Dr. J told her that the wires were not for shock treatment. He then told her that they would begin medication the next day, and that then she would feel better. The patient apparently received the medication without any further decisions being made.

A few days later, they changed the mode of administering Ms. C's medication from oral to intramuscular injection. This decision was made at the staff meeting. Shortly thereafter, a staff member asked our observer to come with him because "I'm going to tell Lila about her change in medication." The observer's notes are worth quoting:

He told Lila that she had been getting Prolixin through pills, but now this was going to be changed to injections. Lila said "Oh, I'm going to get an injection," and wrinkled her nose and didn't look happy about it. The staff member was explaining it very slowly, and Lila was leaning on the counter. He put his hand on her arm when he was talking to her, calming her down a bit. She said "Yeah, I don't really like them. Am I going to get them in my 'tush'?" He said "Yes, Brenda's going to give them to you." She then said OK and walked away.

While Ms. C consented in a formal way, it is clear that because a lower staff member rather than the doctor was the participant, and because the staff member's comment to our observer was that he was going to "tell her" about the change, the consent was largely *pro forma*.

A similar phenomenon occurred when orders were written to increase Ms. C's Prolixin dosage. When she got the shot the next morning, she was told that the dosage had been increased to get rid of the music she was hearing in her imagination and the TV and radio messages that were not real. She simply nodded.

Several other similar examples from Ms. C's history could be presented, as well as innumerable ones from the histories of other patients. Most interesting is that Ms. C seemed to accept and take for granted this process of decision-making. She did not object that her rights had been violated by giving her medication or by changing her dosage without her consent.

It was not only psychotic patients like Ms. C who were so acquiescent to staff decisions about their medication changes. Janice Q, one of the most active patients on the ward and probably one of the least psychologically impaired, had the following interaction with her doctor during Walking Rounds just before she was to complete her period of being on the Protocol:

DOCTOR: If it turns out you are on placebo, I want to put you on Aventyl. [He then told her that Aventyl was a metabolite of Elavil that she may have been taking while on the research study.]

PATIENT: Uh-huh. (*She smiled.*)

DOCTOR: It is easier for us to measure your blood level. We're sure about the therapeutic level of Aventyl but we're not sure about the Elavil. . . . So if you are on placebo, I'd like to start you on Aventyl.

NURSE: We're going to open the capsule today [to find out whether the patient was on Elavil or placebo].

PATIENT: What if I was on Elavil?

DOCTOR: Then we'll need to think. I also want to see your sleep studies before I make any decisions.

The assumption of the doctor that he would decide what the drug should be, and Ms. Q's apparent acquiescence by smiles and silence to this assumption, should be noted.

Another indication of the locus of the decision was that when disagreements arose about medication, the staff won. For example, Eloise T, admitted to the Hospital for detoxification from drug addiction, decided at one point that she needed some pills to help her sleep. The staff, suspicious of her motives because of her history of drug addiction, refused her request. The argument went on for several days, but the staff won, and Ms. T did without her sleeping pills.

Likewise, Clyde Z developed an edema of the face and tongue, possibly as an allergic reaction to the Elavil he was taking. Although he complained about this repeatedly, the staff raised his medication level twice in the succeeding week. He had also complained about being nervous since getting "the medicine." He was told this sometimes happened when the depression lifted. While the staff eventually did discontinue the Elavil, citing his increased anxiety as the reason, they waited much longer than Mr. Z would have if he had been making the decision.

None of this is meant to say that the patients had no say whatever about the medications they received. In general, the staff tended to be responsive to patients' requests when these were framed in the proper manner, such as by citing the effectiveness or noneffectiveness of past treatments. Patients could not always affect medication choice this way, but usually they could, as an experience of Dwayne T's demonstrates:

> Dwayne T complained in Walking Rounds that he was feeling miserable and very anxious, that his legs were shaking, and that he was depressed and desperate. He told the doctor, "You said you would increase the medicine." The doctor responded, "Yes, the question is which." He took the patient's pulse and asked him if he was feeling any restlessness. The patient responded that he definitely was. Dr. J asked the nurse who was accompanying them what she thought about increasing the Cogentin. She responded that it was possible. Dr. J turned to the physician's assistant and suggested giving the patient one Cogentin instead of a half each day. He then turned back to the patient and said, "I want to change one thing at a time. So we'll increase the Cogentin." Mr. T asked, "What is it supposed to do?" Dr. J said "Well, the Haldol has the effect of restlessness so we will try Cogentin, but if it's anxiety we will need to increase the Valium and the Haldol. But why don't we try the Cogentin first?" Mr. T responded, "I would suggest Valium because it has helped me in the past." Dr. J then asked the physician's assistant how much Valium Mr. T was getting. Dr. J then turned back to Mr. T and said "OK, we'll begin with Valium if that is what you want." Mr. T thanked him, and the doctor moved on to the next patient.

Such efforts by patients to influence medication prescription were not always successful. Mr. T clearly had two advantages: He could provide credible information that was useful to the doctor—namely, his past experience—and the doctor was ambivalent about the decision. The case of Noelle H provides a good counterexample.

Although Ms. H was quite experienced with medication, she also had a reputation as a chronic complainer about medication. This reputation affected the way in which she was told that she would be getting medication after her sleep studies had been completed. Dr. J told her that he would start her on medications that night and that he wanted her to remember the symptoms she had been complaining about during the 2-week drug-free period so she would not later attribute them to the medication. However, when she was called to the medication counter, she was told only that she was going to receive Aventyl. The nurse said, "We have an order for some medication. You're going to get Aventyl." Ms. H objected and only took it at the urging of her husband and several other patients as well as the nurse.

The next morning during Walking Rounds, Ms. H said, "Last night when I got the medication I was disappointed, because it was something I already got before. I had hoped to get a tranquilizer antidepressant. However, I will follow any program that you suggest, because I don't know what I need." She continued to complain that her anxiety was more serious than the depression, for which she thought the Aventyl had been prescribed. The following morning at Walking Rounds she asked whether she could get something "for my nerves" because the Aventyl had made her very nervous, and suggested 2 mg Valium. Dr. J responded that he would prefer not to give her that because "I want to give you a good trial on one drug so that when it's over at least you will know whether it works or not. . . . I appreciate that you are suffering but . . ." Ms. H interrupted him, "But I have already suffered for 2 weeks." Dr. J responded, "But you have only been here 2 weeks. You've already been on many things, and it didn't help you. We see a lot of people with anxiety, and it seems to me the most beneficial thing is to have one drug at a time." The next morning during Walking Rounds, Ms. H once again complained about her anxiety and suggested that she had done much better on Sinequan than on Aventyl. The staff member responded that this was very encouraging for the Aventyl, since Sinequan and Aventyl were from the same class of drugs. Ms. H continued to complain about her anxiety on Aventyl for the next few days, and the staff continued to insist that she should spend 10 days on Aventyl. During a Wrap-Up meeting one day she said that while she did indeed have a predisposition to think that Aventyl wouldn't work, this was because it hadn't helped her in the past. She complained that the staff had a predisposition to blame everything she said on her anxiety, adding, "I think if my skin turned blue they would say 'Oh, it's just your anxiety.'"

While the staff did not change Ms. H to Sinequan as she had requested, they did refrain from raising the dosage of Aventyl further as they had planned. After 5 days on Aventyl, Ms. H and Dr. J agreed that if she would wait until 10 days had elapsed, they would let her pick her medication if she was still anxious on Aventyl. Finally on the seventh day of her trial on Aventyl, Dr. J gave up and told her that he was very much against it because she wouldn't be able to find out what the causes of her difficulties with Aventyl were unless they had a blood level at 10 days, but he would allow her to go off the Aventyl any time she wanted to. At this point, Ms. H accepted his recommendation and decided to continue on Aventyl until the end of the 10-day period. After a discussion between Ms. H and Dr. J, the Aventyl was terminated, and she was given Sinequan. In connection with this decision, Mr. H apparently had discussed with a staff member what his wife was going to get, because he said their account did not correspond with his wife's. One of the social workers told him that the staff and not Ms. H formulated the treatment plan on the Research Ward.

What is clear from this case is that both the staff and Ms. H largely took for granted that the decision was fundamentally the staff's. Ms. H complained about the substance of the decision, not the process. Even these objections received no support from other patients.

The difference between patients such as Dwayne T, whose medication was adjusted following his report of side effects, and patients such as Noelle H, whose medications were not changed at her request, seems to have been that the staff saw Ms. H as trying to prescribe for herself. The staff willingly altered medications in order to minimize the side effects and maximize the therapeutic effects, but they seemed very hesitant when they thought the patients were attempting to prescribe for themselves or to control the medication decisions.

The other type of decision that was clearly the staff's decision was whether or not patients should take psychological and physiological tests. In spite of the doctrine of informed consent, both staff and patients seemed to take for granted that it was the staff's responsibility to order tests. As an example, let us consider the way in which Lloyd G's tests were decided upon, although the experience of any other patient would do just as well.

Upon first being introduced to Lloyd G during Walking Rounds, Dr. M noticed a difference in the way Mr. G moved his muscles on one side of his face than on the other. He then gave him a brief examination for imbalances on the right and left side without making any request, but by simply telling him to do one thing or another. At the end of this, he said, "The most important thing you will have to go through in the next few weeks is medical and neurological exams. . . . One side of your face is less responsive than the other, and we should give you a good neurological exam." Mr. G then got a full neurological exam as well as a CT [computed tomography] scan, which were scheduled for him without further discussion.

Several patients objected to having prescribed tests, but the objections were easily overridden. During Walking Rounds, Eloise T complained of having had indigestion, nausea, and a headache the previous night and asked whether it might be her nerves.

DOCTOR: Maybe. We'll do tests to make sure you are physically well—also an EEG, to make sure that you don't have seizures.

Ms. T: Last night I really vomited . . . I didn't eat anything, and I had a terrible headache and nausea and I threw up.

DOCTOR: Nick, schedule her for a GI and a gall bladder [test]. (*He then turned to the patient.*) We'll give you X-rays.

Ms. T: Maybe it's only nerves.

DOCTOR: Well, since you're here, we'll do it anyway.

In no case did a patient's objection prevent a test that the doctor or another staff member wanted from being carried out.

COLLECTIVE DECISIONS: PASSES, PRIVILEGES, AND STATUS

As noted in Chapter 9, unlike the other wards in the Hospital, the Research Ward operated as a therapeutic community. This meant that the staff shared with the patient group the power to make certain decisions, such as the granting of "privileges" to patients.

The mechanism of this sharing of power consisted of the right of the patients' Advisory Board to decide on a patient's "status" (which in turn regulated the patient's freedom of movement around the Hospital and outside) and to grant patients weekend passes to visit friends and family. This power was subject to a staff veto in any particular case. Although the criteria differed for deciding upon pass requests and status increases, the procedure was the same. The patient in question was required to turn in a slip requesting a status increase or a pass, in the latter case filling out the time for which the pass was requested and what the patient intended to do with the time. These were then discussed by the staff to determine what sort of a response they would make to the proposal at the Advisory Board Meeting. After this the Advisory Board Meeting was held, and any patient could comment on any pass or status request except his or her own. However, only the five elected Advisory Board members were allowed to vote. The nursing staff also routinely attended and discussed the requests. Following the Advisory Board Meeting, the staff met again to discuss the Advisory Board's decisions, and then the staff and patients met together in what was called the Patient-Staff Meeting in order to finalize the decisions.

Some examples of the functioning of the Advisory Board are given in Chapter 9. However, it can be said that the Advisory Board generally approved patients' requests for both passes and status increases, except when it was quite clear that the staff opposed them. The requests disapproved by the Advisory Board were ones of which the staff members had, among themselves, already indicated disapproval. Thus the Advisory Board Meeting did not function so much as an occasion for decisionmaking as it did as a forum for the patients to try to persuade the staff that their friends deserved higher statuses or passes. The veneer of democracy did not fool either staff or patients. The medical director of the ward told our observer that he was a "benevolent dictator"; and a number of patients, explaining the Advisory Board mechanism, told the patient-observer that the staff "really" made the decisions because the patients could not be relied on to make them objectively.

Staff members did not always have to explicitly veto passes or status increase requests that they opposed. By expressing their thoughts about the matter during the Advisory Board Meeting, they could often persuade enough patients to win their point. Consider the case of Noelle H, already discussed with reference to her medication:

Ms. H's relations with the staff were not good, and she complained frequently about her treatment. Toward the end of her Aventyl trial period, Ms. H applied for a status change to advance to "2-hour open" status. In their closed meeting, the staff decided that she was in no psychological shape to handle such an advanced status and would use the status against the staff and her husband. However, the observer's notes on the Advisory Board Meeting show that the patients' impression was somewhat different.

> Phyllis began by saying that Noelle handled her pass outside with her husband pretty well. She said that Noelle felt bad that day, but she has control when she leaves the ward. Helen then commented that Noelle had told her that when she was outside the last couple of times, she didn't have the panic attacks that she had had a week previously; also that when she did have that panic attack, she had the good judgment to ask her husband to bring her back to the ward. Thus she deserved the pass. Karen said that everyone has an occasional bad pass and that Noelle was capable of handling the highest status because the last couple of times her trips outside had gone well.
>
> [A nurse] then expressed her concern about Noelle's ability to handle her anxiety when she was by herself. Karen responded that if Noelle felt badly she wouldn't go out, and anyway she wouldn't be by herself. Eloise also said that she wouldn't be by herself if she was anxious and nervous. If she did go out, she would be able to handle it. [A second nurse] then said that this was a request for a "2-hour open" status, which assumed that the patient would go out by herself. Thus the question was whether she felt better or worse than she did last week.
>
> Phyllis then suddenly responded that she felt worse, and Janice agreed. "She has feelings of hopelessness about whether the medicine worked at all. This morning her anxiety increased greatly. She has mixed feelings about whether to stay in the hospital or to go home. I hope she will decide to stay. . . ." [The second nurse] then asked to hear the opinion of some of the patients who hadn't spoken. Lila said that she thought that Noelle should wait a while before she went out by herself. She should wait until she was more ready and felt better. Janice said that the same issue had come up a number of weeks ago when Lila herself had applied for that status. The question was then brought to a vote and the promotion was turned down, 3 to 1.

None of this means that the staff had unrestricted power over these decisions. For example, when Faye C applied for "2-hour open" status, the staff was very hesitant to approve this, knowing that she was both alcoholic and suicidal. However, they concluded that since she had complied with all the rules of the community and had fulfilled all the requirements for a "2-hour open," they could not easily turn it down, and thus she was promoted. On the other hand, when Lila C applied for the third time to be a monitor, the staff was very hesitant to turn her down for fear that she would become discouraged and believe that she was never going to get well. Nonetheless, since she did not meet any of the criteria for being a monitor, they could not see how she could be passed. The Advisory Board, equally reluctantly, voted her down.

These decisions did not resemble patient decisionmaking of the kind envisioned by the doctrine of informed consent. A patient was not even allowed to speak in favor of his or her request at the Advisory Board Meeting. On the other hand, to the degree that the goal of informed consent is enhanced by patient participation in decisionmaking, this system clearly did encourage such participation. Although the major responsibility for the decision still lay with the staff, patients did play important roles in these decisions—at least as advocates, and occasionally as decisionmakers.

MUTUAL PARTICIPATION:
ECT, DISCHARGE, AND POSTDISCHARGE PLANNING

Some decisions on the Research Ward were typically made by a process similar to the decisionmaking pattern of mutual participation that informed consent theorists have held out as a model. While not all actual decisions about ECT, discharge, and postdischarge planning were made in this manner, mutual participation was the norm in these decisions.

Electroconvulsive Therapy

As we note in Chapter 10, patients had mixed feelings about ECT. The collective understanding of the patients about ECT was that it was a useful treatment, but there were also many fears of its unintended consequences.

Perhaps modal, if not typical, of the decisionmaking process was the ECT decision of Velma B, a 62-year-old unemployed widow who came into the Hospital diagnosed as depressed.

We did not observe Ms. B's admission, but the staff thought that she was in the Hospital specifically to get ECT, and a pre-ECT workup was scheduled for her on the day she was admitted. However, Ms. B told our observer that ECT had not been discussed with her prior to her admission. The day after her admission, Dr. J noted that she had moved into a manic phase of her disorder. He simply told her, "Yesterday we talked about ECT, but if you feel better, maybe we won't need to do it." For the next few weeks, the staff treated Ms. B's mania and subsequent depression with medications. However, when after 3 weeks of hospitalization she did not improve, Dr. J decided to schedule a pre-ECT workup and to propose it to her at the next morning's Walking Rounds. However, when he suggested ECT to her, Ms. B looked a little surprised and upset.

PATIENT: I don't want it. I know how I was before when I had ECT.

DOCTOR: Well, we're only thinking about it. Are you worried you'll get high?

PATIENT: No.

NURSE: Well, last time the ECTs are what helped you. Granted, it caused you to be sky-high.

PATIENT: (*Interrupting her.*) I don't want it, I don't want it.

DOCTOR: We're only thinking about it. You don't think much of it?

PATIENT: No. I was high. I was happy, but it was a fool's paradise. I think that what I'm taking now will help me with my slurred speech.

NURSE: Well, if you're worried about your slurred speech, what about your depression?

PATIENT: I'm fighting it every day.

DOCTOR: We just wanted to know your thoughts on it. Now we know.

NURSE: But we'll ask you again.

Perhaps better than anything, this interchange typifies the nature of the decisionmaking process over ECT. While the staff conceded to the patient the right to say no, they also insisted that if they decided it would be good for the patient, they would insist on discussing it repeatedly.

Three days later, while the physician's assistant and the nurse were doing Walking Rounds, Ms. B complained, "I really feel horrible."

PHYSICIAN'S ASSISTANT: We just started you on antidepressants last night. It may take a number of days.

PATIENT: I know that.

NURSE: So you won't give up any hope. You have to remember ECT helped you in the past. Even though you called the time after the ECT a "fool's paradise," ultimately it did help you. You don't always have to feel the way you do now.

PATIENT: Am I required to take ECT or whatever you call that?

PHYSICIAN'S ASSISTANT: We want to give the medicine a chance, 10 to 12 days, before we think about ECT. In a number of days we'll see if ECT helps.

NURSE: But remember, there have been things that have helped you.

Despite the physician's assistant's timetable, 4 days later in Walking Rounds Dr. J—after hearing from Ms. B that she wasn't feeling any better—said, "I know you aren't really keen on ECT, but I think that you might think about it if you aren't getting better on Elavil."

PATIENT: I don't know. I had it in the past, and it made me high.

DOCTOR: It was only for a short time. When you did come down, you felt good. We aren't going to force you if you don't want to, but I think you need to think about it.

Again, at the next morning's Walking Rounds, the physician's assistant told Ms. B, "I'm thinking more and more about a course of ECT." Ms. B responded, "I don't want it." After some discussion, the physician's assistant concluded, "We will continue to try the medicine a few days. I think that you need to start thinking about it [ECT]."

Finally, exactly a month after Ms. B was admitted, Dr. J went to her room to discuss it with her. After some preliminary discussion about her progress on the medication, this exchange took place:

PATIENT: They want me to take ECT. The attendant suggested to me that I try it before I go completely out.

DOCTOR: I know that you are afraid you will be high.

PATIENT: Well, at least I was better off when I was high. I sang, I could talk with people.

DOCTOR: My suggestion is that we give you ECT again. What we can do is go more slowly, and if we see you are getting high, stop it. So we'll do it more slowly, and even if you are high, you yourself say you are better off there.

PATIENT: When will it be done?

DOCTOR: I think we will begin on Friday. Do you want to give it a try?

PATIENT: I know whoever gives it knows what he is doing. I had 18 when I was very young, but then I was another person, and I didn't have anything to lose.

Dr. J got the forms; after an explanation of the risks and benefits of ECT, Ms. B asked him whether she had to read it. Dr. J informed her that she didn't, and she agreed to sign.

This rather lengthy and involved decisionmaking process concerning ECT was typical for those patients who eventually got it. In the most extended process we noted, our observers recorded 17 instances when Brenda N discussed the possibility of getting ECT at public meetings, including Walking Rounds, group therapy sessions, and Wrap-Up sessions, before she actually received it.

However, we did see one instance of "prior decision" to get ECT. Stella L was admitted on May 13. She later told our patient-observer that she had come to the Hospital specifically to get ECT. She got her first ECT on May 14 and received three more in the next week. She was discharged 10 days after her admission. Unlike all the other patients, who received ECT only after extended discussions on the ward, Ms. L came to the Hospital with her mind already made up.

Not all patients to whom ECT was proposed accepted it. Whether or not to have ECT was, in most cases, a fairly autonomous choice.

After he had been in the Hospital a month, the staff decided that Timothy M should have ECT. Anticipating difficulty, nobody on the staff wanted to talk to him about it. When the topic was proposed to Mr. M the next day, he flatly rejected it. He told them that he had had it before, and it hadn't worked at all. They suggested that perhaps he was confused when he had it the last time, and it had actually helped him. However, when Mr. M again refused to consider ECT the next day, the orders that had previously been given for him to have ECT were canceled.

For Timothy M as well as several other patients, the ability to refuse depended upon a determined rejection of the staff's recommendation. However, other patients managed to avoid it in different ways. Perhaps the most interesting was the case of Brad C.

Brad C told everyone that he would do "whatever was necessary" in order to get over his depression. One reason for this clearly was that his wife told him she didn't want him back home in the condition he was in. Apparently his marriage depended on his doing something about his depression. However, he repeatedly stated that he didn't want to have ECT. Every time it was proposed to him over a period of 3 weeks, Mr. C agreed to "consider" it. However, the day after Dr. J proposed seriously that Mr. C receive ECT, Mr. C reported feeling much better and commented that the medicine seemed to be working. This led Dr. J to decide to "take his word for that" and to wait before administering ECT. The next day he told our observer that he had "dodged" ECT. For the remaining 2½ weeks of his hospitalization, the staff occasionally suggested ECT to Mr. C, but since he continued to make slow progress, they never insisted.

Discharge and Planning

Decisionmaking procedures for both discharge and the planning for postdischarge follow-up could also be characterized as mutual decisionmaking. Explicit statements about the time of discharge varied a great deal, from the case of Christine E, who was told it was up to her if she wanted to stay, to that of Edward M, who said he would stay until his doctor said he was good and ready to leave. However, the diversity was more apparent than real. Christine E was also told many times by the staff and by her family that it would be in her best interest to stay longer than she had planned. While Edward M said it was up to the doctor, he also did not hesitate to object to the doctor's plans when he didn't like them.

The assumption behind this pattern of mutual decisions was the belief that patients should be discharged only when they had received the maximum therapeutic value from their stay in the Hospital. The process of mutual decision about discharge that we observed among the majority of patients was perhaps best illustrated by the case of Lila C.

Lila C was a rather charming 18-year-old woman in her first year of college who was diagnosed as schizophrenic or as having a schizo-affective disorder. As noted earlier, she believed that both the radio and the television were communicating to her personally, even when they were not turned on. Ms. C's extended dialogue with her doctor about discharge began on April 15 during Walking Rounds.

> PATIENT: Do you think I will need to stay here longer than May 4?
> DOCTOR: Do you want to stay here longer?
> PATIENT: No.
> DOCTOR: Well, it's OK with me if you want to stay longer if you still think that you aren't well enough.
> PATIENT: How many weeks longer?
> DOCTOR: I want to rely on your own judgment.

Ms. C responded that she thought she would be better by May 4, and the doctor responded, "It's OK with me; but if on May 4 you don't feel OK, just tell me and I'll have you stay here another week, OK?"

Five days later, after Ms. C told Dr. M that she thought she would die at 33 because "that's the way Jesus had died," the following conversation took place:

> PATIENT: You promised me that I'll go back home.
> DOCTOR: You will, but it's important that you go back home when you feel well.
> PATIENT: I'm not going to shoot myself.
> DOCTOR: Yeah, but I also don't want you to hang yourself [this was a reference to her previously saying she was afraid she would die by hanging].
> PATIENT: I won't. Are you ashamed of me? Are you mad at me?
> DOCTOR: Not at all.
> PATIENT: Am I getting better?
> DOCTOR: Yes.

Nine days later, the discussion about her leaving again came up in Walking Rounds with the physician's assistant.

> PATIENT: How long will I have to stay here?
> PHYSICIAN'S ASSISTANT: How long do you think you will have to stay?
> PATIENT: I don't know.
> PHYSICIAN'S ASSISTANT: It depends on how you feel. Do you think you are close to feeling well?
> PATIENT: Yes. [Here she mumbled something about her symptoms, which were not yet showing any significant improvement.]

NURSE: You may well need to leave here with some of the symptoms, but that doesn't mean you won't be able to leave.

The general communication that Ms. C should stay until she felt better but that she could leave whenever she wanted to continued throughout her stay. However, it is important to note that there was a sense of mutuality on both sides, as is evident in the final discussion about when she wished to leave.

PATIENT: How long am I going to have to stay?
DOCTOR: We always play this game. You ask me, and I tell you about 2 or 3 weeks, and then when the time comes, you say you will stay here a little longer. When do you want to get out?
PATIENT: You should figure it out because I don't know.
DOCTOR: Is the last Friday of the month OK?
PATIENT: OK with me.

Although Ms. C was sicker than many of the patients on the ward, this pattern of decisionmaking was typical. Variations on this pattern were the cases in which the staff wanted the patients to leave, but the patients were reluctant. For example, Brad C, discussed previously in connection with his ECT decision, was extremely anxious about going back to work and about leaving too early, because during an earlier hospitalization he had left early and had had to be rehospitalized almost immediately. His departure from the ward was postponed three times. Likewise, Mildred L expressed a number of times the fear that she would not be able to handle life on the outside; she even more frequently expressed the related fear that she would be discharged too soon. However, since her diagnosis had been anorexia nervosa and she had been gaining weight, on April 19 the staff decided that she should be discharged a week later. Oddly enough, 5 days went by without any staff member's remembering to tell her. Two days before the scheduled discharge, Dr. M announced it at a patient meeting. Ms. L cried during the entire meeting. Afterwards she spoke to Dr. M about it, and he commented that some of the things he had heard about her during the meeting, as well as her crying, had convinced him that she was really depressed and needed to be started on antidepressants. Therefore, he would not discharge her 2 days hence. In the days that followed, Ms. L was repeatedly assured that "we won't throw you out just like that" and was encouraged to prepare herself for her discharge. After about 2 weeks of such preparation, as well as participation in the discharge task group meetings, she felt strong enough to leave and was discharged.

While discharge decisions were almost always made jointly, they were not always based on a complete agreement between the patient and the staff. For example, Felicia E, whom we describe in Chapter 10, pushed and cajoled the staff into discharging her, even though they didn't think that she was ready to leave.

It must be reemphasized that this pattern of mutual decisionmaking was the norm. In practice, it did not always work as we have described it. Two patients whom we observed left AMA. In one case the patient, who was near the end of his treatment, simply did not want to postpone a planned discharge because the doctors had decided to change his medication. Another patient, Max I, signed himself out after 3 days in the Hospital. The staff had predicted that he would sign out AMA after the first full day of his hospitalization. He decided to do so after asking Dr. J to allow him to see his chart. Dr. J told him that he could not, and Mr. I said that there were some philosophical differences between them. Dr. J replied, "If that's the way you feel, you can sign yourself out." Mr. I immediately went to another staff member to get the forms to sign out and did so. The staff did not hold him for the extra 72 hours that they could have. Thus even here there was a consensual element to the agreement that the hospitalization should be terminated, even though Mr. I and his doctor disagreed sharply, and Mr. I signed himself out AMA.

There were two other marked disagreements about discharge. Martin T was thrown off the ward after he violated ward rules, and Cora T was involuntarily committed. We discuss both these cases in more detail later.

We must make one final qualification of the proposition that these decisions were generally made on a mutual basis. The staff apparently did not take seriously any patients' suggestions that promoted actions more serious than the staff thought necessary. Similarly, the staff felt free not to consult patients when canceling treatments that had previously been agreed to but were no longer necessary. Examples of these patterns were numerous. For example, Lloyd G suggested that he ought to be sent to a state hospital, but the staff simply refused to consider that as a serious proposal. Lila C suggested that she ought to have ECT, but the staff dismissed it. When Brad C seemed to improve without the scheduled ECT, the staff decided to cancel it without consulting him. Whether such actions contradict the model of informed consent is not clear. While patients clearly have the right to reject the treatments proposed by their doctors and to get the least restrictive alternative treatments available, it is not clear whether patients have the right to propose treatments that their doctors do not think appropriate or to have more restrictive treatments than their doctors consider necessary.

PRIOR DECISIONS:
PROTOCOL AND GENERAL TREATMENT COOPERATION

We have emphasized throughout this volume that most of the decisions that we observed were made through a long and complex process. Decisionmaking is a process, not an event. This is certainly true of any human behavior that takes place over time. Almost any previously made decision can be reopened at any point. Nevertheless, in some circumstances people behave as though a decision is an event that has occurred in the past and is not open to further review. We call this pattern of decisionmaking "prior decision." Although the doctrine of informed consent insists that any consent is revocable by the patient, in two specific instances both staff and patients treated the decisions made upon signing the form as final. These decisions were to enter and participate in Protocol and to cooperate with the general rules of the ward while in the Hospital.

Protocol

In general, Protocol patients signed a consent form when they were admitted in the Evaluation Center. Dr. J went to the Evaluation Center and presented the risks and benefits of participation in the Protocol to each patient, after which the patient was to decide whether to participate or to be treated on some other ward in the hospital (see Reference 5, Chapter 10). Although in theory this decision could be reviewed at any time, and the patient could leave the Protocol and continue to receive treatment on the same ward, the staff was quite resistant to this in practice.

Consider what happened when Karen H was admitted to the Research Ward:

Karen H had previously decided with her private doctor that she would participate in the special research program on the Research Ward, but there was no evidence that Ms. H signed any forms or was told anything in particular about the Protocol when she was admitted to the Hospital. During her first day on the ward, she told our observer that she planned to be on the Protocol, and she discussed it at some length with the observer. While there were several general discussions about her participating in the Protocol during the first few days of her stay, it was not until the end of the third day that Dr. J asked her whether anyone had spoken to her about the Protocol. She said no, but even then neither Dr. J nor any other staff member discussed it with her. It was not until 2 days later, when she asked the physician's assistant about it, that something was done.

PATIENT: I've been asked a few times by patients if I am on Protocol. Do you know why?

PHYSICIAN'S ASSISTANT: I guess that's what you consented to when you came here.

PATIENT: No one mentioned it to me.

PHYSICIAN'S ASSISTANT: Didn't you fill out forms when you came here?

PATIENT: Yes.

PHYSICIAN'S ASSISTANT: Did they mention sleep studies to you?

PATIENT: I'm certain that they didn't.

PHYSICIAN'S ASSISTANT: I'll check on the chart. That's the reason you came here.

PATIENT: Maybe that was my doctor's idea.

NURSE: All the waiting you went through in the Evaluation Center was because of the forms.

PATIENT: No, no one explained it to me. No one told me about it. I just heard it from patients.

PHYSICIAN'S ASSISTANT: I promise I'll check that, but that isn't my understanding. I understand that you were in the Evaluation Center for 4 hours because you weren't sure you would consent to Protocol. We admitted you here only on the basis that you would.

PATIENT: No.

PHYSICIAN'S ASSISTANT: I'll check that.

They agreed to talk about it further. However, by themselves in Staff Rounds, they were not so generous. They clearly believed that Ms. H had betrayed an agreement made with somebody by questioning whether she should be on Protocol. Dr. M summarized the staff's sentiments by saying that Ms. H should either "shape up or ship out" and that he would insist that she sign the Protocol or leave the ward.

The next morning in Walking Rounds, Dr. M renewed the staff's position by insisting that, even if she had not signed the consent form, she had been told about the Protocol, since she had spent many hours in the Evaluation Center so that the staff could decide whether she fitted into the Protocol. Furthermore, her private psychiatrist must have explained this to her. She insisted that the doctor had explained to her only that she might be given sugar pills for awhile, and that no one had mentioned the word "Protocol" to her. Dr. M then told her that since she did not live in the catchment area and since she did not have her own private insurance, he couldn't keep her on the ward unless she was on the Protocol. She said that nobody explained that to her when she came into the Hospital.

Later that day a social worker talked to Ms. H to see if she would sign the Protocol consent form. The conversation went on for quite a while, but the choice that Ms. H was given can be summed up in the closing exchanges of the conversation.

PATIENT: I don't want to sign anything. I want to talk with Dr. M or one of the other doctors. I don't like what they did here with me. I feel they took advantage of me.

SOCIAL WORKER: Who is "they?"

PATIENT: Everyone. Maybe it was an error, but it is not easy for me to get over that. It's as if you are telling me, "either you're on Protocol or you leave."

SOCIAL WORKER: Essentially, that is what we are saying.

Although we did not directly observe it, Dr. M later told our staff-observer that Ms. H had signed the Protocol form when he had taken her into his office and had given her two forms, an AMA form and a Protocol consent form, and had told her to decide which she wanted to sign.

What needs to be emphasized about this case is that the staff was much more coercive with Ms. H than they were when trying to persuade patients in the Evaluation Center to come into the Protocol (see Reference 5, Chapter 10). They felt she was trying to violate an agreement already made with them. The decision, from their perspective, had already been made, and she was trying to get out of it. Much of the intensity of the staff's reaction to Ms. H resulted from their feeling that she was deliberately lying to them and trying to manipulate them into spending $20,000 to $30,000 on her treatment and refusing to cooperate with the Protocol.

Although most of the patients on Protocol seemed relatively content to be on it and showed no strong inclinations to change their minds, Ms. H was not unique. The staff was, however, no more receptive to Lloyd G when he considered leaving the Hospital because he thought the Protocol treatment was going to take too long.

General Treatment Cooperation

Although being on Protocol was an ambiguous decision for the patient to make, both the staff and the other patients expected that all patients would accept the general rules of the ward, the general pattern of decisionmaking, and the utility of being treated on the Research Ward. Like cooperation with the Protocol, this was understood to be a prior decision. Only three patients failed to accept this concept with any consistency. Lloyd G eventually came to accept it; Cora T was involuntarily committed to the ward until she accepted it; and Max I signed out of the Hospital.

The only formal expulsion from the ward was for failing to accept and live by the general rules of the community. Martin T was expelled from the ward for sexual misbehavior with a female patient after he had been repeatedly warned about it. Once again, the staff did not believe that accepting the rules of the community should be decided anew each time, but rather that the rules were something the patients should accept when coming on the ward. It was not a decision made by the patients or the staff or made collectively, but rather something that needed no decision while the patients were on the ward. Failure to accept these assumptions seemed to lead to expulsion.

SPECIAL CASES AND SERIOUS DISORDERS

Until now, our description of decisionmaking on the Research Ward has emphasized the routine, ordinary, and generally expected ways of making decisions. Needless to say, the actual patterns of decisionmaking were not as uniform as we have described. A number of special circumstances led to decisions being made in radically different ways. Let us now consider those special circumstances.

INCOMPETENCY

We have noted in Section Two that the Evaluation Center staff members seemed to adjust the amount of information they disclosed to their assessment of a patient's competency. This in turn was rather closely related to their perception of the patient's illness.

We observed a somewhat similar pattern on the Research Ward. Although by and large the patients on the ward were more competent than the patients in the Evaluation Center were, we did note that in a few instances the staff seemed to decide that the patients were not competent to participate in the decision. In such cases, the entire decisionmaking pattern changed quite markedly. Even though staff members frequently disclosed information to an incompetent patient in the same way they would to a competent patient, they seemed much less respectful of the incompetent patient's choice. Remembering the general pattern of mutual decisionmaking about ECT that we describe above, consider the way in which the decision about Werner G's ECT was made.

Werner G, a 55-year-old man with a diagnosis of chronic psychotic depression, had been unemployed for the past 14 years and had had five previous psychiatric admissions. Mr. G gave the general appearance of being miserable, rarely spoke to anyone spontaneously, and even when questioned was inclined to give one- or two-word answers. However, he was clear on one thing—he did not want to have ECT. Even before ECT was suggested to him, he repeatedly asked the staff whether he would have "the treatment," which apparently referred to ECT. Several patients told our observer that Mr. G thought the sleep studies he was getting were ECT, and the staff notes say that "he was quite frightened when getting wired up for sleep studies." He was repeatedly assured by both staff and patients that he could not receive ECT until he signed the consent form. However, a number of patients and staff members privately noted that under certain conditions he might have it if his wife signed for it. Although the staff members reported that Mrs. G was in favor of Mr. G's receiving ECT because it had helped 15 years earlier, they decided to try a combination of antipsychotic and antidepressant medications before considering ECT. Whether this was based on Mr. G's continually telling them he didn't want it is not clear. However, after Mr. G had been on the medications for 8 days, one of the staff asked Dr. M at Staff Rounds what he thought should be done with Mr. G. Dr. M responded that Mr. G was Dr. J's patient, but if it were up to him he would shock him. A medical student interjected that Dr. J had told him the only thing that had worked for Mr. G in the past was ECT. Dr. M then responded, "Let's shock him on Wednesday." Several staff members commented that this was the next day and that Mr. G did not want to get ECT. Dr. M asked when Mrs. G was coming in to see Mr. G and then decided to postpone the ECT for 2 days in order to allow Mrs. G to use her influence with her husband.

The next day at Staff Rounds the social worker reported that she had talked with Mrs. G, who thought that ECT had helped in the earlier situation, although

Mr. G himself believed that ECT was the cause of his illness. Mrs. G apparently believed the staff should not explain anything to him, since this would just confuse him; rather, they should just give him a pencil and paper so he could sign. Dr. M said he would take the form to Mr. G.

The next day Mr. G, with "encouragement" from his wife, signed the consent form for ECT. However, the following day when the ECT was scheduled, he refused to have it, promising instead to have it on Monday. According to the staff, Mr. G twice came to the nurses' station over the weekend to tell them he did not want to have ECT. When a patient asked him whether he was going to have ECT on Monday, Mr. G responded, "No." The patients then pressured him to accept it, telling him that he might end up spending the rest of his life in the state hospital if he did not. That Monday, our staff-observer was told by one of the staff members that they had decided "to give it another shot; and if that won't help, we'll kick him out of the ward." Mrs. G also came to the ward that day to encourage him to accept ECT. Mr. G did receive ECT that Monday. Shortly thereafter, Dr. J told our staff observer that he wouldn't have given ECT to Mr. G if he had refused, since he had "never given it to a patient who had refused." Mr. G continued to receive ECT over the following weeks and improved markedly, although the improvement did not persist.

Although other cases were less dramatic, a patient's role as decisionmaker was generally downgraded to the degree that the staff saw the patient as incompetent. This was consistent with the structure of the law, except in two ways. First, the staff made no attempt to get formal adjudication from a court to the effect that the patient was incompetent.[1] Second, while the law treats competency as either absent or present, the staff tended to treat it as a matter of degree.

DANGEROUSNESS

Another factor that changed the way in which decisions were normally made was whether or not a patient was considered "dangerous." In general, "dangerous" patients had their privileges restricted, and the normal processes of processes of collective decisionmaking were ignored or modified.

The most obvious examples were the two highly suicidal patients, Lloyd G and Leonard T, who were maintained on "constant observation" status by administrative fiat. Their statuses and privileges were decided independently of the recommendation of the Advisory Board.

In a somewhat similar vein, the staff considered, but did not implement, a proposal to keep Stanley G from getting "monitor" status because he reported having "murderous" thoughts. While they agreed that he had done everything specified by the rules to obtain such a status, the staff felt he should not be granted it because he was dangerous. Nevertheless, since "monitor" status did not involve allowing him to leave the building, it was not vetoed.

SPECIAL THERAPEUTIC NEEDS

The final factor that could modify the routine decisionmaking procedures was a decision by the staff that there were sufficient therapeutic grounds for modifying the procedures. For example, on one occasion, Stanley G was denied a weekend pass from the Hospital because the staff felt the request indicated that Mr. G was actually testing boundaries and thus needed some discipline. Similarly, although the rules of the ward specified that one was supposed to talk about one's problems as much as possible with other patients, Dwayne T was explicitly forbidden to do so. Mr. T believed his major problem to be a physical one that caused severe pains in his neck. However, the staff believed that this was simply a defensive tactic and that Mr. T should talk about the things that were really bothering him. However, since Mr. T continued to believe what was really bothering him was his neck, they eventually forbade his discussing it.

THE BASIS FOR CONSENSUS: NORMS AND SANCTIONS

We have seen that a fairly general consensus existed on the Research Ward about how decisions should be made about treatment. While patients occasionally objected to specific parts of this consensus as it applied to them, in general the patient community strongly supported this consensus, even when it involved the staff's making decisions for them. We now address the question of why this support existed.

All social groups have power and status differentials within them. These differences are maintained in part by various types of sanctions available to the powerful and in part by the belief that these distinctions are right and just. Over the long run, both are necessary to maintain those differences. This was certainly true on the Research Ward. Although the staff had ample access to sanctions to coerce or induce patients to cooperate, it was rarely necessary to use them. Rather, the pattern of decisionmaking was seen by patients as reasonable.

NORMS: THE DOCTOR-PATIENT RELATIONSHIP

The legal allocation of decisionmaking authority to the patients was seriously compromised by two factors in the doctor-patient relationship: (1) the patients' trust in the staff's expertise and goodwill, and (2) to the societal definition of the patients' role.

Belief in the Staff's Expertise

The belief that the treating staff had a body of expertise much greater than that of the best-educated patient worked against patients' exercising autonomous judgment. In Chapter 10 we note that Justin M, a research patient who had been drug-free for 13 of the required 14 days, was called to the drug-dispensing counter and mistakenly given a pill by the nurse. In reporting this event to the patient-observer, Mr. M said he thought it was strange but then decided, "I'm not going to tell her her job," and took the pill. Only later did he ask, "By the way, what was that pill I took?" Similarly, Timothy M never thought to question the nurse when, although he had not been receiving medication in the evening, he was called to the counter at 9 P.M. and given Trilafon and "something else." His only comment to our observer was, "They usually tell you at the beginning if they're going to give you something extra, but I'm not sure what happened to me this time."

The belief that the doctor is "all-knowing" may have had even more subtle effects. Phyllis D, a depressed patient who felt no better after drug treatment, was reluctant to discuss this with the doctor because "I assumed that the doctor had picked the right medicine and that it should be working, and I also thought maybe he won't believe me because I hadn't had any contact with a psychiatrist before, so maybe he wouldn't believe that I wasn't feeling better if I was getting the right medicine."

The Patients' Status

To some degree, the patients' lack of assertiveness in decisionmaking was a reflection of the societal definition of the status of "patients" and what patients themselves felt about their capabilities as decisionmakers. Because the Research Ward was one to which patients who were considered "treatment failures" were referred, it was considered by many to be a place of last resort. Many patients felt they were not only failing at life but also failing in their treatment as well. This type of despair about their capabilities led Velma B to say, "I just don't see any other way than patients' having trust in the doctors." Similarly, when Brenda N was given ECT after her medication failure, she recounted to fellow patients that she said to the nurse, "You just do whatever you like." The nurse advised her, "No, it's got to be up to you." But Ms. N commented later, "You know, I felt like giving up. I was crying when I went in and crying when I came out."

The fact that patients feel ill can also mean that they feel incapable of expressing their desires. Thus Janice Q recalled that, before an interview, a doctor asked her if she had any objections to medical students sitting in. "I did have objections," she said, "but I was feeling so weak that I just didn't have the guts to say 'Yes, I do object.' I just went in there and felt uncomfortable."

Ms. Q was also interviewed by a journalist interested in depression. Before going to this interview, she mentioned to other patients that she was interested in asking the journalist some questions. When she arrived at the doctor's office, she was asked to wait outside while the doctor entered carrying her chart. Perhaps the knowledge that the journalist would see her chart and thus symbolically be encouraged to view her as a "patient" caused Ms. Q's reaction: "Every feeling that I would ask questions just evaporated."

SANCTIONS

The consensus about how decisions were made on the Research Ward was not completely self-enforcing. Patients did object and disagree. They occasionally believed that they knew better than the staff. For these occasions, a variety of sanctions were available to the staff and to other patients to ensure the proper role for the patients in the decisionmaking process and the proper decision itself.

Physical Force

In general, the types of pressures brought to bear on patients in this setting were much more subtle than those we saw in the Evaluation Center. During our observations on the ward, we saw no one dragged or pushed, nor did we see any patient put in seclusion. One obvious form of restraint—locking the ward door—occurred twice: once when Leonard T was considered to be in imminent danger of committing suicide, and another time when the staff feared that Cora T, who was involuntarily committed, would attempt to leave the Hospital.

Force of Law

As in the Evaluation Center, the Research Ward staff had a strong potential weapon to use in coercing patients, though it was rarely used—the force of law, exercised through involuntary commitment proceedings. Both patients who were originally voluntarily hospitalized and those who were involuntarily committed were subject to this form of pressure. Voluntary patients could be subsequently involuntarily committed if they met the legal criteria for involuntary commitment, and involuntarily committed patients, despite the fixed term of their commitment, could have the original commitment extended. The only person against whom the threat and actual use of involuntary commitment occurred was Cora T, a 33-year-old woman diagnosed as a paranoid schizophrenic. She attempted to sign out AMA and was thereafter involuntarily committed three times.

Family Involvement

Pressure from family members was a major source of sanctions. Almost without exception, family members were supportive of the authority and actual decisions of the staff.

There were many cases in which family involvement supported the staff's point of view. Molly X reported that her husband advised her, "You should do whatever the staff tells you." Similarly, Leonard T said that his parents told him, "Whatever the doctor suggests, you do it." Karen H also said that her mother advised that, whatever the recommendation of the doctor, "it is good to follow it." She told other patients, "Even if they say I will be better off in another country, then she is going to make me do that." Likewise, Pearl M came to the Hospital as a result of encouragement from family members. "My husband's family wanted me to come in, and I thought that maybe I should." Both Eloise T and Felicia E reported very active support for treatment from family members. Both patients wished to leave the Hospital after being drug-free a few days, and both were encouraged by family members to stay. Ms. T's father said, "This is just going to be another example of your giving up on something and quitting, and then you are going to feel really guilty again." Other patients were faced with threats from family members that were intended to make them comply with the treatment plan. For instance, Faye C, a patient who had come to the Hospital for treatment of alcoholism, reported to other patients that her husband would divorce her if she didn't quit drinking.

In only two cases did a family member support a patient who refused treatment, and even these cases are equivocal. Prior to Brenda N's entering the Hospital, her husband promised that under no circumstances would he allow her to receive ECT treatment. However, after a conference with the psychiatrist at which Ms. N was present, and since she seemed willing, he agreed that she should have it. In the other case, Noelle H, who had previously experienced a bad side effect from ECT, told her husband that she didn't want ECT and added, "You're not going to make me, are you?" to which he replied, "Not if it makes you as bad as it did [on the previous occasion]."

Staff Use of Family Pressure

In general, the families and the informal sanctions that were available through them were aligned on the side of the staff, even when the ward consensus was that the decision was to be a mutual one. In some cases, staff members used relatives to ensure that a certain course of treatment was followed. This was done either by alluding to the attitudes of relatives or by using them directly. Brad C, undecided about the recommendation to have ECT, was reminded by the doctor that his wife didn't want him home again. Mr. C responded, "Yes, she won't have me back in this condition."

Martin T's family was used more directly. The staff wanted Mr. T to go to a halfway house and to assume more responsibility for his life. They simply advised his parents not to take him back home. Later at a meeting with his parents and the psychiatrist, after Mr. T had been expelled from the ward for misconduct, his distraught mother told him that he had "lost a doctor and lost a hospital," and that if he wouldn't follow instructions he would also "lose his mother." The staff members also persuaded Cora T's mother to sign an involuntary commitment petition to assure that Ms. T would not be able to leave the Hospital as early as she had hoped.

The Therapeutic Community

As we have noted, an important aspect of the Research Ward was that it operated as a "therapeutic community." In the therapeutic community, the kinds of behaviors for which patients were rewarded were openness about one's own problems and support for others in dealing with their problems. Much of this supportive behavior was organized around attempting to make patients aware of the "true" nature—that is, the psychiatric nature—of their troubles, as well as the ways in which they could be helped (by becoming contributing members of the community and by accepting treatments prescribed by the medical staff). Advocacy of the therapeutic community and of other treatments utilized on the ward was a constant theme in the various meetings among patients; patients and staff; and patients, staff, and family members. The symbolic power of the community was expressed in a previously quoted exchange: A patient asked Werner G, "Do you want to get well?" Mr. G said that he did, and the person who addressed him went on to say, "Well, why don't you show *us* by accepting the treatment that the doctors have given you?" (emphasis ours).

The ability of the patient group to influence the decisions of its members was enhanced by the existence of the therapeutic community's stepladder status system, described in Chapter 9. To gain promotion to a higher status, a patient was required to satisfy other patients that he or she had behaved in accordance with the rules of the community. A typical example was the case of Cora T. As the period of her involuntary commitment began to run out, Ms. T was repeatedly asked by the staff to sign into the Hospital voluntarily, but she refused. During the previous week, Ms. T had been denied an increase in status, based on her denial that she needed hospitalization. On the morning of the next group meeting to decide status requests, Ms. T told the patient-observer that she wanted to sign out. When the meeting was held, however, she was given much positive encouragement for her status increase. When she was asked by patients at the meeting if she wanted to leave or if she would sign out if she were not committed, she said she would stay. She was then granted an increase in status and did not again talk about leaving.

Influence of Other Patients

Even apart from the therapeutic community, patients acted as very effective persuasive agents on one another. One patient aided in assuring compliance with treatment by telling another, "I'm very pleased with the way you are fighting the side effects of the medication. I am very proud of you." On another occasion, a former patient visiting the ward after a meeting with his social worker stopped Velma B and said, "I hear you finally got ECT. You know that's going to get you out of here; you know that." Similarly, on hearing that Ms. B had agreed to have ECT, Werner G slapped her on the shoulder and said,

"I wish you a lot of luck. I hope you'll feel the same as I do after eight [treatments]." Such reassurance was common. Brad C, who was grumbling about the inconvenience of having to return to the Hospital every evening after work and was thus thinking about leaving, was reminded by Janice Q that "they want to see how you get along, and you are a little apprehensive about going to work." By relieving fears, patients also got other patients to accept treatment. When Mildred L expressed doubts about continuing with a drug after having experienced bad side effects from it, Justin M told her, "In this hospital they are really going to make sure that they are giving you the right medicine."

It was not uncommon that patients who came to the ward were reluctant to stay; they found the prospect of being drug-free for 2 weeks and the process of induction into the community difficult to accept. As one new patient expressed it, "I thought the meeting yesterday was a bit gruesome. I really didn't want to talk in front of all those people." Many expressed the desire to leave, but in all but one instance other patients persuaded them to stay. Noelle H thought about leaving during the first few days, but later recalled that Karen H, who had entered the ward at about the same time, said to her "We'll stick it out; we'll stick it out."

Karen H herself was subject to some pressure to stay after she became upset about how the staff treated her after a group therapy session. She began to talk of leaving. Other patients encouraged her to stay, saying that her despair was a result of going through a period of drug withdrawal. A community member also encouraged her to rely on other patients, saying, "Oh, you need a nursemaid. Perhaps none of them [staff members] has had the experience, and everyone around you has, and we are the people who can help you most."

This is a particularly interesting example, because Ms. H encouraged other patients who were thinking of leaving during the same time period to stay in the Hospital. This was not unusual. Patients frequently encouraged other patients to comply with the very same treatment proposals that they themselves had resisted.

MULTIPLE SOURCES OF PERSUASION

We have emphasized that decisions on the Research Ward were processes over time, not unitary events. They tended to involve a large variety of people, not just the doctors and the patients in question. This resulted in pressures being put on the patients from a variety of sources over a substantial period of time. Consider Noelle H's initial decision to accept Aventyl, which we have discussed earlier in this chapter. One evening, after a visit to a neighborhood restaurant with her husband and two other patients, she returned to the ward and was greeted by a nurse with the news, "You're going to get some Aventyl." Ms. H was disturbed by this and indicated that she didn't want to take this drug. Her husband then said, "You should, Noelle. You should take it. That's the stuff that makes you better." Ms. H still objected, saying that the psychiatrist hadn't discussed this medication with her. Another patient joined the conversation, saying, "You can talk about it in the morning. Just take it when Karen takes hers. Just pop it down." Ms. H then said that she would like to take it just before she went to sleep so that she wouldn't worry about side effects. The nurse replied that Ms. H couldn't do that, since it was ordered for 9 P.M. "You have to take it now," she said. Ms. H, surrounded by four people actively encouraging her to take the medicine, reluctantly did so.

Not only were patients influenced by multiple persuaders, but they were also subject to such influence on many occasions. A good example was the case of Felicia E, a divorced woman with a son who lived with his father in a city 200 miles away. During her hospitalization, Ms. E's social worker told her that she should tell her son that she was in the Hospital, since the staff wanted him to come to the Hospital to provide information about her behavior prior to hospitalization. In a community meeting, Ms. E questioned the utility of the enterprise. Her attitude met with no support, and other patients advised her that she ought to do what her social worker suggested. When the chairperson of the community asked whether she was going to make the call, Ms. E responded that she would like to think about it a little more. At that point a staff member interjected, "I'd just like to add that when you do go to the telephone, you should take along a staff member or someone that you are close to for moral support."

A week later, Brenda N asked Ms. E in a Wrap-Up what she was going to do about calling her son. She posed the same question the following morning at a meeting, as well as at an evening meeting a day later. Ms. E appeared reluctant to telephone, saying that she had tried to call home but that no one had answered. Ms. N responded rather sarcastically, "You got a reprieve, huh?"

The issue surfaced again when Ms. E complained to the psychiatrist that her social worker intended to call her son, irrespective of her wishes. In a firm voice, she stated, "She has no right to do that, doctor." She further maintained that since her son was a minor, it would be "wrong legally" to contact him without her consent. The doctor then responded in a harsh, fatherly tone, "If she doesn't, I will," and then turned to another subject. But Ms. E was not content to leave this topic, saying she would speak to her son when she felt ready. Days later, however, Ms. E suffered a "panic" attack and some shortness of breath after another discussion with the social worker. The next day she reported in a group therapy session that she would call her son, since "it must obviously be upsetting me." She reported community members were supportive of this action and had told her that "I won't get so anxious after I've done it." When she was interviewed upon discharge, however, Ms. E had a perception of herself as having been coerced into this course of action.

Another patient who was subject to influence from multiple persuaders on numerous occasions was that of Lloyd G, a Protocol patient. His intention to leave the hospital AMA was brought up by an aide as a topic for general discussion at one of the patient meetings. Mr. G maintained that since he wasn't getting any better, he felt he would be better off at home. The aide challenged him, saying that he couldn't have been functioning all that well; "otherwise, why did you come here?" Five other patients in turn urged him to stay and to get out of his room and to talk more to people, reminding him that he was undergoing a difficult experience in being drug-free.

The next day at the morning meeting, the issue of Mr. G's leaving was brought up again by the community chairperson. Mr. G said that he wanted to go home to attend to personal matters, but he was again strongly urged to stay. One patient told him, "I have been worried that you will throw away a very good chance. It is my understanding that when you sign out AMA you can't come back to this floor," and looked to the staff member, who agreed with the statement. Again, at a patient meeting the next day, Mr. G was asked if he intended to stay. He said that he would like to talk things over with his wife; other patients assured him that he would feel much better when the drug-free period was ended. The following day, during Walking Rounds, the head nurse asked him if his wife's leaving him made it difficult for him to decide about staying. She then continued, "If you stay here and get treatment, it will help keep your marriage going, but if you leave you will stay in the same mess, which is why your wife doesn't want to stay with you." After talking with his wife, who promised to stay with him if he remained in the Hospital, Mr. G eventually decided to stay.

STAFF'S AND PATIENTS' ENCOURAGEMENT OF PATIENTS' DECISIONMAKING

We have discussed the ways in which patients' inclinations to exercise their decisional authority were reduced through pressures from other patients, staff members, and family members; through structural aspects of the Research Ward organization; and through their own internal pressures. These pressures far exceeded the forces propelling patients in the direction of exercising decisional authority, but they did not completely submerge them. In fact in some situations that we observed on the Research Ward, the staff—and especially one of the psychiatrists—strongly encouraged patients to make their own decisions.

At a meeting with Christine E and her parents, Dr. J said that he was willing to discharge her, but recommended that she stay longer in order to benefit from the community setting. He then asked her what she wanted to do. Ms. E did not answer but looked to her father, who told her that it was her decision and something that she should work out with the doctor. Ms. E still did not respond, but at the next meeting in the patient community, she raised her hand and said, "I want some help. I had a meeting with Dr. J, and he says it's entirely up to me whether to stay or to go." Janice Q then asked Ms. E whether she wanted other people to tell her what to do, to which Ms. E replied, "I guess so."

Encouraging patients to make their own decisions may be just as complex and frustrating as getting them to make the "right" decisions. For example, in Chapter 10, we report Dr. J's efforts to get Felicia E to decide whether to take a medication and endure its side effects or to reduce the dosage and risk loss of effectiveness:

Dr. J concluded a long discussion by saying, "I have limited alternatives to go to. You're the one, not me, who has to decide what disturbs you more." Ms. E did not appear to understand these alternatives and asked, "Doctor, is my vision important? Because it is to me." He replied, "I can't tell you; that's your decision." Dr. J later told the staff-observer that he considered Ms. E competent. He appeared a little exasperated with her because she "can't even make a decision whether her symptoms or the side effects bother her more." Ms. E was upset over her interaction with the doctor on this issue and remarked to other patients, "The staff doesn't care very much what happens to you." She also protested about having the responsibility for the decision placed in her hands, explaining, "It seems that they want you to know everything. How do I know all about medicine? I just went to high school and I didn't keep up on all this stuff."

A similar response was evoked by Phyllis D, who was also presented with a number of treatment alternatives and was asked by the psychiatrist to choose among them; this made her so anxious that she talked with the social worker about having the doctor make the decision. Ms. D remarked to the patient-observer, "I think, in a way, it's right to give someone a choice, but I don't really feel that I had enough information to make the decision, and I wasn't going to go to a medical dictionary and figure it all out." Thus even when the staff attempted to promote patients' participation in treatment decisionmaking, the patients sometimes balked at the chance.

The therapeutic community also provided a supportive environment for patients' assertiveness, within certain boundaries. For instance, Christine E was denied a pass because it became evident that she had not asked questions of the staff about her sleep studies, which the chairperson of the community thought she should have done.

Patients sometimes supported each other informally, particularly their friends, in efforts to get information from the staff that they considered important. This was particularly true about the results of sleep studies, which the patients almost unanimously believed to be very important in determining what medications they should receive. We saw three separate occasions in which one or more patients encouraged others to ask about the results of sleep studies. Although less frequently, almost all types of information gathering were occasionally supported by other patients. For example, Mildred L was told by other patients that she couldn't be expected to take medication without obtaining information about it from the staff, and she was urged to do so.

However, it must be reiterated that, as much as staff members and other patients encouraged participation in treatment decisions, this encouragement was limited to decisions that were considered therapeutic. Participation in decisionmaking was done as part of therapy; not for its own sake.

12

Summary of the Research Ward Findings

In this chapter, we provide a brief overview of the major trends on the Research Ward in order to facilitate a comprehensive evaluation of the findings. However, in making such an evaluation, it is important to remember that the Research Ward was not a typical ward, even for the Hospital. It was a highly desired placement for both staff and patients and was generally thought to provide the best care in the Hospital. Moreover, it was based on the principles of the therapeutic community, which substantially affected both the way information was disclosed and the decisionmaking processes.

THE DECISIONMAKING PROCESS

In general, we can say that there were four different decisionmaking patterns, and that these patterns differed depending on which decision was being made.

The first of these patterns was one in which the staff made the decisions. This applied to all decisions about medications and about the type of testing a patient would undergo. For example, decisions about medication were generally made during Staff Rounds in the middle of the day, and were then implemented when the medications were next dispensed to patients in the early evening. When a patient was being given a totally new medication, the medication nurse usually told the patient the name of the medicine, either on her own initiative or after the patient had asked about it. However, this was not an opportunity for the patient to object. When patients did object, they were typically told to take the medication now and to discuss it with the doctor the next morning. By and large, patients did very little except to find out from the doctor the names of the medications they were taking. However, when they objected or provided alternate suggestions, these were sometimes accepted. Whether these suggestions were accepted seemed to be determined, at least in part, by whether the patients accepted the authority of the staff to make the treatment decisions.

The same pattern is shown in the temporal structure of disclosure of testing. Patients were often informed of psychological and physiological testing they were to receive only when taking the tests. Typical disclosures of what was going to happen often involved no more than a simple statement that a patient would be having some tests.

The second pattern of decisionmaking is closely related to the first. This is what we call "prior decisionmaking." For both participation in the Protocol and for general cooperation with the rules and restrictions of the ward, both staff and patients treated the decisions as though they had been made prior to admission to the ward, that is, as though there were no further decisions to be made by the patients at all.

The third pattern of decisionmaking is probably unique to those settings that use therapeutic communities—the pattern we call "collective decision-making." The formal power to decide on patients' privileges was lodged in an elected group of five patients called the Advisory Board, which decided, after hearing the opinions of other patients and sometimes those of the staff, what privileges would be granted to patients. However, the staff reserved the right to veto the Advisory Board's decisions, and it was clear that the Advisory Board listened closely to the staff's opinions. In general, the Advisory Board usually granted the requests, unless the staff opposed them or the requests clearly violated the rules. Thus the Advisory Board Meeting became an opportunity for patients to try to persuade the staff that their friends should be allowed more privileges (patients were not allowed to speak on behalf of their own requests). However, the Advisory Board was supposed to make its decisions on the basis of rules that governed the right to obtain privileges. Thus these rules often constrained the staff members to accept or reject a proposed new privilege for a patient, even when they would rather have done otherwise.

The final type of decisionmaking is one we call "mutual participation." This decisionmaking pattern is close to the one envisioned by the doctrine of informed consent. Two types of decisions were made in this way. Decisions related to postdischarge planning constituted the first of these types. Here the patients and staff cooperated fairly well in making the decisions. The decision-making in this area more closely resembles the decisionmaking in the Out-patient Clinic, which we discuss in Section Four. The greater role for patients in this instance is probably related to the fact that the staff had little control over patients once they left the ward. Thus the patients' active cooperation was necessary in order for the treatment plans to be carried out. The second, more interesting type of decision that was made this way was the decision about ECT. Why the staff conceded such a great role to patients in making this decision is difficult to understand. Perhaps the presence of the consent form that had to be signed prior to the treatment was one factor. Also, given the public nature of treatment decisions and the nature of the patients' feelings about ECT, perhaps cooperative decisionmaking helped to demonstrate to the other patients that those who had received ECT thought it was a good idea. Certainly most patients came onto the ward unreceptive to receiving ECT and tended to resist getting it initially. Sometimes the resistance lasted for several weeks. However, we saw no patient who successfully resisted the sustained desire of the staff to give the patient ECT.

Running throughout the four different types of decisions, even decisions based on mutual participation, was the underlying assumption that it was up to the staff to make medical decisions. The patients essentially reserved for themselves only the right to object. The overwhelming assumption was that the patients should cooperate because the treatments were being administered in their best interests. Even more than in the Evaluation Center, we found that patients on the Research Ward placed great faith in the doctors' expertise. While it is true that pressure from other patients, family members, and the staff members themselves played some role in the high level of patients' cooperation with staff-proposed treatments, the prestige of the staff among the patients was so high as to leave most patients inclined to cooperate. When this was combined with the patients' own view of their limited capacities to make these decisions, they were inclined to give the staff a large benefit of the doubt in making decisions.

It is also noteworthy, however, that—at least as compared with the Evaluation Center—the Research Ward staff gave most of the patients a very substantial role in deciding about their own treatment. Even in such decisions as medication, in which the staff was almost the sole decisionmaker, the patients were eventually told a great deal about the treatment, and they were expected to participate in implementing the treatment.

In general, the staff members were open with the patients, told them what they felt was important information, and listened to the patients' feelings about the issues at hand. There were, however, some exceptions. While decisions about ECT or discharge were mutually made, the staff members felt free to make such decisions for a patient if they believed the patient to be either dangerous or intellectually or emotionally incapable of making a decision. We saw a number of such instances. In doing so, the staff seemed to be consistent with the general spirit of the law, even if their actual practices sometimes violated the letter of the law.

PATTERNS OF DISCLOSURE

As in any system in which people are thrown together for substantial periods of time, there were multiple channels of communication. However, the Research Ward was unique since often the staff disclosed information to the patients collectively—as a unit in public meetings—rather than individually, the way most theorists of informed consent have envisioned. This collective disclosure was done by means of the Walking Rounds, in which each case was discussed between the patient in question and the staff, in front of all the other patients. This meant that whatever information was conveyed to patients routinely about their treatment was also conveyed to all the other patients. Thus most patients, when they were prescribed a drug, had already heard the drug discussed by staff with other patients.

A second major difference between disclosure on the Research Ward and the model of disclosure envisioned in informed consent is that disclosure on the Research Ward usually came from multiple sources. Thus the two psychiatrists on the ward took turns doing Walking Rounds. When both were occupied, the physician's assistant was primarily in charge of Walking Rounds. Moreover, the patients received information from the ward nurses, from volunteers, from psychiatric aides, and from various other ward personnel. Patients also received substantial information from other patients. Beyond the obvious advantage of patients' receiving more information than they might have otherwise received, the multiple sources of information sometimes caused troubles. One problem was that the information sources sometimes conflicted with one another. The second difficulty was that it was not always clear who was responsible for informing patients. As in the Evaluation Center, there was a sense of "floating responsibility."

Another observation we made was that there seemed to be various styles of disclosure. One style of disclosure, which we call "legal-rational," conformed closely with the doctrine of informed consent. However, it seemed that the patients responded more positively to the "charismatic" style of disclosure, which was more reassuring but could also be deceptive.

PATIENTS' UNDERSTANDING

One of the most interesting findings on the Research Ward was that the patients relied much more on other sources of information than on statements from the staff. Thus the patients tended to cite either their own past experience with treatments, their observations of other patients, or the things other patients told them about their treatment. Direct disclosure by staff members was cited relatively rarely, and even then it was often cited with some skepticism. However, this finding must be qualified by the fact that most of what was heard from other patients was a recounting of what other patients had previously been told by the staff. Indeed, the patients' interpretations of their own experiences was strongly affected by the staff's viewpoint.

A second major finding was that the patients seemed to have substantial difficulty in distinguishing research from treatment. In general, they found it hard to believe that the staff was not acting in their best interests in all circumstances. They seemed to have difficulty in understanding the systematic features of the research design and the ways in which these affected the staff's decisions about how to treat them.

A final interesting point about patients' understanding is that, while patients in general understood quite well, it usually took them some time on the ward to do so. Typically, they were still learning important features about treatment and research decisions toward the end of the first week. To the degree that these were continuing decisions, of course, this may well have been an acceptable feature of the decisionmaking.

SANCTIONS AND TRUST

Overall, we found a relatively high degree of consensus among patients and staff about the nature of treatment, its risks and benefits, and the alternatives that were available. Patients did not typically understand all of those issues, but they understood substantial parts of them. The basis of this consensus was both normative and coercive, although primarily the former. Patients had a great deal of trust in the staff in general, and were impressed with staff members' specialized technical expertise. They saw themselves as relatively weak and incapable of making the decisions, and they tended to feel that such decisions were best left to the staff.

Relatively few coercive pressures were brought to bear on the patients. The doors to the ward were locked twice: once when one of the patients was suicidal, and again in the case of an involuntary commitment. Involuntary commitment itself was used in only one case.

A more important type of pressure came from families and other patients. Almost without exception, both in public and in private, both the families of patients and the other patients tended to support what the staff said. They repeatedly encouraged cooperation with the staff's treatment plans and reassured the patients that the treatment plans were in their own best interests. While there was occasional support from other patients for autonomous decisionmaking, the pressures were overwhelmingly in favor of cooperation with the staff. We know of only one instance in which a family member encouraged a patient to make a different decision from the one the staff wanted. The intensity of these pressures was reinforced by the fact that they came from multiple sources, not just from one patient or one family member.

In general, decisionmaking in the Research Ward more closely approximated informed consent than did decisionmaking in the Evaluation Center. However, even here, there were substantial divergences from the model of informed consent. These were due to, among other things, the therapeutic community structure of the ward; the fact that treatment took place over a long period of time; paternalism on the part of the staff; and the patients' assumptions that the staff members were best qualified to make the decisions.

The Outpatient Clinic

13

Introduction to the Outpatient Clinic

Slightly more than 80% of all patients receiving treatment at the Hospital were outpatients; the figure is typical of psychiatric treatment in the United States as a whole. At the Hospital, there were several different clinics that provided treatment to outpatients. Some were organized according to the kinds of mental illness that they treated—there was a clinic for depression, another for schizophrenia, and one for drug addiction. Still other clinics were organized on the basis of the kinds of treatment they provided: individual psychotherapy, group therapy, and family therapy. The "Outpatient Clinic" is the name we gave to one of these clinics, which specialized in treatment of schizophrenia and cared for approximately 10% of the Hospital's outpatients.

The primary treatment for schizophrenia that the Outpatient Clinic provided was a class of antipsychotic drugs known generically as phenothiazines, including Thorazine, Mellaril, Stelazine, Trilafon, and Prolixin. Other patients received other types of antipsychotic medications, including drugs such as Haldol or Navane. All of these medications can be taken orally, but Prolixin is commonly given in the form of "depot" injections; that is, the patient receives injections of the medication at 2- to 3-week intervals. The undesirable side effects of antipsychotic drugs include a potentially permanent one, tardive dyskinesia, which may involve involuntary movements of the lips, tongue, hands, and fingers, and/or other uncontrolled body movements. The best estimates of the prevalence of tardive dyskinesia range between 10 and 20% of chronic patients.[1] This side effect, however, is disabling and/or severe for a smaller percentage of all patients—perhaps 1-3% of them. Reversible side effects of antipsychotic drugs include motor restlessness, muscle spasms or stiffness, and pseudoparkinsonism (tremors, shuffling walk, drooling). Dry mouth, blurred vision, constipation, decreased sexual functioning, dizziness, sensitivity to light, fatigue, and weight gain may also occur. The temporary muscle-related side effects of antipsychotic drugs are typically managed by giving the patient another type of medication known as antiparkinsonian drugs, including Artane, Cogentin, Kemadrin, Benadryl, and Akineton. While easing the muscular rigidity and tremors associated with antipsychotic drug treatment,

239

these drugs do not relieve tardive dyskinesia. In addition, they cause unwanted side effects of their own, including dry mouth and blurred vision.

In the Outpatient Clinic, we observed 60 patient–staff contacts involving 48 patients (see Table 13-1 for a demographic breakdown of patients) and eight staff members. Nine patients were observed on more than one occasion. All but two patients had been diagnosed as schizophrenic. This includes 23 patients whose diagnosis was paranoid schizophrenia, six patients with schizo-affective schizophrenia (disorders of both thinking and mood), and the remainder with various other qualifying diagnoses. Five patients were also diagnosed as having an organic impairment. A total of 46 patients (including the two patients who had not been diagnosed as schizophrenic) were being treated with antipsychotic drugs, and 32 of these (over 60%) were also receiving antiparkinsonian drugs.

The clinic patients virtually all had had considerable prior experience with mental illness and had been treated by the Hospital for prior periods of up to 31 years (see Table 13-1). At least 36 of the 48 patients we studied had already had at least two prior psychiatric hospitalizations.

An additional four patients refused to allow us to study them, and in three instances the Outpatient Clinic staff declined to allow us to observe the interactions.

It could be argued, of course, that there is no reason to expect that we should see informed consent in a setting like the Outpatient Clinic. The clinic did not use consent forms, and there was no positive law or administrative regulation requiring it. Yet on the basis of both legal and ethical theory, the doctrine of informed consent seems relevant here. Tardive dyskinesia is a serious potential risk that might be the basis of a legal suit. Ethically, it would seem important to get consent to any substantial type of prolonged treatment with potentially risky medication. Thus we thought it important to look at this situation from the perspective of informed consent, even though there exists little positive law on the subject.

In this chapter, we try to describe the routine procedures of the Outpatient Clinic by describing three types of patients and their interactions with clinicians. We describe an "experienced" patient, a "new" patient, and a patient we saw several times. Let us begin with the type of patient we saw most often, an "experienced" patient whom we observed only once.

AN "EXPERIENCED" PATIENT

Talcot D was a typical "experienced" patient. He was a 40-year-old black single man, 5 feet 8 inches tall, overweight, with dark hair, dark eyes, and wire-rimmed spectacles. He had been receiving psychiatric treatment intermittently for more than 6 years and had had five hospitalizations, three of which had been in the Hospital. He had first been referred to the Outpatient Clinic more than 3 years before and had been treated there regularly since that time. During

TABLE 13-1. Outpatient Clinic Patients

Patient	Age	Race	Marital status	Education	Occupation	Time from first clinic contact to observation	Diagnosed schizophrenic?	Type	Medication	Number of prior admissions
Marcy N	51	W	M	8G	Homemaker	2 yr	Yes	Paranoid	Thorazine, Cogentin, Tofranil	Unknown
Joshua X	44	B	W	10G	Factory worker	0	Yes	Paranoid	Stelazine, Dilantin	1
Isabelle N	38	W	M	11G	Homemaker	2 yr	—	—	Trilafon, Cogentin	3
Elena D	36	W	S	Coll	College student	2 yr	—	—	Haldol, Cogentin	4
Jerry G	29	W	D	BA	Teacher	3 mo	Yes	Catatonic	Prolixin, Cogentin	6
Bella C	56	W	S	9G	—	6 yr	Yes	Undifferentiated	Trilafon	2
Letty D	33	B	Sep	HS	Homemaker	1 yr	Yes	Catatonic	Stelazine	4
Torno U	41	W	S	TS	Bartender	6 yr	Yes	Paranoid	Thorazine	2
Esther N	64	W	S	9G	Odd jobs	3 mo	Yes	Paranoid	Thorazine	3
Dan D	24	W	S	9G	Sheltered work-shop	4 yr	Yes	Undifferentiated	Prolixin, Cogentin, lithium, Trilafon	10
Emma D	46	B	W	HS	Homemaker	3 mo	Yes	Schizo-affective	Haldol, Cogentin	3
Jon T	45	W	S	Coll	Security Guard	20 yr	Yes	Paranoid	Haldol, Cogentin	Unknown
Dimitri V	36	W	S	—	Steel worker	1 mo	Yes	Paranoid	Trilafon, Cogentin	2
Penny D	41	B	Sep	RN	Nurse	5 yr	Yes	Schizo-affective	Haldol, Cogentin, Thorazine	3
Leslie E	67	B	D	8G	—	2 yr	Yes	Undifferentiated	Mellaril	0
Anita S	53	W	D	10G	Homemaker	9 yr	Yes	None specified	Thorazine, Cogentin	10

(continued)

241

TABLE 13-1. (*continued*)

Patient	Age	Race	Marital status	Education	Occupation	Time from first clinic contact to observation	Diagnosed schizophrenic?	Type	Medication	Number of prior admissions
Efram S	36	B	Sep	11G	Porter	6 mo	Yes	Paranoid with affective components	Trilafon, Cogentin	4
Jake E	62	W	S	11G	Laborer	4 yr	Yes	Undifferentiated	Trilafon, Cogentin	Unknown
Danielle B	70	W	S	MA	Librarian	31 yr	No	Manic–depressive	Mellaril, lithium	23
Jacinta G	32	W	S	TS	Manicurist	15 yr	Yes	—	Prolixin, Cogentin, Pertofrane, Trilafon	12
Aldo H	29	W	S	Coll	Kitchen worker	2 yr	Yes	Undifferentiated	Trilafon, Cogentin	6
Jacqueline M	46	W	W	Coll	Stenographer	6 mo	Yes	Schizo-affective, manic	Haldol, Cogentin, lithium	6
Shaw T	33	W	S	Coll	Sheltered work-shop	2 yr	Yes	Paranoid	No medication	4
Sheldon M	34	W	S	7G	Busboy	10 yr	No	Passive–aggressive personality, mentally retarded	Haldol, Cogentin	1
Wolfgang G	30	B	M	Coll	Free-lance artist	3 yr	Yes	Paranoid	No medication	4
Mimi E	35	W	D	HS	Nurse's aide	2 yr	Yes	Undifferentiated	—	5
Talcot D	40	B	S	Coll	—	6 yr	Yes	Paranoid	Prolixin, Cogentin	4
Hilda H	54	W	S	7G	Factory worker	30 yr	Yes	None specified	Prolixin, Cogentin	8
Alex G	34	W	S	HS	—	15 yr	Yes	Schizo-affective, depression	Thorazine	4
Delbert B	26	B	S	HS	Sheltered work-shop	6 yr	Yes	Paranoid	Prolixin, Cogentin, Haldol, Benadryl	9

Name	Age	Race	Marital	Education	Occupation	Duration		Diagnosis	Medication	
Ann X	26	B	M	10G	Homemaker	5 yr	Yes	Schizo-affective, paranoid	Stelazine, Cogentin	4
Loraine D	49	B	Sep	HS	—	2 yr	Yes	Paranoid	Prolixin, Haldol	11
Ottie G	54	B	M	7G	Laundry worker	10 yr	Yes	Paranoid	Prolixin, Cogentin	6
Pam X	32	W	S	8G	Practical nurse	9 yr	Yes	Paranoid	Prolixin, Cogentin, phenobarbital	5
Audrey N	46	W	S	11G	Sheltered work-shop	2 yr	No	Moderate mental retardation	Mellaril, Cogentin	Unknown
Dick C	33	W	D	Coll	Bookbinder	4 yr	Yes	Paranoid	Prolixin, Artane	5
Jason U	42	W	S	PG	Bookkeeper	14 yr	Yes	Paranoid	Thorazine	6
Hollis N	50	B	S	8G	Porter	6 mo	Yes	Catatonic	Thorazine	Unknown
Holly E	48	W	D	HS	Sheltered work-shop	21 yr	Yes	Undifferentiated	Trilafon, Cogentin	0
Benny I	25	B	S	HS	—	1 yr	Yes	Paranoid	Prolixin	8
Lucy T	66	W	M	—	Grocery clerk	22 yr	Yes	Paranoid	Prolixin, Cogentin	31
Judd D	46	W	S	11G	Janitor	24 yr	Yes	Schizo-affective, paranoid	Trilafon, Elavil	2
Evelyn G	58	W	D	—	—	0	Yes	Paranoid	Haldol, Akineton, Prolixin	3
Andrea V	69	W	W	11G	—	2 yr	Yes	Paranoid	Prolixin, Cogentin	4
Paula B	43	W	D	HS	Waitress	2 yr	Yes	Paranoid	Haldol, Benadryl, Dilantin, Cogentin, Dalmane, pheno-barbital	2
Myrna G	38	W	S	Coll	Homemaker	1 yr	—	—	Haldol, Cogentin	1
Wallace H	26	B	S	TS	Sewer worker	0	Yes	Paranoid	Trilafon	0
Nolan S	37	W	M	PG	College professor	3 mo	Yes	Paranoid	Haldol, Cogentin	1

our observations, he was also participating in outpatient group therapy at another of the Hospital's clinics. Like other clinic patients, Mr. D saw one particular therapist regularly, but occasionally was treated by other clinic staff members when his regular therapist was not able to be present for his scheduled appointment. Thus Mr. D regularly saw Dr. R; but in the interview we observed, he met with Dr. D because Dr. R was not able to be present.

The observers introduced themselves to Mr. D in the Outpatient Clinic waiting area, explained our study, and asked permission to observe his interview. Mr. D agreed, and he and the observers entered Dr. D's office together. The following conversation then occurred:

DOCTOR: I understand that you've been meeting with Dr. R every 2 weeks.

PATIENT: Right.

DOCTOR: This was decreased from every 3 weeks to every 2 weeks. Was it at this time that your medicine was decreased?

PATIENT: Yeah.

DOCTOR: I understand that Dr. R is unable to meet with you today. How did you react to that?

PATIENT: Well, I did want to meet with him, but fortunately I didn't have too much to talk about today.

DOCTOR: What did you want to talk about?

PATIENT: I wanted to ask his advice. There's an opportunity for a job at the Hospital which has come up, and I was thinking of applying for it.

DOCTOR: What kind of a job is it?

PATIENT: Well, it's an administrative assistant under a doctor. I was playing pool upstairs, and there was this guy from Personnel there, and I asked him if there were any jobs, and he said that there were two jobs but that the descriptions hadn't been written up and I should give him my application. I was supposed to call him today, but I'm having second thoughts about that and I'm not sure.

DOCTOR: What's the problem then?

PATIENT: Well, it's the desire, Doctor. When I wake up I'm depressed, and I'm not sure that I can function on the job situation feeling this way.

DOCTOR: Well, our first concern is . . . I think the main thing we can look at today, you and I, is whether the changes in your medicine have affected you and if you feel any different with taking the medicine every 3 weeks instead of every 2 weeks, so we'll talk about that and it will only take a moment. I think that's the main thing that you and I can achieve today, and then we can talk more.

PATIENT: Well, Doctor, I'm feeling good.

DOCTOR: And I think you should raise with Dr. R your question about the job. But since you did ask me, then I will reply. Let's say that there are three views about the ways in which activities and mental state interact. The first is that you should achieve a very good mental state and then get involved in activities. The second view is that doing things helps you attain that good mental state. And the third is a mixture of the two, and it's for you to decide. There's no hard and fast rule one way or the other, but you should decide whether you think you'd like to stay waiting for an ideal state of mind or whether you'd like to get involved in something in the hopes of achieving it. Neither Dr. R nor I can decide for you. It's up to you. [This conversation on this topic continued for several minutes.] Has it been necessary for you to take the Cogentin?

PATIENT: Yes, Doctor, it has. I've been taking one in the morning and one at night. But I haven't taken it all. Just for the stiffness.

DOCTOR: Well, with having Prolixin in between weeks, I think you'll find for a part of that 3 weeks—I think you'll find that the stiffness and the tightness will subside, because overall the blood level of the medicine will be reduced, and you won't need the Cogentin. Do you need another supply of medicine?

PATIENT: I haven't checked, but I think it's a good idea to get something.

DOCTOR: What's the maximum that you'll need?

PATIENT: 40 to 50 tablets.

DOCTOR: You haven't seen Mrs. K for your injection? You should work that out and come in on Monday for your next appointment—3 weeks?

PATIENT: Yeah, 3 weeks. I'd like to come on Monday, OK?

At this point, Dr. D showed Mr. D a standard form used to bill Medical Assistance for patient care.

DOCTOR: Has Dr. R been asking you to fill out this invoice?

PATIENT: Well, he's asked me to sign a couple of them, but he hasn't asked me to fill them out.

DOCTOR: When you get the Cogentin, what supply do you get? 50s or 100?

PATIENT: I get 30 or 40, Doctor.

DOCTOR: And you regulate your own use of it?

PATIENT: Right, I do.

DOCTOR: Let Mrs. K know that the medicine will be the same.

PATIENT: I need to see Dr. R to get a character recommendation. Do you think that would be all right, Doctor?

DOCTOR: I'm not sure if you'll be able to get a character reference from Dr. R. His contact with you has been [of] a professional nature, not a personal one.

PATIENT: OK.

Mr. D left Dr. D's office to schedule his next appointment and to receive his Prolixin shot. Then he met with the patient-observer.

OBSERVER: What did you expect to get out of coming to the Hospital today?

PATIENT: I wanted to see Dr. R to talk about what I'm going to do about the job, but I'm satisfied with what Dr. D told me. I guess it's up to me.

OBSERVER: What kind of drugs are you taking?

PATIENT: At the present time I'm taking Prolixin, but in the past I took a variety of drugs.

OBSERVER: Were you told anything about the side effects of these drugs?

PATIENT: I had discussions about the side effects of drugs I took in the past, and Prolixin causes the least amount of side effects. Even on Prolixin, though, my hands shake.

OBSERVER: What other side effects have you had?

PATIENT: Uncontrolled mouth movements [referring to short-term reversible side effects]. I knew about side effects from when I was in a hospital ward in California. I was given Thorazine and I hadn't been told there were any side effects, and I just wasn't prepared for it. I couldn't walk. I didn't know what was happening, then later they told me that this was a side effect of the medicine. I had been on the hospital ward and had awakened in the middle of the night and was unable to sleep so I went to the nurses' station, and the nurse there gave me a vial of Thorazine. I thought I was just going to get some light sleeping pill and then found that I couldn't function or work the next day or even move because of the Thorazine. That's not what I expected. After that I was pretty wary of the side effects of medication. I was on Stelazine and was affected by that, so I told the doctor and he put me on Prolixin. I take the Prolixin every 3 weeks and take Cogentin whenever I feel I need it, depending on how much my hands are shaking.

OBSERVER: Are there any side effects to Cogentin?

PATIENT: No.

OBSERVER: Why are you taking Prolixin? What's it for?

PATIENT: (*Laughed.*) That's a good question, I guess. Generally speaking, it helps me to think more clearly. I'm not as paranoid with the drug as when I'm off it.

OBSERVER: Do you know that from experience? Have you ever stopped taking it?

PATIENT: Well, I'm not really so sure. I've been on a steady stream of medication since 1968, so it would really be interesting to see. But I want off it anyway, and Dr. R is going to lower it as we go along. It's been cut down, and he's been giving me advice about getting me off it. I don't think that I could function well without it right now.

OBSERVER: Why is it being lowered slowly?

PATIENT: Oh, so that I don't have too much of a radical feeling of change.

OBSERVER: Does anyone encourage you to come here to the clinic?

PATIENT: No, it's up to me completely. I come every time I have an appointment, and I feel good when I come. I come to get the shot, and I also enjoy coming to talk. It's for my self-betterment. I think the people here are very considerate. It isn't a problem at all. I go up to the fourth floor to play pool when I come, and that adds to the enjoyment of coming. In the afternoons I go to group therapy, and my appointments are coordinated with my group therapy sessions.

OBSERVER: Do you have any worries about treatment?

PATIENT: No, I have a long illness. It's going to be very slow. It's one that you can't turn off like a light switch and I'll be coming here for a long time—as long as I need it. But I've been feeling good the last couple of months.

OBSERVER: How long will you need to come here?

PATIENT: I'll follow the doctor's advice about how long I need to come. I discovered that I have the type of schizophrenia that I was born with, and I've really been ill all my life. It was only after I was discharged from the service that they discovered it.

OBSERVER: So you're satisfied with the treatment you've received?

PATIENT: Well, I wish I had been told about the side effects of the drugs I took before I took them. Sometimes they're not completely honest with you about what might happen. For instance, I wouldn't have taken the Thorazine at all. But if I was told what to expect then I could handle it better, maybe.

Meanwhile, the staff-observer had been interviewing Dr. D, who told him that Mr. D had a tendency to take a doctor's word as gospel and didn't think he could function without medical care. "He still keeps in touch with the doctor he saw a few years ago in California." Dr. D explained that a part of Mr. D's treatment consisted of trying to develop in him some independence about making decisions. When the staff-observer asked about the character recommendation, Dr. D explained that he preferred not to mix personal and professional opinions, and added that Mr. D had applied for work at the Hospital as a part of his tendency to want to be protected by and close to the people who saw him here.

Dr. D's note on Mr. D read:

> Pt. says he is feeling "better" on a 3-week Prolixin interval than a 2-week schedule; has talked c̄ Personnel Dept. at the Hospital about obtaining employment as an administrative assistant, is now ambivalent about whether to proceed with application and is in doubt whether he would be considered for the job at all when he reveals his pt. status. Support given to the approach that work activity can improve mental status, in contrast to the notion that a symptom-free mental state needs to be reached before a person is able to look for employment.

A "NEW" PATIENT

Treatment in the Outpatient Clinic took place over a long period of time. Thus the interactions we observed between patients and staff members represented only a cross-section of a much more extensive longitudinal experience that had commenced long before our observations began and would terminate long after they were completed. As a result, there was no way of assessing the extent of information that had been provided to patients about their treatment prior to our observations.

In an attempt to overcome this problem, we stratified our sample so that we observed 10 "new" patients—that is, patients who had never been treated in the clinic before (seven cases) and patients who were returning to the clinic after a significant absence because of hospitalization or treatment elsewhere (three cases). We assumed that this would be the time when a large amount of treatment information would be given to a patient in a single interview. As it turned out, while these patients were "new" to the Outpatient Clinic, only one was "new" to psychiatric treatment. Eight had previously been treated at the Hospital, and the remaining "new" patient had previously been treated at other psychiatric hospitals and thus was not a total stranger to psychiatric treatment. Perhaps one of our most important findings about Outpatient Clinic treatment is that it is a derivative of previous inpatient treatment, and neither staff nor patients saw it as basically a new experience.

A patient who exemplified the "new" patients was Myrna G, a well-dressed, 38-year-old white woman, 5 feet 4 inches tall, and overweight. Although this was her first appointment in the clinic, she was familiar with the Hospital, having been an inpatient for a 17-day period more than a year earlier. A month before this appointment, because she had complained of hearing voices, she had gone to the Evaluation Center at the suggestion of the child care worker who was supervising the care of her children. The Evaluation Center staff had attempted to persuade her to admit herself to the Hospital, but she refused and was referred to the Outpatient Clinic. She was given a prescription for Haldol and Cogentin to take in the interim.

The observers approached Ms. G in the clinic's waiting area, explained the study, and received her permission to observe her interview. She was interviewed by Dr. R.

DOCTOR: This is the first time that you and I have talked?

PATIENT: Yes, sir. . . .

DOCTOR: The only thing I've heard about you is from Mr. N, your child care worker, who came to see me and told me about the contacts that he's had with you about your children.

PATIENT: I'd like to know, when I was first in, what was the reason. When I was first here, with the police and all. [They talked about the events leading to her admission for a while.]

DOCTOR: (*Looking at the chart.*) As far as I can see, we haven't had any contact with you from October '76 to February 1st, until you came to the Evaluation Center.

PATIENT: True.

DOCTOR: Have you been having any treatment during that time?

PATIENT: Well, I was in the Medical Pavilion and I had the X-ray. Then I was at Angels Hospital for a physical. There's a nurse named Donna there who did it. I don't know her other name.

DOCTOR: Can you tell me the reason why you came back here?

PATIENT: Well, I was hearing voices . . .

DOCTOR: But had you ever heard them before, when you were a teenager?

PATIENT: No, it was just when I was first in the Hospital and she asked me about them. When she asked me that one day, and ever since then I've heard them off and on. . . .

DOCTOR: Do you have your two children with you now?

PATIENT: No, they're at my sister's house. She's a foster parent for them. . . .

DOCTOR: Do you understand why they are in a foster home?

PATIENT: Yes, due to the fact that I can't take care of them properly, as far as meals and all, until I'm feeling much better and have myself back together again. . . .

DOCTOR: Did you have any other hospitalization?

PATIENT: Only for pregnancy.

DOCTOR: So, you weren't hospitalized besides that one time for any emotional or mental illness?

PATIENT: No.

DOCTOR: Were you ever taking any medications before you came to the hospital?

PATIENT: No, as far as doctors.

DOCTOR: Well, any tranquilizing medication?

PATIENT: I was taking drugs.

DOCTOR: Street drugs?

PATIENT: Yeah, but other than that, I wasn't taking any.

DOCTOR: When was that?

PATIENT: In 1973, when I was pregnant.

DOCTOR: And what were you using?

PATIENT: Heroin. . . .

DOCTOR: And how long have you been off it?

PATIENT: Since 1973.

DOCTOR: Good. Do you live by yourself?

PATIENT: Yes, I do.

DOCTOR: Do you have any trouble with the neighbors?

PATIENT: No, I don't.

DOCTOR: And what are the voices telling you?

PATIENT: They're not directing me, but sometimes, like when I don't do things right, I guess I feel guilty and I think they say things then.

DOCTOR: So they complain at things that you don't do?

PATIENT: Yeah, like when my kids are fighting, or when I see them doing something wrong to somebody.

DOCTOR: Do they ever tell you to hurt yourself in any way?

PATIENT: No.

DOCTOR: Do they ever tell you to kill yourself?

PATIENT: No, but one thing I'm scared of, and this might be me, is voodoo.

DOCTOR: What things about voodoo scare you?

PATIENT: Well, being rooted.

DOCTOR: What is that?

PATIENT: Well, I don't even think that I can explain it, but I just think it's my handicap that I'm scared of it.

DOCTOR: So, do you think people are responsible for some of these kinds of things?

PATIENT: Well, yeah. When my son was being taken from me, I was very suspicious then. I thought that somebody was doing that.

DOCTOR: Who did you think was doing it?

PATIENT: Well, neighbors and friends of mine.

DOCTOR: Do you think you seem all right now?

PATIENT: I think I'm all right besides hearing the voices. I'm also taking medications.

DOCTOR: Show me.

Ms. G took two bottles of medications from her purse and handed them to Dr. R, who examined them, then resumed the discussion.

DOCTOR: Cogentin, OK, fine. And you're taking two a day of the green ones and one of the white ones?

PATIENT: No, I'm taking one green and one white. I'm not taking two green ones.

DOCTOR: Is that what the doctor at the Evaluation Center told you? Because the directions are that you do take two a day of the green ones and one a day of the white ones. When are you taking them, in the morning or in the evening?

PATIENT: Well, when I don't sleep, I take one white then, and then I get off to sleep easily. But I've had a twisted mouth—it's like this, up to the side. (*She moved her mouth.*)

DOCTOR: How long have you had that?

PATIENT: I had it for a few days, but I kept on taking the pills.

DOCTOR: That's what the white tablets are for, to help you with that, to get rid of anything which is happening with the green tablets, and it seems like it did help and that taking one of the white ones is enough and it hasn't happened again. But if it does, then you should take extra white ones and it'll go away.

PATIENT: OK.

DOCTOR: Well, apparently you're a lot better than you were when you came to the Evaluation Center. They said that you were staring out into space and you couldn't figure out what was happening. So the medicine or something is helping with something since you were here last.

PATIENT: Yeah.

DOCTOR: Well, since you're better, why I think that we'll continue with one of each for a while. It doesn't look like you need more than one a day. And if you're getting better, I don't see there's any sense in your taking more than you need. [Dr. R and Ms. G then discussed her sleep for a few minutes.] Well, the reason why the people in the Evaluation Center sent you here is because this is a clinic for people who have the same problems you do, such as hearing voices, being suspicious, and we'll try to set up some appointments to see you and talk and give you prescriptions for your medicines and see how things are going. It's a month now since you were here, and I think I'd like to see you more than once a month. I'd like you to come every 2 weeks 'til I get to know you better, and you can get to know this place better. And then after that, why, we can space out your appointments, and then you could come once a month and then once every 6 weeks. But I would like to see you every 2 weeks the first two or three visits, if that's all right with you.

PATIENT: OK. [Dr. R then asked about Ms. G's physical problems and the side effects of the drugs.]

DOCTOR: That's all I have to ask. Do you have any questions for me?

PATIENT: That's all, but I was wondering about why I'm hearing things and wondering if there was something I could do about it.

DOCTOR: Well, that's part of your illness, and that's why you're taking the medicine. And that should cut down on that some. But if the voices don't improve, then we'll increase you to two and that should be enough to cut down the voices. But we should wait and see what's happening after awhile.

PATIENT: Well, I've had this desire when I was on drugs to take them and I will with this medicine, but I don't want to get dependent on the drugs in the same way.

DOCTOR: This is medicine. You won't have that problem because it's not addictive at all. But I understand your concern, given the troubles that you had before. But it's not addictive and, in fact, it might help, because sometimes people take street drugs to help them feel better when they are not taking anything else. But these drugs are not dangerous in terms of their being addictive.

PATIENT: OK. [Here they talked about the way to get "welfare" to pay for her medication.]

DOCTOR: I think you have enough green ones to last you for 2 weeks. I'll give you a prescription for the white ones and I'm going to give you different ones. The ones you have now are football-shaped, and the ones that I'm giving you will be round. The reason is that they'll be a little better because they're bigger, and that will help prevent the trouble with your mouth and the trouble with the jitteriness that you're having. These work best if you take one of the green ones at night before you go to sleep and then you take one white one when you wake up and that'll prevent the jitteriness when you're awake.

PATIENT: OK.

The appointment over, Dr. R directed Ms. G to schedule another appointment for 2 weeks later and escorted her to the secretary's office to do so. After she had arranged for the appointment, the patient-observer explained our study again and obtained Ms. G's permission to be interviewed. The observer began by asking her how she had come to the Outpatient Clinic.

PATIENT: Well, I was afraid that I could feel myself going backwards, like I was before. I didn't understand things I'd done, so I came here to get some help.

OBSERVER: Had they told you anything about the clinic at the Evaluation Center?

PATIENT: No. They didn't tell me anything, but I think when I went to the financial thing, that that's how I came to get here.

OBSERVER: What did you hope to get from coming here today?

PATIENT: I hoped that they would tell me that I was doing better and to give me a time period for when I could get back to being myself, because I feel like I have a lot of problems I can talk about here. [She said she wanted the doctor to explain the voices and to tell her how she'd end up.]

OBSERVER: Are you satisfied with what went on today with Dr. R?

PATIENT: Yes.

OBSERVER: What medications are you taking?

PATIENT: Haldol and Cogentin.

OBSERVER: How many are you going to be taking?

PATIENT: Haldol is a white tablet. I'm going to take two of those a day and I'll take one at night. The Cogentin I'll take in the morning. Just a minute, I'm going to make sure. (*She took out the bottle of pills from her purse and looked at the instructions on the bottle.*) I never check this, but I should because after I talked to the doctor, he told me I wasn't taking enough.

OBSERVER: Do you think the doctor should explain things to you about the treatment?

PATIENT: Yes, I thought it was a good thing, and I sometimes ask questions as well.

OBSERVER: Do you have worries about the treatment?

PATIENT: (*Smiled.*) The only worry I have is whether it's going to help me enough to get my children back.

OBSERVER: Do you think it will help you?

PATIENT: Yes, I hope so. [She said she left the Hospital before because she thought that the treatment wasn't doing her very much good, so she'd stopped taking the medicine.] And this is how I ended up.

OBSERVER: Did they tell you anything about the medicine before you were taking it, anything about the side effects, when they had given you the medication on the unit?

PATIENT: I can't think. I don't remember.

OBSERVER: Did they tell you what the medications are for, what they gave you in the Evaluation Center?

PATIENT: It's to help me sleep and get my proper rest. It helps me with that problem. No, they didn't tell me anything about side effects.

OBSERVER: Do you know what side effects are?

PATIENT: Yes, it happened to me upstairs when they were giving me a liquid. I got really still and I felt much different. I didn't know myself, but there was a doctor there and I was really scared, but I'm no doctor and I don't know. I'd be scared again if it happened to me.

OBSERVER: Well, what would you do if you got any bad side effects?

PATIENT: I'd probably get back here to the Hospital. [She said she wasn't told anything about a special diet to follow.]

OBSERVER: Did they tell you what other kinds of treatment they could give you besides drugs?

PATIENT: No. Well, I could leave the Hospital myself, because I didn't think the treatments were doing me any good, but that wasn't the right answer because look where I am.

OBSERVER: Did you feel any pressure on you to come to the Hospital? Were you encouraged in any way?

PATIENT: Yeah. My mother encourages me. She says that I'll soon be all right. She's very religious and she says it helps to believe in God. She says it's good to see what the doctor wants because that's the way I'll get well—if I follow what they say.

OBSERVER: Do you feel you have any choice about accepting the treatment?

PATIENT: It was given to me for the way I appeared to be. I was confused. I have a guilty complex.

OBSERVER: How long do you think you'll be coming to the clinic?

PATIENT: I think for one more year, and then I'll be back to normal.

OBSERVER: Who would decide on when you should stop coming?

PATIENT: I'd better leave that to the doctors this time, because it didn't turn out right before when I took it in my hands.

While this interview had been going on, the staff-observer had been questioning Dr. R about his assessment of Ms. G. Dr. R said that the diagnosis given her during her previous hospitalization had characterized her as having suffered an "acute psychotic episode." However, he disagreed with this, because she had been behaving in a paranoid manner for some time and had a family history of paranoid schizophrenia. Although she misunderstood the instructions given by the Evaluation Center and had taken only half as much Haldol as had been prescribed, she had improved markedly in the interim period between her visit to the Evaluation Center and her first clinic appointment. He was surprised that she had responded so well to a relatively small dose of medication, as her behavior prior to coming to the Evaluation Center was described as bizarre, including giving away all her money and hanging naked out the window. He added that it was common for patients to continue to experience hallucinations after their other symptoms had gone, and that it was the staff's dilemma whether to work then on decreasing the hallucinations too.

Dr. R explained that Ms. G's jitteriness may have been due to akathisia (motor restlessness), a side effect of Haldol. It was his assessment that Ms. G would cooperate with treatment because, according to Mr. N (the child care worker), it was Ms. G herself who had made the decision to seek treatment and because she had kept the appointment despite the month-long delay. While it was difficult to be sure specifically what she did or did not understand about treatment, as he had not questioned her extensively, Dr. R believed that he and Ms. G had communicated very well and that she had understood everything.

Dr. R's summary of the interview with Ms. G was as follows:

Patient seen for first time on referral from Evaluation Center. Was hospitalized here on Oct. '76 with a psychotic illness, signed out AMA and had no followup treatment. Family and child care worker have been encouraging her to seek help for many months. In Feb. she came to the Evaluation Center on her own, was quite psychotic, refused hospitalization, but agreed to outpatient care. Has been taking less Haldol than was prescribed but has improved markedly. Still has 2 residual S_c—SCD [sleep continuity disturbance] and auditory hallucinations. But is getting 8 hr. sleep/night, is less suspicious, hallucinations are not as loud, is able to talk spontaneously and appropriately, etc.

Dx: schizophrenia, chronic paranoid type with beginning response to Haldol.

Plan: (1) maintain on present dose of meds as she had EPS [extrapyramidal syndrome, a reversible side effect of antipsychotic drugs]. Will evaluate need for increased dosage on subsequent visits. (2) see at 2 wk. intervals initially for continued support and psychotherapy. (3) contact Angels Hosp. about medical care. (4) maintain contact with [Mr. N].

[He recorded Ms. G's medication as follows:]

HALDOL 5 HS #0 (NO CHANGE)
COGENTIN 2 AM #30 (INCREASE)

As had been expected in the case of a new patient, Ms. G was given information about the Outpatient Clinic itself. Information about risks, benefits, and dosage of her medication, while given, was not communicated in a clear, unambiguous manner. Her discussion with the patient-observer about side effects and dosage and her responses to Dr. R's questions about side effects indicate that she misunderstood much of it.

REPEAT OBSERVATIONS

The hallmark of the Outpatient Clinic from the perspective of medical decision-making, as we have emphasized, is the fact that each patient-staff encounter that we observed was merely a slice of a long-term relationship. We were able to observe nine patients between two and four times each.

One patient observed twice was Elena D, a college student who had been a clinic patient for 2½ years at the time of our first observation. She was a slender, 36-year-old white woman about 5 feet 4 inches tall, with long straight brown hair, brown eyes, and a very pale complexion. She kept her coat on throughout the interview, played nervously with her purse, and talked very rapidly. She was interviewed by a nurse/clinician, Ms. J, who obtained her permission for our observers to be present. As they entered the interview room, the clinician was questioning Ms. D about her physical problems.

CLINICIAN: Did you have trouble with your asthma before today?

PATIENT: Today and the other night, not before. I'm allergic to the day, and then walking up the hill I can't breathe in the cold somehow, it's terrible. And then I can't sleep. I didn't go to school today. I was so tired. I'm nervous. Maybe I need a different medicine. I'm not sleeping.

CLINICIAN: Do you have any questions about the medicine?

PATIENT: It's not helping.

CLINICIAN: Are there any other things that you're concerned with?

PATIENT: I'm depressed.

CLINICIAN: Well, what's worse about this week?

PATIENT: Well, it was going home, with my mother, you know. I want to ease my way out, but there isn't a chance I can do it. Then I stayed home from school because it was so cozy to stay there and I was in bed all day. I don't think I can do it.

CLINICIAN: How are things with your mother?

PATIENT: Well, I'm used to doing nothing, nothing when I'm with her. My mother is so easy on me. So I stay in bed and then I do a few chores and then I just don't do anything.

CLINICIAN: How do you feel at home?

PATIENT: I feel good. I feel happy with my mother.

CLINICIAN: Well, do you feel it's not good for you to be at home?

PATIENT: Yeah, because I get into a rut. It's comforting to be there. Every minute my mother's with me, all the time, which isn't the case when I'm in my apartment, when I have to be independent.

CLINICIAN: Do you find that difficult then—having to be more independent, going to school, and not being at home?

PATIENT: Yeah, I do. I sometimes find it hard, and I get depressed, and then I think that it seems like I haven't got a lot of things going for me. I'd like to try and feel as good as I did before. I want that feeling back.

CLINICIAN: Do you ever feel it beginning to come back?

PATIENT: Well, sometimes I do find it's coming back, and then I get scared. One time I was exercising and it was coming back. I could feel it. But then I got scared and took some pills, and I went to bed and went to sleep. I was so nervous.

CLINICIAN: When you felt good, how were you feeling?

PATIENT: I don't know. I didn't know what to do. I took two pills and I went to bed.

CLINICIAN: Can you identify your feelings about that?

PATIENT: I don't know. I don't like to think about it enough.

CLINICIAN: How are you dealing with school this term?

PATIENT: Well, I'm lonely there. I have classes in the morning and afternoon, and there's nowhere to go. I have no friends there. There is one group that I used to go around with, but now they seem to want to avoid me. And I'm not imagining it. It is true. They don't want to talk to me. [They talked about this for a while.] I feel so tired. I took the pills today before I came, and I think I'm taking too many.

CLINICIAN: You think taking the pills has to do with your tiredness?

PATIENT: Well, I hadn't thought of that, but I think they could be milder. But it's not my mind that's messed up. I'm depressed and anxious, but I don't think that I'm psychotic.

CLINICIAN: Do you think that your thoughts are disorganized?

PATIENT: I'm not sure what that means.

CLINICIAN: Well, I've seen you when you thought you were mixed up and confused and disorganized.

PATIENT: I don't know that. I don't know if that's true or not. I think that my problem is different than being disorganized.

CLINICIAN: Well, what do you understand about your diagnosis?

PATIENT: Well, I was diagnosed as being psychotic, as having bizarre behavior and that my thinking processes were not responsible, but I think I'm depressed and anxious and my thinking is OK.

CLINICIAN: Well, do you think you're always OK?

PATIENT: No, not when I was in the Hospital here. Then when I was in the other hospital, even there the medicine they gave me was terrible. It was just horrible.

CLINICIAN: Why were you in that other hospital?

PATIENT: Oh, 'cause I was nervous and I was thinking people were talking about me. But some of them were. That's true.

CLINICIAN: What was strange about the way you acted?

PATIENT: I can't explain it.

CLINICIAN: You said that you had a problem with depression rather than thinking? How do you see the periods which I call "confusion"? How do you view those?

PATIENT: Well, I think that a lot of things were happening at the time. Things were going well at school, but with my father—I was facing his death. I was thinking that I was mixed up. You know, I always thought that he was trying to hurt me, but then I thought if he died it would be a disaster.

CLINICIAN: Would you like to say how you thought it was?

PATIENT: I don't really know.

CLINICIAN: Yeah, I think you needed help to some extent. You took some medicine, and that worked and then you worked on your own, but the medicine was helpful with that. You're taking Haldol. That's one of the medicines which is least prone to make you drowsy. But there is another kind, Prolixin, and before we go we could talk about that. It's possible that would make you less drowsy.

PATIENT: How about weight gain?

CLINICIAN: Well, Haldol is best for that.

PATIENT: You mean with the Prolixin you'll probably gain weight?

CLINICIAN: Yeah. It's probably six of one and half a dozen of the other.

PATIENT: Even without eating?

CLINICIAN: Well, Prolixin is not really that bad, and something might be managed. Maybe you are more prone to the side effects such as tremor and stiffness.

PATIENT: Is Haldol better for that?

CLINICIAN: Well, it's probably better than Prolixin, but you can always take Cogentin to deal with that.

PATIENT: I'm afraid of getting into something worse.

CLINICIAN: Well, it's different and you would tend to gain weight—from eating, though. There's an imbalance caused in what you're using up. If you eat less and burn more calories, then I think that your weight problem won't be any worse and it will be manageable, and you'll be less drowsy. And then with the Cogentin . . .

PATIENT: Cogentin isn't for sleeping, is it?

CLINICIAN: A little bit. If you take 2 milligrams at bedtime, then you might notice that you feel drowsy and go straight off to sleep. If you feel drowsy during the day, then you might consider taking it at bedtime.

PATIENT: I always sleep all right.

CLINICIAN: So do you want to talk about changing the medicine?

PATIENT: Well, I'm nervous about that. I might need to take Valium. I'm very nervous.

CLINICIAN: Well, Valium is a totally different kind of medicine, and it's not recommended at this point.

PATIENT: Oh, it won't work in me?

CLINICIAN: Well, there are major tranquilizers and minor tranquilizers. The major ones organize thinking, and Valium does not. It has also been found to be addictive, so that's not really recommended for you. The major reason why Haldol is recommended is that it organizes your thoughts. So, you're leery about changing?

PATIENT: Yes, I am a little bit. I don't know who I am. It's hard to act when you don't know who you are and where you're coming from, and the medicines don't help.

CLINICIAN: Well, the medicine isn't going to give you a sense of who you are. It's you who will help yourself, and going to your group counseling sessions, that'll help some too.

PATIENT: It's hard for me to explain things today. But I suppose it's better because it's OK, it's early in the term. I can make up for what I missed. Sometimes I feel like I just want to go to bed and to sleep and forget everything. It's very comforting. Then, it was all so cozy at home with my parents and after 3 days there it's hard to get away from it.

CLINICIAN: Yes, when it's comforting you like to stay in place and it's not easy to go away. Yeah, that's true, isn't it?

PATIENT: Yeah.

CLINICIAN: It's difficult to leave.

PATIENT: It sounds childish, but that's the way I am. Whatever happened to me, the good parts died, and the only thing that's left is the worse and that's there all the time. I don't understand why.

CLINICIAN: Well, when you were exercising the good feeling was coming out, but it seems that you were afraid of it and wanted to push it back.

PATIENT: Why do I do that?

CLINICIAN: I'm not sure about that. There could be many reasons. Do you have any thoughts?

PATIENT: It's hard to think right now because I'm on the medicines. My mind's not working. The medicines make me drowsy.

CLINICIAN: I suggest now that you think over the question and give some thought to what the fear is about. It'll be something to come back to. [The discussion about her identity problems went on for quite a while.] I think that you're not letting yourself feel, and that's related to not wanting to feel good things too. I think that's a thought you should take away with you for next time, and I think you should also try to focus on what's happening now. What medication do you want?

PATIENT: I'll stick to the Haldol.

CLINICIAN: You need to take two at bedtime, right?

PATIENT: Yeah, I usually do, except today I took one before I came.

CLINICIAN: Do you have any meds at home?

PATIENT: Yes, I have five Cogentin and a few Haldol.

CLINICIAN: Now, with regard to the appointments. How often would you like to come? We've been seeing each other on a monthly basis. How about coming every 2 weeks?

PATIENT: Well, the only trouble is the only time I have is Thursday afternoon.

CLINICIAN: Well, I have a problem with my schedule, because one afternoon a month I go to another hospital. But if you come for a couple of Thursday afternoons, we can possibly work something out.

PATIENT: Well, I'm in school from 9 to 4, and then it takes me an hour and a half to get home.

CLINICIAN: I'm here on Tuesday evenings.

PATIENT: OK, the evenings would be OK. I could come around 6.

CLINICIAN: Do you want extra meds, or don't you think you need it?

PATIENT: I think I would like to have it.

CLINICIAN: Is 10 extra enough for 2 weeks?

PATIENT: Yes.

The patient and the clinician then went to the reception office, where they arranged a time for her next appointment. The patient-observer then approached Ms. D and asked if she would answer a few questions.

OBSERVER: How did you first begin coming to the clinic?

PATIENT: Well, I was told it was the best in the area and my brother came here. But I, myself, started coming here after I was in the Hospital. The floor I was on as a patient referred me. I was brought here to be admitted by a neighbor who saw me and thought I was really sick and brought me here on a bus. I'm glad I was brought here. I was scared to death because of the hallucinations I was having.

OBSERVER: What do you expect to get from coming to this clinic?

PATIENT: Drugs. The first time I was in the Hospital I was very sick, but now I feel somewhat better. I think that's due to the medication. It helps me; it gives me clear thinking.

OBSERVER: Were you told anything about the risks and benefits of the medication?

PATIENT: The risks and benefits of the drug I'm taking were explained to me, and I talked it over. This was after the drug had been given to me. They knew that they could see it was working and that's why they gave it to me.

OBSERVER: Do you have any worries about treatment?

PATIENT: I sometimes wonder what it does to my brain, but if I had any big worries I'd go to my counselor and tell her that I want the medicine stopped. The Haldol makes me nervous sometimes, but then when I was back home without any pressures I was fine.

OBSERVER: What medication are you taking now?

PATIENT: Haldol and Cogentin. Haldol's a chemical which works on the brain for some reason. The side effects are that it sometimes gives you tics in the face and makes you drowsy. I'm also taking Cogentin, which takes care of the side effects of Haldol, like stiffness, restlessness, visual things—something to do with vision.

OBSERVER: Why did you decide to continue taking Haldol rather than change to Prolixin?

PATIENT: Oh, I heard that Prolixin makes you stiff.

OBSERVER: Who did you hear that from?

PATIENT: Other patients.

OBSERVER: When?

PATIENT: When I was on the [inpatient] floor.

OBSERVER: Do you think any pressure was put on you to accept the treatment?

PATIENT: No. I think it was given to me on the basis that it was working for me and I'd accepted that and also the fact that it was helping me. I was also afraid not to take the medicine. The people here have a lot of power over me because I'm frightened. I don't want to get sick again.

While this interview took place, the staff-observer discussed Ms. D's case with the clinician, who said that she had been seeing Ms. D for 2 years; that she thought her case chronic; that she did not seem to change; and that she did not see hope for improvement. Since coming to the clinic, Ms. D had had paranoid ideation. She was currently receiving 20 mg Haldol, which the clinician was afraid to decrease. As Prolixin and Haldol are the major tranquilizers that cause the least drowsiness, she thought Ms. D was probably tired from school rather than from the medication. However, she thought it might be better to switch to Prolixin rather than to decrease the Haldol, thus achieving the same antipsychotic effect but with less drowsiness. She did not want to give her an antidepressant because it would just harm her, since Ms. D was not depressed but paranoid. The clinician also said that it was best for Ms. D to focus on present problems and that she would stress this focus in the future. She noted that Ms. D was very dependent on her, a fact that was reflected in her frequent phone calls for advice.

The clinician wrote the following note in Ms. D's chart:

> Still S/W paranoid, loose and anxious. Still hypersomnic when needed to get up for school and do homework. Attributed some of this to meds which I'm not sure about but did not want to change to Prolixin. Considering part-time school.
>   [She recorded Ms. D's medication as follows:]
>   HALDOL 10 MG TT HS #30 (No Change)
>   COGENTIN 2 mg T HS #15 (No Change)

In many ways, Ms. D's case is typical of other Outpatient Clinic cases. Perhaps the most striking way such interactions differed from the Evaluation Center interviews was the friendly way in which information was shared with these patients by the staff. After a lengthy discussion, Ms. D was allowed to make the final decision whether to change medication. She also knew a great deal about her medication and had gleaned information not only from the staff but also from other patients. Another striking feature of the Outpatient Clinic was the degree to which the staff members were called upon for advice on all aspects of a patient's life, such as Ms. D's problems in dealing with school.

Elena D returned to the clinic for her next appointment 2 weeks later.

CLINICIAN: How is it going for you today?

PATIENT: Oh, pretty good. I think the extra medicine helped. I've been taking one extra Haldol and I feel much better.

CLINICIAN: What especially did you notice was different?

PATIENT: Well, I didn't think about or get depressed about a lot of things.

CLINICIAN: You look more relaxed.

PATIENT: Yeah, I stopped sleeping a lot. That was my problem. I would sleep a lot and then I would get so far behind in my studies. I didn't do anything during the day. But now I'm not getting behind.

CLINICIAN: Good, you said you were going to get caught up last time we talked. How's your appetite? Has that been good?

PATIENT: Yeah, it's good. I hate sleeping. I don't like to sleep late. I want to study for school and I've been exercising. I think I'll go to the "Y" and do some swimming.

CLINICIAN: Yeah, exercise can help.

PATIENT: Yeah, I don't want to do anything too strenuous. You know, I was in a bus wreck yesterday.

CLINICIAN: Oh, was anybody hurt?

PATIENT: No, it wasn't a bad wreck. I was just reading and I didn't really know what was going on. And I'm going to get my hair cut pretty short on Tuesday. I want to get it styled. [They chatted casually for a few minutes about Ms. D's desire to change her hair style and a new boyfriend.]

CLINICIAN: OK, so you need a prescription for Haldol. How about the Cogentin?

PATIENT: I have a lot of Cogentin.

CLINICIAN: Do you want to come back in 2 weeks again?

PATIENT: OK.

CLINICIAN: Anything else you want to talk about?

PATIENT: No.

CLINICIAN: OK, we'll make an appointment in 2 weeks.

The staff-observer asked the clinician whether it was common for patients to increase their medication without consulting her. She laughed and said that usually they decreased it on their own, but if they felt like increasing it they would usually call her first. She was surprised that Ms. D had increased the Haldol because in the past they had had to decrease it.

In her note, the clinician wrote:

Much improved. Increased Haldol on her own which has made a difference. Less anxious and ruminative. Visited old boyfriend. Keeping up with school work better.

[She recorded Ms. D's medications as follows:]

HALDOL 10 mgs . . . HHS (Increased)

#3 2/23 DC. #45

THE OUTPATIENT CLINIC
AS A SETTING FOR INFORMED CONSENT

The relevance of informed consent to the Outpatient Clinic, unlike the Research Ward or the Evaluation Center, is not immediately apparent. As we have seen, the role of treatment personnel was largely confined to modifying drug dosages and giving advice. Yet the question of patients' participation remains important, and treatment with antipsychotic drugs was a serious issue. Clinics of this sort provide an increasing percentage of all psychiatric services for patients, and therefore we cannot ignore this sort of setting. In the next two chapters, we analyze the interactions in the Outpatient Clinic from the point of view of informed consent and try to determine whether or not what occurred was informed consent and what difficulties for informed consent arose in that context.

14

Information and Understanding
in the Outpatient Clinic

There were a number of features in the Outpatient Clinic that made information flow different from information flow in the other two settings we observed. First, contact between the clinicians and the patients in the Outpatient Clinic was different. Unlike the situation in the Evaluation Center, staff-patient contact was an ongoing and often personal relationship, not a "one-shot" visit. This was also true of the Research Ward; but unlike the situation in the Research Ward, Outpatient Clinic patients were usually seen by the same clinician each time they came to the clinic, and the functional differentiation among psychiatric nurses, residents, and staff psychiatrists was minimal. The entire issue of "who informs the patient about what" that was so crucial in the other settings was insignificant in the Outpatient Clinic. A second difference was that Outpatient Clinic patients did not have to sign consent forms relating to their treatment or rights. Information disclosure was thus generally informal and not the bureaucratic procedure we observed in the Evaluation Center. Another difference between the Outpatient Clinic and the other two settings was the paucity of third-party involvement. This fact and the absence of legal compulsion meant that patients came only when they wanted to, and thus staff disclosure had to be more persuasive.

As with the other settings, however, before we can analyze the disclosure, we must consider what the standard of disclosure should be. This must be entirely deduced from the doctrine, since there exist no statutory and almost no common-law guidelines.

What, then, should be the standard of disclosure in this context? Arguably, "new" patients might, of course, be informed of and understand the standard elements of informed consent—the risks, benefits, alternatives, and nature and purpose of the treatment, including at least the idea that the patients have a "disease" or "symptoms" that will be helped by treatment. Patients might also be told, and might be hoped to understand, that the drugs might also have some side effects—particularly the one potentially permanent side effect, tardive dyskinesia. While there was no reason to expect the Outpatient Clinic staff to disclose very unusual or infrequent risks from antipsychotic drugs (such as liver

263

damage or effects on the blood-forming organs, which are clearly very rare), we did expect to see some disclosure of rather frequent side effects, such as dystonia (muscle spasms), muscle stiffness, akathisia (motor restlessness), and possibly others, such as dry mouth, constipation, dizziness, blurred vision, and weight gain.

In accordance with the doctrine of informed consent, we might also have expected to see discussion with patients of the limits of medications. Moreover, since at least some physicians maintain that long-term drug treatment of schizophrenia may not necessarily be helpful for all patients,[1,2] information about the alternative of no drug treatment might possibly be disclosed, at least in those cases where the patients clearly did not wish to take drugs.

Such information as this might be disclosed to "new" patients, in accordance with the doctrine of informed consent. As for patients who were not new to the clinic, they might be informed of the same things periodically, the frequency depending on what evidence they exhibited of understanding the issues. Also, when the staff recommended a drug change in accordance with the informed consent doctrine, they might be expected to explain why they recommended it, and the patients might be hoped to understand why the change was recommended.

THE PURPOSE AND BENEFITS OF TREATMENT: STAFF DISCLOSURE AND PATIENTS' VIEWS

We have noted elsewhere that presenting the purpose and the benefits of a specific treatment is the aspect of disclosure most susceptible to vagueness, perhaps because most medical treatment aims at the restoration of a "normal" state that is itself vague.

This problem was also present in the Outpatient Clinic. For example, clinicians told Myrna G that the medication would "help" her, and Lucy T that her medication was related to her becoming "alert" and "healthy." Likewise, Jacinta G was told only that Prolixin would "help" her, and Torno U that the medication he was taking seemed to help him.

In most cases in the Outpatient Clinic, the staff was somewhat more explicit simply by focusing on symptom relief. Thus Anita S was told that the medication would lift her mood; Leslie E, that the medicine would help her fall asleep; Jerry G, that Cogentin would help with his restlessness; Dick C, that if he took the Prolixin he might not have the problems of fatigue and inability to concentrate that he had when taking other drugs; and finally Aldo H, that Cogentin would help with the "queasiness" in his stomach, as well as with the restlessness caused by Trilafon.

It is important to make clear that while the benefits of treatment were rarely given in an explicit and detailed manner, they were often clearer in context. We noted above that Myrna G was only explicitly given the vague statement that the medication would help. However, a detailed look at the discussion between her and the doctor (parts of which we have given in the previous chapter) before that vague phrase occurred shows that the word "help" did a complex job.

DOCTOR: This is the first time you and I have talked.

PATIENT: Yes, sir. . . . I'd like to know when I was first in [the Hospital], what was the reason. When I was first here, with the police and all.

DOCTOR: Well, I don't know if I could answer that. . . . (*Leafing through the chart.*) It says here that the police were called in by your neighbors. . . . It says they were concerned because you were feeling strange, that you stopped talking to your family and friends, and you were alone for long periods of time by yourself.

PATIENT: At the time they came and confiscated my son from the house. I was alone, but earlier in the day I wasn't completely by myself.

DOCTOR: And they thought you were also suspicious of people.

PATIENT: True, that's true. [The doctor asked a bit about her medical history.]

DOCTOR: Can you tell me the reason why you came back here?

PATIENT: Well, I was hearing voices. . . . [now I'm hearing] them off and on. . . . one thing I'm scared of, and this might be me, is voodoo.

DOCTOR: What things about voodoo scare you?

PATIENT: Well, being rooted.

DOCTOR: What is that?

PATIENT: Well, I don't even think that I can explain it, but I just think it's my handicap, that I'm scared of it. . . .

DOCTOR: Well, apparently you're a lot better than you were when you came to the Evaluation Center. They said that you were staring out into space and you couldn't figure out what was happening. So the medicine or something is helping with something since you were here last.

While the doctor's actual concluding statement presented the benefits of medication very vaguely, his meaning of what the medicine would do for her seems clearer in context.

We should add that when patients were compliant, the clinicians generally focused upon the symptomatic relief that would result from the medications; hence the emphasis on the medicine's regulation of one's "sleep" or "nerves." On the other hand, in the case of patients who did not want to take medications, the clinicians tended to emphasize more the risk of rehospitalization.

If staff members were often vague, it is not because they were not trying to communicate the general purpose of treatment. Mostly they were quite open about this. Evelyn G was told,

"It was the thoughts of Dr. D and Dr. J that you were having problems with thinking—a thought disorder. That's the reason for the medication and the reason for coming to the clinic."

Similarly, Hilda H was told that people who lived with her in the transitional living facilities

". . . are concerned about your health. The staff who work there are worried about you . . . That was one of the reasons Mark [a counselor] brought you in today."

This type of information was not given to the patients systematically. It was given only when it "came up in the conversation." For example, the clinician told Wallace H nothing about why she thought that he should be coming to the clinic, probably because he so dominated the conversation that it was hard for the clinician to convey her definition of what was going on. In general, however, new patients were given some sort of orientation about the clinic and why they were there.

Clinic patients were usually told why a particular treatment had been recommended. Thus Dimitri V was told that because he felt numbness in his extremities, certain physical examinations were recommended. (On the other hand, Jerry G did not hear his clinician tell another staff member that she had recommended group therapy for him in part because the leader of one particular group had asked to be sent some patients.) Patients were usually also told why a particular treatment that they wanted was not recommended for them. Thus Jake E was told that since the last decrease in his medication was not giving him any problems, the same dosage probably should be maintained. Likewise, Efram S was told that his Trilafon would be decreased only after 3 or 4 months, because they wanted to make sure he was sleeping well.

The Outpatient Clinic staff members provided patients with fairly substantial information concerning their rationales for not having made changes in treatment. They also provided explicit information when they did make changes, such as increasing or decreasing a particular medication, stopping it altogether, or introducing a new one. Of the 14 cases we observed in which changes were made, six patients received explicit information as to why they were made. When the clinician told Isabelle N that her Trilafon was to be decreased, the reason given was that Ms. N was jittery, nervous, and unable to sleep well. Danielle B's Mellaril was decreased, she was told, because it made it difficult for her to read. When Alex G's Elavil was decreased, he was told by the clinician,

"I think that another thing we should try is to cut down the dosage of Elavil, because that tends to make you gain weight, and it's a year since we changed the dosage."

The decision to decrease Jacinta G's Cogentin was related explicitly to the fact that her Prolixin would also be decreased. On her next visit to the clinic, she complained about feeling bad. Her clinician suggested that they return to her previous pattern in which she came for a shot, and resisted the patient's desire to come in every week. The clinician pointed out that "it's only in this past week that you have been on edge." The clinician told Ottie G, whose Prolixin was being decreased, "I'll cut down the shots, but only a little. If we cut them down too much, you'll be nervous again." Likewise, Myrna G was told she would be given medication because it "will help prevent the trouble with your mouth and the trouble with your other jitteriness that you're having."

Aside from those six patients, other patients were not told explicitly the rationale for a change in medication, yet the rationale could be implicitly understood. Efram S was not told explicitly why his dosage of Trilafon was increased, but the rationale for that decision was implicit, since he had complained of having trouble sleeping when on a lower dose. Similarly, while Dan D was not told explicitly why Trilafon was prescribed for him, the rationale was implicit in his having refused Mellaril because of side effects that Trilafon did not have. The rationale for decreasing Dimitri V's medication could be inferred from his complaint about its adverse effects and from his and the clinician's agreement that his symptoms were in partial remission. Similarly, the rationale for increasing the medications for Penny D, Elena D, and Myrna G was implicit in their requests for increases because their symptoms were reappearing.

In only two cases, no explicit or implicit reason for treatment changes was given. Though the clinicians who decreased Joshua X's and Mimi E's medications entered into the patients' charts "adverse effects" and "remission of target symptoms" as the official rationales for the changes in medications, the reasons were never explained to the patients and were not clear from the context of the discussion.

We note in Chapter 13 that, unlike the situation in the Evaluation Center, treatment in the Outpatient Clinic was a continuous process, and the clinicians might in theory be expected to provide repeated disclosure. It is thus interesting to note that the staff members reminded patients of the past history of their treatment, so that discussions of present and future plans would make sense to the patients. Information about treatment that had already been given to a patient was presented as a context within which the patient's present situation and prospective treatment plans could be understood, and against which they could be rationalized and accounted for. Thus, before Isabelle N was told that she would be taking only two Cogentin tablets a day, she was reminded that until then she had been taking three. Similarly, before Sheldon M was told that in a month or two his Haldol would be decreased and maybe even stopped, the clinician reminded him that his medication had been reduced in the past from three to two tablets a day and finally to one tablet a day. Mr. M was also reminded that the Cogentin he had been taking to control the side effects of the

Haldol had been reduced from two tablets to one tablet a day, and if at his next clinic visit he still felt good, it might be decreased even further.

This does not mean that this information was necessarily given to help the patient decide what to do. Rather, this "historical summary" was often provided as a context within which patients could answer clinicians' questions, as the clinician's question to Jake E illustrates:

> "Last time you were here, you saw Dr. R, and he cut down the medication. What are the differences you have noticed?"

The same questions were asked of other patients, including Loraine D, Anita S, Ottie G, and Emma D. Similarly, before Mimi E was asked if she had felt any changes during the past few months, she was reminded that her Prolixin dosage had not been changed since the last decrease in June. All such reminders functioned to provide the patients with a context within which they could understand the questions from the clinicians that immediately followed. They were intended to guide the patients' answers by making clearer what the clinicians were after when they asked the questions.

Given this fairly substantial level of disclosure, what did patients understand about the reasons for their treatment? In trying to assess this systematically, we were forced to look at what patients understood about the general purposes of treatment, rather than the specific purposes of the changes in treatment that were made on the particular days of observation. Since an understanding of a particular change requires an understanding of the general purpose, this does not seem to be a serious loss.

Unlike patients in the Evaluation Center, who often did not understand their situation in the same way the staff did, patients in the Outpatient Clinic almost uniformly held a view of the goals of treatment that was close to that of the staff. Their reasons for coming to the Outpatient Clinic, the problems they felt needed attention, and the improvements they sought generally were similar to the staff's view of these matters. Like the staff, most patients accepted the idea that they were afflicted with a chronic disease that could be managed but usually not cured with major tranquilizers. Of the 48 patients we observed, 38 seemed to accept this view of the purpose of treatment. Since in five cases we lacked the data to make such a judgment, only five patients expressed any significant differences in their understanding of the purpose of treatment from that of the staff.

Acceptance of the staff's view of the purpose of treatment showed up in three ways. First, 25 patients made some reference to coming to the Outpatient Clinic because of their sickness or condition, or because they wished to avoid relapse and inpatient rehospitalization. For example, Delbert B explained that "I'm sick in the head"; Isabelle N, that she needed treatment because her "nerves were bad"; Mimi E, that she took the medicine because "it keeps me well"; and Andrea V, that "I get nervous and upset and I get medication here." While few patients were as sophisticated in their understanding as Talcot D, who told our observer that he was a "paranoid schizophrenic" and had been all his life, as a group they understood that something was wrong with their psychological makeup that required them to come to the clinic for treatment.

Another group of seven patients can be roughly distinguished from the first 25. Their understanding of the purpose of treatment was similar, but more focused on specific symptoms. Perhaps it was only a turn of a phrase, but these patients seemed less involved with the idea that they had a chronic disease than that they had a particular discomfort that the Outpatient Clinic could alleviate. For instance, Elena D wanted treatment because she was "nervous and can't sleep." Jerry G saw himself as having a disorder, but he focused his complaints specifically on his alienation and confusion. Paula B understood that the purpose of treatment was to quiet her voices.

A final group of six patients who were included among the 38 "understanding" patients is perhaps the most questionable. They said they came to the Outpatient Clinic because the treatment helped them, but what the help consisted of was either more restricted than the staff's view or was unclear. Holly E thought the drugs helped her, but primarily as an aid in sleeping. Ottie G saw the drugs as helping her nervousness and letting her sleep. Others, like Hollis N, just said they came to get the medications because they didn't feel well without them.

Thus there were really only five patients who did not view the purpose of treatment as generally corresponding with the staff's view, and even two of these patients shared part of the general institutionalized model. Jacqueline M said she came primarily because she enjoyed socializing with other patients and the staff. She used the Hospital not only as a resource for nonpsychiatric medical care, but also because she said she "needed" the pills. Pam X could give a normatively prescribed answer, but her main reason for coming seemed to be to keep her parents and boyfriend "off my back." Although we classified these two patients as not understanding the purpose of treatment, it is possible that they understood the staff's view but did not accept it.

Of the remaining three patients, we can say very little about Jake E. He was not very expressive of any understanding about treatment, but he did deny that he had been ill. The two remaining patients were new to the Outpatient Clinic. Wallace H, who acted in a paranoid manner (perhaps with good cause), was brought to the clinic by his mother. He seemed to want protection from his enemies, not treatment. Likewise, Wolfgang G felt he was not sick, but only wanted the doctors to sign papers allowing him to receive disability and welfare benefits. He saw the purpose of treatment merely as undercutting the attentiveness of patients and keeping mental health professionals employed.

THE NATURE OF THE TREATMENT

What were patients told about the nature of their treatment, and how did they view it? To begin with, almost every new Outpatient Clinic patient we observed was told by the interviewing clinician that he or she would be the person seeing the patient during clinic appointments. The only exception was one patient who was quite ambivalent about returning. However, his discussion made it clear that, although he was not explicitly told, even he understood that he was choosing between the particular clinician and his previous doctor. The same information was provided to two patients who returned to the Outpatient Clinic after an extended absence, including hospitalization, and one patient previously seen by a resident who had completed a rotation period in the clinic. The clinician-patient relationship was the core of the functioning in the Outpatient Clinic, and the clinicians tried to build it up in various ways. While we did not explicitly ask patients about this, they seemed to understand it in all cases for which we have evidence.

Patients new to the Outpatient Clinic were also usually informed about the frequency of their future appointments. This was important information for patients, since whether they were to come to the clinic every week or every 6 weeks would deeply affect the sort of treatment they would get. Thus Evelyn G, Benny I, and Dick C were told that they would be seen every other week. Lucy T was first told that she would come every week, but that in time her visits might be reduced to only once every other week. Similarly, Myrna G was first told that she would come every other week; but when her doctor knew her and she knew the clinic better, she would be able to come every 4 weeks and eventually every 6 weeks.

Such information was also given to experienced patients, especially when the clinician contemplated a switch in the frequency of visits to the clinic. Thus Jacinta G was told that she would be given shots every 4 weeks, and that at the next visit they would decide where to go from there, possibly even reducing the frequency of her visits. The clinician told Sheldon M that if everything went well until his next visit he might have to come in only every 8 weeks.[3]

Most of the information given to patients about the nature of their treatment concerned the future course of their medication, particularly the dosage. Here are a few examples: Joshua X was told that the next thing to do was to cut back on his Dilantin; Isabelle N, that the staff wanted gradually to reduce the Trilafon she was taking; Emma D, that if she still felt well at her next visit, her dosage of Haldol would probably be decreased; and Jerry G, that at some point in the future his Cogentin would be decreased. When Aldo H's Cogentin dosage was increased, the clinician told him that it might be reduced to the previous dosage at his next clinic visit. There are many more examples of this sort of disclosure in our notes.

We did not ask patients what modifications of their treatment were decided upon, but we did ask them what drugs they were getting. In general, patients knew the names of the drugs fairly well. Just under 75% of the 45 patients for whom there is adequate data could name the psychoactive drugs they were taking. In most of the remaining cases, the patients were at least partially correct about what drugs had been prescribed for them. For instance, five patients taking several drugs did not mention all of them. Another patient said she could not remember what drugs she was taking, but she knew that the names were written on the bottles. Only five patients could not name the drugs they were taking.

Perhaps equally important, these discussions did convey to the patients the idea that medications were the core of their treatment. Only one patient clearly described something else (psychotherapy) as the core of the treatment. About one-third of the patients made references to the interviews with clinic staff as part of the treatment, but more than one-third of these did so either to disparage its importance or to say they didn't like it. For example, Wolfgang G, a new patient, was asked at the end of the interview about returning for further treatment:

PATIENT: It depends on who I was talking to, the personal concepts and what it turned into.

CLINICIAN: The person you would be seeing is me. Are you willing to see me again?

PATIENT: So I would be the recipient of conversation. I don't know. I can't see too much benefit. But I don't want to talk for no reason. I don't need that.

Sheldon M expressed lack of interest in the psychotherapy in a different way. He told our observer that his mother encouraged him to come to the clinic, but he didn't like to because he didn't like to talk to people.

This is not to say that all of the patients disliked talking with the staff. For example, Danielle B appreciated it, as our observer noted:

She wanted to discuss with the clinician what was going on with respect to her involvement with a community group. She said she liked coming to the clinic because she felt that after hospitalization she needed support and someone to talk to. She said, "I don't want to sound snobbish about this, but I have a master's degree, and I find it difficult to find people who understand me."

Likewise, Aldo H expressed his pleasure with his clinician, who "really talks" to him. In all, 10 patients expressed positive feelings about the verbal side of treatment. But it was also quite clear that few patients saw this as the center of their treatment, but rather as an adjunct to the pharmacotherapy. Thus, although Aldo H clearly liked talking to his clinician, he also asked her help in arranging psychotherapy for him. He did not ask for more frequent appointments, as he probably would have if his Outpatient Clinic visits were seen by him as being psychotherapeutic.

While patients were told and understood that the treatment focus was on medication and that the primary decisions had to do with the dosage modifications, disclosures about the length of treatment were infrequent. Patients were not told that they might have to stay on drugs for the rest of their lives. Thus, although Andrea V was told that the clinic generally planned to maintain her on medication to keep her out of the Hospital, and Lucy T was told that she would be brought down to the minimal dose required to keep her alert, neither was told how long she would have to keep coming to the clinic. When Benny I asked his clinician how long he might be on medication, the clinician said she did not know.

Perhaps the staff avoided this topic because they feared that a discussion of long-term prognosis or of the need to take medication forever might frighten patients. Even though the Outpatient Clinic was defined as one that took care of chronic schizophrenic patients, we observed only one instance when the possible chronicity of the patient's disorder was even mentioned (and that was only after the patient had brought up the issue). In that case, Dick C's question produced a fairly clear answer:

PATIENT: Can mental health like this be cured in a few years?
CLINICIAN: (*Smiling.*) Well, it's the word "cured" that's the problem, because it implies that it is cured, gone for good, and won't ever come back, and we can't ever predict that. It can be treated, yes, and well treated.

Although the fact was rarely disclosed, most patients knew that their treatment would not end quickly. In fact, 43% of the patients in our study said, in one way or another, that they expected to come for the rest of their lives. Marcy N explained her need for continuous treatment to our observer by noting that the last time she had gone off the drugs she had had to be hospitalized. Penny D commented that a doctor had told her, "Some people need these drugs just the way a diabetic needs insulin." As noted earlier, Talcot D said, "I have a long illness. . . . It's one that you can't turn off like a light switch." He believed he had had schizophrenia all his life. As a group, these patients were resigned to the idea of continuous treatment. Another 32% of the patients also assumed that they would need continuous treatment, but reported that how long they would be treated was their doctors' decision. Of these patients, only Isabelle N even suggested an expectation of terminating the medication, saying, "I hope it will be soon," but she accepted the clinician's comment that it probably would not be soon.

Four patients said they did not know when the treatment would end, but even in those cases the predominant tone was one of resignation to continued treatment with medications. "The only thing that keeps me going," remarked Delbert B, "is the medicine. I don't know when I'm going to be well." Anita S said she didn't know and didn't care when she could leave treatment. And Joshua X complained, "I don't know how long I have to keep taking Stelazine." He requested a reduction, but seemed unconvinced that he would get one.

Only three patients explicitly said they expected an end to their drug maintenance treatment, but even they expressed expectation in qualified ways. Aldo H hoped to substitute psychotherapy for the medications. Efram S expected to end treatment, but only when he was his "old self again." Dimitri V, whose attitude toward the Outpatient Clinic was quite ambivalent, once said he expected to get off drugs, but on four other occasions he expressed doubt that he would ever be able to stop treatment.

THE RISKS OF TREATMENT

The risks of treatment were generally presented in substantial detail. However, the risks were presented not to aid patients in deciding whether or not to accept treatment but rather to enlist the patients in monitoring the drug effects to determine dosage. A clinician told the following to Dick C before increasing his dosage of Prolixin:

> "There is a feeling that people describe as restlessness, like in a chair. It's not a mental thing. It's a bodily thing. And then sometimes people move around like this [demonstrating by moving her foot to and fro], and it's only if you pay attention to it that you can stop it. And sometimes you get weak in the limbs and experience some stiffness. *Well, I wanted to go over them with you so you know what they are and you are aware of them.*" (emphasis added)

The clarity and depth of this description of the side effects was exemplary; furthermore, unlike the information disclosure in the Evaluation Center, it was not simply *pro forma* compliance with the law. However, neither was it motivated by the values of informed consent. Rather, it was designed to educate the patients to monitor their reactions to the medication and to recognize trouble when it occurred. Our methodology prohibits clear-cut assessment of how many patients received such warnings, but they were very frequent, even during the limited period in which we observed each patient-staff relationship.

Another way in which patients learned about side effects was that the staff identified them as such when patients complained. For example, when Pam X complained about having experienced a spasm in her knee, she was told it might have been caused by the change in her Prolixin dosage. Similarly, when Letty D complained of dizziness, she was told that it might be from a side effect of the medication that lowered her blood pressure, so that when she sat up the blood did not go to her head as quickly as it normally would have. Shaw T, who complained of an arthritic sensation in his elbow, was told that the experience was characteristic of some people taking medications such as Haldol. Alex G, who complained of fatigue when getting up in the morning, was told that the medication, when taken late at night, might slow him down in the morning. There were many other similar examples. It is also interesting that when the side effects of antipsychotic drugs were discussed, the clinicians usually added that they could be managed by taking Cogentin.

A third and indirect way in which information about the drug side effects was provided was in the form of questions from the staff. Consider, for example, the case of Sheldon M.

DOCTOR: We cut down the Cogentin in November. You were taking two before that.

PATIENT: Something like that.

DOCTOR: Have you noticed any change, any difference in any way?

PATIENT: No, it's the same.

DOCTOR: Cogentin is primarily for the side effects of Haldol. Are you aware of any effects of Haldol?

PATIENT: No.

DOCTOR: Have you been dizzy?

PATIENT: No.

DOCTOR: Have you had any blurred vision?

PATIENT: No.

DOCTOR: Have you had any trouble reading?

PATIENT: No.

DOCTOR: Have you been shaky?

PATIENT: No.

Such questions educated patients in an indirect manner, so that if they might have any of these experiences in the future, they could relate them to the medication they were taking. However, this manner of disclosing information did not encourage patients to see this as part of their role as decisionmakers, any more than the first two ways of disclosing this information did.

While the Outpatient Clinic staff members were usually fairly informative about the side effects of prescribed drugs, there were nevertheless a number of cases in which they deliberately withheld information about the risks from the patients. The resident seeing Wallace H had received permission from the Outpatient Clinic Director to tell Mr. H about the side effects of Trilafon he was going to prescribe, but he decided that paranoids like Mr. H might misinterpret these effects, and thus the resident did not tell him. Likewise, Dimitri V's doctor told our observer that, although he suspected Mr. V had parkinsonism, he had not checked this so as not to alarm the patient.

The Outpatient Clinic staff often seemed to withhold information about risks not only because they were afraid of the effect on patients' decisions but also because they expected the patients might become upset. In this way, they were exercising the "therapeutic privilege" to withhold information when disclosure would interfere with the patients' health.[4] This occurred in at least 10 cases that we observed. The following case is illustrative:

Aldo H, a 21-year-old student, was awaiting placement in the Hospital's Individual Psychotherapy Clinic as an adjunct to the treatment in the Outpatient Clinic. However, the clinician pointed out that the waiting list in the Individual Therapy Clinic was long.

CLINICIAN: Another thing they have is group therapy.

PATIENT: I don't like group therapy. I've been through it before, and I didn't get much out of it. It could be that I didn't put much into it, I guess. But the individual counseling—now that would be something I possibly would like.

The clinician expressed pleasure that Mr. H did want therapy, whether individual or group, and agreed to check on the referral.

During the following session, the patient noted that the referral process was taking a long time and wondered whether he really required therapy.

PATIENT: I've been trying to get along without a psychologist. I just wonder if it will ever happen that I'll get to see one. I'm doing without it now, and why get yourself into something that you may not need?

CLINICIAN: Am I correct in assuming that you have definitely decided against group therapy?

PATIENT: Yeah, I was talking to someone from Group [Psychotherapy Clinic], and judging from my own experience in Day Hospital before and group therapy, well, I just don't really think it's helpful. Maybe it is, but I don't think it would be.

CLINICIAN: I sort of have the feeling that I could talk you into the group, but in the back of your mind you're thinking "no."

PATIENT: Yeah, that's right.

CLINICIAN: I hear your "no."

Eventually the clinician offered to see him in individual therapy herself, a suggestion that Mr. H accepted.

The above dialogue illustrates the cordial and supportive nature of the interchange between the clinician and Mr. H. However, the very supportive nature of the interaction limited the clinician's disclosure. She later told our observer that she wanted Mr. H to join group therapy because "individual therapy may be too intense for him. Mr. H already has had two breakdowns. His ego defenses are not that intact." Thus although the clinician felt Mr. H should have group therapy, she felt that she could not disclose why. He eventually received supportive therapy with the clinician herself.

Other examples of the "therapeutic privilege" occurred in our observations. Elena D, whose case is discussed in Chapter 13, requested that her medication be lowered because it was making her drowsy. The clinician then proposed that Ms. D consider another antipsychotic medication that might make her less drowsy. Ms. D, however, eventually chose to stick with the medication because change "might get her into more trouble." However, the clinician did not tell Ms. D that she believed Ms. D was tired from the stress of her school work, not from the medication she was taking, and that at any rate the clinician was worried that a decrease in total medication would lead to a recurrence of the psychosis.

Similarly, in the lengthy discussions with Dimitri V in which Mr. V complained about impotency and lack of sexual urge, the clinician tried to explain that even though impotency might be a side effect of the medication, Mr. V's lack of sexual desire was not. However, the clinician was not being entirely truthful with Mr. V, as he later told our observer, that he believed Mr. V's impotency was not due to the medication but rather due to psychological reasons, "but when you tell that to him, then, of course, he will become paranoid."

However, the Outpatient Clinic staff withheld one type of information in a systematic manner that could not legitimately be thought of as an exercise of the therapeutic privilege, although the staff may have felt it was in the patients' best interest. This was information concerning tardive dyskinesia.

Although it is estimated that about 10-20% of all patients treated for long periods with antipsychotic medication develop tardive dyskinesia, a neurological syndrome characterized by repetitious involuntary movements such as grimacing, cheek puffing, lip smacking, chewing motions, and so on,[5] we did not see this potentially irreversible side effect of antipsychotic drugs mentioned to a single patient, even those patients for whom the presence of side effects was already an issue in treatment. While in one case tardive dyskinesia was not diagnosed until after we saw the patient in question, we also saw five cases where the staff had already diagnosed or were considering diagnosing tardive dyskinesia when we saw the patients. In none of these cases were the patients told about the cause of the problem. In one of these cases, the clinician began asking the patient about abnormal tongue movements, but the patient misunderstood the clinician's remarks and the discussion did not progress. Evelyn G, a 58-year-old new patient at the Outpatient Clinic, was referred from the Evaluation Center after having been treated elsewhere for many years. During the conversation, the clinician had difficulty understanding Ms. G.

CLINICIAN: There seems to be some difficulty with your tongue. It seems to be thick. I'm having problems understanding you sometimes. Are you having problems with thickness of your tongue?

PATIENT: No.

CLINICIAN: Stick your tongue out, OK?

PATIENT: (*Did so.*) I don't have any problems putting things in my mouth like that. Are you accusing me of that?

CLINICIAN: Sometimes the medication does things to your tongue. Does it bother you at all?

PATIENT: No. Are you accusing me of taking food?

CLINICIAN: What was it you are thinking I was accusing you of?

PATIENT: Of taking food. That's what my roommate does.

After this exchange, the topic changed. The patient later told our observer that she did not know why the clinician had asked her to put out her tongue. She also said that she knew nothing about the side effects of the medication. When asked directly whether "bad" things could happen from the medication, she denied it. Following her interview with Ms. G, the clinician told the staff-observer that she believed Ms. G had tardive dyskinesia and that she "has to consider this in her treatment plan."

Lucy T, a 65-year-old woman who had had more than 35 admissions to the Hospital, had chin movements that the clinician thought must be either mannerisms or symptoms of tardive dyskinesia. The potential tardive dyskinesia was not discussed with either Ms. T or her husband on the day of our observations. The clinician, however, told us that Prolixin was necessary for Ms. T because "if the side effects were not too bad, it was worth it." The patient knew only that her medication was prescribed because of her "nerves," and said that the medication was a "vitamin shot."

We cannot, of course, conclude from our observations that the staff never told patients about tardive dyskinesia—only that this issue was not discussed systematically in the cases we observed. The cases of tardive dyskinesia and possible tardive dyskinesia that we saw were all at relatively early stages. A review of these patients' charts did indicate that when at a later stage the patients' movement disorders were more pronounced, the staff did discuss with them in more detail the nature of the problem.

Subsequent to our observations, the Outpatient Clinic staff did a study of the results of informing patients more extensively about tardive dyskinesia. The proposal generated heated discussion among the Hospital's research committee about the very existence of the syndrome and the ethics of informing patients about uncertain risks, especially since the disclosure might cause some patients to stop taking the medications.

Perhaps understandably, no patient showed signs of understanding that tardive dyskinesia was a possible side effect of antipsychotic drugs. However, patients did understand substantially that antipsychotic drugs do have side effects. In more than three-fourths of the cases, the patients mentioned something that they felt was or might be a side effect of a drug, or reported something that their clinicians thought might be a side effect. Of the patients who reported side effects, over 80% reported recognized side effects of the drugs they were taking. Of course these are, from one perspective, retrospective understandings of what the law calls "materialized risks." We do not know whether or not patients understood the risks of side effects before they experienced them. However, it is important to remember that these were continuing treatments. The patients may or may not have known about the existence of side effects before they took the drugs, but they knew about them when they made the decision either to continue or to stop taking the drugs. Thus the fact that these were reported as side effects argues persuasively that most patients had some understanding of the short-term risks involved in the treatment.

Most patients described the side effects with very little alarm. They complained about side effects, but did not seem seriously bothered by them. For example, Jason U complained that the drugs made him drowsy and that he didn't wake up properly refreshed. Myrna G told our observer that, when she began taking the drugs, she had some involuntary mouth movements that later went away. Nolan S, a professor, complained that the blurred vision from the drugs made it hard to read.

For a few patients the side effects were a reasonably serious matter, or at least they complained a lot about them. Talcot D, for example, described himself as "pretty wary of side effects" following an incident in another hospital when he was overmedicated with Thorazine. He said that the Prolixin he was now taking had fewer side effects, but nonetheless his hands shook and he had had involuntary mouth movements. Only a few patients reported "side effects" that the Outpatient Clinic staff did not believe were side effects of the medication. The psychiatrist believed Dimitri V's complaints (the most vigorous of any patient in the clinic) were a mixture of things: side effects (dry mouth, drowsiness, lightheadedness when he changed positions, stiffness, and constipation), symptoms of the disorder (impotence, nervousness, and confusion), and a few others for which the staff had no explanations (upset stomach and numbness of the extremities).

However, none of the above-mentioned facts means that patients in the Outpatient Clinic adequately understood what risks they faced in taking the drugs. While by and large they knew about the acute drug risks that materialized in their own case, they understood only some nonmaterialized risks and none of the long-term risks. For example, only one of the patients mentioned that antipsychotic drugs often produce weight gain, a side effect that may have accounted for the large number of overweight patients in our sample. No patient gave us an adequate list of the possible side effects that had *not* materialized in his or her own case. While some of these limits in the patients' failure to understand were a result of the staff's failure to disclose information, patients were sometimes not able to repeat back to our observer what they had just been told about the risks. For example, Leslie E was told that she was getting Mellaril, but a few minutes later, in an interview with our observer, she could not remember the name of the drug.

Perhaps part of the difficulty patients had in describing risks is that the problem is inherently confusing. Which unpleasant experiences were symptoms of the disease, which were effects of life stress, which were side effects of the antipsychotic drugs, and which were side effects of the antiparkinsonian drugs used to deal with other side effects was not easy to understand. Thus the resident who saw Nolan S told him,

> "Have you been feeling like a heavy weight is on your shoulders? This happens too. It could be that your arms and legs will get stiff in the future, so we give you the white pill just to protect you, to prevent that from happening. And the white pill is called Cogentin. The green pill is the one that will make you stiff, and the white pill is to help you with that. But guess what the white pill does? It helps you not to get

stiff, but the side effect of the white pill is that it gives you blurred vision. We are giving you the white pills so you won't get stiff, but with the white pill you can't always see when you want to read."

Perhaps because of the complexity of such an explanation, Aldo H, when explaining to our observer why he thought Cogentin didn't have side effects, relied on his common sense and came up with the wrong answer:

"You wouldn't expect that a medicine you were taking for side effects of another medicine would also have side effects, would you?"

The inconveniences caused by the medications were equally confusing and not always easy to separate from those caused by the disease itself. While the boundaries between these two types of inconveniences may have been distinct for the clinicians, they were not always that obvious for the patients, since pain does not come with causal labels attached.

Whether an inconvenience was defined as a symptom or as a side effect was a matter requiring some negotiation between clinicians and patients; the staff often went to great pains to clarify the distinction. The clinician who saw Penny D, for example, questioned her for quite some time about her getting "jittery and nervous, especially at work." But when Ms. D commented about possibly needing more medication, the clinician commented:

"Well, it works the opposite way than you seem to imagine. The longer you're on it, the more good it does you. It isn't something that you might develop a tolerance to. I wonder if the way you feel might not be more related to what is happening in your life."

Likewise, when Jon T asked the same clinician whether his dry mouth was caused by either anxiety or the medication, he was told it might be either or a combination of both. However, it is important to point out that the effort to distinguish the side effects of one drug from another and both from the disease was a rarity. Most patients remained confused about these issues.

The effort to separate these sources of discomfort was not a simple process and could produce considerable conflict, as is illustrated by the case of Dimitri V.

On his second visit to the Outpatient Clinic following his discharge from the Hospital, Mr. V complained to his doctor of having thrown up and of having a dry mouth. He attributed both difficulties to the medication. The doctor responded that, on the contrary, his medication had been known to have a calming effect on the stomach. He also complained that the medication increased his appetite and consequently caused weight gain. The doctor reminded him that he had a history of having attributed things to the medication that were not related to it.

On his next visit to the clinic, Mr. V complained that the medication made him drowsy and lightheaded. The doctor admitted that those were probably side effects of the Trilafon he was taking, and added that this was why he was taking Cogentin. He also admitted that the Cogentin was responsible for the dry mouth about which Mr. V also complained. However, he refused to accept Mr. V's complaints that several other problems he had were side effects of the medications. On three different occasions during the meeting, Mr. V complained that the medication was responsible for the numbness in his fingers, and each time the doctor replied that it was not a side effect of the medication, but rather a neurological problem about which Mr. V ought to talk with a neurologist. When Mr. V said that the medication made food taste stale, the doctor responded that the only way the medication could affect his taste was as a result of the dry mouth. When Mr. V stated that the medication caused problems with his memory, the doctor replied that if the medication had any effect on his memory, it could only be a positive one, since it helped with his thoughts. The discussion came to a head when Mr. V complained that he just could not function with the medication, and the doctor replied, "But Mr. V, I think it is the other way around—that you can function only with the medicine." Later he added, "I think you should also separate the side effects of the medicine from other difficulties you have been having, such as the numbness, which isn't a side effect."

At their next meeting, the doctor again agreed that one problem of which Mr. V was complaining—namely, constipation—could indeed be attributed to the medications. However, he informed Mr. V that the results of Mr. V's physical examination showed no relation between the numbness in his fingers and the medication. He also had to deal with a new difficulty that Mr. V attributed to the medication, a lack of sexual urge. He conceded that many patients report impotence as a typical effect of the medication, but added that no one had ever mentioned that it affected sexual urge.

Although Mr. V's was an extreme case, it exemplifies the process of negotiation about a certain definition of the situation. It should be noted that Mr. V and his physician agreed on the factual existence of the difficulties. Their only disagreement was about how these difficulties ought to be interpreted—that is, whether they were side effects of the medications, were caused by the disease, or were unrelated to either.

The patients often seemed to operate on the assumption that their problems must come either from the disorder itself or from the side effects of the drug. But they were not always correct in attributing them to one or another cause. When discussing why he was wary of side effects, Talcot D described symptoms from overmedication, not from side effects. At first Danielle B thought that her dizziness, a side effect, might come from her disorder, and Jon T discussed with the clinician the possibility that his drug-related dry mouth might be from anxiety. Likewise, a few unrelated discomforts were reported as side effects, such as Jerry G's belief that his boredom might be a side effect of the drug.

Although from the patients' perspective, the drugs' side effects were the main risk of treatment at the Outpatient Clinic, they were not the only ones. A number of patients complained about being socially categorized as mental patients. Talcot D spoke of the "stigma" that society places on the mentally ill. Dan D said, "Some things that mental patients do, other people can do and get away with. But ex-mental patients get locked up." While both of them felt that this was the large price paid for being involved with the Hospital, they did not connect it specifically with treatment in the Outpatient Clinic. Paradoxically, the same view of mental patients, but from the other side, was seen by Jacinta G as the biggest disadvantage of treatment at the clinic. She resented having to sit next to other patients in the waiting room and was worried that one of them might follow her home. However, these were disadvantages of treatment that they "discovered" for themselves, not ones that the staff disclosed to them.

ALTERNATIVES

This was the only area of information disclosure in which the Outpatient Clinic did not approach the ideal model of informed consent any more closely than the Evaluation Center did. Of the patients we observed, only a handful were presented with two or more alternatives to consider. This, of course, does not necessarily mean that patients in the Outpatient Clinic did not make choices. It may only reflect the facts that the consideration of alternatives was not a continual process and that most of the patients were not faced with decisions about treatment on the days they were observed. However, only 17 of the 48 patients we observed made any mention, either in the interview with the staff or later when questioned by our observer, of an alternative of any kind whatsoever. Of course, this may also be only a reflection of a strong commitment to their course of treatment. This interpretation is supported by the fact that seven of the 10 patients who were new to the clinic on the days we observed their interviews did discuss alternatives with their clinicians or with our observer.

While the alternatives theoretically available to Outpatient Clinic patients were diverse, medications predominated, as in all other aspects of the patients' perspective on the clinic. Seven patients considered some modification of the medications.

Dan D is typical of the patients who considered alternatives. As the dialogue below demonstrates, the discussions between Mr. D and the clinician were focused on alternatives to his current medicine. Mr. D complained to the clinician about having trouble sleeping because of the medicine, thus raising the issue of changing treatment.

PATIENT: I think it [the sleeplessness] is because of the medicine, and I think it is going to be bad unless it gets cut down.

CLINICIAN: We are cutting down the dose, and you're also getting [Prolixin]. I think it would be bad to cut down on two things at once.

PATIENT: I know, but I'm not sleeping at night.

The clinician then asked several questions about the specifics of his medication and the origins of his difficulties sleeping. Eventually Mr. D conceded:

PATIENT: I can't sleep at night, and then during the day I sleep. It might not be the medicine, though. It could be that I'm worrying about stuff.

Then they talked about the substance of his worries. Finally, the clinician asked:

CLINICIAN: Have you ever had Mellaril?
PATIENT: Doesn't that . . . stop the production of sperm?
CLINICIAN: It doesn't stop that, but it stops erections.
PATIENT: I don't want to try that.
CLINICIAN: I think we'll give you some Trilafon.

With few exceptions, the patients who, like Mr. D, considered alternatives or treatment modifications assumed that the treatment would be centered around medications. The same thing is illustrated by Elena D, who complained about being drowsy.

CLINICIAN: You're taking Haldol. That is one of the medicines that is least prone to make you drowsy. . . . It's possible that [Prolixin] would make you less drowsy.
PATIENT: What about weight gain?
CLINICIAN: Well, Haldol is best for that.
PATIENT: You mean with Prolixin you'll probably gain weight?
CLINICIAN: Yeah. It's probably six of one and half a dozen of another. . . . Maybe you are more prone to . . . tremor and stiffness.
PATIENT: Is Haldol better for that?
CLINICIAN: Well, it 's probably better than Prolixin, but you can always taken Cogentin to deal with that.
PATIENT: I'm afraid of getting into something worse.

The discussion continued for several minutes, and Ms. D decided to stay on Haldol.

Although there was a great deal of discussion in these two cases about the relative merits of two different drugs, in neither case did the clinician mention or did the patient consider either a nonpharmacological therapy or a marked reduction in dosage of the medication.

Likewise, the staff sometimes described two alternatives, neither of which involved medication. We observed three such cases. Aldo H was informed about individual psychotherapy and group therapy as two alternative courses of treatment for him. Dimitri V's psychiatrist gave him a choice between two other alternative "extra" treatments, partial hospitalization and vocational rehabilitation. Jacinta G was informed about both of these as well as about group therapy, all in a manner that would enable her to compare these three alternative courses of treatment:

> "It seems like you need some activities of some complexity, and partial hospitalization will supply you with some complexity of occupation that you require. You will be doing a lot of things, and it will be better than meeting with groups just once a week. . . . There are some other possibilities of activity besides the Day Hospital, which would be less therapy and more activity. The first is seeing about a job."

Eight patients, including the three who had alternatives suggested to them, mentioned some consideration of alternatives to our observer. Four of these (including Jacinta G and Dimitri V) included a partial hospitalization or other resocialization program among their possible choices. The other four considered other types of nonpharmacological therapy.

In summary, both patients and staff considered some alternatives to medications, but only with other medications. They also considered some nonmedication treatments, as supplements to medications.

THE GENERAL NATURE OF THE DIALOGUE

POSITIVE ASPECTS

In general, the staff of the Outpatient Clinic encouraged and responded to patients' questions. However, we did observe several instances in which patients' questions were ignored by clinicians. Wallace H, who asked the resident interviewing him what medications he would be getting, got the laconic reply, "Pills." Jacinta G asked her psychiatrist three times whether she could get her shot every week, but she still did not receive a direct answer. When Dimitri V asked whether there was anything wrong with him, since he kept forgetting things and losing his sense of direction, the doctor simply asked him more questions about his previous hospitalization. When he asked, just before leaving, how he was doing in general, he was told only that he ought to consider vocational rehabilitation or partial hospitalization.

Yet these were exceptions. On all other occasions, patients' questions were answered. Eleven patients we saw were asked explicitly whether they had any further questions, and Andrea V was asked that question no fewer than four times.

This differed strikingly from the situation we saw in the Evaluation Center. The nature of the therapeutic relationship in the Outpatient Clinic, which involved long-term, ongoing contact between clinicians and patients as well as personal responsibility of the former for the latter, certainly affected the quality of information that clinicians provided to patients about their treatment and produced a rather high level of understanding from substantially impaired patients. While, paradoxically, there is no evidence that the clinic staff was motivated by the doctrine of informed consent, the Outpatient Clinic was the closest approximation to a model of informed consent that we saw.

SOME QUALIFICATIONS

On a statistical basis, element for element, the patients understood many aspects of their situation in a manner similar to that of the staff. However, there are a number of serious limits to this picture that might not be apparent in the analysis presented above.

To begin with, although there is no clear cutoff line, 10-20% of the patients had very little or no understanding of the issues at hand. Although a small minority, such patients are nonetheless important to consider in any policy seeking to promote patients' interest. Jake E is typical of these patients.

Jake E's only active request was that he be allowed to postpone his next appointment 1 week if at that time the weather was still cold. [The interview took place in the middle of winter.] Otherwise he volunteered nothing and generally answered in monosyllables. When interviewed by our observer, Mr. E could not recall the name of his medication, nor what it was for. When the observer suggested that people sometimes take medicine because they are sick and asked if he had ever been sick, Mr. E responded that he didn't think he had ever been sick. When asked why he came to the clinic, Mr. E said, "Because she wants me to come." When the observer asked who "she" was, he responded, "The woman I just saw." He could not explain the purpose of the form he had just signed [it was a third-party payment form].

The understanding of about another 10% of the patients was severely affected by their psychosis. Their understanding of treatment was quite unusual by conventional standards and was related to other unusual beliefs that they had, as the case of Wallace H demonstrates.

Wallace H, a 26-year-old man who had just been released from an inpatient ward, came to the Outpatient Clinic for help in dealing with a number of agencies from whom he was seeking money. His sentences were often confused or tangential to the topic. When asked why he had been hospitalized, Mr. H responded:

PATIENT: It was always the police bringing me here. That's what you call red tape, police quota systems.

CLINICIAN: Yeah, but aside from that . . .

PATIENT: There is nothing much aside from that. I'm also on the wrong side of the stick. [He talked bitterly about how people are manipulated.]

CLINICIAN: Do you mean that it's intentional on their part?

PATIENT: Yes, I do believe in conspiracies.
CLINICIAN: What do you hope to get from the outpatient treatment?
PATIENT: I don't know. I hope to get help to secure a specific position.

Then he said that it wouldn't help his paintings, make his father younger, get him to see his children, or make his wife more truthful. However, he agreed to return for treatment if the clinician would give him "something official, on paper, for the agencies." He agreed, even though he described the Hospital and its staff as deliberately abusing and mistreating him, and he did not know any way the treatment could help.

While Mr. H understood some elements of the treatment decision, his overall framework for understanding was unusual and even bizarre.

Another difficulty that we observed, which was not necessarily reflected in the previous summaries, is that the ability of some patients to understand fluctuated from session to session. Thus the first time we observed Letty D, she was well organized and focused, and she remembered more about some of the past details of her treatment than the doctor did.

DOCTOR: You seem better than the last time I saw you.
PATIENT: Yes, I was upset because of my grandmother.
DOCTOR: What happened to your grandmother?
PATIENT: Oh, she passed on, but I'm learning to cope with it better now.
DOCTOR: How long ago did she die?
PATIENT: Going on 3 months . . . I think that changing the medicine also helped.
DOCTOR: I increased the medicine at the beginning of January [2 weeks before].
PATIENT: Yes, that's right, and then you told me that I should come back today for a blood test.
DOCTOR: (*Seeming a little puzzled.*) Oh! I'll have to have a word with my secretary. Can you remind me about that?

During her interview with our observer, Ms. D seemed to have a good grasp of the issues of her treatment, but at her next appointment she had difficulty following the clinician's dialogue.

CLINICIAN: Do you still have trouble perspiring?
PATIENT: I take Joe [her son] to the clinic sometimes. . . .
CLINICIAN: I was going to ask you if you have trouble perspiring.
PATIENT: Yeah, I have trouble with sweating at night.
CLINICIAN: I see that Dr. C had you get a blood test last time.
PATIENT: I haven't heard nothing from my sister. . . .

In this interview, Ms. D generally had trouble staying with the clinician's conversation. In her interview with our observer, her understanding of treatment was clearly not as good as it had been the previous time. For example, during the first interview, she knew that the medication was supposed to make her less nervous; however, in the second interview, when asked why her medication had been increased, she said, "It might be for my eyes. I don't know." Likewise, while on the first occasion she described drowsiness as a side effect, on the second she could describe no side effects at all. In our count of patients who understood, Ms. D was scored as knowing that drowsiness was a side effect, but she did not have that fact available during her second interview.

Finally, it must be noted that since most of the patients understood most of the information most of the time, this did not mean that they used this information to produce autonomous, rational decisions. But this is something that we take up in the next chapter.

15

The Outpatient Clinic: An Opportunity for Voluntary Patient Participation

In observing the Outpatient Clinic, we encountered another type of problem for the vision of autonomous decisionmaking. The Outpatient Clinic was a relatively free and open place for patients, compared with either the Evaluation Center or the Research Ward. In the Evaluation Center, patients were often brought by others, sometimes by the police; the threat of involuntary commitment always loomed over the decisionmaking process. In the Research Ward, although most of the patients were technically free to leave whenever they liked, still the exercise of their will in opposition to the staff meant that the patients had to take the initiative to leave, and the possibility of involuntary commitment remained.

The situation in the Outpatient Clinic was quite different. Patients were not only free to leave whenever they chose, but they were also free not to come at all. If they did not like what they were getting, they did not have to come. The setting approximated an economist's free market, with a willing seller and presumably a willing buyer.

The question at hand is whether such a situation produces a decisionmaking pattern that approximates the informed consent vision of a voluntary, informed choice. As soon becomes clear, the answer is no, with a few qualifications. This chapter documents the patterns of decision and attempts to explain the situation.

STAFF DECISIONMAKING

By continuing to come to the Outpatient Clinic, patients may have been expressing their views that "taking the medicine was worth it," but more concrete evidence of patients' participation in decisionmaking was hard to come by in most cases. Despite evidence (which we present below) that the staff sometimes solicited the patients' opinion and that between sessions some patients took treatment into their own hands, the predominant pattern of decisionmaking in the Outpatient Clinic was that treatment decisions were made by the staff.

Evidence for this proposition comes from several sources. One way of seeing this pattern is in the temporal relationship between information and disclosure. Here, only the first interaction that we observed between a patient and his or her clinician was included.

In 20 of 48 patient-staff encounters, the patients indicated a decision about the proposed treatment only after some information relevant to their choice had been presented to them. Typically, the staff asked the patients a few questions about side effects of medication to check on the patients' progress, told the patients a few things about medication, and suggested to the patients that the medication be increased, decreased, or stay the same. From the point of view of who made the actual decisions, these were mixed cases. Sometimes the patients only acquiesced to decisions made by the staff; as soon becomes clear; in other cases they played an active role.

In 28 of 48 cases, however, the pattern is clearer: The decisions were made without any information disclosure to, or even agreement from, the patients. In 17 of these cases, the patients expressed no decision at all. The working assumption of the interchange between the staff and the patients seemed to be that the patients were already committed to do whatever the staff recommended, even before treatment recommendations were articulated by the staff. Seven of the 17 patients specifically told the staff or our observer that it was up to their doctors, not them, to make treatment decisions. For example:

TORNO U: I'm not a doctor. I didn't study medicine. Oftentimes what they do is they try you out on medicines to see whether you need them or how you respond. It's the doctor's opinion.

JAKE E: [I come to the Clinic] because she [the clinician] wants me to come.

The temporal aspects of the staff's decisions in the Outpatient Clinic was also revealing. In 37 of 48 cases, the staff clearly indicated to the patients what should be done prior to the patients' making any statement or suggestion as to what should be done. In the other 11 cases, the staff members reserved any expressed decision as to what would be done until after the patients had been given some information and the patients' opinion about treatment had been solicited. We discuss these 11 cases below under "Solicited Decisionmaking." Interestingly, in none of the five treatment decisions in which management of the patients' tardive dyskinesia or potential tardive dyskinesia was involved were the patients' preferences about medication solicited. Instead, the staff in effect made the decision for the patients. The clinic staff was not neutral about important decisions and felt that they could not be left to the patients.

Another piece of evidence that the staff made most of the decisions was, as we mention in Chapter 14, that there were very few instances when the staff simultaneously told patients both the risks and benefits of continuing treatment or of alternative treatments, so that the patients could choose which treatments they wished to pursue. More frequently, the staff discussed the side effects of medication only as clinically necessary to monitor the patients' response to treatment, or presented only the benefits of the proposed treatment when patients refused the staff's recommendations.

Moreover, explicit weighing of risks and benefits by the patients, including nonspecific risks or side effects, occurred in only 15 of 60 treatment decisions we observed, and only three of these involved choices between alternative medications. None involved choices between medication and nonpharmacological treatment. In almost all cases, the weighing of risks and benefits was done at the patient's, rather than the staff's, instigation.

This leads us to the final piece of evidence demonstrating the predominance of the staff in Outpatient Clinic decisions. As in the other two settings, the Outpatient Clinic staff members were far more successful in changing the patients' minds about what should be done than were patients in changing the minds of the staff members. Even those patients who, on their own initiative, gave reasons for treatment choices different from those of the staff almost always changed their minds after discussing the matter with the staff and ultimately accepted what the staff believed was best for them. We observed nine instances in which the staff changed patients' minds, but only two instances in which the patients, despite opposition from their clinicians, persisted in their decisions. This does not mean that the staff was "coercive" or threatened patients in order to achieve what they wanted. Indeed, the majority of interactions we observed in the Outpatient Clinic were very cordial, and patients indicated they were pleased with the interaction and with attending the clinic. However, as in the Research Ward and the Evaluation Center, the staff was generally persuasive in securing the patients' consent to what the staff wanted.

There are, in addition, several other patterns of decisionmaking worth examining.

SOLICITED DECISIONMAKING

Within a general pattern of staff decisionmaking, it is interesting that the staff sometimes solicited the patients' opinions about possible treatment options. Staff members sometimes directly told clinic patients that it was "up to them" to decide whether or not to comply with the staff's recommendations. While the patients did not always weigh risks against benefits, and while the information disclosure was not complete, this pattern of decisionmaking more closely resembled informed consent than any other pattern.

SOLICITING THE PATIENTS' OPINIONS ABOUT MEDICATIONS

We saw only three instances in the Outpatient Clinic when staff members asked for the patients' opinions about changing medication. One such instance involved Isabelle N, a 38-year-old homemaker who was taking Trilafon and

Cogentin and who had been seen for more than 2 years in the clinic. After discussing Ms. N's recent purchase of a sewing machine and her difficulties in learning how to use it, the clinician referred Ms. N to a local patient recreation center where sewing lessons were given. Towards the end of the interview, the clinician inquired:

CLINICIAN: Are you nervous at this time?
PATIENT: Not that I know of.
CLINICIAN: Since the last time I saw you, how have you felt? Have you felt any different? Is there anything else that is bothering you?
PATIENT: Not that I know of.
CLINICIAN: Well, the reason I'm asking is that we are thinking of reducing your Trilafon.
PATIENT: Do you mean to decrease it?
CLINICIAN: Yes. What is your thinking about that?
PATIENT: It's OK. Pretty soon I won't be taking it at all.
CLINICIAN: Not pretty soon. We want to slowly decrease it and see how you go on from there. You are taking three Trilafons at bedtime, right?
PATIENT: Yeah.
CLINICIAN: Well, let's do it slowly. There are different sizes of Trilafon. Do you read the labels when you take them?
PATIENT: Yeah.
CLINICIAN: OK, well, that's not a problem. The pills come in 2, 4, 8, and 16 sizes. I don't want to take away the 16 sizes, but we will take away the 2. I'm thinking of your getting jittery and nervous. In the meantime, if you get more nervous and you are not resting, give me a call.
PATIENT: OK.
CLINICIAN: Do you have any questions?
PATIENT: No.

In Ms. N's case, the clinician's request for an opinion seems to amount to "Are you ready for the next step in the treatment?" However, in Penny D's case, the clinician's willingness to listen to the patient's point of view was a response to the patient's desire for a change.

Unlike many of the other patients in the Outpatient Clinic, Penny D, a 41-year-old registered nurse, was presently working and was actively involved with her family. However, she complained about recently becoming "jittery and nervous" because of having to take more responsibility at work.

CLINICIAN: Do you feel that a change in medication is needed?
PATIENT: Let's see. I'm not too sure about that. Sometimes I don't feel too good. I used to be able to manage on what I have. I really don't understand because I take it faithfully.
CLINICIAN: Well, it works the opposite way than you seem to imagine it. The longer you are on it, the more good it does you. . . . Well, sometimes

when the stress level is high, the medication needs adjusting—you need to get more just for that. You need more, but it is related to a certain period in your life. . . . If you feel like changing medicine, you are getting two different kinds, Haldol and Thorazine. Both of these affect the level of sedation, but Thorazine will make you more sleepy. I don't see that there is any point in increasing both the Haldol and the Thorazine. The Thorazine is going to make you more drowsy than the Haldol.

PATIENT: I think we should up it temporarily.

CLINICIAN: Do you feel you want an increase right now?

PATIENT: I can try it.

CLINICIAN: I would suggest the Haldol.

PATIENT: Then if I get too sleepy I can stop it myself.

CLINICIAN: Well, go back down. I would suggest the Haldol. If you have any questions, give us a call.

SOLICITING THE PATIENTS' DECISIONS
ABOUT PSYCHOSOCIAL TREATMENT

While staff members rarely asked patients' opinions about medications, and then only about adjusting the levels, there were other matters about which the staff usually solicited the patients' decisions. These concerned patients' participation in group therapy or attendance at day care programs designed to assist the patients' psychosocial rehabilitation. We witnessed several instances in which staff members suggested that patients participate in such programs, and the patients were noncommittal or clearly refused the recommendation. Staff members then usually responded that it was the patients' decision. The staff seemed to be trying to persuade the patients to participate without alienating the patients from continuing to attend the clinic. The dialogue between Hollis N, a 50-year-old unemployed man, and the clinician illustrates this point.

CLINICIAN: Have you been spending much more time out of the house than you were?

PATIENT: Oh, I've been spending time around the house all winter helping clean up and stuff like that.

CLINICIAN: I think we have talked before about your getting involved in some kind of social activities. There are a variety of them available going from one day a week to a couple days a week. Have you heard of _____ House?

PATIENT: No.

CLINICIAN: It's a social organization. They have social activities. You can go and play cards once a week. Are you interested in getting into anything like that?

PATIENT: Not right now. I'll have to ask my mother.

CLINICIAN: Why do you have to ask your mother?

PATIENT: Oh, sometimes she says that she wants me to stay with her for awhile. (*The patient paused.*) When does it start?

CLINICIAN: Well, it goes on all year round. Another thing, Mr. N, is that we have a person here who is an activities specialist. One thing I could do is set up an appointment for you to see him about activities, and you could talk about what days you wanted to come and how often.

PATIENT: Well, I haven't really got the time, and then there's the bus fare.

CLINICIAN: You're hesitating a bit. Maybe you could discuss it with your mother. [The subject was then dropped, and the clinician checked the patient's progress with the medication. However, as the interview concluded, the clinician said:] OK, Mr. N, we'll send a prescription to you by the 14th of April, OK? Call me if you decide about the _____ House.

In many ways, the staff's pattern of soliciting decisions from patients reflected what patients expected from them. Patients in the Outpatient Clinic did not differ greatly from patients in the Evaluation Center and in the Research Ward in their understanding of the allocation of decisional authority. As we discuss below, they continually expressed trust in the judgment of the clinic staff as to what medications they should take and for how long; but when the discussion turned to other types of treatment or additional activity programs, patients seemed much less willing to relinquish responsibility for these decisions.

In interviews with our observer, patients frequently said they could not determine by themselves the proper medications or dosage levels of drugs. For example, Audrey N said of the clinician, "She's good to you. She tries to help . . . I used to take two [pills] a day, but then she decided it would be better if I have one. I don't know why." However, decisions about any type of treatment other than medications were rather tightly guarded by the patients as their own. Jacinta G, a patient whom the doctor was trying to persuade to move away from her mother, expressed her feelings this way:

DOCTOR: [M]ight you consider a change in your life, either immediate or long-range?

PATIENT: (*Emphatically.*) Dr. R, right now I'm satisfied. I have the apartment to myself and my mother all day. I do things on my own and that's just how I like it.

DOCTOR: Are there any other things you'd like to call to my attention and talk over?

PATIENT: No.

DOCTOR: I'll give you the medicine.

PATIENT: Yeah, I need them.

In this case, the patient was quite clearly drawing the boundary between what was and what was not the doctor's acceptable role.

The cases of solicited decisionmaking involved 11 of the 48 Outpatient Clinic patients and were relatively clear-cut examples of the staff's directly involving and reinforcing the right of the patients to decide about treatment. However, only three of them involved medications, and these involved only relatively minor modifications in the pharmacotherapy. Moreover, the patients' right to decide about treatment was not solicited in the two instances we observed when the patients did not initially view their problems as being amenable to medication and therefore refused. Nor did the staff remind the patients that it was their right to decide when trying to persuade recalcitrant patients to continue taking medication, despite its side effects. It is also interesting that the pattern of solicited decisionmaking occurred mainly in the "older," continuing cases and not in the "new" cases, in which, *a priori*, we might have expected to find informed consent procedures. Among the "new" patients we observed, only Benny I was told by the staff that it was up to him to decide about the alternatives (i.e., whether to be treated at the Outpatient Clinic or elsewhere).

PROXY DECISIONMAKING

There were few potential proxy decisionmakers available at the Outpatient Clinic. In several cases, patients were accompanied to the clinic by someone else who played no role in the negotiations. For example, Jerry G and Evelyn G were accompanied by roommates; Loraine D, by her boyfriend; Dimitri V, by a girlfriend; and Emma D, by her sister. However, none of these third parties participated in the discussions.

There were five cases in which third parties played a direct role in negotiating treatment for the patient. However, unlike many third-party cases in the Evaluation Center, none involved clear-cut conflicts of interest between the third parties and the patients. The third parties seemed to have been trying to help the patients, not to ease their own burdens. Lucy T, a 65-year-old woman who had recently been discharged from the Hospital and still seemed somewhat confused, was brought to the Outpatient Clinic by her husband. It was her husband, not Ms. T, who received instructions from the staff about Ms. T's need for Prolixin, Cogentin, and Digoxin, a heart stimulant. Ms. T could not name the medication she was taking or give their side effects. She told our observer that she was at the clinic to receive "vitamin shots" to calm her nerves. Wallace H, a 26-year-old sewer worker, came to the clinic with his mother. They both tried unsuccessfully to persuade the staff to write Mr. H an excuse from work because of his illness. Case workers from a Goodwill training program accompanied Delbert B to the clinic. With Mr. B's active participation, a "behavioral contract" was arranged among Mr. B, the caseworkers, and the clinician that if Mr. B took his medications properly and did not come late for work, he would be permitted to attend a dance with female patients. Nolan S's wife helped her foreign-born husband by translating the clinician's questions.

Of all the patients we observed, only Hilda H, a 54-year-old unemployed woman who lived in a halfway house, had her Outpatient Clinic treatment significantly affected by third parties. Nursing students who had visited Ms. H at the halfway house reported to her clinician that Ms. H was not doing well. The clinician asked Ms. H's counselor to bring her to the clinic for an evaluation and possible admission. The counselor sat in on the session with the patient's clinician, a psychiatrist, and the patient. The clinician began the interview as follows:

CLINICIAN: It seems that a lot of people are concerned about you lately. They say that you are not feeling good like you were several weeks ago.
PATIENT: I am feeling good. I am taking my medicine. I am taking it early. Maybe I should start to take it late.
CLINICIAN: You don't look quite as cheerful as you were 3 weeks ago.
PATIENT: My transistor radio is broken.
CLINICIAN: What happened to your pretty clothes?
PATIENT: They're at home in the wash.
CLINICIAN: When did the student nurses come to see you?
PATIENT: Today.
CLINICIAN: How did the visit go?
PATIENT: All right.
CLINICIAN: Well, they were concerned about you. Is anything wrong?
PATIENT: No, I'm feeling fine, I can't see very good, I need better glasses.
CLINICIAN: You have a crust on your eyes. Is something wrong with your hearing aid?
PATIENT: Yeah, I ran out of batteries.
CLINICIAN: Do you have any money to get some more?
PATIENT: No, I don't have any money. It's all in the bank.
CLINICIAN: Are you feeling any different from when I saw you 3 weeks ago?
PATIENT: No.
CLINICIAN: Because there are some people living with you who seemed to be concerned about you.
PATIENT: But it's none of their business, those people about me.

The clinician decided that the patient's reported behavior might be due to a number of causes, including a recent medication change, in which Haldol and Thorazine had been increased. These problems were compounded by an absence of sensory stimulation because of the broken hearing aid and radio. After getting more information from the counselor about the patient's behavior, the clinician decided, without consultation with the patient, to reduce the patient's Thorazine by 100 mg and to check her diabetes in the medical clinic.

CLINICIAN: We're going to ask the doctor at Medical Services to see you and to check your blood sugar and blood pressure, and we will have the results back in a few days. We are thinking that you might need to come into the Hospital. I don't think that we are going to do that today, but we will see how you get along on the outside. Do you feel you need to come into the Hospital?

PATIENT: No.

DOCTOR: What things do you think might make you think you might need to be in the Hospital?

PATIENT: (*No reply.*)

DOCTOR: What would have to happen?

PATIENT: I'd have to be sick.

DOCTOR: In what way?

PATIENT: Melancholy, I guess, something like that.

DOCTOR: OK. A number of people are concerned about you right now, but if we can help you without putting you into the Hospital, we'll do that. But if we feel that you need to be in the Hospital, we'll talk more about it, OK?

Of all the patients in the Outpatient Clinic, Ms. H was the most pressured by third parties and might have been handled in the Evaluation Center. However, even in this case the patient was ultimately consulted about the question of her possible hospitalization.

Indeed, clinicians generally tried to keep third parties out of the discussions. Thus when Loraine D's boyfriend asked to sit in on the interview, he was refused; and the clinician told the patient, "It was, after all, you that I wanted to talk to." On the chart, the clinician also noted that Ms. D's boyfriend was "belligerent." In this case and also elsewhere, it seems that clinicians found that third parties often interfered with rather than helped their relationships with patients.

However, the fact that third parties played a small direct role in treatment negotiations does not mean that there were no third-party pressures on Outpatient Clinic patients. While pressure from family members was not as apparent in the Outpatient Clinic as in the other settings, this may have been due in part to the fact that the vast majority of the patient's time was spent outside the clinic and thus unobserved. It is, therefore, likely that a great deal more third-party pressure was exerted than was apparent during the patients' clinic visits.

One important way in which third parties became involved in the treatment of Outpatient Clinic patients was by instigating the initial contact between the patients and the Hospital. Usually this resulted first in inpatient hospitalization, then after discharge in referral to the Outpatient Clinic. For instance, Shaw T, a student in his 20s, was committed to the Hospital by his brother, and Wolfgang G, a 30-year-old art student, said, "I was brought by the police because me and my wife had a slight difference of opinion, and that was expressed through her calling the police."

Although none of the clinic patients had been involuntarily committed by a court for outpatient treatment, some patients bore memories of past commitments to inpatient treatment. Shaw T told our observer that his brother, who had once had him committed to a state hospital when Mr. T did not feel he was sick, now urged him to come to the Outpatient Clinic for treatment. Ottie G, telling about how she had been committed for inpatient treatment by her husband and brother, said, "So if I need the medicine, then I take it." The lesson of these past commitments probably influenced the patients to go along with their current treatment in the clinic.

Third parties not only initiated treatment, but also provided encouragement to continue. For example, Myrna G, a 38-year-old woman with a college education, was told by her mother, "It's good to do what the doctor wants, because that way you'll get well if you follow what they say." And 34-year-old Alex G told the observer that his aunt was in charge of giving him medication and always asked about his discussions after each of his clinic visits.

For those patients without families or not living with their families, other persons with whom they lived or associated exerted the same sorts of pressures as did family members. Dimitri V's girlfriend exerted a significant influence on his continuing treatment. When he felt that the medicine was his main problem and he was considering stopping it, he decided that his girlfriend's wanting him to continue was enough reason not to stop. "She's blind and she depends on me a great deal, so that's why I keep taking it." Mr. V also said that it was his girlfriend who got him to come back for his appointments. In our interviews with patients, we found that many who lived in halfway houses tried to arrange appointments to coincide with those of their roommates. Jerry G, a 29-year-old man last employed as a teacher, continued to attend the clinic because his roommate also came. "If he didn't come," Mr. G told us, "then I would probably quit too."

While the above discussion shows clearly that there was some third-party pressure on patients both inside and outside the Clinic, this was a minor problem for informed consent in the Outpatient Clinic, compared to the Evaluation Center. The pressure mainly took the form of general support for treatment.

PATIENT DECISIONS OUTSIDE THE CLINIC

We have seen that, by and large, the staff made decisions in the Outpatient Clinic and the patients accepted them. This was true despite the absence of significant pressures from the law or from other outside forces. Indeed, much of the involvement of patients in decisionmaking seemed to come from the staff's efforts to involve the patients.

Now we add to this paradox by showing that many patients did seem to be able to make deliberate decisions for themselves about treatment. In fact, outside the Outpatient Clinic context, they seemed to do it frequently. Let us, then, consider two other patterns of patient decisionmaking that we observed in clinic patients: patient self-regulation of medications between appointments, and what is usually called "noncompliance" with staff recommendations.

SELF-REGULATION: INTERIM DECISIONMAKING

Some patients in the Outpatient Clinic were encouraged by the staff to manage their own medications between visits. Not only were such patients given some information about the rationale for medication, but their clinicians also recommended either explicitly or implicitly that the patients ought to be responsible for adjusting the dosage of medication between appointments. Typically, this self-regulation involved the patients' adjusting the dosage of antiparkinsonian drugs (e.g., Cogentin) that combat some short-term side effects of antipsychotic drugs, such as restlessness, muscle stiffness, slowness, or tremors. Ten of the patients we observed were told by their clinicians that it was their responsibility to manage their Cogentin levels or even to decide how much antipsychotic medication to take between visits. For example, once it was decided that Dan D's Trilafon would be increased, he was told to take between one and three additional Trilafon pills at night to go to sleep.

A more frequent example of interim self-regulation was, however, that the patients were given the responsibility for managing their Cogentin, with permission to vary either the amount or the time that the drug would be taken. We saw eight instances of this. In some cases, these instructions were given by the clinicians after changes had been made in the patients' antipsychotic medications, which meant that the level of Cogentin might need adjusting. Thus the patients were given the responsibility to adjust the dosage between appointments as necessary.

Of course, since we usually saw patients only once in the Outpatient Clinic, we could not tell how often patients actually adjusted their dosages after receiving staff permission, but we do know that patients often changed dosages between visits.

PATIENT-INITIATED CHANGES IN MEDICATIONS BETWEEN VISITS

We consider here what are usually referred to in medicine as "compliance" problems. These are situations in which a patient fails to comply with a clinician's advice. However, from the perspective of informed consent, these can be considered situations in which a patient unilaterally adjusted his or her treatment between visits to the Outpatient Clinic.

Patient-initiated changes in medications between visits occurred in 25% of the cases that we observed. However, these changes did not always seem to be part of a rational process of modifying treatment to deal with overmedication or undermedication. At least two patients did not seem to be sufficiently well organized psychologically to continue a routine process of taking medication. For example, Audrey N, a 46-year-old woman who worked in a sheltered workshop, was extremely compliant in her interactions with the staff, who believed that she was somewhat mentally retarded. Since Ms. N sometimes took too much medication, using up a month's supply of medication in a week, and since community workers who visited her apartment noted that there were many pills lying around, the staff arranged for her to come once a week to regulate her medication.

Several other patients accounted for their noncompliance by saying that they had not understood. For example, Aldo H had been prescribed three pills of Cogentin per day, but he told the clinician that he took only two. When she told him that he was supposed to take three, he responded, "I used to think it was strange, because I always had more Cogentin [remaining] than I should have." While it is possible that this was simply his way of exercising a conscious decision to take less medication, he misunderstood what Cogentin was for and thus probably misregulated it.

However, some patients said they deliberately took more or less medication because they felt they needed it or because of the side effects. For example, Elena D, a 36-year-old patient diagnosed at various times as either schizophrenic or depressed, increased her own Haldol between the first and second of our observations. She noted to the clinician, "I think the extra medication helped. I've been taking an extra Haldol and feel much better." Although Ms. D had complained about being on too much medication at a previous session, she nevertheless decided between sessions that increasing the dose would help her feel less upset and would help her sleep better.

On the other hand, Jon T chronically took only half the Cogentin prescribed for him. He found the side effects of Cogentin worse than the side effects that the drug was intended to relieve. Somewhat less deliberately, Shaw T simply stopped taking medication when he ran out and missed several appointments. He apparently felt well enough to stop taking it. At his next appearance at the clinic, the clinician made the same assessment and discontinued the medications, with the warning that Mr. T should monitor his feelings carefully and call immediately if he found himself in need of medication.

Finally, a small group of patients seemed to reduce their medications in an angry and/or paranoid state. Dan D personifies this type of patient.

Dan D, a 24-year-old man who worked intermittently at a sheltered workshop, was evaluated by the staff as psychotic. On the first occasion that we observed him, Mr. D showed relatively good understanding of treatment and was able to converse clearly with the staff. During this session, Mr. D asked for a reduction of his medication, but more Trilafon was added instead. At his next interview, Mr. D noted that he still did not sleep at night. "I don't need any medication. I took Trilafon just half the time, and half the time I found it wasn't working." The clinician insisted that the medication was very important for him, but Mr. D continued to insist, "I don't think I need all that medication."

CLINICIAN: Is there anything else you wanted to talk about?
PATIENT: I don't need medicine today.
CLINICIAN: Yes, you will. I don't see you for 2 weeks, and I'm going to give you a little more.

During the interview with the clinician, Mr. D was extremely talkative. He spontaneously brought to the dialogue a number of seemingly irrelevant subjects. When the interview concluded, the clinician said:

CLINICIAN: You should get your lithium today and also your shot [Prolixin].
PATIENT: I don't like Prolixin shots.
CLINICIAN: Relax, you're doing pretty good.
PATIENT: People like you are going to put me away.
CLINICIAN: Relax.

Immediately following this dialogue, Mr. D told our observer that the purpose of his lithium-level test was to see if the Prolixin shots had entered his body. He also noted, "I feel they are trying to kill me. My heart beats so strong I swear that when they inject it they are trying to kill me. Then I realize that nobody is going to harm me because if they were going to harm me they would have got rid of me before now."

In summary, although patients sometimes were encouraged to monitor their own medication levels, a relatively small percentage deliberately changed the levels.

WHY PATIENTS DID NOT DECIDE

We now try to answer the paradox that the Outpatient Clinic raises: If patients were relatively free from outside pressures and were free to come or not to come to the clinic, why did the staff make almost all of the decisions?

We have already noted one and probably the most important reason why patients were typically not the decisionmakers—staff members and most patients believed that the staff members should make the decision because of their superior technical competence. However, even when the patients were inclined to take a more active role in the decisionmaking, there were other reasons why they did not.

STRUCTURAL PRESSURE

Certain aspects of the operation of the Outpatient Clinic encroached upon patient autonomy. Foremost among them was that the clinic was organized as a "medication" clinic. The fundamental assumption of the Hospital administrators who established the clinic and the staff members who worked there was that some form of neuroleptic (antipsychotic) medication was essential for the well-being of the patients who were seen in the clinic. This belief was a corollary of the fact that almost all of the patients bore the diagnosis of chronic schizophrenia and that most psychiatrists believed that the only effective treatment for such a condition was medication with antipsychotic drugs. Although the staff viewed various forms of psychotherapy and other activities (such as attending community centers) as useful adjuncts to medications, only medication was viewed as essential. These views impinged on patient autonomy in significant ways. For example, Wolfgang G, a patient who refused to take medication as an inpatient, came to the Outpatient Clinic to talk and to obtain help in sorting out some problems with various welfare agencies. He was informed at the outset that unless he accepted medication, the clinic would not be able to help him with his other concerns. Thus, for the most part, patients could not avail themselves of whatever other benefits they perceived the clinic as providing unless they agreed to take medication. Of course, since most of the patients came primarily to get medications, this was not a constraint on them.

This case also highlights a significant source of power possessed by mental health professionals. As personnel engaged in treatment, the Outpatient Clinic staff members had a series of relationships with other health and welfare agencies, and with such relationships went the capacity to become brokers for the patients with these agencies. The ability to negotiate for other services for the patients meant that staff members had the potential to become very significant in the lives of patients who attended the clinic.

In almost all cases, discussions about concerns other than the medications took place, and staff members provided advice and referrals to other institutions. Much of this advice and most of the referrals were medically related. During her interview with the clinician, Letty D complained of night sweats, which the clinician arranged to get checked by a physician in another part of the hospital. Aldo H was told that he should see the same physician for his cough, while Esther N was given advice as to which low-tar cigarettes she should smoke. Numerous patients were told that they should attend a recreation center. Staff members were frequently perceived as significant help-givers in critical areas of the patients' lives. As Anita S, a 53-year-old white woman, expressed it, "I like her; she's a really nice doctor. She's helped me with a lot of things."

Another source of staff influence was based on the facts that patients' lives were often devoid of close personal relationships, and that patients lacked economic resources. These facts often led them to place a great deal of emphasis on their relationships with their clinicians. The literature describing schizophrenic patients indicates that they suffer from social as well as economic "poverty." The demographic breakdown of the patients we saw in the Outpatient Clinic appears to confirm this picture. Of the 48 patients seen, only six were married; 23 were unemployed, and most who worked were engaged in low-paying, unskilled occupations. In such circumstances, contact with clinic personnel had the potential to become extremely significant in patients' lives. Thus most patients sustained a rather long-term relationship with the clinic, a mean of 11.4 months among the patients we observed. Patients seemed to have developed strong attachments to the clinic staff; these attachments probably lessened their degree of vigilance with respect to treatment negotiation. For example, Judd D said that he had no worries about his medications "because I think they're concerned about me here." A clear example of dependence on a clinician and its effect on treatment choice is that of Aldo H, who was reluctant to move into other forms of therapy because "I'm afraid I'm going to lose her" [the clinician]. Danielle B, an ex-librarian who resided in a transitional-living home, reported to our observer that she enjoyed coming to the clinic because she liked to talk to people on her own educational level. She was encouraged to attend the clinic, she said, because "people are glad to see me."

The patients' reliance on the treating clinicians for access to desired resources and the nature of the patient–clinician relationship may have made it harder for patients to enter into conflict with the staff over treatment issues. In a situation where patients lacked economic resources and social contacts, the patients' dependence on the staff was even greater than simple transference theory would suggest.[1]

STAFF PRESSURE

Within this context, let us now examine the way in which staff members used their influence. Among the most important objectives of treatment, as viewed by the Outpatient Clinic staff, were the efforts to persuade patients to take their medications and to impress upon patients the importance of taking medications. A variety of techniques had been developed, many no doubt unwittingly, toward this end. One technique was to threaten tacitly to withdraw treatment. For instance, after interviewing Wallace H and talking to his mother, the doctor recommended that he take pills prescribed to help him sleep.

PATIENT: But I didn't plan on taking no pills. I plan to undertake my own mental well-being.

DOCTOR: Well, it sounds like you weren't making a whole lot of progress. With the medicine, it seems like you'd start doing a whole lot better.

The patient still appeared reluctant to take the medication, and at this point the doctor became slightly exasperated.

DOCTOR: (*In a stern voice.*) I don't know why you came here, Wally. How did you see that I could help you?

One moderate and routine technique that the clinic staff used to attempt to assure that patients would take their medication was to emphasize what they believed were the negative consequences of stopping medications. Torno U, a 41-year-old man of Greek extraction, suggested that his medication be reduced because of drowsiness. The doctor said he did not think it was a good idea to change the medication. While writing the prescription, the doctor reiterated that taking the medication was essential: "It seems that you're doing fine, and there is no likelihood that you will be hospitalized again if you take the medicine."

Another way in which the staff attempted to get patients to follow treatment prescriptions was to remind patients that they were ill. The case of Dimitri V, who somewhat assertively complained about the side effects of the medication, graphically illustrates this point. The doctor adopted a scolding tone with the patient, saying that he was under the impression that Mr. V had made a commitment to take the medication. He also conveyed the impression that not taking the medication was pathological. "You have a history of this . . . and I think you should be alerted to the fact that you ascribe things to the medication that aren't always so."

At the next interview some weeks later, Mr. V complained again about the side effects of the medication, and announced that once he got a job he was going to stop taking the medication, because "I can't function." The doctor responded, "But, Mr. V, I think it is the other way around—that you can function only with the medicine." The doctor then emphasized how sick he had been and how the medication had helped: "Mr. V, when you were hospitalized, your thinking was unrealistic in a lot of ways, and these medications helped get your thinking back on realistic levels." Again, Mr. V protested that there were few jobs he could hold while on the medication and mentioned his intention to stop the medication once he had a job. The doctor reiterated that he thought Mr. V would jeopardize his health if he stopped the medication.

Although medications were the essential ingredient of treatment in the Outpatient Clinic, group therapy was also recommended to patients, and patients often resisted this form of treatment. When the staff was committed to the idea that therapy was important for a particular patient, they used the same persuasive techniques that they used when prescribing medication. For instance, Jerry G, for whom group therapy was suggested, continued to resist participation because his past experience with group therapy had not been effective for him. In response, the clinician suggested that Mr. G's "mental state" was affecting his decision and recommended that he take lithium, explaining, "It would help if you would try to take lithium because it would moderate the fluctuations in your mood, which might be affecting your willingness to take part in the group therapy program." Mr. G was also reluctant to take lithium because it had not relieved his depression on former occasions, and also because if he were to take lithium, he would continually have to undergo blood tests that he did not like. The clinician let the conversation on this point lapse for a while, but later said, "I wish you would consider lithium at this point." Mr. G even more adamantly refused, saying forcefully, "I don't want that needle in my arm. I had 900 mg of that stuff and it didn't help me." The clinician thought it was worth a try, at which point Mr. G reminded her that he took the drug for about 6 months and it did not help him. Furthermore, it had the undesirable effect of making him gain weight. The clinician agreed, but continued to urge him to take the drug and to become occupied in such things as a group. Mr. G promised to think about the medicine but said that he was definitely not interested in group therapy.

Not only did the clinician insist on persuading Mr. G to get involved in group therapy and to take lithium through repeated arguments during their first meeting, but on Mr. G's next visit, she again suggested that he begin group therapy and continued to discuss this recommendation, despite his expressed skepticism about its efficacy for him. This case illustrates how, as on the Research Ward, the opportunity for cumulative pressure existed because of the ongoing nature of the relationship between staff and patients.

Various other techniques were used to increase compliance. Staff members attempted to create alliances between themselves and their patients by talking as though both parties were involved in adjusting the treatment. This sense of partnership was reflected in the use of the term "we." For instance, in talking to Marcy N, the clinician said, "I really think *we* should supplement the medicine because I think you need the Cogentin. Last time you were here, *we* stopped the phenobarb." And with Dan D, "What I think *we* should do is add to that medicine until you fall asleep." The staff also used their authority to remind patients of their own expertise by letting patients know the experience of fellow patients, thereby mobilizing their desire to be like the others. In one interview, the psychiatrist said, "Most patients do take them at night, and it works well."

PATIENTS' ROLE AND SELF-CONCEPT

The final category of explanations as to why patients typically allowed the staff to make treatment decisions concerns the patients' views of themselves and the staff.

The Staff's Superior Knowledge

In large part, patients perceived the staff as possessing a significant body of knowledge and an understanding of patients that was superior to the patients' own. A remark by Torno U exemplified this belief:

> "It's a good idea to come to the clinic, because doctors can see you're not doing fine when you think you're OK; and a lot of times you don't realize, especially with mental experience. They know that you really need help—so you have to listen to the doctor."

The consequences of this belief in the superior knowledge of the staff members—and especially doctors—were that patients were deferential to the staff's recommendations, hesitated to express their own views, and denigrated their own ability to make any contribution to decisionmaking about treatment. For instance, when a clinician suggested an increase in medication to Anita S, she responded, "Well, it's up to you. I don't think I need it. But you're the doctor." Jacinta G agreed that her medication level be reduced, stating, "OK, you're the doctor." When the clinician requested that Delbert B participate in defining the treatment goals they were formulating, he responded, "I'd like to hear your point of view. Maybe yours would be better than mine." On a previous visit Mr. B had requested readmission to the Hospital as an inpatient, but the clinician felt this was not necessary. Later Mr. B admitted that he had failed to pursue the issue with the clinician because "she's a nurse and she feels that I shouldn't be in the Hospital, and she's dealing with me pretty good and I respect that."

Deference to Professional Status

Closely related to the staff members' actual or assumed expertise was their position. They were professionals, and not mere professionals but medical professionals.

Patients' deferential attitudes toward doctors was best illustrated by Mimi E, who, in talking about her treatment, said that she would rely on the doctor's judgment because "he's the physician and he's trained. He knows about these things, and besides, he wouldn't give me any medicine that would harm me. He's the one that's familiar with all the medications, isn't he?" Some patients were so deferential to the staff that, like Holly E, they thought that they should come to the clinic so as not to disappoint the doctors.

As in the Evaluation Center and in the Research Ward, patients did not always make their real needs felt in the presence of staff members. When, for example, Hollis N was asked by the clinician if he would like to go to a recreation center for patients, he said that he would have to check first with his mother, who did not like him to leave the house often. Afterward, when the clinician was not present, Mr. N was more specific and forceful about his desire not to go, saying, "It takes time and also extra bus fare, and just for recreation I don't think it's worth it."

One important consideration was the extent to which patients thought they were able to contribute to their treatment plans. Many patients perceived their relationship with the medical staff as being entirely subordinate; they had no sense of themselves as entitled to information that would enable them to choose whether or not to receive treatment. When indicating that the staff gave him no information about his medication, Dan D said, "I guess they'd rather you ask them, because that shows that you're showing more interest in it and in your surroundings." And Jacinta G said she thought it was good for patients to know the medications that they were taking, not for themselves but as an aid to the medical profession when taking medical histories. Even Talcot D, who had suffered particularly bad side effects from Thorazine said he would like to have known the side effects so that he could have been prepared to cope with them, rather than saying that he would have liked information with which to make a decision whether or not to accept this particular treatment.

Chronic Mental Illness

Also influencing patients' views of themselves as decisionmakers was their personal self-image. In interviews with our observer, patients often gave the impression of being plagued by a sense of failure and inefficacy in their lives. Jerry G's account, though more articulate than most, is typical in expressing this feeling:

> "I just feel stagnant and useless. I don't like myself. I've withdrawn from society and from life. I feel that I'm an audience and I'm not a participant anymore. I feel alienated from the rest of the world. I'm not well. I don't really think that I can plan for the future. I just want to let it happen."

Some patients specifically eschewed responsibility for their lives on the basis of their illness. Elena D commented, "People have a lot of power over me because I'm frightened. I don't want to get sick again." Others recognized that their ability to act was circumscribed by the very fact that they were mental patients. Dan D remarked that he would never get into an argument with his clinician, because "sometimes what normal people can do, mental patients can't." In a similar vein, Jerry G remarked, "I've had a mental illness, and mental illness changes your life and your view of yourself as sick, and you don't think you can do too much. You can't do too many things." The stigma associated with having been in a mental institution was considered by some to be a limiting factor in their lives. Talcot D, for instance, felt he would have great difficulty finding a job: "Once they find out that I was a patient, they won't hire me anyway." This patient, as noted in Chapter 13, also manifested feelings of dependence on the Hospital and on mental health professionals. He had been hospitalized 8 years before in California and still called the psychiatrist who had treated him there. The only work for which he had applied had been in the Hospital itself.

These feelings of dependence and passivity manifested in their dealings with the Hospital staff were also apparent in other aspects of patients' lives outside the Outpatient Clinic. For example, according to her account, Penny D's supervisor frequently did not come to work, leaving her with large amounts of work to do, and she never protested or asked her supervisor to give her forewarning of these events. Leslie E talked about spending her life alone in a tenement building, where her major contact with other people occurred when her upstairs neighbor would occasionally drop by to see how she was feeling. In the transitional living center where Jacqueline M lived, counselors had a large amount of power, and this reduced the number of decisionmaking areas in patients' lives. Ms. M complained to our observer, "They tell you what to cook and what to buy."

Acceptance of the Necessity for Treatment

Partly because of the efforts of the Outpatient Clinic staff to convince patients that their ability to function depended on their taking the drugs, and partly because the patients' own past experiences in the world bred a sense of inefficacy and failure, patients believed they had no option but to take medication if they were to avoid a relapse with consequent rehospitalization. Acceptance of this view severely limited patients' playing an active role in treatment decision-making. Once having accepted the necessity for medication, there was little scope for discussion of that treatment. Seven patients spontaneously told us that they believed they would not be able to function without taking some medication. Jerry G, for example, believed that although the clinic had not done too much for him besides give him drugs, he felt the drugs were extremely important, since he was unable to function without them. Other patients, although objecting to and disliking the drugs, continued to take them because, as Mimi E said, "I know I have to, and they keep me well, so I really don't mind that much." Perhaps the patient who acknowledged the value if not the absolute necessity of the drugs most articulately was Delbert B:

> "I'm a sick person. The only thing that keeps me going is the medicine. I don't know when I'm going to be well. I'm a schizophrenic. I do need the medicine because I can't socialize or comprehend without it. I was a wild man. I was really spaced out before I started taking the medicine. The medicine gives me my mind back."

Some patients experienced a relapse after they ceased taking medication. As a result, they were even more committed to relegating responsibility for their treatment to the Outpatient Clinic staff. This sentiment was expressed by Myrna G, a patient who had stopped taking medication and had subsequently been rehospitalized. When asked by our observer who would decide when to stop coming to the Clinic, she replied that she would leave it to the doctors because, "it didn't turn out right before when I took it in my hands."

In some cases, the medications contributed to the patients' feelings of inefficacy. Jacinta G told our observer that she felt embarrassed because she was falling down on the street, which made her feel as if she was "acting like a baby." Only after she saw a doctor other than the one who had first prescribed the medication did she learn that her behavior was caused by too much medication. When the dosage was cut, she was better able to cope with her environment. Some patients were more keenly aware that the medications caused some problems for them. Elena D reported, "It's hard to think right now because I'm on the medicines. My mind's not working. The medicines make me drowsy." Even though they reported some dissatisfaction with medication, these patients and many others continued to take it.

16

Summary of the Outpatient Clinic Findings

INTRODUCTION

The Outpatient Clinic was an interesting setting in which to study the disclosure and decisionmaking processes, because it was markedly different from the other two settings. In general, the relationship between clinician and patient was more isolated from external pressures and seemed to operate more autonomously. One aspect of this isolation was the existence of no black-letter law about informed consent in outpatient settings. Moreover, there exists almost no common law about informed consent in outpatient psychiatric settings. Consequently, there were no consent forms that attempted to structure the disclosure and decisionmaking processes. There was almost no direct participation by third parties, such as friends or relatives of patients, in the decisionmaking processes. Furthermore, since only one clinician dealt with each individual patient and had personal responsibility for that patient's care, we did not see the ambiguous structures of responsibility for informing patients that we saw in the other settings.

Another feature absent from the Outpatient Clinic was that of legal coercion. The possibility of hospitalization was considered seriously only once by the staff, and even then it was not clear that such a hospitalization would have been involuntary. Moreover, in most cases the patients were perfectly free not to show up for treatment and thus seemed free of any obligation to participate except for their own perceived need for treatment. While there were some exceptions to this pattern, they were not many.

However, the most important difference between the Outpatient Clinic and the other settings was the personal relationship between the clinicians and the patients. Although we saw some of this on the Research Ward, the treatment there was mostly collective. The Outpatient Clinic was much more like the traditional one-to-one, doctor–patient relationship. Thus, at least in some ways, the Outpatient Clinic resembled the type of setting that the informed consent doctrine envisions.

PATTERNS OF DISCLOSURE AND UNDERSTANDING

In general, the staff members were quite forthcoming. They attempted to inform the patients of what was going on and to elicit the patients' cooperation with the treatment plans. This is not to say that the staff disclosed everything that the doctrine of informed consent envisions; however, with few significant exceptions, they seemed eager to tell the patients whenever they thought the patients could understand. However, unlike the settings in which the information disclosure was primarily presented on a consent form, information seemed to be disclosed "whenever it came up in the conversation." There was no systematic effort to disclose information.

Moreover, the disclosure was often quite vague. This was evident in the way in which the purpose of treatment was disclosed. Staff members often simply talked about providing "help." However, it was our impression that this vagueness was not so much an effort to obscure as it was a reference to a shared understanding with patients. Our interviews seemed to confirm this. The patients seemed, in general, to share the staff's view that they had a condition that needed treatment. Some of the patients were vague about this or used expressions to describe their troubles that are now considered archaic (e.g., "There's something wrong with my nerves"). However, there seemed to be a general agreement between staff and patients about what the problems were. Few patients attributed their difficulties to something other than personal problems of their own.

It is essential to understand that the information presented to the patients was not presented in order to facilitate the patients' decisionmaking. Rather, it was presented to facilitate patients' cooperation with treatment. For example, the side effects of the medications were presented to help the patients tell their clinicians what side effects they had been experiencing. For this reason, the risks of medications were often presented fairly clearly. However, they were usually presented in the form of questions about whether the patients had experienced such side effects, rather than declarative statements that the patients might experience them. This same concreteness about the risks of treatment was present when we asked the patients what the risks were. Typically, they tended to list those risks that were actually experienced, rather than the ones that might possibly be experienced.

As far as the nature of treatment went, patients were repeatedly told, and generally understood, what drugs they were taking. They knew who was treating them and that the core of treatment would be the taking of medications. They were generally not told, as far as we were able to determine, how long they could expect to be in treatment. Since the Outpatient Clinic assumed that schizophrenia was a lifelong disease and that it could be managed only with maintenance doses of antipsychotic drugs, it seemed reasonable to expect that the patients would be treated for the rest of their lives. However, even though they were not told this, most patients seemed to share this perception of the duration of their treatment.

Both patients and staff assumed that treatment in the Outpatient Clinic centered around medication. In all the treatment discussions we saw, the staff never proposed an alternative to medication, and most patients seemed to believe that there was none. The staff did, however, present a number of additional possible treatments. These included group therapy, individual therapy, and recreational and other social contacts. The patients seemed also to treat these as additional rather than alternative forms of treatment, and were generally quite resistant to them.

There was only one area in which the staff systematically did not give information. This concerned the possibility of developing tardive dyskinesia as a result of taking the antipsychotic drugs. While in a few instances the staff was aware that these risks might already have materialized for patients, there was no systematic disclosure about tardive dyskinesia even to those patients for whom tardive dyskinesia was already an issue in their treatment, to say nothing of patients for whom it was only a future possibility. None of the patients seemed to understand the problem of tardive dyskinesia.

Two final comments must be made about patients' understanding. In spite of what we said about the general pattern of patients' understanding, between 10 and 20% of the patients had almost no understanding of their treatment. These patients had such serious cognitive disorders (disorders of thought) that even repeated discussions about such issues as the drugs they were taking and their side effects had little impact. Second, it is important to note that in some patients whom we saw more than once, understanding seemed to fluctuate between visits. In several cases, these fluctuations were quite dramatic.

PATTERNS OF DECISIONMAKING

The overwhelming pattern of decisionmaking was that the staff made the decisions, with very little input from the patients as to what the decisions should be. In 11 instances in which there was a clear change in either the patients' or the staff's opinion because of what the other person said, nine involved the staff's changing the patients' minds, and only two went the other way.

Perhaps more important, patients seemed to abdicate or waive their right to make the decisions. Implicitly or explicitly, they told their clinicians to decide. There were a number of reasons for this. First, the patients seemed to view medications as essential to their well-being. This is not to say that they felt they were doing extremely well on medication, but rather that they would do worse without it. Second, they assumed that the staff knew much more than they did about how to make medication decisions. In a more general way, patients saw themselves as weak, passive, and incapable of effective action owing to their condition, while they saw the staff members as competent professionals. Within what they saw as the professional expertise of the staff—namely, prescribing medications—they followed the staff's suggestions. However, when they had to deal with decisions concerning other matters than medications (mainly referrals to other types of treatment), they often ignored and resisted the staff's suggestions.

We saw very few proxy decisions. Indeed, individuals accompanying patients played almost no role in the decisions. Although there were a substantial number of cases in which other people accompanied the patients to the Outpatient Clinic, only in five cases did they participate in interviews. Several times the clinicians prevented third parties from participating for one reason or another.

In the five instances in which others were involved in interviews or decisionmaking processes, they usually seemed to be trying to help. In several cases, the third parties acted as advocates or translators for the patients. In another case, the third party was taught how to administer the medication. Only in one case did a third party seem to be acting against a patient's perceived self-interest. In this case, the counselors from a halfway house brought the patient to see the clinician in order to consider whether she needed to be admitted to the Hospital.

A more common pattern than proxy decisionmaking was what we called "solicited decisionmaking." In these cases, the staff members requested the patients' opinion before decisions were made. This pattern was relatively rare in decisions about medications and usually seemed to be an opening for the clinicians to suggest changes in medication. In nonmedication decisions, where the patients' cooperation was somewhat more tenuous, this pattern was more frequent. Thus when suggesting various types of psychotherapy or participation in group activities, the clinicians usually began by asking the patients' opinion about a particular procedure. We also noticed that this occurred more often when the patients had been in treatment for a relatively long period of time and the clinicians and patients seemed to have developed good rapport.

The other situation in which the patients played a significant role in making decisions was when the decisions were made outside the Outpatient Clinic. There were two ways in which medication decisions were made outside the clinic. First, the clinicians sometimes suggested that the patients adjust their dosages of medication, depending on the effectiveness or the side effects of medication. Even in the absence of the clinicians' suggestions, patients sometimes increased or decreased their dosages, either because of side effects or for reasons that the clinicians did not consider legitimate. Some of these decisions would conventionally be called "failures in compliance."

Notwithstanding our earlier description of the Outpatient Clinic as a place in which patients were relatively free to make decisions, the staff members were not without power to affect the patients' decisions. They had numerous sources of power that came from their position as clinicians. First, they had legitimate power to intervene with other agencies for the patients' benefit. These agencies included other sections of the Hospital, which could provide patients with medical care and other types of psychiatric care; welfare agencies; criminal justice agencies; and so on. A second source of power was their ability to withdraw treatment. Because patients saw treatment generally as beneficial to them, the clinicians' ability to withdraw treatment made patients feel that they had to cooperate on specific details of the treatment.

The staff also had other ways of influencing the patients. One of these was to emphasize the negative consequences of the patients' failure to receive treatment or, similarly, to emphasize that the patients were indeed ill and needed treatment. Another, although more subtle, type of influence that the staff members had over the patients came simply from their being human beings who were willing to listen to and associate with the patients. Like many chronic mental patients, many of the Outpatient Clinic patients were socially isolated. The ability simply to talk to somebody who would listen to them was often cited as a major benefit of coming to the Outpatient Clinic. Thus the clinic provided some surcease from the pain of loneliness.

CONCLUSION

Although Outpatient Clinic patients were better informed in general than were those in the Evaluation Center, and even though they were not subject to the same types of pressures that both Evaluation Center and Research Ward patients were, the staff usually ended up making the decisions. This seems to have evolved in part from the patients' belief that they could not or should not make the decisions, and in part from the belief that the staff made the decisions in their best interests. Disclosure, although not systematic, was probably as good as it was on the Research Ward and better than in the Evaluation Center. The failure to disclose anything about tardive dyskinesia was the major exception to that otherwise fairly full disclosure.

Conclusion

17

Summing Up

The methods by which we chose to study informed consent in a psychiatric hospital do not, as ought to be apparent by now, yield findings that lend themselves to a concise summary. Yet for the same reason that a concise presentation of the findings is difficult, it is also necessary, and thus we attempt in this chapter to do just that. This is done largely as a basis for putting forth our thoughts about the implications of these findings for the practice of psychiatry and for lawmaking.

Our primary goal was descriptive: to determine what psychiatric hospital personnel tell patients about the hospital—about admissions and discharge procedures, about confidentiality, and about diagnostic, therapeutic, and research procedures; to establish what patients understand and are capable of understanding; to describe the process of decisionmaking; and to define the pressures that are exerted on patients in the decisionmaking process. However, contained within these questions was an assumption that we made—namely, that something approximating "informed consent" would be found in the routine of a psychiatric hospital.

Informed consent in the pristine form envisioned by law and by ethicists[1] was only rarely, if ever, to be found in the Hospital. As with all of our findings, we hesitate to generalize to other settings; but our review of other studies, other work in which we are currently involved,[2] and the shared experiences of other clinicians and investigators both in psychiatry and in other branches of medicine confirm our intuitions that our findings are substantially close to the norm that prevails in many other institutions as well.

The fact that we did not find informed consent in its pristine form does not mean that we did not find, from time to time, some of its constituent parts. Nor does it mean that there are not other patterns of decisionmaking in a psychiatric hospital that conform to a greater or lesser extent to the patterns envisioned by law and embodied in the informed consent doctrine. We thus turn to a brief review of the highlights of what we did discover about the decisionmaking process and the role of the patients and staff in it.

SUMMARY OF FINDINGS

DISCLOSURE

One of the most striking findings is the difference in the patterns of communication between staff and patients in the different settings. While communication in the Outpatient Clinic involved the one-to-one personal communication between staff and patient that the informed consent doctrine is based upon, communication on the Research Ward, by contrast, was largely collective. Patients were told things as a group more than they were told things individually. The Evaluation Center differed in basic ways from either of the other two settings, in that the patients were typically under a great deal of pressure (either from their friends and families or from their own psychic pain) to get into treatment, and staff disclosure was very limited and sometimes deceptive. Despite these differences, there are certain important common findings.

1. Regardless of the setting, patients were typically given information after, rather than before, decisions were made. This reflects the fundamental finding that whatever information was provided was given not in order to facilitate patients' making autonomous *decisions*, but rather to aid patients in carrying out their part of the *treatment* plan.

2. Except in the Outpatient Clinic, information was given to patients by a variety of people, rather than by "the doctor," as envisioned by the informed consent doctrine. This typically meant that in some cases relevant information was not disclosed, and that in other cases, information presented by one person contradicted that given by another. It was unclear to both staff and patients who was responsible for telling a patient what was going on. We label this phenomenon "floating responsibility."

3. Overall, disclosure was brief and incomplete. The disclosure of alternatives was particularly poor, reflecting, we think, the manner in which doctors are trained to and do practice medicine. Doctors view their goal as being the maximization of patients' health by the provision of the technically best medical care. The doctor's skill is to be able to choose the best treatment for a patient's condition. Only rarely do doctors believe that there are two "alternative," equally good treatments available for a particular condition. Rather there are more desirable treatments and less desirable treatments, and it makes little sense to inform the patient of the alternative treatments, since the patient lacks the skill and experience necessary to make the right choice.

4. In every setting, the staff was least likely to provide information to patients whom they considered of limited intelligence and/or less psychologically healthy, thus making their own informal judgments of competency and restricting disclosure accordingly.

5. We saw no evidence that disclosure produced any harm. Occasionally something that a doctor or a nurse told a patient caused the patient some anxiety, but we never saw patients making decisions that markedly interfered with their treatment or their well-being on the basis of something the staff told them. However, it is possible that this was true only because there was so little disclosure of risks or alternatives by the staff.

UNDERSTANDING

1. Patients' understanding was also typically incomplete and occasionally badly misdirected. Perhaps more important, it seemed often to be idiosyncratic and experientially based. That is to say, disclosure by the staff, even when fairly substantial, seemed to play a relatively small part in the patients' understanding of their problems. For example, on the Research Ward, patients tended to cite their own and other patients' experiences much more frequently than they cited information they had received from the staff in justifying their decisions.

2. Patients' understanding was not only often idiosyncratic; it was also technically limited. Moreover, this limited understanding was often due to factors unrelated to the patients' psychiatric disorders. Specifically, patients often lacked the necessary background understanding of mental illness to be able to formulate problems in a way that properly incorporated the staff's disclosures. Because they lacked the requisite background knowledge, their understanding of what the staff told them often bore no relationship to what the staff intended to convey.

3. What understanding patients did develop occurred over time. Like the process of obtaining information, the process of understanding is not instantaneous. Thus, when patients made decisions or when decisions were made for them, they came to understand the basis for the decision and its implications, if at all, only after the lapse of days, weeks, or even months. This had less serious consequences in settings where treatment decisions took place over a period of time, rather than in the Evaluation Center, where decisions were made rapidly and their consequences could not easily be undone.

4. Patients who participated in psychiatric research protocols were not able to distinguish clearly between the therapeutic and nontherapeutic goals of the research. They therefore could not appreciate the costs of participation in the research. Despite the small size of the sample of patients who participated in research, we are satisfied that these findings are valid, in part because they are consistent with the findings of others[3] and in part because further studies that we have performed on psychiatric patients as research subjects support this finding.[4]

DECISIONS

Our observations about the patterns of decisionmaking were quite striking. Although the patterns differed quite markedly from one setting to another, certain elements were common.

1. Most patients believed that the decisions about what treatments they were to receive were up to their doctors. This was true in all three settings, but particularly in the Outpatient Clinic. Patients felt that the doctors were very competent and had highly esoteric knowledge about how to treat their disorders. On the other hand, patients saw themselves as weak and largely incapable of understanding the issues involved. There were some exceptions to this pattern, but very few patients felt that they could be the primary decision-makers.

2. Almost equally important, the staff seemed deeply committed to the outcome of the decisions and to making sure that patients received the best treatment they could provide. They did not act like a grocer who is indifferent to whether one buys apples or pears, as long as one buys something. They felt, often very strongly, that there was a "right" decision, and they tended to present the information in a manner designed to convince patients of that viewpoint.

3. One of the general analytical categories with which we began the study was the concept of "voluntariness." However, we found that this was an extremely difficult matter to study. We have been unable to develop any clear-cut way of determining whether or not a decision was voluntary. About all we were able to say is that there were only a few cases of overt coercion. However, particularly in the Evaluation Center, patients often made decisions under intense pressure from their families as well as from their own psychic pain. As a result, decisions were often made without the sense of deliberateness one might have hoped for.

4. Consent forms played an insignificant role in the decisionmaking process.

a. Consent forms were generally presented to patients only *after* the decision was made and agreed upon by all parties.

b. The forms were typically too complex for the average patient.

c. Particularly during the admission process, patients often did not read consent forms before signing them; even when they did, they rarely seemed to have much understanding of the material contained in them.

d. Decisions were made in a real sense without regard to consent forms. The information in consent forms never changed a decision that had already been made.

e. Staff viewed consent forms as bureaucratic obstacles to be surmounted before treatment could commence, and thus as something that did not require attention either from them or from patients.

f. Consent forms were treated by both patients and staff as a ritual for confirming a decision already made, rather than as a step in the decision-making process. In effect, consent forms merely symbolized that the patients had agreed to the particular procedure, thus providing some evidence (though of dubious legal value) of consent. If consent forms were meant to ensure that patients understood and consented voluntarily to the decisions, then these consent forms at least were failures.

THE EVALUATION CENTER

1. The Evaluation Center was the locus of most of the legal and administrative requirements (and certainly the clearest ones) for the staff to obtain informed consent from patients. Nonetheless, it was the farthest from the ideal of informed consent of any of the three settings we observed. Staff members usually felt that the patients' commitment to getting the required treatment was marginal, and thus an important part of the staff's role was to persuade patients to accept treatment and not to raise "unnecessary" fears.

2. The predominant pattern of decisionmaking involved patients' presenting a problem and the staff's agreeing to help. However, although the staff and the patients both agreed that the patients had problems that needed to be dealt with, they often did not conceptualize the problems, and hence the "solutions," in the same way. Patients often saw the benefits of hospitalization or treatment in nonmedical terms, such as providing a rest or a way of getting somebody off a patient's back.

3. The pattern of decisionmaking varied from case to case. Sometimes the patients sat passively by and allowed the staff to make the decisions alone. In other cases, families got intensely involved in negotiations; and in still others, the patients were actively, if not necessarily effectively, involved in the decisionmaking process.

a. By and large, the staff made decisions with passive acquiescence from patients, or, in some cases, over patients' objections.

b. In several instances, family or friends were significant participants in the decisionmaking process, sometimes strongly pressuring the staff about what the treatment should do.

THE RESEARCH WARD

1. There was a diversity of sources of information that patients relied on.

a. When discussing their decisions and feelings about their treatment, patients continually cited their own experiences and the experiences of other patients, rather than the disclosure of staff, as reasons for their opinions.

b. The continual discussions among these patients seemed to be the major source of information and basis for forming opinions about treatment on the ward.

2. Disclosure was continual and essentially conversational. Patients were informed about treatment whenever the topic arose. No systematic effort was made to inform patients before deciding to begin a new treatment.

3. The pattern of disclosure was largely collective. The major location of disclosure was the daily Walking Rounds, when the entire patient group was assembled in a circle, and the doctor and head nurse went around discussing with each patient his or her problems and treatment. This provided information not only to the patient being directly addressed, but also to the rest of the patient community as well. Thus patients often knew a great deal more than they had personally been told about their treatment.

4. Decisionmaking patterns differed not so much according to the particular patient who was involved, but according to the type of decision that was being made. Decisions about medications, medication levels, and tests to be performed were made almost exclusively by the doctors on the Research Ward. Patients were often told about changes in medications *after* they had been begun. On the other hand, decisions about privileges within the Hospital and passes to leave the Hospital were made collectively by the Advisory Board of elected patients and by the staff. Still other decisions (about ECT and post-discharge planning) were made through a process that looked somewhat more like the mutual decisionmaking that the informed consent doctrine envisions.

5. Discussions among patients were also the major source of pressure on the patients to go along with the staff-recommended treatment. With very few exceptions, patients encouraged one another to cooperate with the treatment. Patients who refused to cooperate were told repeatedly by other patients that it was in their best interests to go along with whatever the staff was proposing.

THE OUTPATIENT CLINIC

1. As was the case on the Research Ward, disclosure was continual and took place in a conversational manner. That is, no systematic efforts were made to inform patients; rather, patients learned about treatment whenever the topic arose.

2. Unlike the situation on the Research Ward, the topic of treatment often "arose" when a patient experienced side effects of a medication that he or she was taking. This then became the occasion for discussion of that and other side effects of the drug.

3. Two things were systematically not disclosed to patients in the Outpatient Clinic. The first was the expected length of treatment. Except when a patient explicitly asked, the staff member did not disclose their belief that the patients were chronically ill and would need lifelong maintenance on antipsychotic drugs. The second and more serious disclosure failure was the staff's resistance to saying anything about tardive dyskinesia. This serious and potentially irreversible side effect of antipsychotic drugs was not discussed with patients during the period we observed, and patients had little or no knowledge of the possibility that their drugs could produce tardive dyskinesia. Furthermore, in the few instances we observed in which patients possibly already had tardive dyskinesia, the patients were not told about it.

4. Patients seemed to feel that treatment decisions about medications were up to their doctors to make. This seemed to be tied, at least in this clinic, to their deep and profound feeling of being incapable of making the decisions. The fact that most of these patients had been in treatment for serious psychiatric disorders for many years seemed to have undercut their sense of self-worth and

autonomy. Providing them with the opportunity to participate in their treatment decisionmaking, something that some clinicians did fairly actively, did not alleviate patients' doubts about their ability to make decisions.

5. As was the case in the Evaluation Center, patterns of decisionmaking varied from case to case. Decisions about medications and medication levels were made almost exclusively by the staff. Occasionally staff members solicited the patients' opinions, and they always considered patients' reports of side effects and symptoms before making decisions. However, decisions about non-medication-related issues were made by patients after their clinicians had made suggestions. Both decisionmaking patterns reflect the patients' and the staff's assumptions about the legitimate authority of the staff. For example, patients believed that only the staff had the specialized knowledge necessary to make decisions about medications. However, they strongly resisted suggestions about how they should conduct their lives outside the Outpatient Clinic, viewing these issues as not within the expertise of the clinicians.

CONCLUSIONS AND IMPLICATIONS

For those who have harbored great hopes for the doctrine of informed consent as a vehicle for social reform within the mental health care system, the findings of this study will come as a disappointment. We saw no evidence that informed consent law, as currently implemented, had substantial positive effects. It is difficult to point to an instance during our observations when legal requirements to make disclosure and obtain patients' consent made a substantial, positive contribution to patients' participation in treatment decisionmaking. We found no evidence that the existence of the law of informed consent promoted better staff-patient communication, improved patients' cooperation with treatment, led to better patient understanding or greater patient autonomy, or achieved any of the other goals envisioned by the doctrine.

Although supporters of the informed consent requirement will find little in our findings about which to be hopeful, detractors should not take much comfort from them either. We did not see large numbers of patient refusals, substantial patient anxiety about the risks of treatment, or improper treatment because physicians were unable to obtain consent to proper treatment. The absence of substantial consequences, either positive or negative, may be in part due to the minimal levels of staff compliance with the legal doctrine. Even in those cases where there was compliance (whether substantial or *pro forma*), obtaining informed consent did not impose much of a direct burden on the staff, nor did we see any compromise of patients' welfare. It is true that some time was spent in making explanations to patients, in attempting to clear up confusion that the explanations engendered, and in signing forms; however, the commitment of resources to these activities was not very great and probably had no effect on the quality of care delivered. Perhaps the most serious cost was a certain amount of cynicism engendered among the staff members who were required by law to perform a rite that, in their professional judgments, contributed little toward the achievement of their professional goals.

In large part, the findings of this study do little either to credit or to discredit the legal and ethical requirement to obtain informed consent. Although we attempted to perform a study of how informed consent is obtained in a variety of psychiatric treatment settings, this goal was impeded by the fact that the entire constellation of behavior that ought to constitute informed consent was rarely observed. Doctors talked to patients, as did other staff members; patients agreed to treatments; patients even signed consent forms. But, by and large, decisions about treatment were not made as one would have supposed they would have been had the informed consent doctrine shaped the decisionmaking process.[5] To say that informed consent is feasible or not, to determine whether it benefits patients or inconveniences staff, or to verify any one of a multitude of other claims made about the doctrine requires of necessity that doctors and patients first engage in behavior that bears some close resemblance to that behavior as envisioned by the doctrine. Since we did not see such behavior, our data cannot be said to support or refute any such claims.

Thus, our primary finding about informed consent is that it did not often exist in the settings in which we looked for it. This general finding gives rise to two rather fundamental questions: Why was this the case? And how likely is it that this finding is widespread?

We believe that informed consent in the clinic is unlike informed consent as the courts envision it—in fact, the difference is so great that "informed consent" is a largely inappropriate term for medical decisionmaking in the settings we studied—in part because of the manner in which mental health workers are trained and socialized into their profession; in part because of the manner in which psychiatric care is provided in an institutional setting; and in part because patients seem little interested in exercising their right to informed consent.

Earlier, in connection with the presentation of the findings about the disclosure of alternatives to patients, we mentioned that doctors do not view their role as one of providing patients with information about alternative forms of treatment and then letting patients choose among them. We suggested that the reason for this reluctance is that physicians are taught to search for the best treatment for a given problem and to recommend that treatment to patients exhibiting that problem—indeed, to attempt to convince the patients to accept the treatment if the patients exhibit any resistance to the recommendation. And, for a physician, the "best" treatment is almost always defined in technical medical terms—that treatment most likely to alleviate a patient's illness—rather than in terms of a patient's personal preferences, which might incorporate such things as the patient's aversion to or preference for risk, the way in which particular illnesses or treatments affect the patient's life style, the patient's willingness to trade off short-run pain for long-run well-being, and other considerations that are highly particular to individual patients. The entire structure of medicine, including medical training, encourages physicians to search for the technically most efficacious treatment. Indeed, the physician who obtains informed consent in conformity with the legal vision is the deviant. Thus, the values of the healing professions are substantially at odds with the values that underlie the informed consent doctrine.

The social context and structure within which psychiatric care is usually provided today, including the settings that we studied, interfere further with the implementation of informed consent. The practice of institutional psychiatry—whether in an admission and referral center, an inpatient unit, or an outpatient clinic such as the ones investigated, or in any one of a number of other institutional settings—is far different from the practice of medicine as envisioned by the informed consent doctrine. The historical model of the doctor-patient relationship upon which the doctrine is grounded is that of a single physician in private practice administering a discrete hospital-based treatment, which is usually (but not always) a surgical procedure. Certainly the common-law rules for obtaining informed consent are premised on this model of the doctor-patient relationship, as are some of the more recent legislative enactments and administrative regulations, including the ones in force at the Hospital during the time of our study. These rules are unrealistic for a variety of reasons, not the least of which is that they fail to take into account the fact that medical research and practice often bear little resemblance to the model on which the informed consent doctrine is based.

In a contemporary institutional setting, there are a large number of persons responsible for providing a portion of the patient's care. No single person is solely responsible, as the informed consent doctrine assumes. As a matter of law, the hospital director, or even a single physician, is "legally" responsible for the patient's care; however, in a day-to-day sense, care is provided by a team of people, often under only the nominal supervision of a physician. For instance, when a person is hospitalized as an inpatient, there are three shifts of people; even in an outpatient clinic, there is no assurance that the patient will have an appointment with the same clinician on each visit (though patients at the Hospital usually did). It is therefore easy to understand why each staff member, even if sincerely interested in keeping patients well informed, might reasonably assume that someone else has done the informing. Thus, the provision of information to patients closely parallels the provision of care itself: They are both fragmented, along no clear lines of responsibility.

The pressure imposed by lack of time and other scarce resources is another feature of the contemporary mental health care system of which the informed consent doctrine takes no account. We are not prepared to say that patients are poorly informed and uninvolved in the decisionmaking process because "obtaining informed consent" as envisioned by law takes too much time or because the cost of a doctor's time is substantial (we observed no clear evidence of this); rather, patients are uninvolved because there is a strong pressure permeating the practice of institutional psychiatry today to achieve results in a far shorter period of time than historically has been the case, especially when care is being provided on an inpatient basis. This concern is generated in large part by the policies of third-party payers for care (insurance companies and government agencies), which restrict payment of inpatient hospitalization and create an atmosphere in which all staff members are aware of the need to treat and discharge rapidly. In such an atmosphere, informed consent must seem a luxury, even assuming that staff members are otherwise motivated to involve patients in the decisionmaking process.

Ironically, another barrier to the informed consent doctrine is inherent in the mechanisms chosen to implement that doctrine. We are referring, of course, to the state regulations governing informed consent to admission to inpatient status. Yet it was in the setting most governed by these regulations—the Evaluation Center—that informed consent worked least well, not only in relation to the clarity of the legal requirement but also in an absolute sense. In the Evaluation Center, there were less disclosure (or disclosure more perfunctorily performed), less comprehension by patients, more reliance on form than on substance, and more pressures placed on patients to make the "right" decisions than there were in the other two settings studied.

We believe that the overwhelming failure of the regulations to produce anything more than ritualized compliance is explicable in part by a clash of bureaucratic goals. The informed consent regulations were promulgated by one bureaucracy with one set of goals and values, and were intended to be implemented by another with different goals and values. The first (the state department of welfare) had as its goal compliance with statutory and judicial mandates.

The other bureaucracy, the one charged with implementation of the regulations, was composed of admission staffs like those in the Evaluation Center. The primary goal of this bureaucracy was to make sure that patients were properly evaluated and referred to an outpatient clinic, an inpatient service, or some other social service or health care agency, or merely sent home. The problem for the Evaluation Center bureaucracy was that the flow of patients, while irregular, was also inexorable. Patients had to be dealt with expeditiously, not only because they might be in serious need of attention, but also because whether they were or not, there would soon be yet another patient to be dealt with.

The informed consent regulations were not only not designed to achieve the primary goal of the Evaluation Center; they probably impeded the expeditious processing of patients, or at least they were perceived that way by the center's staff. Forms had to be signed that previously did not have to be signed; patients had to be given information that previously did not have to be revealed. All of this took time and was therefore resented by the staff, because it did take time, because it was in the nature of a fiat, and because it did not concur with the values of the staff.

Thus, one of the clear lessons of this study is that even the promulgation of clear and precise regulations for obtaining informed consent does not neces-sarily result in greater compliance. The complaint that many doctors have about the law of informed consent is that it does not really tell them what they are supposed to tell patients. Yet, when precise and detailed regulations were issued as to what patients were to be told, they were resented—and perhaps rightly so—as a bureaucratic intrusion upon a professional province. In the final analysis, it is not clear that the net result is any better than it would have been had the regulations and consent forms not been issued, and indeed it may well be worse.

However, even if all of the above problems were somehow resolved, implementation of the informed consent doctrine would still have to face the problem of patients' indifference. While patients often felt that they were not sick and did not need treatment, once in treatment they rarely seemed interested in playing any role in deciding what their treatment should be. They, too, seemed to have been trained to act as though decisionmaking were the province of the doctors and not their own.

Is it likely that what we found prevails in other settings too? First, we wish to state emphatically that we do not believe that any implications can be drawn from our study for the private, office-based practice of psychotherapy. There are so many different structural features that we are loath even to speculate about the operation of informed consent there. Second, we must remember that our study was conducted in a single psychiatric hospital during a particular time period. The Hospital was a university hospital. It was not typical either of exclusive private hospitals, since it largely served a catchment-area population, or of state hospitals, since it had many more resources and treated patients for much shorter periods. The time in which our study was conducted was also out of the ordinary, coming as it did in the wake of substantial legislative and regulatory changes in the jurisdiction's basic mental health law. To generalize our findings to other psychiatric hospitals in other places at other times is thus a somewhat risky undertaking. Yet neither the empirical literature nor informal discussions with colleagues give us reason to believe that our findings are atypical of institutional practice in general.

Certainly, as far as the institutional practice of psychiatry is concerned, we are less reticent about the generalizability of our findings. In institutions such as the Hospital, where patients are treated exclusively by hospital-employed doctors (rather than by their own private physicians with staff privileges) in combination with an array of nurses, social workers, therapeutic aides, and physicians' assistants, both the socialization process of the physicians (and other staff members) and the structure of the delivery of care should also militate against the operation of medical decisionmaking in the manner en-visioned by the informed consent doctrine. However, in addition to limiting our findings to the *institutional* practice of psychiatry, we also advocate caution in drawing implications from this study for the operation of informed consent outside of psychiatry. To make extrapolations from this setting to general hospitals is a risky enterprise, since the patients we studied often had obvious psychological deficits and, in any case, were usually perceived by the staff as having such deficits. Whatever mental illness is, the belief that patients are mentally ill affects both the staff's and the patients' perceptions of patients' abilities to participate in decisionmaking, regardless of the legal presumption of competency.

Informed consent has not "restructured" the doctor-patient relationship, as some have hoped and others have feared. In fact, if anything, the doctor-patient relationship—or, more precisely, the existing structure of mental health care delivery—has restructured informed consent.

Informed consent has been "restructured" in a number of ways. When information about contemplated treatment is provided to patients, it ordinarily follows, rather than precedes, decisionmaking. Decisionmaking is not typically a mutual process, but one undertaken predominantly by health professionals, with information given to patients after decisions are made in order to obtain compliance with treatment regimens. Whether even the existence of this pattern has anything to do with the legal requirement for informed consent is difficult to say.

Both doctors and patients have accommodated themselves very nicely to informed consent by largely ignoring it. True, there is a certain awareness of the requirement among mental health professionals, and in the one setting where state law rather clearly and precisely required that informed consent be obtained, consent forms were signed and explanations made without undue difficulty. But medical decisionmaking is not a joint venture between well-informed, autonomous patients and physicians bent on educating patients to make intelligent choices. This is not to say that the level of patient participation in decisionmaking has suffered on account of the legal requirement, only that it has not changed much at all.

To be sure, we have not (and we do not believe that others have) conducted a "before-and-after study," so we cannot be certain what effect legal requirements for obtaining informed consent have had, if any.[6] Yet we can be sure that informed consent has not produced the results contemplated by its most ardent advocates.

RECOMMENDATIONS

It is not unduly harsh to conclude that current informed consent policy has been a dismal failure in the settings we studied, at least when measured against the loftier goals of the doctrine. We simply did not witness a consistent pattern of behavior by staff members that was directed toward providing patients with adequate information on the basis of which they might make intelligent decisions; nor did we witness much enthusiasm by patients for making decisions when they were given the opportunity to do so.

In light of these fundamental findings, what should be done with the legal requirement to obtain informed consent?

In theory, there are three general approaches that can be taken. First, in recognition of the finding that there is minimal compliance with the requirements of informed consent, those requirements could be abandoned altogether, especially the requirement that disclosure be made to patients.[7] In effect, doctors would be legally obligated merely to obtain patients' "consent" to treatment. This approach attempts to conform law to behavior, acknowledging the disrespect for law in general generated by any law that is not enforced, that people know is not enforced, and that may not be enforceable.

Another approach would be to attempt to conform behavior to law, on the assumption that if the end is a desirable one, then reasonable efforts should be undertaken to achieve that end. Specifically, this would require that stronger measures be taken to assure that doctors make disclosures to patients and try to involve patients in the decisionmaking process. At some point, efforts to produce informed consent either might not be worth the cost or might become so inherently disagreeable that they should be abandoned.

The third and final approach would seek to change neither the law nor behavior, though it would welcome positive changes in behavior should these result. This approach recognizes that a law, the full extent of which may never be fully complied with, serves as an ethical beacon; it establishes an ideal toward which those it affects may strive. The ideal itself may strengthen and grow in the process, even though attainment is still difficult to achieve, and thus a gap is always maintained between the actual and the ideal. Further, the existence of such a law may prevent actual practice from deteriorating at any given time. That is, without an unattainable ideal, practice might be far worse than it presently is. Finally, the existence of idealistic law is a source of flexibility in the regulation of human behavior, for it permits the reconciliation of conflicting values in a fluid, rather than a rigid, balance to be applied somewhat more in favor of one value in one instance and more in favor of another value in another.

Before recommending that the doctrine of informed consent be retained, abolished, or modified, it is first necessary to examine the ethical justifications for the requirement. There are two primary traditions in current ethical thought: the deontological and the consequentialist. The deontological tradition derives from the work of Immanuel Kant, whose categorical imperative was intended to be a nonreligious, absolute grounding for moral judgment. The importance of Kant's position for present purposes is that the moral quality of an act is said to be independent of the outcome or consequences of the act. "Right" and "wrong" are categorical judgments of types of acts, not situationally specific judgments of results. In contrast, the consequentialists, whose views were best expounded by Jeremy Bentham and John Stuart Mill, held that the key to the morality of an act is to be found in its consequences. Whether or not it is right to lie, for instance, cannot be settled categorically, but must be determined by reference to whether or not the consequences of the lie are mostly positive or negative. If the benefits exceed the costs, then a particular lie—indeed, any given action—is morally justified.

The doctrine of informed consent has been justified on the basis of both of these ethical theories. Most deontological analyses of informed consent start from the value of autonomy. Since the autonomy of the individual is a highly regarded value and one to be fully implemented, at least in all spheres where it does not enter into substantial conflict with other significant values, the requirement of informed consent is justifiable to the extent that it is reasonably calculated to promote the autonomy of individuals. A further deontological justification for informed consent arises from the fact that it also promotes another important and widely held value, rationality. Informed consent provides patients with information that enables them to make rational decisions.

The findings of social science contribute little if anything of value to the analysis of a deontological justification for or against a particular policy, since it is not the consequences of the policy (which an empirical investigation ascertains), but the values sought to be promoted by that policy that are the policy's ultimate justification. The most that social science can say is that the value on which an ethical principle is based is either widely held or not widely held within a society. However, when investigators seek to justify a policy from a consequentialist ethical position, empirical studies may be relevant. Since the ultimate justification for the policy is to be found in the benefits that it confers and the costs that it imposes, an effort that ascertains these benefits and costs is essential to an adequate consequentialist analysis. For informed consent to be justified on consequentialist principles, we must be able to say that the doctrine produces more good than harm.

At one level, on the basis of our findings, we find it difficult to conclude anything about the good and evil that informed consent produces, simply because we rarely saw anything like it. The behavior we did see that most closely resembled informed consent produced no harm to patients in terms of their medical well-being, and what can only be characterized as mild inconvenience to staff members. Nor did we see much in the way of benefit.[8]

The doctrine of informed consent cannot be justified on consequentialist grounds on the basis of our findings, at least in part because it did not produce very much behavior resembling informed consent. This leads us to the next question: Is a policy leading to informed consent behavior possible? And, if so, is it justifiable?

If it turns out that the benefits of informed consent behavior, whatever they may be, do not exceed the costs of getting doctors to make disclosure and of getting patients interested and involved in the decisionmaking process, then it is unnecessary to ask the question: Do the costs of informed consent behavior exceed its benefits? That is, first we must focus on the costs (and benefits, if any) of putting informed consent into practice before we can address the costs and benefits of informed consent itself.

Here we face a substantial difficulty. The informed consent doctrine, while relatively new, has had a long infancy. When our study began, the first informed consent case[9] was only a year short of its 20th birthday; the landmark cases of the early 1970s[10] were well known to first-year law students and taught to many medical students as well; and the requirement to obtain simple consent to treatment was decades if not centuries old. Further, a great deal of discussion had been taking place in the psychiatric literature for several years preceding our study about the right to refuse psychiatric treatment. Yet, despite a climate in which only the most obtuse could have reasonably claimed ignorance of the general legal obligation to obtain informed consent, most staff members did not take this obligation seriously.

Perhaps more could and should be done to make health care personnel aware of the ethical obligations and legal requirements to obtain informed consent and to encourage patients to believe that they can and should participate in decisionmaking. Eternal vigilance is necessary to assure the enforcement of most rights, not just of informed consent. The tendency to assume that the new generations of doctors and patients will be adequately inculcated with the newest of ideas must be resisted, for what seems like old hat to the old may not even be a new hat to the young. And further, the old tend to forget and revert to older patterns of behavior, especially when they are simpler patterns of behavior. Thus, continued reinforcement must be provided to doctors and patients alike to participate in a decisionmaking process that reflects the spirit of informed consent if we wish for that spirit to be realized.

One approach is to promulgate detailed regulations and forms, such as the ones mandated for use in the Evaluation Center when we studied it. However, our observations do not show this method to be very effective. Another approach is to designate some individual to be responsible for monitoring informed consent practices, for conducting training sessions for those responsible for obtaining informed consent, and possibly for imposing administrative sanctions on those who fail to comply.

No doubt there are a variety of ways in which informed consent might be made to work better—perhaps the creation of an informed consent "police force" and the assignment of one "police officer" to each doctor or each patient might be necessary. The particular merits and drawbacks of such solutions are not our present concern. What is of concern here is that such enforcement measures entail costs—costs in time, money, and good will, all of which are scarce resources and, in the consequentialist view, should not be expended without countervailing benefit. Needless to say, as the enforcement costs increase, the corresponding benefits must also increase if the underlying policy is ultimately to be found justifiable.

We are skeptical that a system of enforcement for informed consent would not entail substantial costs in all three of these scarce resources, and we doubt that the beneficial consequences could justify those expenditures. *Yet we believe, on deontological grounds, that informed consent must not be abandoned.* Representing as it does values fundamental to our society, to the community of societies of which we are a part, and to a long religious, ethical, and political tradition, abandonment of informed consent represents a partial abandonment of these fundamental values as well.

To say that informed consent must be preserved *avoids* the question central to consequentialist analysis of how informed consent is to be implemented, but does not *resolve* it. The matter of implementation, while not relevant to deontological justification, is still of concern, if for no other reason than the fact that every aspect of implementation may also be judged as to its ethicality in deontological terms. It is not right, for example, to compel compliance through the use of techniques that are highly invasive of the rights of physicians or patients, such as covert surveillance. Thus, it is still necessary to discuss the matter of implementation of informed consent.

To date, the technique primarily employed to encourage the implementation of informed consent has been the minimalist, though time-honored, one of retrospective, private enforcement through judicial remedies. The basic problem with this means of enforcement is tightly bound up with the twin problems of current informed consent policy. The reason that the doctrine requires doctors to make disclosure is that it is presumed that patients are unaware of important information—both information about their medical condition, and information about their right to participate in the medical decisionmaking process. Unfortunately, patients who have not been informed by their doctors may also be uninformed about their right of participation; and when that right is breached, the patients are unaware of that too. Thus the existing remedy depends upon patients' knowledge of their doctors' obligation to obtain informed consent, and for that reason it is unlikely to be invoked. The other major problem we observed was the general passivity of patients in decision-making, and it is hard to see how giving patients the right to sue doctors will do much about this problem. Even when it is invoked, a lawsuit will be unavailable or unavailing for both practical reasons and legal ones if the patient has suffered no bodily harm as a consequence of the failure to obtain informed consent. It is no wonder, then, that despite all the avowed talk among doctors about their fear of lawsuits, suits for the failure to obtain informed consent seem to have had little effect on the behavior of many doctors.

We do not believe, however, that the failure of the minimalist approach requires a resort to heavy-handed means of enforcement, certainly not in the first instance. There are other minimalist means of promoting informed consent besides lawsuits, and these may be more effective in achieving their goals.

PATIENT EDUCATION

We doubt that there is much sentiment in support of the view that the duty to disclose is a good in itself; instead, there may be support for the idea that the duty exists for instrumental rather than symbolic reasons—namely, to provide patients with a *sine qua non* for participation in the decisionmaking process. If patients can acquire information in ways other than or in addition to classical "disclosure" from their doctors, they will be prepared to participate in the decisionmaking process. One way to improve the flow of information to patients in institutional settings is for the institution to hire an individual to educate patients. This is already being done in some institutions for purposes such as teaching patients how to deal with chronic diseases and preparing patients for the ordinary consequences of surgery.

PRETESTED ADMINISTRATIVE REGULATIONS

Our findings in the Evaluation Center do not give much encouragement for improving informed consent through the promulgation of detailed and precise regulations that specify what information should be disclosed and when. It is possible, however, that the failure of these regulations lies in their particulars, rather than in the regulatory approach per se. Before detailed regulations are used, they should be developed and pretested on site in order to assure that they blend in, rather than conflict with, the existing structure for providing care.

SIMPLIFIED CONSENT FORMS

We have mixed feelings about the use of consent forms in obtaining informed consent. Consent forms are viewed by many doctors as a substitute for talking to patients and by many patients as nothing but paperwork. The abolition of consent forms (and of laws requiring their use where they exist) might do something to encourage doctors and patients to talk to each other. And if they did not, nothing would be lost except possibly a small measure of legal protection for doctors, which is unwarranted where in fact disclosure has not occurred.

Our experience leads us to believe that consent forms that provide minimal information and a place for the patient's signature may be preferable to forms giving details of a procedure, since the former are less likely to be used as a substitute for discussion. If consent forms with substantial written information are to be used, they should be subjected to review by parties other than those who have drafted them, and ought to be tested on "normal" and clinical populations to assure that they are reasonably comprehensible. We believe that a copy of the consent form ought to be given to each patient, and that it is preferable for patients to be given written information (where medically feasible) long in advance of their actually being requested to make a decision, so that they may have some time to study the information and talk about it with friends, family, other patients, and doctors and nurses[11] in an unpressured atmosphere.

PATIENTS' DUTY TO ASK

A more substantial modification of current law is to replace the doctor's "duty to disclose" with a patient's duty to ask questions. This approach has been adopted by statute in Oregon, under which physicians are required only to "explain . . . [i]n general terms the procedure or treatment to be undertaken" and to tell the patient whether there are alternative procedures and/or risks.[12] The doctor is not required to tell the patient what the alternatives or the risks are, but merely to "ask the patient if he [or she] wants a more detailed explanation"[13]; if the patient requests additional information, then and only then is the doctor obligated to provide it. However, without substantial measures to encourage patients to get involved, this seems to be little different from abandoning the attempt to encourage informed consent.

PATIENT GROUPS

One way of encouraging patients' participation that impressed us, both on the Research Ward and in other contexts, is promoting discussions among patients. While this is hardly a substitute for effective implementation of the informed consent doctrine, patients do seem to be able to communicate information quite effectively to other patients.

CONSIDERATION OF THE STRUCTURE OF MEDICAL CARE

Greater attention has to be paid to the structure in which medical care is provided, in order to determine how doctors may best provide information to patients and involve them in decisionmaking. We are convinced that patients are more likely to learn over a longer period of time than they are in a short, compressed period. Thus the techniques for obtaining informed consent, or at least for educating patients, may have to be modified, depending upon such things as whether the patient is acutely or chronically ill and whether the patient is hospitalized or being treated as an outpatient.

CHANGES IN MEDICAL EDUCATION

The future of informed consent lies in part in the hands of the current generation of medical and nursing students, house staff, and young physicians and nurses. Significant efforts are well under way in medical education to inculcate students and young professionals in a "humanistic" approach to dealing with patients. We doubt that these approaches can be anything but beneficial in terms of implementing informed consent, but we believe that there must be a constant effort in all of medical education, clinical and didactic, toward encouraging doctors to talk with patients about their treatment—not simply because the law requires it, but because decency does. Informed consent should be the result of the natural interaction between medical care personnel and patients, rather than of attempts to "obtain informed consent" in a reifying manner.

EXPANDED LEGAL REMEDIES

At this time, almost the only recourse available to a patient who has been treated without informed consent is a lawsuit, which is expensive, time-consuming, and energy-draining, and will ultimately be unavailing if the patient has not been physically harmed by the treatment. Simpler and broader forms of recourse might be considered for patients who have not been given adequate information. One approach is to amend state medical licensure statutes to make the failure to make disclosure and/or obtain consent a basis for professional discipline. Aggrieved patients could then file complaints with medical licensing authorities, and ultimately doctors could be disciplined for this infraction. We are, of course, aware of the difficulties with the existing system of professional discipline in most states, which, if uncorrected, will dilute the force of this recommendation; however, that is a problem beyond the scope of our current concerns.

FINAL REMARKS

Informed consent policy is not currently working in the settings that we studied, and on the basis of other studies we are performing, our conversations with colleagues, and our own knowledge as patients, we believe that it is not working very well in most other medical care settings either.

But informed consent has yet to be really tried. Rather, the courts (and legislatures) have spoken and assumed that all care-providers would follow their mandate unquestioningly. In fact, some have not heard the mandate, and those who have, have been provided with insufficient incentive to take it seriously.

Before either dismantling the requirement on the one hand or resigning ourselves to winking at it on the other, we believe that bona fide and reasonable efforts at implementation ought to be attempted. Finally, we believe that, over time, as new generations of health care professionals and patients are socialized in a climate that takes informed consent more seriously, informed consent may well be taken more seriously in practice. None of the remedies that we have suggested either singly or together are likely to be solutions for the problems that now exist in the implementation of the informed consent doctrine, and the path to achieving the goal of involving patients in a decisionmaking partnership will be, at best, a long, slow, gradual, difficult, and winding one. However, the moral commitments of our society do not permit us to turn back.

APPENDIX

INTERVIEW GUIDELINES: EVALUATION CENTER PATIENTS

What kinds of things do you think they do here? How do you think that might benefit you?

(After psychiatric interview and treatment decision:) Can I now ask you a few questions about what just went on with the doctor and the clinician?

1. What kind of treatment are you going to have? What do you expect to get from it?
2. Did you know anything about this kind of treatment from before? Either you were given it or you know somebody who had it?
3. Do you have any worries about the treatment? (Coming into the Hospital?)
4. Do you feel that you were given enough information about the treatment? (If no:) What else would you like to know? Do you know anything about alternative kinds of treatment?
5. Do you think it's necessary for you to understand the treatment? (If not:) Why not?
6. Do you feel that there was any pressure put on you from the staff or others to accept this treatment? (If yes:) How do you feel about this?
7. Why do you think you were asked if you would consent to this treatment? Do you think you might have refused it?
8. Do you feel that you came to a decision about this treatment, or that it was just presented to you? (If answer is "I came to a decision":) At what point did you decide? What kinds of information led you to the decision?
9. Can you tell me a little bit about what you understand your rights are?
   When can you leave the Hospital?
   What do you have to do in order to leave?
   How long do you think you will stay here?
10. Can I now ask you about the forms you signed? Can you tell me which ones they were?
11. What kinds of information did you agree to have released when you signed the financial form?
12. Can you explain about the release of information to the county?

INTERVIEW GUIDELINES: RESEARCH WARD PATIENTS

When you first came to the Hospital, what did you think were the benefits and the disadvantages? What do you think now after treatment?

Are you glad you came here? Did it help you? How?

Did you get the treatment you wanted? Needed?

Anything here happen that surprised you that you weren't prepared for or didn't expect—in the Evaluation Center or the Ward?

Who helped you most—the staff or the patients? Is there a difference in the kind of help that they did?

Who do you think should decide which treatment a patient gets—the doctor or the patient? In your case, do you think that you or the doctor decided most of your treatment for you?

Do you think that the doctors are too wishy-washy and give too much power to the community—or do you think the community has too little power?

Do you feel yourself qualified to make decisions about treatment?

Was enough information given to you about treatment? Do you understand it?

I'd like to ask a few questions about treatment on this ward:

ECT

What is the purpose of ECT? How do you think it works?

What are its advantages and disadvantages?

(If ECT was given or proposed:) What did your family think about your getting ECT?

Do you think you have improved because of this treatment? If so, how?

SLEEP STUDIES

What is the purpose of sleep studies? How do they work?

What are the advantages and disadvantages of being on the sleep studies?

Did you ever talk about the sleep studies to your family? What did they say?

PROTOCOL

What is the purpose of the Protocol setup? How does it work?

How do they decide who gets the active drug or the placebo?

What good does it do for you? What are its disadvantages?

(If on Protocol:) Did you talk to your family about it before agreeing to go on Protocol? What did they think?

14-DAY DRUG-FREE PERIOD

What is the purpose of the drug-free period?

What do you think is good about it for the patient?

What are its disadvantages?

How did you feel about them?

LEAVING

Did you ever consider leaving AMA? When? Why didn't you?

Do you think you are ready to go home now?

Were you ready earlier?

Did staff discuss it with you?

What does your family think?

What did the doctors tell you that your problem was? What will be the treatment for the future?

You may remember that when you came they gave you a Patients' Bill of Rights. Can you remember anything about them? Do you think they are important and relevant to your stay here?

Looking back on all of your treatment here, can you remember a time when things seemed to be going badly for you and then began to get better? If yes, why do you think that was?

INTERVIEW GUIDELINES: OUTPATIENT CLINIC PATIENTS

1. Can you tell me if you had anything special in mind today that you wanted to talk to the people here about (refer to the interview where possible, changes in medication)? What do you think of the outcome of your visit? Are you going to make any changes in the way you take your medicines? Which ones? How will you take them? I.e., Will you take more or less pills and when? Is that what you remember the physician recommending?

2. Why have your medicines been changed?

3. How did you start coming to this clinic? What were you told about it? What do you expect will happen as a result of coming to the clinic?

4. What kinds of medicines are you taking? Why are you taking them? What else does the treatment here consist of aside from the medicine? What does that do?

5. Do you have any worries about the treatment?

6. Why do you think that they asked you about _____? (Refer to interview topics— discussions of blurred vision, etc.)

7. What have you been told about when to take your medicines? When was this told to you? Were you told anything about the side effects attached to taking this medication? Have you experienced any? (If yes: When and what were they?) Were you told anything about any dangers attached to taking this medication? (If so: When and what were they?) How would you recognize any of these side effects/ dangers? What would you do next?

8. Is there any special diet you need to follow while you are taking these drugs? Who told you that? When? Were you told anything about drinking alcohol while you are taking these drugs? What were you told and when? Were you told anything about what might happen if you took too many pills? What were you told and when?

9. Does it matter to you that the doctors explain things about your treatment to you? How much would you like to be told about the kind of treatment that you're

getting? When the doctors explain treatment, do you ask questions to try to learn more about what they're saying?

10. Do you know anything about alternative kinds of treatment?

11. Do you feel that there was any pressure (encouragement) put on you by anyone like members of your family or the staff here to accept this treatment? To continue treatment? What happens if you stop coming to the clinic? What do you think will happen next?

12. Do you feel you had any choice about accepting this treatment? (If answer is "No, I decided": At what point did you decide? What kinds of information led you to the decision?)

13. How long do you think you will be coming to the clinic? Can you foresee a time when you might not? Who would make the decision concerning that? Could you stop treatment if you wanted to?

14. If forms were signed: Can you tell me which ones they were and a little bit about what they concerned?

15. If changes in medications/treatment were recommended: Do you think that you're going to do what he/she suggested in your meeting?

*   *   *

Other publications from this project include the following (in order of publication):

Meisel A. The expansion of liability for medical accidents: From negligence to strict liability by way of informed consent. *Nebraska Law Review* 1977; 56:51-152.

Meisel A, Roth LH, Lidz CW. Toward a model of the legal doctrine of informed consent. *American Journal of Psychiatry* 1977; 134:285-289.

Roth LH, Meisel A, Lidz CW. Tests of competency to consent to treatment. *American Journal of Psychiatry* 1977; 134:279-284.

Ashley MJ. Identity work and field-work in a psychiatric setting. *Humanity and Society* 1979; 3:238-247.

Meisel A. The "exceptions" to the informed consent doctrine: Striking a balance between competing values in medical decisionmaking. *Wisconsin Law Review* 1979; 1979:413-488.

Ashley M, Sestak RM, Roth LH. Legislating human rights: Informed consent and the Pennsylvania Mental Health Procedures Act. *Bulletin of the American Academy of Psychiatry and the Law* 1980; 8:133-151.

Lidz CW. The weather report model of informed consent: Problems in preserving patient voluntariness. *Bulletin of the American Academy of Psychiatry and the Law* 1980; 8:152-160.

Lidz CW, Gross E, Meisel A, Roth LH. The rights of juveniles in "voluntary" psychiatric commitments: Some empirical observations. *Bulletin of the American Academy of Psychiatry and the Law* 1980; 8:168-174.

Meisel A, Kabnick L. Informed consent to medical treatment: An analysis of recent legislation. *University of Pittsburgh Law Review* 1980; 41:407-564.

Zerubavel E. The bureaucratization of responsibility: The case of informed consent. *Bulletin of the American Academy of Psychiatry and the Law* 1980; 8:161-167.

Appelbaum PS, Roth LH. Clinical issues in the assessment of competency. *American Journal of Psychiatry* 1981; 138:1462-1467.

Appelbaum P, Roth L. What would it mean to be competent enough to consent to or refuse participation in research?: Psychiatric overview. In Reatig N (ed), *Competency and informed consent* (papers and other materials developed for the workshop, Empirical Research on Informed Consent with Subjects of Uncertain Competence). Washington, DC: Department of Health and Human Services, Alcohol, Drug Abuse, and Mental Health Administration, 1981.

Kaufmann CL, Roth LH. Psychiatric evaluation of patient decisionmaking: Informed consent to ECT. *Social Psychiatry* 1981; 16:11-19.

Kaufmann CL, Roth LH, Lidz CW, Meisel A. Informed consent and patient decisionmaking: The reasoning of law and psychiatry. *International Journal of Law and Psychiatry* 1981; 4:345-361.

Meisel A. The "exceptions" to informed consent: Part I. *Connecticut Medicine* 1981; 45:27-32.

Meisel A. The "exceptions" to informed consent: Part II. *Connecticut Medicine* 1981; 45:107-109.

Meisel A. Informed consent: Who decides for whom, when, and if. In Hiller M (ed), *Medical ethics and the law: Implications for public policy.* Cambridge, MA: Ballinger, 1981.

Meisel A. What would it mean to be competent enough to consent to or refuse participation in research?: Legal overview. In Reatig N (ed), *Competency and informed consent* (papers and other materials developed for the workshop, Empirical Research on Informed Consent with Subjects of Uncertain Competence). Washington, DC: Department of Health and Human Services, Alcohol, Drug Abuse, and Mental Health Administration, 1981.

Meisel A, Roth LH. What we do and do not know about informed consent. *Journal of the American Medical Association* 1981; 246:2473-2477.

Appelbaum PS, Roth LH. Competency to consent to research. *Archives of General Psychiatry* 1982; 39:951-958.

Roth LH. Competency to consent to or refuse treatment. In Grinspoon L (ed), *The American Psychiatric Association annual review.* Washington, DC: American Psychiatric Association, 1982.

Roth LH, Appelbaum PS, Salee R, Reynolds CF, Huber G. The dilemma of denial in the assessment of competency to refuse treatment. *American Journal of Psychiatry* 1982; 139:910-913.

Roth LH, Lidz CW, Meisel A, Soloff PH, Kaufman K, Spiker DG, Foster FG. Competency to decide about treatment or research: An overview of some empirical data. *International Journal of Law and Psychiatry* 1982; 5:29-50.

Lidz CW, Roth LH. The signed form—informed consent? In Boruch RF, Cecil JS (eds), *Solutions to ethical and legal issues in social research.* New York: Academic Press, 1983.

Meisel A, Roth LH. Toward an informed discussion of informed consent: A review of the empirical studies. *Arizona Law Review* 1983; 25:265-345.

NOTES AND REFERENCES

CHAPTER 1

1. Restructuring informed consent: Legal therapy for the doctor-patient relationship. *Yale Law Journal* 1970; 79:1533-1576.

2. Katz J. Informed consent—a fairy tale? Law's vision. *University of Pittsburgh Law Review* 1977; 39:137-174.

3. Szasz TS, Hollender MH. The basic models of the doctor-patient relationship. *Archives of Internal Medicine* 1956; 97:585-592.

4. Freidson has demanded an even greater change and has proposed that "the profession's role in a free society should be limited to contributing the technical information men need to make their own decisions on the basis of their own values." Freidson E. *Profession of medicine.* New York: Harper & Row, 1970, p. 382.

5. Annas GJ, Glantz LH, Katz BF. *Informed consent to human experimentation: The subject's dilemma.* Cambridge, MA: Ballinger, 1977. Katz J, Capron AM. *Catastrophic diseases: Who decides what?* New York: Russell Sage Foundation, 1975.

6. Meisel A, Roth LH, Lidz CW. Toward a model of the legal doctrine of informed consent. *American Journal of Psychiatry* 1977; 134:285-289.

7. Durkheim E. *The division of labor in society.* New York: Free Press, 1933.

8. Roth LH. A commitment law for patients, doctors, and lawyers. *American Journal of Psychiatry* 1979; 136:1121-1127.

9. Compulsory treatment has begun to be challenged, reflecting the slow, general process of extending individual rights to previously excluded sectors of the population. See Marshall TH. *Class, citizenship, and social development.* Garden City, NJ: Doubleday, 1964. In the last three decades in the United States, starting with the landmark Supreme Court ruling in Brown v. The Board of Education, this process has accelerated and has begun to include not only racial and ethnic minorities but also women, prisoners, the handicapped, and psychiatric patients.

The core of the argument against involuntary commitments, made most fervently by Thomas Szasz, is that involuntary hospitalization is, in effect, imprisonment. For Szasz and his followers, such imprisonment is a violation of basic Western freedoms, because it is done with a minimum of procedural safeguards for an indeterminate length of time and typically in the absence of any crime having been committed. Szasz TS. *Law, liberty and psychiatry.* New York: Macmillan, 1963. Thus Szasz sees involuntary psychiatric treatment as more a violation of individual autonomy than criminal punishment. Furthermore, Szasz and other civil libertarians have urged that psychiatric hospitalization may not serve the individual's best interests, functions as a degradation ceremony, and tends to serve as a dumping ground for people who are troublesome to their families and communities. In many ways, the argument for the right of informed consent for psychiatric patients is an extension of the arguments against involuntary treatment. It is an argument that psychiatric patients, presumably like other medical patients, have a right to make their own knowledgeable decisions whether to receive treatment.

CHAPTER 2

1. Portions of this chapter are reprinted with permission from Meisel A. The expansion of liability for medical accidents: From negligence to strict liability by way of informed consent. *Nebraska Law Review* 1977; 56:51-152; and from Meisel A. The exceptions to the informed consent

341

doctrine: Striking a balance between competing values in medical decisionmaking. *Wisconsin Law Review* 1979; 1979:413-488. The chapter is further adapted from Meisel A. Informed consent: Who decides for whom, when, and if. In Hiller M (ed), *Medical ethics and the law: Implications for public policy*. Cambridge, MA: Ballinger, 1981.

2. Beecher HK. Consent in clinical experimentation—myth and reality. *Journal of the American Medical Association* 1966; 195:34-35.

3. Laforet EG. The fiction of informed consent. *Journal of the American Medical Association* 1976; 235:1579-1585.

4. Burnham PJ. Medical experimentation on humans. *Science* 1966; 152:448-450. Irvin WP. Now, Mrs. Blare, about the complications . . . *Medical Economics* 1963; 40:102-108. Middleton EB. Informed consent. *Journal of the American Medical Association* 1975; 233:1049. Ravitch MM. Informed consent—descent to absurdity. *Medical Times* 1973; 101:164-171.

5. Meisel A. The "exceptions" to the informed consent doctrine: Striking a balance between competing values in medical decisionmaking. *Wisconsin Law Review* 1979; 1979:418-488. Specific reference is made to p. 413, note 3.

6. Young v. Yarn, 222 S.E.2d 113 (Ga. App. 1975); Georgia Code Ann. §88-2901 et seq. (Supp. 1977).

7. Meisel A, Kabnick LD. Informed consent to medical treatment: An analysis of recent legislation. *University of Pittsburgh Law Review* 1980; 41:407-564.

8. It is worth stating clearly what informed consent is not: It is not the same as traditional medical malpractice. A physician may be liable for injuries to the patient caused by a procedure that the doctor has administered, even if informed consent was obtained, if the doctor was negligent in one of several ways: (1) the failure to possess a reasonable degree of learning and skill; (2) the failure to exercise reasonable care and diligence in the exercise of skill; (3) the failure to use best judgment in the exercise of skill and application of knowledge; (4) the failure to keep abreast of developments in medicine; and (5) a departure from generally approved or used methods. Pike v. Honsinger, 155 N.Y. 201, 209-210, 49 N.E. 760, 762 (1898).

9. Informed consent and the dying patient. *Yale Law Journal* 1974; 83:1632-1664.

10. Salgo v. Leland Stanford Jr. University Board of Trustees, 317 P.2d 170 (Cal. App. 1957).

11. Meisel and Kabnick, supra note 7.

12. Slater v. Backer and Stapleton, 2 Wils. 359, 95 Eng. Rep. 860 (K.B. 1767).

13. Natanson v. Kline, 350 P.2d 1093, opinion on denial of motion for rehearing, 354 P.2d 670 (Kan. 1960).

14. Mitchell v. Robinson, 334 S.W.2d 11, opinion on denial of motion for rehearing, 360 S.W.2d 673 (Mo. 1962).

15. Canterbury v. Spence, 464 F.2d 772 (D.C. Cir.), cert. denied 409 U.S. 1064 (1972).

16. Cobbs v. Grant, 502 P.2d 1 (Cal. 1972).

17. Wilkinson v. Vesey, 295 A.2d 676 (R.I. 1972).

18. Modern status of views as to general measure of physician's duty to inform patients of risks of proposed treatment. *Annotated Law Reports* (3rd ser.) 1978; 88:1008-1044.

19. Some courts refer to these risks as "hazards" or "discomforts" or "side effects."

20. Meisel, supra note 5, p. 421.

21. The physician is required to know about those risks that a reasonable medical practitioner would know about. For a further discussion of the term "reasonable," see Natanson v. Kline, 350 P.2d 1093, 1106 (Kan. 1960).

22. Cobbs v. Grant, 502 P.2d 1, 11 (Cal. 1972).

23. Modern status of views as to general measure of physician's duty to inform patients of risks of proposed treatment, supra note 18.

24. Natanson v. Kline, 350 P.2d 1093, 1106 (Kan. 1960).

25. Id.

26. Prosser WL. *Handbook of the law of torts*. 4th edition. St. Paul, MN: West, 1971, p. 165. Louisell DW, Williams H. *Medical malpractice*. Albany, NY: M. Bender, 1969, p. 200.

27. For further references to these jurisdictions and cases and for discussion of this issue, see Meisel A. The expansion of liability for medical accidents: From negligence to strict liability by way of informed consent. *Nebraska Law Review* 1977; 56:51-52.

28. The courts have clearly rejected a subjective patient-oriented standard in which the physician would be obliged to disclose what the particular patient would have wanted to know.

29. Canterbury v. Spence, 464 F.2d 772, 786 (D.C. Cir. 1972).

30. Id., p. 790.

31. Goldstein J. For Harold Lasswell: Some reflections on human dignity, entrapment, informed consent, and the plea bargain. *Yale Law Journal* 1975; 84:683-703.

32. Id., p. 691.

33. Shetter v. Rochelle, 409 P.2d 74, 83 (Ariz. App. 1965).

34. Plant ML. An analysis of "informed consent." *Fordham Law Review* 1968; 36:639—672. Comment, "Informed consent in medical malpractice." *California Law Review* 1967; 55:1396—1418.

35. Cobbs v. Grant, 502 P.2d 1 (Cal. 1972); Funke v. Fieldman, 512 P.2d 539 (Kan. 1973); Fogal v. Genesee Hospital, 344 N.Y.S.2d 552 (App. Div. 1973); Scaria v. St. Paul Fire and Marine Insurance Company, 227 N.W.2d 647 (Wis. 1975).

36. Poulin v. Zartman, 542 P.2d 251 (Alaska 1975); Wilkinson v. Vesey, 295 A.2d 676 (R.I. 1972); Shetter v. Rochelle, 409 P.2d 74 (Ariz. App. 1965).

37. Dunham v. Wright, 423 F.2d 940 (3d Cir. 1970); Mohr v. Williams, 104 N.W. 12 (Minn. 1905); Moss v. Rishworth, 222 S.W. 225 (Tex. App. 1920).

38. Sullivan v. Montgomery, 279 N.Y.S. 575, 577 (Bronx Cty. City Ct. 1935).

39. Roth LH, Meisel A, Lidz CW. Tests of competency to consent to treatment. *American Journal of Psychiatry* 1977; 134:279-284.

40. Miranda v. Arizona, 384 U.S. 436, 475, 476 (1966).

41. Comment, "Informed consent: The illusion of patient choice." *Emory Law Journal* 1974; 23:504.

42. Nishi v. Hartwell, 473 P.2d 116, 119 (Haw. 1970).

43. Ferrara v. Galluchio, 152 N.E.2d 249 (N.Y. 1958); Kraus v. Spielberg 236 N.Y.S.2d 143 (Sup. Ct. Kings Cty. 1962); Williams v. Menehan, 379 P.2d 292, 294 (Kan. 1963).

44. See, for example, Franklyn v. Peabody, 228 N.W. 681 (Mich. 1930).

45. See, for example, Wilkinson v. Vesey, 295 A.2d 676, 689 (R.I. 1972).

46. The National Commission for the Protection of Human Subjects of Biomedical and Behavioral Research has eschewed the use of the term "consent" when a research subject is unable to participate in decisionmaking. Instead, it speaks of "permission," when given by a third party. For a further discussion of consent when research subjects are involved, see The National Commission for the Protection of Human Subjects of Biomedical and Behavioral Research. *Protection of human subjects—research involving children.* Washington DC: US Government Printing Office, 1978.

47. Health Law Center. *Hospital law manual.* Germantown, PA: Aspen Systems, 1974, p. 58. King JH. *The law of medical malpractice in a nutshell.* St. Paul, MN: West, 1977, p. 140.

48. In re Quinlan, 70 N.J. 10, 355 A.2d 647 (1976); Superintendent of Belchertown State School v. Saikewicz, 370 N.E.2d 417 (Mass. 1977); In re Spring, 405 N.E.2d 115 (Mass. 1980); Eichner v. Dillon, 426 N.Y.S.2d 517 (App. Div. 1980); Severns v. Wilmington Medical Center, Inc. 421 A.2d 1334 (Del. 1980).

49. Rogers v. Okin, 634 F.2d 650 (1st Cir. 1980); Mills v. Rogers, 50 U.S.L.W. 4676, 1982; Rennie v. Klein, Nos. 79-2576, 79-2577 (3d Cir. July 9, 1981); Davis v. Hubbard, No. C-73-205 (N.D. Ohio, Sept. 16, 1980); Colyer v. Third Judicial District Court, 469 F. Supp. 424 (D. Utah 1979); In re K.K.B., 609 P.2d 747 (Okla. 1980).

50. Cal. Admin. Code, title 9, art. 5.5, 851.

51. Meisel A, Roth LH, Lidz CW. Toward a model of the legal doctrine of informed consent. *American Journal of Psychiatry* 1977; 134:285-289.

CHAPTER 3

1. Meisel A, Roth LH, Lidz CW. Toward a model of the legal doctrine of informed consent. *American Journal of Psychiatry* 1977; 134:285-289.

2. Golden JS, Johnston GD. Problems of distortion in doctor-patient communications. *Psychiatry in Medicine* 1970; 1:127-149.

3. Boreham P, Gibson O. The informative process in private medical consultations: A preliminary investigation. *Social Science and Medicine* 1978; 12:409-416.

4. Gray BH. *Human subjects in medical experimentation.* New York: Wiley, 1975.

5. Schultz AL, Pardee GP, Ensinck JW. Are research subjects really informed? *Western Journal of Medicine* 1975; 123:76-80.

6. Grossman L, Summers F. A study of the capacity of schizophrenic patients to give informed consent. *Hospital and Community Psychiatry* 1980; 31:205-206.

7. Alfidi RJ. Informed consent—a study of patient reaction. *Journal of the American Medical Association* 1971; 216:1325-1329.

8. Alfidi RJ. Controversy, alternatives, and decisions in complying with the legal doctrine of informed consent. *Radiology* 1975; 114:231-234.

9. Meisel A. The "exceptions" to the informed consent doctrine: Striking a balance between competing values in medical decisionmaking. *Wisconsin Law Review* 1979; 1979:413-488.

10. Faden RR, Beauchamp TL. Decisionmaking and informed consent: A study of the impact of disclosed information. *Social Indicators Research* 1980; 7:313-336.

11. Lankton JW, Batchelder BM, Ominsky AJ. Emotional responses to detailed risk disclosure for anesthesia: A prospective, randomized study. *Anesthesiology* 1977; 46:294-296.

12. Denney MK, Williamson D, Penn R. Informed consent: Emotional responses of patients. *Postgraduate Medicine* 1975; 60:205-209.

13. Roth LH, Meisel A, Lidz CW. Tests of competency to consent to treatment. *American Journal of Psychiatry* 1977; 134:279-284.

14. Leonard CO, Chase GA, Childs B. Genetic counseling: A consumers' view. *New England Journal of Medicine* 1972; 287:433-439.

15. Robinson G, Merav A. Informed consent: Recall by patients tested postoperative. *Annuals of Thoracic Surgery* 1976; 22:209-212.

16. McCollum AT, Schwartz AH. Pediatric research hospitalization: Its meaning to parents. *Pediatric Research* 1969; 3:199-204.

17. Klatte EW, Liscomb WR, Rozynko VV, Pugh LA. Changing the legal status of mental hospital patients. *Hospital and Community Psychiatry* 1969; 20:199-202.

18. Garnham JC. Some observations on informed consent in nontherapeutic research. *Journal of Medicine Ethics* 1975; 1:138-145.

19. National Commission for the Protection of Human Subjects of Biomedical and Behavioral Research. Institutional review boards: Report and recommendations. *Federal Register* 1978; 43:56174-56198.

20. Grundner TM. On the readability of surgical consent forms. *New England Journal of Medicine* 1980; 302:900-902.

21. Morrow GR. How readable are subject consent forms? *Journal of the American Medical Association* 1980; 244:56-58.

22. Epstein LC, Lasagna L. Obtaining informed consent—form or substance? *Archives of Internal Medicine* 1969; 123:682-688.

23. Morrow G, Gootnick J, Schmale A. A simple technique for increasing cancer patients' knowledge of informed consent to treatment. *Cancer* 1978; 42:793-799.

24. Faden RR. Disclosure and informed-consent: Does it matter how we tell it? *Health Education Monograph* 1977; 5:198-214.

25. Barbour GL, Blumenkrantz MJ. Videotape aids informed consent decision. *Journal of the American Medical Association* 1978; 240:2741-2742.

26. Williams RL, Rieckmann KH, Trenholme GM, Frischer H, Carson PE. The use of a test to determine that consent is informed. *Military Medicine* 1977; 142:542-545.

27. Soskis DA. Schizophrenic and medical inpatients as informed drug consumers. *Archives of General Psychiatry* 1978; 35:645-647.

28. Olin GB, Olin HS. Informed consent in voluntary mental hospital admissions. *American Journal of Psychiatry* 1975; 132:938-941.

29. Palmer AB, Wohl J. Voluntary-admission forms: Does the patient know what he's signing? *Hospital and Community Psychiatry* 1972; 23:250-252.

30. Pryce IG. Clinical research upon mentally ill subjects who cannot give informed consent. *British Journal of Psychiatry* 1978; 133:366-369.

31. Sacks MH, Carpenter WT, Strauss JS. Recovery from delusions: Three phases documented by patient's interpretation of research procedures. *Archives of General Psychiatry* 1974; 30:117-120.

32. Carpenter W. A new setting for informed consent. *Lancet* 1974; 1:500-501.

33. Siris S, Docherty J, McGlashan T. Intrapsychic structural effects of psychiatric research. *American Journal of Psychiatry* 1979; 136:1567-1571.

34. Jacobs L, Kotin J. Fantasies of psychiatric research. *American Journal of Psychiatry* 1972; 128:1074-1080.

35. Park LC, Covi L, Uhlenhuth EH. Effects of informed consent on research patients and study results. *Journal of Nervous and Mental Disease* 1967; 145:349-357.

36. Singer E. Informed consent: Consequences for response rate and response quality in social surveys. *American Sociological Review* 1978; 43:144-162.

37. Roling GT, Pressgrove LW, Keeffe EB, Raffin SB. An appraisal of patients' reactions to "informed consent" for peroral endoscopy. *Gastrointestinal Endoscopy* 1977; 24:69-70.

38. Rosenberg SH. Informed consent—a reappraisal of patients' reactions. *California Medicine* 1973; 119:64-68.

39. Stuart RB. Protection of the right to informed consent to participate in research. *Behavior Therapy* 1978; 9:73-82.

40. Flanery M, Gravdal J, Hendrix P, Hoffman W, *et al.* Just sign here. . . . *South Dakota Journal of Medicine* 1978; 31:33-37.

41. Priluck IA, Robertson DM, Buettner H. What patients recall of the preoperative discussion after retinal detachment surgery. *American Journal of Ophthalmology* 1979; 87:620-623.

42. Appelbaum PS, Gutheil TG. Drug refusal: A study of psychiatric inpatients. *American Journal of Psychiatry* 1980; 137:340-346.

43. Fellner CH, Marshall JR. Twelve kidney donors. *Journal of the American Medical Association* 1968; 206:2703-2707.

44. Fellner CH, Marshall JR. Kidney donors—the myth of informed consent. *American Journal of Psychiatry* 1970; 126:1245-1251.

CHAPTER 4

1. Pennsylvania Mental Health Procedures Act, 50 P.S. §7101, et seq. (1976).

2. Id. at §7203.

3. Blumer H. What is wrong with social theory? *American Sociological Review* 1954; 19:3-10.

4. Lidz CW, Walker AL. *Heroin, deviance and morality.* Beverly Hills, CA: Sage, 1980.

5. While it is not possible to provide a quantitative measure of the reliability of the observations by this technique, we were consistently impressed by the similarities of the overall accounts that they produced. Dialogue was usually similar in the two sets of notes, but much more fully recorded by the observer who used speed writing.

CHAPTER 5

1. Pennsylvania Mental Health Procedures Act, 50 P.S. §7101, et seq. (1976).

2. Treatment of mentally ill persons in accordance with the mental health procedures act of 1976. *Pennsylvania Bulletin* 1976; 6:2113-2181.

3. No official hospital statistics on Evaluation Center cases were compiled during the period of our observations, September–December 1976. The figures presented here are based on the Evaluation Center monthly reports for September–December 1977.

4. Section 203 of the Act states that a voluntary admission must involve an explanation (50 P.S. §7203):

> Including the types of treatment in which he may be involved, and any restraints or restrictions to which he may be subjected, together with a statement of his rights under this Act. Consent shall be in writing. . . . The consent shall include the following representations: That the person understands his treatment will involve inpatient status; that he is willing to be admitted to a designated facility for the purpose of such examination and treatment; that he consents to such admission voluntarily, without coercion or duress; and, if applicable, that he has voluntarily agreed to remain in treatment for a specified period of no longer than 72 hours after having given written notice of his intent to withdraw from treatment.

5. The regulations require that a full explanation of the types of treatment in which the patient may become involved is to be written on a form and signed by both physician and patient. Such written explanations were usually very general and very brief, consisting of a statement that "patient will be observed and further treatment discussed with the attending physician" and covering less than three of the seven lines provided on the form. In addition, the patient was usually (14 cases) given some further explanation, such as "You will be on the 10th floor," "You will probably be given medication," "You will be given tests," and so on. In one case, the patient, a young woman whose admission diagnosis was schizophrenia (paranoid type), asked many questions and was given an extremely detailed explanation of a prospective drug and testing:

D: You'll be here for observation and pharmacotherapy.
P: What's that?
D: Well, it's a type of medication used to slow down thoughts. It's used for two things: one, to slow down thoughts . . .
P: I don't like that idea at all.
D: It will make you less tremulous and anxious.
P: I'm not really anxious. I'm just anxious today because I'm in a strange place.
D: . . . And, two, it will make your voices decrease. Not all of a sudden, but gradually. . . . Well, you may not be put on those kinds of medications right away, but after the evaluation we'll put you on medications, probably within a certain spectrum.
P: Called . . . ? What are the names of some of those?
D: Well, you can refuse drug treatment. But the names of some of them might be Thorazine, Mellaril, Prolixin . . .

It was stressed to one other patient, a heroin addict, that he would receive no drugs to aid in his withdrawal. In two of the cases, no information other than that appearing on the form was offered, and in one of these cases, that of a man ordered to sign in by a police officer, the form was blank when signed. The information was then filled in above the signature, resulting in a finished product indistinguishable from a properly completed form. Surprisingly, this description of a proposed treatment was more detailed than most, reading:

1. Hospitalize for purpose of protecting others from violent behavior;
2. Reinstitution of butyrophenone (Haldol);
3. Referral to outpatient service.

One other patient who received no explanation was considered an emergency case, in that he had suffered a suspected seizure during the initial interview and was thereafter rushed through the admission process with minimal delay. In three cases, the data was insufficient for analysis.

6. This type of brief explanation of possible restrictions and restraints for the patient occurred in 14 of 22 voluntary-admission cases.

7. This explanation of the initial findings is about as detailed as those given to seven other voluntary-admission patients. Two patients heard similar explanations given to their relatives in their presence. Two other patients received slightly more detailed explanations—for example,

> I have some information about you. See if you can read this and see if you agree. It says that you talked with the doctor . . . and this is his initial evaluation. . . . It says you are suicidal and ideational. That means you might have the possibility of hurting yourself . . . and you have diabetes.

This is considered a more detailed explanation, because it incorporates evaluative information not present on the form itself. Five other patients were simply shown the form without a verbal explanation or restatement of the information contained there. Two patients were given no information and signed blank forms. One of these patients, Jason X, appeared to suffer a seizure during the admission process, and the staff cut corners to hospitalize him as quickly as possible. Another patient, Reavis C, was not subjected to involuntary-commitment procedures, although he was considered dangerous. Instead, the university police officer who had brought him to the admission unit was permitted to be present when he signed the papers and in fact ordered him to do so. The information was then filled in above his signature, resulting in a finished product indistinguishable from a properly completed form. The following chart summarizes our findings on the information given to patients about initial findings:

Amount of information given about initial findings	*Number of patients*	
Oral restatement/explanation of information on form plus additional information	2	9%
Oral restatement/explanation of information on form to patient	8	36%
Oral restatement/explanation of information on form to relative in patient's presence	2	9%
Written information on form	5	23%
No information	2	9%
Unknown	3	14%
TOTALS	22	100%

8. The Department of Public Welfare regulations required that patients be provided with a "Bill of Rights." A signed receipt for the Bill of Rights was to be obtained from the patient, stating that the patient had received and understood these rights. If it was impossible for the facility to obtain such a receipt, this fact was to be documented in the patient's record. In addition, this Bill of Rights was to have appended to it the names, telephone numbers, and locations of legal and other available advocacy services. None of these procedures was ever carried out in the Evaluation Center during our observations. The Bill of Rights was neither provided nor explained to patients, because the Evaluation Center staff wrongly believed that this was the responsibility of the treatment staff on the ward.

9. At the time of our study, the Mental Health Procedures Act required that all applications for voluntary admission be filed with the county mental health administrator. The Hospital protested this rule, arguing that it breached the confidentiality of voluntary patients, and they refused to forward the information to the county administrator without the patient's express consent.

The Evaluation Center staff generally asked voluntary-admission patients whether they would agree to this release of information and, if they objected, told them to write on the bottom of the "Voluntary Consent to Inpatient Treatment" form (see Figure 5-1) that information could not be released to the county.

10. The admission form indicates that the patient, not the staff member, should fill out this section. Yet only 11 patients checked one of the boxes themselves and wrote in a number of hours when applicable, and one of these patients did this only after she had already signed the form. The following chart summarizes who filled out this form in each of the 22 voluntary admissions we observed:

Form filled in by	Number of patients
Patient	11
Partly by patient, partly by staff	2
Staff, before patient signed	2
Staff, after patient signed	3
Staff, time unknown	1
Unknown	3
TOTAL	22

The form also states that the reasons for giving notice have been explained to the patient. Only 12 patients received any such explanation. Generally, these explanations were vague, as in Ms. E's case; if more detailed, they were used as a persuasive device by the Evaluation Center staff to encourage patients to agree to give 72 hours' notice. For example, one woman was told by the doctor:

> There's one other thing. You can inform us of a time you're going to leave; you can give written notice 72 hours before you leave that you are going to do so. We do this because some people leave before they have made appropriate plans, and this gives us the opportunity to keep them awhile longer. So if you want to do that, put "72" here and then check this block.

The extensiveness of these explanations is more fully discussed in Chapter 6.

11. Pennsylvania Mental Health Procedures Act, §302.

12. The "rights form" to which the clinician was referring was to be given to patients on the inpatient ward. At the time of our observations, this form had not yet been made available to the Hospital by the Department of Public Welfare.

13. Involuntary-admission requirements were, on the whole, more closely adhered to by Evaluation Center staff than were the voluntary-admission requirements. We saw no instances in which the doctor filled out the "Findings of the Initial Examination" section of the involuntary-admission form before at least talking briefly with the patient.

14. Three referral patients of the 15 observed were given explanations of what outpatient treatment involved that was equivalent to the explanation received by Ms. E, which by comparison was a detailed explanation. Eight other patients were given only very general information, such as that they would "see a counselor" or "talk to a psychiatrist." The remaining four patients were given no explanation of possible treatment.

15. Six patients (of 15) were given some information about what the physical examination would involve, ranging from the very general to the very detailed, such as the explanation given to one 14-year-old girl by the doctor:

> We're going to do some lab tests, and we'll do some brain wave tests. . . . They'll paste some buttons on your head, and then you think of something pleasant like . . . going to a movie. We want to make sure that you're in good health. . . . We're going to send you to the lab, and then you can have your physical done.

The other nine patients were told nothing of this examination.

CHAPTER 6

1. Five cases were eliminated for insufficient data on this issue.

2. The legality of such a "rule"—which, from our conversations with personnel from other hospitals around the state, seems to be widespread—has not been tested, but it clearly violates the spirit of the regulations.

3. Their reluctance was not atypical of the attitude of psychiatric hospitals around the country. See Gilboy J. Informed admission of patients to state psychiatric institutions. *American Journal of Orthopsychiatry* 1977; 47:321-330.

4. Garfinkel H. *Studies in ethnomethodology.* Englewood Cliffs, NJ: Prentice-Hall, 1967.

5. Robinson G, Merav A. Informed consent: Recall by patients tested post-operatively. *Annals of Thoracic Surgery* 1976; 22:209-212.

6. Sharpe G. The proper format and function of consent forms. *Canadian Medical Association Journal* 1978; 118:1001-1004. It should not be regarded as more than that, however. At the outset, the consent form must be recognized for what it is—nothing more than evidence that informed consent has been obtained. See Vaccarino J. Consent, informed consent and the consent form. *New England Journal of Medicine* 1978; 298:455.

7. Ashley M, Sestak RM, Roth LH. Legislating human rights: Informed consent and the Pennsylvania Mental Health Procedures Act. *Bulletin of the American Academy of Psychiatry and the Law* 1980; 8:133-151.

8. Lidz CW, Roth LH. The signed form—informed consent? In Boruch RC, Cecil JS (eds), *Solutions to ethical and legal issues in social research.* New York: Academic Press, 1982.

9. Goffman E. *Encounters.* Indianapolis: Bobbs-Merrill, 1961.

10. In the exceptional case, that of Sally N, it appeared that the resident did the informing himself because he did not want to risk "losing" the patient, whom he considered exceptionally paranoid.

11. Legally speaking, of course, the physician is the one who is held responsible and accountable for the patient.

CHAPTER 7

1. The doctor had inspected some of Sally N's personal papers, which made reference to "he," "she," and "it." The patient explained to the doctor that, at the time of the writing of these papers, "He, she, it, they're all me—not exactly, though."

2. Lidz CW. The weather report model of informed consent: Problems in preserving patient voluntariness. *Bulletin of the American Academy of Psychiatry and the Law* 1980; 8:152-160.

3. Nor can we think of any methods compatible with our commitment to studying the process in the natural setting that would make the actual decisionmaking process more accessible.

CHAPTER 8

1. Zerubavel E. The bureaucratization of responsibility: The case of informed consent. *Bulletin of the American Academy of Psychiatry and the Law* 1980; 8:161-167.

CHAPTER 9

1. While not intended mainly to benefit patients, research procedures may have that consequence nonetheless. Similarly, efforts are made to assure that research procedures do not harm patients either. In some instances, "research" consists of nothing more than a systematic effort to ascertain the safety, efficacy, or both of an accepted diagnostic or therapeutic procedure, the value of which has been assumed but never formally demonstrated; thus it is true that a particular procedure may be both therapeutic and experimental at the same time.

2. Almond R. *The healing community: Dynamics of the therapeutic community.* New York: Jason Aronson, 1974.

3. Baldessarini RJ. *Chemotherapy in psychiatry.* Cambridge, MA: Harvard University Press, 1977.

4. American Psychiatric Association. *Electroconvulsive therapy* (Task Force Report No. 14). Washington, DC: Author, 1978.

5. Research involving human subjects must comply with federal law only when it is supported by federal grants or contracts. US Department of Health and Human Services. Final Regulations Amending Basic HHS Policy for the Protection of Human Research Subjects, 46 Fed. Reg. 8366, 8386 (Jan. 26, 1981), to be codified at 45 C.F.R. §46.101.

6. Noelle H had previously reported to staff members that she had suffered severe side effects when on Sinequan. This apparently constituted the basis for their refusal to give it to her again. Their reason for encouraging her to continue on Aventyl for a set time was to determine the amount of it in her blood. Eventually, she was given the opportunity to decide on treatment, and Aventyl was discontinued.

CHAPTER 10

1. It should be noted that such "expertise" was not necessarily granted to the other psychiatrist, the one who had not admitted the patient originally. For example, when Christine E asked the other psychiatrist whether she would be discharged on Friday, he replied that she would have to wait until the admitting psychiatrist would be back in town from a conference. When Harriet L and Mildred L asked the psychiatrists who were not "their own" about the results of their sleep studies, each was told that she ought to talk with the psychiatrist who had admitted her.

2. Weber M. *The theory of social and economic organization.* New York: Free Press, 1947.

3. This was the only instance we observed in which a patient was asked to weigh the risks of ECT against its benefits. Interestingly enough, the latter were not specified to her.

4. Additional research data (using other research methods) gathered during this research project about patients' understanding of ECT administered at the Hospital are reported in Roth LH, Lidz CW, Meisel A, Soloff PH, Kaufman K, Spiker DG, Foster FG. Competency to decide about treatment or research: An overview of some empirical data. *International Journal of Law and Psychiatry* 1982; 5:29–50.

5. In this section, we describe the extent of patients' understanding and staff disclosure about research that we observed and documented during our 7-week study of the Research Ward. Patients' understanding of the research was based on information given to them by the staff, as well as upon their actual participation in the research. Because patients' initial consents to research were most frequently obtained in the Evaluation Center (prior to the time the patient was admitted to the Research Ward), we were, for a number of logistical reasons, unable to observe such initial consents. We therefore also studied patients' understanding of research through another research approach relying upon questionnaires and videotaped studies. The results from this more structured portion of the research generally confirmed the observational data reported here. See Roth *et al.,* supra note 4. See also Lidz CW, Roth LH. The signed form—informed consent? In Boruch RF, Cecil JS (eds), *Solutions to ethical and legal issues in social research.* New York: Academic Press, 1983.

We were, however, able to observe the obtaining of initial consents of two patients to the Protocol. The following illustrates the process of obtaining, in the Evaluation Center, a patient's consent to be hospitalized on the Research Ward and to enter the Protocol:

Phyllis D, a 35-year-old married housewife, was referred to the Hospital by her outpatient psychiatrist, who recommended that she be hospitalized in the Research Ward. Ever since suffering an episode of sexual abuse several years ago, Ms. D had been intermittently depressed. She was accompanied to the Evaluation Center by her husband. After her initial evaluation by the Evaluation Center staff, Ms. D agreed to admission to the Hospital. At this point, Dr. J, the physician who was responsible for obtaining consents for research (and for patients' admission to the Research Ward, as opposed to a regular ward of the Hospital) came to the Evaluation Center to tell her about the research. Dr. J (who treated patients on the Research Ward and who was also responsible for carrying out the depression research) asked Ms. D, "I understand that you have agreed to come in?"

PATIENT: Yeah.

DOCTOR: Well, we have two types of wards we can admit you to here. The first is the one on which I work. It is a special ward for clinical research on depression.

Dr. J then told Ms. D that most of the patients on the Research Ward are especially referred by other doctors because the Research Ward has a great deal of experience in dealing with depressed patients.

DOCTOR: It also has some interesting properties about it. For example, we have sleep-EEG machines on the ward.

Dr. J explained to Ms. D that the Research Ward does EEGs on patients while they are asleep because "we are trying to find a better way to determine what sort of patients will respond well to drugs." He then added that if Ms. D were to come onto the ward, "You will be expected to participate in the sleep studies."

Dr. J next noted that on the Research Ward they "do placebo research" with drugs.

DOCTOR: At any given time, there is a 50% chance you will get an active drug and a 50% chance you will get a placebo. Another thing is that if you were on one of the other wards, you'll be here probably for a shorter time. We try to keep people [on the Research Ward] on the average of about 8 weeks.

The discussion then turned to the advantages and disadvantages of being on the Research Ward.

DOCTOR: I think the advantages are that, of course, we have a great deal of experience treating problems like you have, and we do have some special equipment like the sleep-EEG machine that is more difficult to get on other wards. The other thing is that we will pay any costs above what your insurance covers during the period you are in the Hospital, so that you won't have to pay for any of the treatment at all. I think the disadvantages are that, of course, you've got to participate in the sleep studies, and the stay does average 8 weeks, and that is longer than on the other wards.

At this point Ms. D's husband inhaled deeply and said, "That is a long time." Dr. J then told Phyllis D and her husband that she would get very good care on either ward.

PATIENT: Well, but you can't guarantee, right? I mean if I was feeling bad and I get on the ward and I feel worse, do I have to deal with that all by myself?

The doctor responded that the Research Ward had very active care, that Ms. D would be expected to do a great deal in the way of participating in ward activities with other patients, and that she would not have to deal with it all by herself. He noted that Ms. D could drop out of the research at any time, but added:

DOCTOR: Obviously we would prefer that you do not. I think you will get excellent care on either ward, and I think in the end it is probably pretty close to an even bet, but I came down here so that I could explain this choice. There are others who would disagree with that.

PATIENT: All right. I'll try your ward.

Dr. J left the room to get the consent form. He returned shortly and gave the consent form to the patient. Ms. D read the form (see text) carefully and signed it. Following this interchange, we questioned the patient. Ms. D indicated that she had been feeling bad for about 2 years.

PATIENT: I've just got to do something about it. I figured that they specialize in working with this type of problem, so they'll probably work harder with me because they are studying it.

Concerning disadvantages of the Research Ward, Ms. D mentioned that primarily she was concerned about "the amount of time I'll have to spend on the ward because I'm sick of hospitals; I don't like them at all." She noted that the sleep-EEGs would be perfectly "OK" with her because she had had them before. She noted that for her the advantages of being hospitalized on the Research Ward were that her "private doctor had recommended it," and thus "it probably was a good idea."

6. This matter is actually extremely complicated. As the research progressed, the investigators came to feel that the sleep patterns of patients on Elavil allowed them to distinguish those who would improve on Elavil and those who would not. Thus the extra sleep studies given to research patients potentially could have been an advantage, since they might have been used to decide whether or not Elavil would be helpful to them. However, as far as we can determine, at this point in time neither the regular sleep studies nor the research sleep studies were actually used in a significant number of cases to determine which drugs the patient should receive.

7. Roth J. *Timetables: Structuring of passage of time in hospital treatment and other careers.* Indianapolis: Bobbs-Merrill, 1963.

8. Zerubavel E. *Patterns of time in hospital life.* Chicago: University of Chicago Press, 1979.

9. The single exception to this was one patient, Max I, a highly intellectual young man who was diagnosed as paranoid and who left the ward within 3 days. His views of the ward were close to those of such writers as Thomas Szasz and Erving Goffman. He described to us, with considerable clarity, various subtly coercive features of ward life.

CHAPTER 11

1. This is not to say that the staff never sought incompetency proceedings for patients whom they believed incompetent to consent to treatment. These situations, however, were rare. Through other methods employed in the overall research project (reported elsewhere), we found that for three of 70 patients for whom the staff had proposed ECT (and who were persistently refusing ECT), the competency of these patients was eventually ruled upon by a court. All three were found legally incompetent. See Roth LH, Lidz CW, Meisel A, Soloff PH, Kaufman K, Spiker DG, Foster FG. Competency to decide about treatment or research: An overview of some empirical data. *International Journal of Law and Psychiatry* 1982; 5:29-50.

CHAPTER 13

1. American Psychiatric Association. *Tardive dyskinesia* (Task Force Report No. 18). Washington, DC: Author, 1979.

CHAPTER 14

1. Baldessarini RJ, Lipinsky J. Risks versus benefits of antipsychotic drugs. *New England Journal of Medicine* 1973; 289:427-428.

2. Gardos G, Cole J. Maintenance antipsychotic therapy: Is the cure worse than the disease? *American Journal of Psychiatry* 1976; 133:32-36.

3. We should add that patients were also typified and classified by the Outpatient Clinic staff, according to the frequency of their visits. This reflected the staff's trust in the patients' willingness and ability to comply with the recommended treatment. Consider, for example, the difference between seeing patients every week or once every 6 weeks, with the interval between visits being "covered" by the patients' self-regulation of the medication.

4. Meisel A. The "exceptions" to the informed consent doctrine: Striking a balance between competing values in medical decisionmaking. *Wisconsin Law Review* 1979; 1979:413-488.

5. American Psychiatric Association. *Tardive dyskinesia* (Task Force Report No. 18). Washington, DC: Author, 1979.

CHAPTER 15

1. Katz J. *Experimentation with human beings.* New York: Russell Sage Foundation, 1972, pp. 635-642.

CHAPTER 17

1. Lidz CW, Meisel A. Informed consent and the structure of medical care. Appendix to President's Commission for the Study of Ethical Problems in Medicine and Biomedical and Behavioral Research, *Making health care decisions.* Washington, DC: US Government Printing Office, 1982.

2. See, for example, Barber B. *Informed consent in medical therapy and research.* New Brunswick, NJ: Rutgers University Press, 1980.

3. See Chapter 4.

4. Roth LH, Lidz CW, Meisel A, Soloff PH, Kaufman K, Spiker DG, Foster FG. Competency to decide about treatment or research: An overview of some empirical data. *International Journal of Law and Psychiatry* 1982; 5:29-50.

5. To conduct an investigation that sheds substantial light on the operation of informed consent, per se, may be an impossible task if the findings of this study and others that are in progress in medical specialties other than psychiatry are generally valid. That is, if for the most part informed consent is not obtained—disclosure is not made and patients are not involved in the decisionmaking process—it is impossible to answer many of the questions suggested by the doctrine, such as the extent of understanding that patients have of disclosed information. Although some of this information could be obtained from experimental (rather than naturalistic) studies, the validity of such data is open to questions. See Meisel A, Roth LH. What we do and do not know about informed consent. *Journal of the American Medical Association* 1982; 246:2473-2477.

6. We did do some observations of procedures in the Evaluation Center prior to the major change in state law that occurred just prior to the commencement of this project and before detailed regulations for obtaining informed consent to hospital admission had been promulgated. Although we do not have fully comparable data to report, pilot observations made in this same Evaluation Center on 23 patients prior to the change in the law showed that the newly mandated procedures had little effect in altering the general nature or extent of information disclosure by staff to patients. There was more information given about the "72-hour hold provision" under the new law than there was under the old law. At the time of our pilot observations, the Pennsylvania law allowed for retention of voluntary patients for up to 10 days (after they asked to leave), but this provision was hardly ever discussed in the Evaluation Center. Of course, even under the 1976 law, the information that was given by the Evaluation Center staff to patients about the "72-hour hold provision" was frequently incomplete or misleading. See Ashley MA, Sestak RM, Roth LH. Legislating human rights: Informed consent and the Pennsylvania Mental Health Procedures Act. *Bulletin of the American Academy of Psychiatry and the Law* 1980; 8:133-151.

7. It might be unconstitutional to abolish the right to sue for damages for battery, for failure to obtain consent, or for misrepresentation in response to a patient's inquiry, but probably not merely for abolishing the disclosure duty.

8. This may largely be a matter of definition, a problem that permeates utilitarian analysis in general. Certainly we cannot say that we saw any better medical outcomes for patients because they chose a course of treatment different from what they would have gotten had the staff alone decided on treatment. (In part, this may have been the case because patients rarely had the opportunity to choose among two or more treatments, but merely had an opportunity to consent to or decline a particular treatment). Nor did we see any benefits accrue to patients (or to family members or to staff) as a result simply of the patient's sheer exercise of choice. Few patients could be found who overtly characterized themselves as "autonomous decisionmakers" and felt pride (or self-hatred) because of this characterization. Very simply put, where informed consent existed, the consequences differed very little, had decisions been made in another manner.

9. Salgo v. Leland Stanford Jr. University Board of Trustees, 317 P.2d 170 (Cal. App. 1957).

10. Canterbury v. Spence, 464 F.2d 772 (D.C. Cir. 1972); Cobbs v. Grant, 502 P.2d 1 (Cal. 1972); Wilkinson v. Vesey, 295 A.2d 676 (R.I. 1972).

11. Silberstein EB. Extension of two-part consent form. *New England Journal of Medicine* 1974; 29:155-156.

12. Oregon Revised Statutes §677.097(1)(a)-(c) (1977).

13. Id. at §677.097(2).

INDEX